VICTOR *and* EVIE

VICTOR

and

EVIE

*British Aristocrats
in Wartime Rideau Hall*

DOROTHY ANNE PHILLIPS

McGill-Queen's University Press

Montreal & Kingston • London • Chicago

ISBN 978-0-7735-5135-0 (cloth)
ISBN 978-0-7735-5221-0 (ePDF)
ISBN 978-0-7735-5222-7 (ePUB)

Legal deposit fourth quarter 2017
Bibliothèque nationale du Québec

Printed in Canada on acid-free paper that is 100% ancient forest
free (100% post-consumer recycled), processed chlorine free

McGill-Queen's University Press acknowledges the support of the
Canada Council for the Arts for our publishing program. We also
acknowledge the financial support of the Government of Canada
through the Canada Book Fund for our publishing activities.

Library and Archives Canada Cataloguing in Publication

Phillips, Dorothy Anne, 1938–, author
Victor and Evie : British aristocrats in wartime Rideau Hall /
Dorothy Anne Phillips.

Includes bibliographical references and index.
Issued in print and electronic formats.
ISBN 978-0-7735-5135-0 (cloth).
ISBN 978-0-7735-5221-0 (ePDF).
ISBN 978-0-7735-5222-7 (ePUB)

1. Devonshire, Victor Christian William Cavendish, Duke of,
1868–1938. 2. Devonshire, Evelyn Cavendish, Duchess of. 3.
Aristocracy (Social class)–Great Britain–Biography. 4. Governors
general–Canada–Biography. 5. Rideau Hall (Ottawa, Ont.)–
History–20th century. 6. World War, 1914–1918–Canada.
I. Title.

FC556.A1P55 2017   971.061'20922   C2017-903752-8
                                         C2017-903753-6

To Ashwin and to Catherine, who have been with me through
this whole long journey

❧

Contents

Figures • ix

Foreword • xv

Acknowledgments • xxiii

List of Major Characters • xxvii

1 Canada Beckons • 3

2 Getting Settled in the Colony • 23

3 Maintaining Imperial Standards • 49

4 Honours: The First Conflict • 64

5 The Blossoming of Lady Maud • 72

6 Summer Adventures, 1917 • 87

7 Crises of State • 110

8 A Most Notable Wedding • 120

9 Travels from Coast to Coast • 134

10 A Troubled Winter, 1918 • 148

11 Honours: The "Unmitigated Nuisance" Returns • 172

12 Blue Sea Lake and Other Summer Pleasures, 1918 • 179

13 Influenza, Armistice, and Aftermath • 193

14 Parliament Rejects British Hereditary Honours – Again • 211

15 Evie in England, 1919 • 216

16 The Winnipeg General Strike • 223

17 The Duty and Pleasure of Summer 1919 • 229

18 The Prince of Wales, and Other Peacetime Pleasures • 250

19 Dorothy and Harold • 262

20 The End of an Era • 275

Afterword • 296

Notes • 305

Bibliography • 363

Index • 377

❧

Figures

F.1 His Excellency Duke of Devonshire – Governor General of
Canada (1916–1921) • xvi
Source: Library and Archives Canada/Historical photographs of
individuals and groups, events and activities from across Canada
collection/C-001013.

F.2 Evelyn Emily Mary Cavendish (née Petty-Fitzmaurice), Duchess
of Devonshire, 29 April 1920 • xvii
© National Public Gallery, London. NPG X120545

F.3 Devonshire Coat of Arms • xviii
© Devonshire Collection, Chatsworth. Reproduced by permission
of Chatsworth Settlement Trustees.

1.1 Wedding of Victor Christian William Cavendish and Lady
Evelyn Emily Mary Petty-FitzMaurice, 30 July 1892 • 11
Reproduced by permission of the Trustees of the Bowood
collection.

1.2 Photo: (World War I 1914–18) Major General Sir Sam Hughes
talking to wounded Canadians at Red Cross Special Hospital,
Buxton (England) • 15
Source: Library and Archives Canada/Ministry of the Overseas
Military Forces of Canada fonds/PA-022662.

1.3 Photo: Canada Steamship Lines CALGARIAN, ca. 1925–1935 • 19
Source: Library and Archives Canada/George Ayoub fonds/
PA-032967.

2.1.a The Great Seal of Canada, George V • 27
Source: Dorothy Anne Phillips photograph taken at Library and
Archives Canada, Gatineau Preservation Centre.

2.1.b Privy Council Seal of the Duke of Devonshire as Governor
General of Canada • 27
Source: Library and Archives Canada C-018585.

2.1.c, 2.1.d The Governor General's Academic Medal of the Duke
of Devonshire • 28
Source: Library and Archives Canada C-077965 and CO-77966.

2.2 Duke and Duchess of Devonshire arrive at Ottawa Grand Trunk
Railway Central Station, 13 November 1916 • 32
© Devonshire Collection, Chatsworth. Reproduced by permission
of Chatsworth Settlement Trustees.

2.3 Photo: The Right Honourable Sir Robert L. Borden • 34
Source: Library and Archives Canada/Post Office Department
fonds/e000611519.

2.4 Arthur Lismer, Olympic *with Returned Soldiers* • 38
Beaverbrook Collection of War Art, Canadian War Museum, CWM
19710261-0343.

2.5 Duke of Devonshire and his four children at Rideau Hall – L.
to R.: (Front row) Lord Charles, Lady Anne; (Back row) Duke of
Devonshire, Lady Dorothy, Lady Rachel • 39
Source: Library and Archives Canada/Department of the Interior
fonds/PA-041385.

2.6 Rideau Hall, Ottawa, Ontario, 1927 • 42
Source: Library and Archives Canada/Department of the Interior
fonds/PA-043904.

2.7 Aides de Camp on the staff of the Duke of Devonshire, 1916 • 44
© Devonshire Collection, Chatsworth. Reproduced by permission of
Chatsworth Settlement Trustees.

5.1 Duke of Devonshire at Deer Lodge, Winnipeg • 73
Source: Library and Archives Canada/Collection Victor Christian
William Cavendish, 9th Duke of Devonshire/Mikan 14182.

5.2 Rt. Hon. C. Arthur Balfour (Left), British Foreign Secretary, Lord
Devonshire (Centre), Governor-General of Canada at Rideau Hall,
Ottawa, 1917 • 84
Source: Library and Archives Canada/Topley Studio fonds/PA-
042936.

5.3 Rt. Hon. Arthur C. Balfour (seated fifth from left), the British
Foreign Secretary, and Lord Devonshire (seated sixth from left),
the Governor-General of Canada, at Rideau Hall, 1917 • 85
Source: Library and Archives Canada/Topley Studio fonds/
PA-042944.

6.1 View of Quebec [P.Q.]. from the Citadel • 88
Source: Library and Archives Canada/Collection de photographies
par Jules-Ernest Livernois/PA-023910.

8.1 Wedding of Lady Maud Cavendish and Captain Angus Mackin-
tosh, 3 November 1917 [Top row, L–R: Capt. A.A. Mackintosh,
Lady Maud Mackintosh, Capt. Ridley/ Lower row – Lady Rachel
Cavendish, Lady Dorothy Cavendish, Lady Anne Cavendish, Master
Roderick Henderson, Miss Peggy Henderson, and Lady Blanche
Cavendish], 1917 • 131
Source: Library and Archives Canada/Madge Macbeth fonds/
PA-127353.

8.2 Group at Rideau Hall after wedding of Lady Maud Cavendish and Captain Angus Mackintosh • 132
© Devonshire Collection, Chatsworth. Reproduced by permission of Chatsworth Settlement Trustees.

10.1 Sir Cecil Spring Rice • 157
George Grantham Bain Collection, Library of Congress, Prints & Photographs Division, LC-B2-2719-9.

10.2.a and 10.2.b Duke and Duchess of Devonshire • 170
Source: Library and Archives Canada/Public Archives of Canada collection, Mikan 4932895 (Duchess of Devonshire: signed "Evelyn Devonshire") and 4932896 (The Duke of Devonshire: signed "Devonshire May 13, 1918").

12.1 Matapedia Restigouche Salmon Club, 1914 • 180
Source: Library and Archives Canada/Department of the Interior fonds/PA-021676.

12.2 Staff and Government House Party, Rideau Hall, ca. 1900–1939 • 189
Source: Library and Archives Canada/Samuel J. Jarvis fonds/PA024975.

13.1 Duke of Devonshire driving a binder in Manitoba, 1918 • 195
© Devonshire Collection, Chatsworth. Reproduced by permission of Chatsworth Settlement Trustees.

13.2 Sir Wilfrid Laurier, ca. 1907 • 210
Source: Library and Archives Canada/William Daum Euler fonds/c000688.

17.1 Blue Sea Lake Cottage • 234
© Devonshire Collection, Chatsworth. Reproduced by permission of Chatsworth Settlement Trustees.

17.2 Prince of Wales' Visit, Reception 9–10 Sept. 1919 • 243
Source: Library and Archives Canada/National Archives of Canada
fonds/PA-022338.

17.3 Prince of Wales' Visit to Canada, H.R.H. greets General Currie
at Government House, Ottawa, Ont. 28 August 1919 • 247
Source: Library and Archives Canada/PA-003215.

17.4 (Prince of Wales' visit to Canada) Group at Government House,
Ottawa, Ont., 28 August–1 September • 247
Source: Library and Archives Canada/Arthur George Doughty
fonds/PA-022278.

17.5 (Prince of Wales' Visit to Canada) H.R.H. The Prince of Wales
laying the cornerstone of the Peace Tower, Ottawa, Ont. 1 September
1919 • 248
Source: Library and Archives Canada/Department of Public Works
fonds/PA-057515.

18.1 Map of the Duke and Duchess's trip on the west coast of British
Columbia, 1919 • 255
Map by Wendy Johnson (Johnson Cartographics).

18.2 (Prince of Wales' visit to Canada) H.R.H. with the Duke of
Devonshire before leaving Halifax N.S. for home, 25 November • 259
Source: Library and Archives Canada/Arthur George Doughty
fonds/PA-022274.

19.1 The wedding of Dorothy Cavendish and Harold Macmillan,
21 April 1920 • 272
© Devonshire Collection, Chatsworth. Reproduced by permission
of the Chatsworth Settlement Trustees.

❖

Foreword

This book began as an idea for an article about the cottage, or summer house, that had belonged to the Duke of Devonshire, Canada's eleventh governor general, at Blue Sea Lake north of Ottawa in Quebec's Gatineau Hills. A friend, Bob Cameron, whose grandfather had built a cottage on what would become Cameron Bay, told me stories about the lake's residents. I too had a cottage in the Gatineau and I was surprised that the duke's cottage was not well known.

Searching for information, I came upon a diary belonging to the duke held in Library and Archives Canada that covered his years in Canada, from 1916 to 1921, and contained a few summer entries about the lake and the cottage. And that was it. I could find no pictures, no plans, despite the architect having been well known in Ottawa, no references at all, not even a biography of this 9th Duke of Devonshire. But the duke's diary itself was a revealing account of a family living at Rideau Hall, Canada's Government House, and travelling extensively across the country.

On a trip to England, I visited the wonderful National Archives in Kew, where I discovered Colonial Office correspondence suggesting that our governor general, the Duke of Devonshire, had defended Canada's positions on two important issues concerning the nation's desire for greater independence from Britain: a request for a Canadian ambassador to the United States, and a request that the king should not offer honours such as knighthoods to those living in Canada. Both of these had resulted in the governor general receiving reprimands from his British colleagues.

Figure F.1 His Excellency the 9th Duke of Devonshire, Governor General of Canada. The sash and the medal with the cross denote the Order of the Garter, awarded by King George V in January 1916.

Figure F.2 *Opposite* Lady Evelyn Cavendish, Duchess of Devonshire, April 1920.

Figure F.3 The Coat of Arms of the Dukes of Devonshire. The shield with three stags' heads represents the Cavendish family, and has two stags as supporters. The motto, *Cavendo Tutus*, means "safe through caution."

Later, reading about those years in Canada, I realized that the duke and his family lived through several important historical events. In his diary, the duke frequently mentioned that a "big English mail" had arrived in the sporadic mail delivery of wartime, so I wrote to the archivist at Chatsworth, the Devonshire ancestral estate in England, to inquire whether any of these letters had survived. The archivist confirmed that there were some letters and, with the current duke's permission, arranged for me to spend two weeks at the Chatsworth archives, where I took photographs of the letters from 9:00 a.m. to 5:00 p.m. each workday. Though I had no time to read them I came away with a trove of almost 1,300 letters and documents, over 7,500 photographs of the many-paged material. I met the current, 12th Duke of Devonshire, Peregrine Cavendish, great-grandson of the governor general, who invited me for luncheon with his wife, Amanda, the duchess, and arranged for me to meet his mother, the Dowager Duchess of Devonshire, Deborah Cavendish. My husband joined me for the weekends and we became tourists, viewing the parts of the house and grounds open to visitors. While in England, we also visited Bowood House in Wiltshire, the home of the Marquess of Lansdowne, father of Lady Evelyn, the Duchess of Devonshire. The archivist there arranged for me to see the duchess's letters to her mother written from Canada. In Ottawa, in Library and Archives Canada, I later found the letters of one of their aides-de-camp, Captain Vivian Bulkeley-Johnson, who had offered them to the archives through his friend Vincent Massey.

What I had discovered was the record of a governor general of Canada and his family who came to Canada in the midst of the most destructive war in history to that time. In 1916, when the Duke of Devonshire accepted the invitation of King George V to become Canada's governor general, his wife, the duchess, was less than enamoured of the idea. To the duke, the position offered a chance to do what he could for King and Empire during the Great War, to participate in the defence of his country and his way of life; it also offered the possibility of adventure in a land he had visited but did not know well. To the duchess, his acceptance of the position meant leaving family and friends who were suffering the privations of wartime, leaving her eldest son who was in the British army, and exposing her six younger children to life in what she considered a British colony, though Canada had in 1867 progressed to semi-independent status as a Dominion. The duchess knew well what the position would entail. She had lived in Canada during her teens when her father, Lord Lansdowne, had been governor general. In 1916, she was particularly concerned about her young daughters, then reaching marriageable age, living in close quarters with young men who would serve her husband as aides-de-camp. She would have to be the guardian of propriety at Government House.

The duke, with the duchess and their two eldest daughters, arrived in Halifax on a bleak November day in 1916 to be greeted by the populace and sworn in. The ceremony was dignified but shortened in keeping with wartime restraints. At that time Canada was struggling to meet its commitment to the Allies to keep 500,000 men active in the killing fields of France, a struggle that would lead within a year to conscription and later to anti-conscription riots.

The story of the Duke of Devonshire's tenure as representative of the head of state of the Dominion of Canada, during a period often referred to as Canada's maturing as a nation, has three interwoven strands. The first involved the British government's expectations of the governor general of Canada, which were only partly written. While the role gave him ultimate authority – with what are known as "reserve powers" the governor general could refuse to give oral assent to a bill, reserve it for consideration in Britain, or invite a member of Parliament to form a government – he had little or no power to influence government policy. He could and did confer with his ministers, but after 1848, when Britain had granted the Canadian colony the right to make its own decisions regarding domestic policy, the governor general's hands were tied. He could not enter the House of Commons. He could use only his personal relationships with government ministers to influence conscription and other policies during this difficult period. However, all correspondence between this British Dominion and the Imperial authorities in London still went through his office. He was required to send regular reports about conditions and events in Canada to the secretary for the colonies; he swore in ministers and others, presented the Speech from the Throne, and prorogued Parliament. There were also unwritten, ceremonial traditions that both the duke and duchess were expected to perform, some of which had to be curtailed during the war.

A second related strand is Canada's growing desire for independence as a country within the confines of the British Empire. When every schoolroom in the country proudly displayed a map showing in red the countries of the Empire on which the sun never set, no one wanted to follow the American lead and take Canada entirely out of the Empire. Still, Prime Minister Sir Robert Borden led campaigns for a little more independence – in foreign policy, in having a Canadian representative to the United States, and in removing the granting of British honours to those living in Canada. While people in Canada wanted to remain part of the British Empire, most did not want a British-style aristocracy, which they feared would result from the granting of large numbers of hereditary titles to the surviving heroes of the Great War. In each of these campaigns, the governor general supported the desire for more independence, but his actions were misunderstood in Britain, leaving him in an awkward position between the two governments.

A third strand of the story involves the family's reactions to Canada, and to the dramatic events of those years: the entry of the United States into the war in April 1917; the Halifax Explosion in December 1917; the influenza epidemic of 1918; the Winnipeg General Strike of 1919; the visit of the Prince of Wales in 1919. The letters of these two strong-minded British aristocrats reveal how the duke and duchess managed, despite their differences, to navigate the major issues of these years, and to emerge with their strong and loving marriage intact. When not at Rideau Hall with their six children, the duke and duchess were travelling across the troubled and developing Dominion to represent King and Empire, or escaping the summer heat and social whirl of Ottawa at their cottage at Blue Sea Lake. The duke thrilled at his fishing and hunting adventures in Canada's backcountry. And just as the duchess had anticipated, two of their daughters, Lady Maud and Lady Dorothy, found themselves at the centre of their own romantic dramas.

The family's Blue Sea Lake cottage has not appeared in publications to date, nor has much been told about the Duke and Duchess of Devonshire. Other than the duke's diary, the material about their personal lives went undiscovered for years and released only in the twenty-first century. Although many authors have written about Canada's part in the Great War, the story has never before been told from the point of view of the Duke of Devonshire and his family. As well, this is the first publication of the part played by the governor general in Canada's efforts to gain more independence from Britain while remaining part of that great Empire, then at its height.

Acknowledgments

My thanks to Bob Cameron, a retired Canadian ambassador, whose boat tour of Blue Sea Lake and stories about the Duke of Devonshire's cottage set me on this path. Bob took an interest in the manuscript as it developed but unfortunately did not live to see its completion.

When I visited Chatsworth in 2010, I was told this story of the letters and papers that were not released until 2005. The 11th Duke of Devonshire, Andrew Cavendish, apparently was so upset by his brother William's death in 1944 that he put all papers away in a storeroom under the theatre at Chatsworth, and no one was allowed inside. His son, the 12th Duke, after his father's death in 2004, decided to open the storeroom. There he found the letters and diaries of the 9th Duke, including several documents about his becoming governor general, the letters his family had written to his mother and to each other, and a few letters from Evie to her mother. Blanche Egerton's letters were also there, and some letters the duke had received from friends. My thanks to the 12th Duke, who allowed me access to these letters for the period from 1916 to 1921, for a lovely luncheon with his wife in their Chatsworth apartment, and for introducing me to his mother, the Dowager Duchess of Devonshire, then ninety, with whom I had a delightful conversation about writing.

The staff and volunteers of the Chatsworth archives were cataloguing the 9th Duke's documents but were far from completing the process. Archivists Andrew Peppitt and James Towe were particularly helpful in providing the letters and photo librarian Diane Naylor at finding the photographs at Chatsworth. Rosie Brewer, a volunteer who was cataloguing the letters when I was at Chatsworth, was an unfailing source of information about the family.

Aide-de-camp Captain Vivian Bulkeley-Johnson wrote letters to his parents during his tenure in Ottawa from 1916 to 1918. He later offered them to his friend, Vincent Massey, whom he had met at Oxford, and who was Canada's high commissioner to Britain (1935–46), asking that they be housed in the archives in Canada and not opened until the year 2000.

Much of the story of the honours struggle came from documents housed at Library and Archives Canada, both the Colonial Office records copied from Britain and the letters and diary of Sir Robert Borden, which, when matched by date with the diary of the Duke of Devonshire, make clear the interaction between these two men with the high commissioner in London, Sir George Perley, and the colonial secretaries, Andrew Bonar Law and Walter Long.

Many people helped to bring this story to fruition. I thank all of them for their information and advice. Thanks to the Marquess of Lansdowne and the archivists at Bowood, Kate Fielden, who gave me access to the letters from the Duchess of Devonshire to her mother during their time in Canada, and later Jo Johnston. The staff of Library and Archives Canada were all very helpful throughout the process, as were staff at the library of the National Capital Commission in Ottawa and staff of the Public Archives of Nova Scotia in Halifax. At Matapedia, Quebec, Peter Dubé and Gilles Dubé were funds of knowledge about fishing. My thanks to Mary Robertson, coordinator of the Cascapedia River Museum, Cascapedia-St-Jules, Quebec; Patricia Belier and later Francesca Holyoke, head of the Archives & Special Collections, University of New Brunswick Libraries, Fredericton, New Brunswick; Bruce Patterson, Deputy Chief Herald of Canada; Glen Lockwood, Diocese of Ottawa Archives of the Anglian Church of Canada; and to Marjorie Norris and Wendy Davis for loans of hard-to-find books. The staff of Apple Canada helped me deal with the large volume of images. My friend Catherine Richards, spent many hours listening and making suggestions about the manuscript. My writing group offered helpful comments on early sections of the manuscript. Thanks to cartographer Wendy Johnson and to editors Ann Fotheringham and John Metcalf for helping to get the manuscript into shape, to Catherine Marjoribanks for a detailed copy-edit, and to Mark Abley and the staff of McGill-Queen's University Press for seeing it through to publication.

My husband, Ashwin Shingadia, deserves my deepest gratitude for his unfailing encouragement and patience in listening over and over again to the stories, and for enjoying the travels with me.

❧

List of Major Characters

DUKE'S AND DUCHESS'S FAMILIES

Victor Christian William Cavendish, 9th Duke of Devonshire (1868–1938), Governor General of Canada 11 November 1916 to 11 August 1921
Lady Evelyn Emily Mary Petty-FitzMaurice Duchess of Devonshire (1870–1960), called Evie
Victor and Evelyn were married 30 July 1892

Children of Victor and Evelyn
Lord Edward William Spencer Cavendish, later 10th Duke of Devonshire (1895–1950)
    Married Lady Mary Alice Gascoyne-Cecil (called Moucher), 21 April 1917
Lady Maud Louisa Emma Cavendish (1896–1975)
    Married Angus Alexander Mackintosh, 3 November 1917
    Their child Anne Peace Arabella Mackintosh born 24 September 1918 and baptized at St Bartholomew's Anglican Church in Ottawa on 14 November 1918
Lady Blanche Katherine Cavendish (1898–1987)
Lady Dorothy Evelyn Cavendish (1900–1966)
Lady Rachel Cavendish (1902–1977)
Lord Charles Arthur Francis Cavendish (1905–1944)
Lady Anne Cavendish (1909–1981)

The Duke's Parents

Lord Edward Cavendish, MP (1838–1891)
  Lady Emma Elizabeth Lascelles (1838–1920), called Granny
  Emma by her grandchildren; Mother by the Duke; Mummie by
  the Duchess; Aunt Emma by her nieces; and Lady Edward by
  anyone else

The Duke's Siblings

The Right Honourable Lord Richard Frederick Cavendish
(1871–1946)
Major John Spencer Cavendish (1875–1914), killed in battle

The Duke's Immediate Ancestors

Spencer Compton Cavendish, MP, the 8th Duke of Devonshire
(1833–1908), Victor's uncle
Lord Frederick Charles Cavendish, MP (1836–1882), Victor's uncle,
assassinated in Ireland; survived by his wife, Lucy Cavendish
William Cavendish, the 7th Duke of Devonshire (1808–1891),
Victor's grandfather

The Duchess's Parents

Henry Charles Keith Petty-Fitzmaurice, 5th Marquess of Lansdowne,
6th Earl of Kerry (1845–1927), Evie's father
Lady Maud Evelyn Hamilton (1850–1932), Evie's mother

The Duchess's Siblings

Lord Henry William Edmund Petty-FitzMaurice, 6th Marquess
of Lansdowne (1872–1936)
Major Lord Charles George Francis Mercer Nairne Petty-
FitzMaurice (1874–1914), killed in battle
Lady Beatrix Frances Petty-FitzMaurice (1877–1953)

THE STAFF AT RIDEAU HALL

James Crowdy, the duke's clerk
Colonel Harold Greenwood Henderson, military secretary
(1875–1922)

His wife Lady Violet Henderson, and children Roderick (b. 1902)
and Peggy (b. 1904)
Miss Saunders, the duchess's secretary
Miss Schofield, the children's governess, from 1919
Arthur Sladen, the duke's secretary
Miss Walton, the children's governess, 1916–19

AIDES-DE-CAMP (ADCS)

Lieutenant Colonel Oswald Herbert Campbell Balfour (1894–1953),
later military secretary to the Duke of Devonshire
Captain Vivian Bulkeley-Johnson (1891–1968)
Lieutenant Colonel Henry John (Harry) Cator (1897–1965)
Lord Victor Gilbert Lariston Garnet (Larry) Elliot-Murray-
Kynynmound, 5th Earl of Minto (1891–1975)
Lord George (Geordie) Haddington, 12th Earl of Haddington
(1894–1986)
Major Robert Orlando Rodolph (Rody) Kenyon-Slaney (1892–1965)
    Married in Ottawa Lady Mary Cecilia Rhodesia Hamilton, cousin
    of the Duchess of Devonshire
Captain Patrick Kinnaird (1898–1948)
Captain Angus Alexander Mackintosh of Mackintosh (1885–1918)
Captain Harold Macmillan, later Prime Minister of the United
Kingdom (1894–1986)
Lord Hugh Molyneux, 7th Earl of Sefton (1898–1972)
Captain Mervyn Ridley (1878–1951)
Lord Walter John Montagu Douglas Scott, later 8th Earl of Dalkeith
and 8th Duke of Buccleuch (1894–1973)

BRITISH

Andrew Bonar Law (1858–1923), Secretary of State for the Colonies,
1915–16
The Duke of Connaught (1850–1942), Governor General of Canada,
1911–16

Edward, Prince of Wales (1894–1972), later King Edward VIII of the
United Kingdom and the Dominions of the British Empire, Emperor
of India

Walter Hume Long, 1st Viscount Long (1854–1924), Secretary of
State for the Colonies, December 1916 to January 1919

Alfred Milner, 1st Viscount Milner (1854–1925), Secretary of State
for the Colonies, January 1919 to February 1921

Winston Leonard Spencer-Churchill (1874–1965), Secretary of State
for the Colonies, February 1921 to October 1922, later Prime
Minister of the United Kingdom, 1940–45, 1951–55

Sir Cecil Spring Rice (1859–1918), British Ambassador to the United
States, 1913–18

CANADIANS

Sir James Albert Manning Aikins (1851–1929), Lieutenant-Governor
of Manitoba

Pierre Édouard Blondin (1874–1943), Secretary of State

Sir Robert Laird Borden (1854–1937), Prime Minister of Canada,
1911 to 1920

Sir Louis Henry Davies (1845–1924), Justice of the Supreme Court

Sir Charles Fitzpatrick (1851–1942), Chief Justice of the Supreme
Court, 1906 to 1918; Lieutenant-Governor of Quebec, 1918 to 1923

Sir George Eulas Foster (1847–1931), Minister of Trade and Commerce

Sir Lomer Gouin (1861–1929), Premier of Quebec, 1905–20

Sir Hugh Graham, 1st Baron Atholstan (1848–1938)

Sir John Strathearn Hendrie (1857–1923), Lieutenant-Governor
of Ontario

Sir Sam Hughes (1853–1921), outgoing Minister of Militia and
Defence in 1916

Albert Edward Kemp (1858–1929), incoming Minister of Militia and
Defence in 1916

William Lyon Mackenzie King (1874–1950), Liberal member of the
Opposition; later Prime Minister of Canada, 1921–26, 1926–30,
1935–48

Admiral Sir Charles Edmund Kingsmill (1855–1935), director of the Canadian Naval Service

Sir Henri Charles Wilfrid Laurier (1841–1919), Prime Minister of Canada, 1896–1911; Leader of the Opposition, 1911–19

Sir Pierre-Évariste Leblanc (1853–1918), Lieutenant-Governor of Quebec, 1915 to 1918

Sir Joseph Pope (1854–1926), Under-Secretary of State for External Affairs

Frank Ross, owner of the seigneury at Magdalen River, Gaspé, Quebec

Clifford Sifton (1861–1929), owner of the *Winnipeg Free Press*

VICTOR *and* EVIE

CHAPTER 1

Canada Beckons

On a typical summer morning, when he was in London, the 9th Duke of Devonshire would set out from Devonshire House, his London residence, past the sphinxes that guarded the great gates in the long cement wall in front of Devonshire House, across Piccadilly to Green Park, where he would stride through a canopy of sycamore and lime trees in the peaceful surroundings of this lovely forty-acre Royal Park. That was his custom. On the morning of 23 June 1916, however, he was headed in the opposite direction – toward Lansdowne House, a short block away. Two days earlier, his father-in-law, Lord Lansdowne, had sounded him out about King George V's proposal that the duke go to Canada as governor general. The idea had sent the duke's household into a tailspin. His children, especially the girls, were very excited about the possibility of living in Canada for five years, the usual length of the posting. The duchess was not. She brought out many arguments against the plan. She worried about leaving behind her eldest son, Lord Edward Cavendish (called Eddy), then serving in the Derbyshire Yeomanry with his regiment in France; she worried about their daughters now approaching marriageable age – where would they find suitable husbands? She argued that they both had aging parents, and that their large estates could be properly managed only by themselves. The duke, from his position as a Civil Lord of the Admiralty, consulted his good friend Arthur Balfour, First Lord of the Admiralty, who encouraged him to go to Canada. Lord Lansdowne and his wife had both given their wholehearted approval. Still, the duke agreed with the duchess that leaving the estates for so many years would be difficult, and they would all feel the isolation from their close-knit families. He had decided to refuse the appointment.

The Duke of Devonshire was accompanied that morning by his eldest daughter. Lady Maud Cavendish went to Lansdowne House each day to work with her grandmother, Lady Maud Lansdowne, who oversaw a charity supporting the families of soldiers who had been killed or injured at the front. Both the duke and his daughter were sad that they would not be going to Canada. Five years in the Dominion would have been an adventure for them all, and a great opportunity for the duke's career.

The duke and his father-in-law were closeted in conversation for a considerable time. Lord Lansdowne probably reviewed many aspects of the duke's life and the current environment in an effort to persuade him to take the position. Finances might have been among the first topics. Both men knew that temporarily closing their large estates or leaving them with fewer staff could alleviate some of the financial troubles that had plagued the family for several generations. Enormous duties had been levied on the estate of the 8th Duke of Devonshire at his death. The aristocracy had been subject to modest death duties since 1894, but with the passage of the Parliament Act of 1911, the House of Lords lost control of financial decisions in Parliament, leaving the House of Commons free to pass laws that increased taxes on the large estates, something the Lords would never have allowed.[1] At the same time, rental revenues from agricultural lands, on which the Devonshire duchy relied for much of its income, continued to fall.[2] Burdened also by the debt accumulated by the expenditures of the 6th and 7th Dukes – though the 8th Duke of Devonshire managed to reduce the obligation to some extent – the present duke found himself left in a precarious financial position.[3]

Lord Lansdowne's next argument might have been the current state of the Great War. In the past two years the Allies had suffered several major defeats and, though the Central Powers had not won the war, these were worrying signs. The Duke of Devonshire's diary, in which he had been writing daily since 1905, expressed his concerns. In earlier days, his diary entries had often begun with the weather – he was a farmer at heart and watched the weather carefully – but since the start of the war, news of battles had taken precedence.

The war had affected both families personally from the beginning. In 1914, the duke and his wife had each lost a younger brother, and both families were still grieving. Then, in April 1915, the duke's eldest son, Lord Edward – Eddy to his family – had shipped out with the Derbyshire Yeomanry, their destination a secret. Eddy wrote one letter from Alexandria, Egypt, but then nothing more. Months later, the duke heard that Eddy's regiment was in Gallipoli, part of the ill-fated expedition inspired by Winston Churchill, then First Lord of the Admiralty. Churchill had argued that the stalemate in France and Flanders required bold moves to break the impasse.[4] He suggested forcing passage through the Dardanelles to the Sea of Marmara to induce the Turkish government to sue for peace and bring the surrounding countries into the war on the Allied side. However, in March 1915, the Turkish forces laid mines after the British minesweepers had gone through the narrow channel. Three ships were sunk and three disabled.[5] The British then tried to take the peninsula with ground forces.

Eddy's regiment took part in the British landing at Suvla Bay on the Gallipoli Peninsula in August 1915. For several difficult months, the British soldiers were on the beaches trying again and again to scale the cliffs and take Gallipoli. As he worried about Eddy, the duke's diary is peppered with references to what became known as the Battle of Gallipoli. When the autumn rains came, Eddy, ill with jaundice, malaria, and dysentery, was evacuated to Greece, where he nearly died.[6] In January 1916, under the noses of the unsuspecting Turks, the British evacuated their troops from the Suvla and Hellas beaches in a manoeuvre similar to the evacuation of Dunkirk some twenty-five years later. On 3 January 1916, while the duke was dining at the exclusive Turf Club, he was called to the phone to speak to "Lord Hartington." "I was quite terrified," he wrote.[7] Lord Hartington was Eddy's formal name, which he had inherited as the son of the Duke of Devonshire. After those long months of waiting for news, he was startled by the use of the ancient title.[8] Eddy told his father he had landed in England still suffering from dysentery, and was in a hospital in Southampton. Both the duke and duchess were enormously relieved. Since then, however, Eddy had tried several times to be reinstated as an active soldier in his regiment, but he was never well enough; instead, he had been assigned to a desk job in Paris.

While the Battle of Gallipoli was ruining Eddy's health, British troops had been sent to garrison the Anglo-Persian Oil Company installations on Abadan Island at the head of the Persian Gulf. Rather than using coal to fuel warships, the British had just begun using oil as the primary fuel. Finding little opposition, the British troops had pushed up the Tigris River past Basra to Kut-al-Amara. By late 1915, when the failure at Gallipoli was obvious, the British ordered General Townshend to move on from Kut toward Baghdad as a countermove against the Turks. On the way, the troops met resistance and retreated to Kut, where they dug in. The Turks followed, also dug in, and besieged the garrison. Britain's subsequent efforts to break the siege and rescue the more than ten thousand surviving British troops failed. Running out of food and supplies, the defenders surrendered on 29 April 1916. The duke's diary tells of his distress: "News arrived of the fall of Kut. Afraid it is very bad. The Turks can claim that they have beaten the English army in Europe and Asia."[9]

As though that were not bad enough, reports of the German offensive to capture Verdun reached the duke on 23 February 1916, two days after it had begun, with news of a French reverse and heavy German losses. In the next months the duke followed the Verdun news closely, referring almost daily to that fierce battle. Although the duke had a tendency to look on the optimistic side of the reporting – he often remarked that the French were holding their ground – by March, his optimism had flagged and he had to admit that the Germans had gained ground. "News was not altogether satisfactory," was his diary comment.[10]

On 31 May 1916, just three weeks before the duke and Lord Lansdowne had their extended conversation, the British Grand Fleet met the German High Seas Fleet in the North Sea near the Jutland Peninsula of Denmark in what became known as the Battle of Jutland. The British had 28 dreadnoughts and 9 battle cruisers, the Germans 16 dreadnoughts and 5 battle cruisers; both had other, smaller ships – in all 250 vessels met in battle. During the course of the battle several ships sank. The British lost more ships than the Germans, and more men, including Rear Admiral Sir Horace Hood, but the German fleet fled. Both nations claimed victory: the Germans asserted that they had won on the basis of sinking more British ships; Britain's Admiral Jellicoe took the position that he had preserved the British navy and forced the Germans to retreat. Two days after the battle, when the press reported the results, the duke wrote one of his most vehement reports: "Shocking bad news. Our losses in naval engagement very heavy and nothing to indicate that we have done much damage to the Germans. … Most serious and disappointing. Everyone very miserable. … Great gloom in the evening."[11] In the following days the press reported that the German losses had also been heavy, but the gloom continued.

Five days later, the "appalling news" of Lord Kitchener's death arrived. HMS *Hampshire*, with Lord Kitchener and his staff on board, was sunk off the Orkneys by a mine or a torpedo.[12] Kitchener had been on his way to Russia on a secret mission.[13] As secretary of state for war, he had been well regarded by the British people, though his reputation with his colleagues in government had suffered, in part because of his support for the failed Gallipoli campaign. The following week the duke and his father-in-law attended the memorial service at St Paul's Cathedral.[14]

So, by 23 June, the duke must have felt bombarded by bad news from the war fronts. Gallipoli, Kut-al-Amara, Verdun, Jutland – the Allies had not won any of these – however, Germany and the Central Powers had not won them either. The atmosphere of gloom persisted as the stalemate continued with mounting horrific losses in men and *matériel*.

With all of these tragic events in mind, how could the duke refuse to do his duty for King and Empire? Though he must have considered the safety of his family during the war, by mid-1916 there was no longer the danger of Zeppelin raids. British fighter aircraft had learned to shoot down the huge, balloon-like, hydrogen-filled airships that had, earlier in the war, dropped bombs on the English coastal military and industrial sites, and a few on London. Even if the Germans developed other weapons, they would likely bomb the main cities, and the family could retreat to Chatsworth in Derby, far away from likely targets. Safety on the voyage across the Atlantic was another concern; German U-boats had sunk RMS *Lusitania* off the south coast of Ireland in 1915 with the loss of more than a thousand passenger lives. The voyage presented a risk, but once in Canada the family would be far away from any bombs.

There were other inducements to becoming Governor General of Canada that might have influenced the duke. The position carried considerable prestige. Lord Lansdowne, after serving in the same role, had gone directly to India as viceroy and returned to a sterling career in politics: secretary of state for war, then foreign secretary. The Earl of Minto, governor general from 1898 to 1904, had also moved to become Viceroy of India. As well, the duke knew that royalty often served the Empire: he would succeed the king's uncle, the Duke of Connaught. He knew, too, that the king had intended the next Governor General of Canada to be Queen Mary's brother, Prince Alexander of Teck. However, the Teck family was German. Conveniently for the king, who may not have wanted to send a prince with a German name while Britain was at war with Germany, Prince Alexander was on duty in the British Army.[15] Nor did Lord Lansdowne need to mention the pleasurable adventures the duke might have in Canada. Stories of Lord Lansdowne's fishing lodge on the Cascapedia River in Quebec were part of the family lore.

Whatever arguments Lord Lansdowne used, they were successful. When the two men emerged from their conference, Granny Maud Lansdowne whispered jubilantly to her granddaughter that her father had accepted.[16]

The 9th Duke of Devonshire, born Victor Christian William Cavendish in 1868, was Victor to his family and friends. During Victor's childhood, he would not have expected to become the duke. His grandfather, the 7th Duke of Devonshire, had three sons; Victor's father was the youngest. However, the second son, Lord Frederick Cavendish, while on government duty in Ireland in 1882, was murdered. When the 7th Duke of Devonshire died in 1891, his eldest son, Spencer Compton Cavendish, still a childless bachelor, became the 8th Duke of Devonshire. Victor's father also died in 1891, so that Victor became the heir apparent to one of the wealthiest estates in Britain. Uncle Cav, as the family called the 8th Duke, could still marry and have a child; however, in 1892, he chose to marry his aging mistress, assuring Victor that he would be the heir. When Uncle Cav died in 1908, Victor became the 9th Duke of Devonshire and took on the responsibility of the estates.

The Devonshire estates had been founded by their formidable ancestor Bess of Hardwick, a friend to Queen Elizabeth I in the sixteenth century. Bess had purchased much of the property and built the first Chatsworth while her fourth husband, the 6th Earl of Shrewsbury, was occupied being keeper of the imprisoned Mary Queen of Scots, Queen Elizabeth's cousin and a threat to her throne. When Bess died in 1608, she left her large estates, including Chatsworth, to William Cavendish, one of her sons by her second marriage, who became the 1st Earl of Devonshire. There followed three more earls, but the 4th Earl, in 1688, was a leader in the Glorious Revolution, which invited the Dutch William of Orange and his wife Mary to depose the Catholic James II. For this the earl was honoured as 1st Duke of Devonshire.

Victor began his political career in 1891. When his father, Lord Edward Cavendish, who had held the post of member of Parliament for West Derbyshire, died suddenly, Victor, then twenty-three, fresh from Cambridge, won the seat as a Liberal Unionist, the youngest member of the British House of Commons at the time. He served under the First Lord of the Treasury, Arthur Balfour, as financial secretary to the Treasury – a key position for an up-and-coming politician.[17] Balfour became prime minister in 1902 but his government was defeated in 1905, leaving Victor to continue as a member of Parliament in the Opposition. However, with the death of the 8th Duke of Devonshire in 1908, Victor inherited the title and had to leave the rough-and-tumble of his beloved House of Commons for the staid and often boring House of Lords – Victor called it "the Mausoleum."[18] He was elected mayor of Eastbourne, where he had property (1909–10), and then mayor of Chesterfield (1911–12), a town close to Chatsworth. In 1915, Arthur Balfour replaced Winston Churchill as First Lord of the Admiralty and asked Victor to join him as a Civil Lord. Victor was thrilled to be working again under his good friend Balfour.

Victor was forty-eight in 1916 when he decided to take up the position of Governor General of Canada. He was often taller than those with whom he was pictured, broad-shouldered, and his girth suggested that he was overweight though not excessively fat. He made an impressive figure with his silvery hair and dark, drooping walrus moustache. Besides politics, Victor loved farming: at Chatsworth he raised prize-winning Shorthorn cattle as well as Shire horses – large, gentle animals distinguished by hair, called "feathers," below the knees. He also loved fishing and hunting and could indulge these passions on his many estates.

The Duchess of Devonshire, born Evelyn Emily Mary Petty-Fitz-Maurice in 1870, was the daughter of the 5th Marquess of Lansdowne. Evie to her family and friends, she was thirteen in 1883 when she travelled to Canada with her parents to live in Canada's Government House, Rideau Hall in Ottawa, while her father was Canada's fifth governor general. When her father accepted the appointment as viceroy and left Canada for India in 1888, Evie was eighteen. In India Lady Evelyn enjoyed riding with her father, but it was not long before her mother, with an eye to her future, brought her back to England to appear before Queen Victoria as a debutante and take part in the London "season." Evie became engaged to the man who was heir to the Devonshire title and estates; they married on 30 July 1892, just two weeks before Uncle Cav, who had kept his plans secret, married his aging mistress and assured Victor's ascent to the duchy.

Lady Evelyn was shorter than her husband, and in 1916, when she was forty-six, still had a svelte figure after bearing seven children. She had a good sense of style, and always dressed elegantly. A portrait of her by John Singer Sargent, painted when she was thirty-two and already the mother of five, is housed at Chatsworth; it shows an attractive, rather withdrawn woman with a mass of brown hair carefully arranged around her thin face, which was very like her father's. Every picture of her shows her long neck and slim figure, enhanced by her notable fashion sense. An article in the newspaper the *Montreal Standard*, which appeared at the time of their arrival in Canada, noted that the duchess was "distinguished by her charm of manner" and had a reputation as "a very capable organizer."[19] Indeed, she had founded and become president of the Derbyshire Red Cross Society.[20] Lady Evelyn was chatelaine of several large country houses in England and one castle in Ireland. Though she was not enamoured of city living – she much preferred the countryside and adored her home at Chatsworth in the rolling hills of Derbyshire – she did enjoy the London "season" from April to August, which was often one long party.

Figure 1.1 Victor Christian William Cavendish, heir apparent to his uncle, the 8th Duke of Devonshire, married Lady Evelyn Emily Mary Petty-FitzMaurice on 30 July 1892. They became the 9th Duke and Duchess of Devonshire on the death of the 8th Duke, 24 March 1908.

Three years earlier, Evie had been interested in the possibility of going to Canada, with her husband in the position of governor general. She had been Mistress of the Robes to her friend Queen Mary – a ceremonial position no longer having anything to do with the queen's apparel – which meant she accompanied the queen to state ceremonies and processions.[21] In March 1913, Evie heard that the king's uncle, Prince

Arthur, the Duke of Connaught, then governor general, was bringing his wife back to England for treatment of a serious illness. Evie consulted her father about the possibility of Victor taking the post should the prince be unable to return. Her father wrote back at length, pointing out that the savings they would realize from closing up their expensive houses would be enormous and would certainly relieve their financial worries. They could do the work with ease, would probably be very popular, and her husband would win the hearts of farmers with his solid knowledge of agriculture. Lord Lansdowne thought the children would thrive "in that glorious climate." He did note that, while he was as anxious as she that Victor fill a big place in public life, her husband might need to give a few more speeches in the House of Lords to solidify his reputation before such a long absence. The Canadian appointment, he wrote, "is that of a constitutional ruler and does not afford the tenant much real opportunity to make his influence felt."[22] In March 1913, Victor was happily hunting near Chatsworth and made no mention in his diary of possibly going to Canada.[23] Probably Evie did not tell her husband about her idea. In any case, the Duchess of Connaught recovered sufficiently and returned with her husband to Canada, so there was nothing to tell.

While Evie may have aspired to the role for her husband in 1913, three years later, when Victor came home to announce that he had accepted the post, Evie was incensed. Her feelings were still raw two weeks later when she wrote to Aunt Lucy, the widowed wife of Victor's uncle, Lord Frederick. "I never dreamt that Victor would accept and frankly was horrified when he went out to refuse and came home having accepted," she wrote. "He thought it a great opportunity for usefulness which no doubt it is – on the other hand we both have many irons in the fire here and I feel that we are deserting a lot of faithful friends and local helpers in this country and elsewhere."[24] Evie, whose main concern was always her family, worried about leaving Victor's ailing mother, Lady Edward Cavendish, then seventy-seven. Lady Edward was still grieving for her youngest son, Major John Cavendish, killed at the First Battle of Ypres, and also worried about her middle son, Lord Richard, who had returned injured from the battlefield in 1915. However, Evie's own parents, who had also lost their youngest son, Lord Charles, in the First Battle of Ypres, both wholeheartedly approved of the Canadian adventure. The hardest part for Evie would be leaving her own elder son, Eddy. She expected him to look after the family estates when the war was over, "if he is spared," she wrote to Aunt Lucy. She worried, too, about taking her young daughters to Canada. "We are much exercised over staff. The nicest available men are mostly quite penniless and with so many daughters the risk is great!"[25] She had four daughters approaching marriageable age: Lady Maud, twenty, and Lady Blanche, eighteen, who would accompany their parents on the crossing to Canada, and two younger daughters, Lady Dorothy, sixteen, and Lady Rachel, fourteen, who would follow shortly after. The younger two were not an immediate concern, but before the end of the five-year posting they too would be ready for marriage. There were also two younger children, Charles, eleven, and little Anne, just seven.

Victor knew that his wife would not be pleased; he had his own doubts, and spent several days wondering whether he had done the right thing. Finally, he took a long walk around his Chatsworth estate and noted that night in his diary: "Really looked beautiful. Sometimes one felt that it was all the more reason to be doing what one could."[26] Though earlier he had been a major in the Derbyshire Yeomanry, he was too old at forty-eight to be part of the military effort. The younger men, like his son Eddy, were taking that responsibility. However, he could take this position, for which his training and his experience fully qualified him. He could help to preserve the way of life that his ancestors had so carefully cultivated. Many of the former Dukes of Devonshire had served the Crown with distinction. Now it was his turn.

Both Victor and Evie made preparations for their departure. Evie cleaned cupboards and drawers and listed everything, especially fancy dresses, in case she might want them sent out to Canada.[27] Victor tried on an old uniform but it was "quite hopelessly small" so he ordered a new one.[28] He also paid a visit to Scotts, the Hatters of Old Bond Street, where he left a silk hunting hat to be repaired and ordered two best silk hats, three caps, two stiff felt hats, a straw hat, and a wooden box in which to transport them.[29] Victor got out the old carriages and decided they would do for Canada.[30]

The Duchess of Connaught wrote with advice to bring everything Evie wanted such as tablecloths, ink stands, and cushions, but not furniture. The letter noted that, because of the war, the duchess had let some of the carpets get rather worn, but advised Evie to "put up with things as we have them (until you can make better arrangements) ... Being on the spot you will know exactly what is wanted." She also advised Evie to bring her own housekeeper and "a friend as Lady Secretary ... who could attend as your representative less important meetings of charitable institutions." These were, she wrote "the monthly meetings of the Red Cross, Daughters of the Empire, Victorian Order of Nurses and National Council of Women ... You will be asked to go to the big ones only."[31] Presumably she meant that her secretary would go to the monthly meetings and she would attend the more important events.

During the summer, Evie met Sir Sam Hughes, Canada's minister of Militia and Defence, when she opened a new Canadian hospital at Buxton near Chatsworth, and she was photographed smiling in his presence.[32] The duke termed the picture "rather unlucky."[33] The duke knew already that there may be trouble about Hughes. They also met the Canadian minister of Trade and Commerce, Sir George Foster, and entertained him at Chatsworth. Foster's diary records his reaction to that visit: "I think we shall like our GG's very much, but what a sacrifice for them!"[34]

In the fall, Victor, Evie, and their eldest daughter, Maud, spent a few days with King George V and Queen Mary at Windsor Castle.[35] The king invested Victor as Knight Grand Cross of the Most Distinguished Order of Saint Michael and Saint George.[36] This was a special honour which the king often granted to officials for important and loyal service in foreign and imperial affairs before the official left for a colonial post. The investiture included appropriate insignia which the duke could wear on ceremonial occasions. Just a few months earlier, the king had invested Victor with the Order of the Garter, the highest order of chivalry in Britain, which also included a sash and medal.[37] During their visit, while Maud rode with the king and Victor was invested with his knighthood, Evie received a seal from the queen, presumably a personal seal to be used on her correspondence. She had also been asked to return to her position as Mistress of the Robes on her return to England. In July, the king had granted Victor the use of the Royal colours on their carriage while in Canada, which Victor pronounced "really a great relief."[38] He probably meant that he could use the Royal Arms on the viceregal landau, indicating that he was acting for the king. Altogether,

Figure 1.2 The Duchess of Devonshire and Sir Sam Hughes, Canada's minister of Militia and Defence, visiting injured soldiers in Buxton Hospital, 1916. A photo accompanying an article in the *Montreal Standard*, 30 September 1916, headlined "Wife of Canada's Governor-General Designate Opens New Canadian Hospital at Buxton Near Historic Chatsworth," does show the duchess smiling beside Hughes as they leave the hospital.

with the carriage colours, knighthood, and medals, Victor and Evie had the viceregal ceremonial accoutrements to establish their credentials in Canada. This satisfying visit, and Evie's expected return to the royal circle, cemented their relations with the royal family and their connections to the Empire.

Two weeks before they left for Canada, Victor had a long talk with the Duke of Connaught, who had just returned. Victor found the old duke to be "quite engrossed" with Sir Sam Hughes, Canada's minister of Militia and Defence. During his tenure as governor general, the Duke of Connaught, who had extensive military experience and was a field marshal in the British Army, had judged Hughes to be incompetent, and he had pressured the prime minister, Sir Robert Borden, to get rid of him. Despite Hughes's excitable nature and eccentric behaviour, Borden had refused; Hughes was still at his post. The conversation made Victor fear that major difficulties awaited him.[39]

A few days before his departure for Canada, Victor visited the Canadian troops in France, where he saw with his own eyes the terrible effects of the war. On 24 October, with Lieutenant Colonel Harold Henderson, his newly appointed military secretary, he crossed the Channel, arriving in Boulogne for luncheon. That day they visited a Canadian hospital and an Army Veterinary Camp and met Sir Douglas Haig, commander of the British Expeditionary Force. Though they passed several military camps, Victor remarked in his diary that everything looked normal, with well-tilled fields, and a few children about. That night they were billeted in a plain but comfortable house.

The next day they reached the devastated Somme battlefield, where the battle had been ongoing since 1 July 1916. Nearly 20,000 British soldiers were killed that first day and 37,000 were wounded, the worst day in British military history. However, in his diary of the first week of July, Victor had noted, based on newspaper reports, that "the advance seems to be favourable so far" (2 July) and "we seem to have made a big advance and the reports generally are not unfavourable" (3 July). By 4 July, he must have been hearing a few negative comments, as he wrote: "Newspapers paint a better complexion on the course of events, but of course everyone here will crabb [sic] everything." Although he did have a tendency to look on the bright side, in this case Victor was not using rose-coloured glasses. The newspapers at the time did report positive results: many prisoners taken, damage to the German army. There seems to have been a concerted attempt to avoid lowering the morale of the British people. General Haig was said to have reported that the situation was for the most part favourable. Since lines of communication had broken down, possibly even General Haig did not know at that time exactly what had happened.

Thus, nothing in the news reports between July and October had prepared Victor for what he would see on the Somme: little wonder at his shock. "October 25: Most remarkable sights. Men, horses and wagons everywhere and the mud is indescribable. No confusion or worse and perfect temper. First we made for Albert. Wish everyone in England could see the desolation. Went on to Fricourt. Saw the show German dug out – Montauban – and tried to get through to Contalmaison, but road was impossible … The whole sight is too strange and weird. Saw what was Pozières [a small village] – not a trace left."

Amid German shelling overhead, he visited the 4th Canadian Division under Major General David Watson, who reported that they were feeling low as they had had a failure that morning. Major Watson's division, as part of the 2nd British Corps, had arrived on the Somme in mid-October, a group of raw, untried troops assigned to take Regina Trench, a deep system of fortified trenches strongly defended by the Germans. The 4th Division had already captured most of Regina Trench using heavy shellfire and direct attack. The 44th Battalion, soldiers from Manitoba, was ordered to take the remainder on the morning of 25 October. They began the battle at 7:00 a.m. It had been pouring rain for twenty-four hours. Tragedy struck immediately. The artillery barrage had been woefully light and ineffective. The Germans were able to sweep no man's land with intense enfilading machine-gun fire. Most of those who were not killed outright sought cover in shell holes and disused trenches; there they lay till darkness, though a few managed to crawl back in daylight to their own front lines. The 44th Battalion withdrew to their original position and all was quiet by 11:00 a.m.[40] They reported 30 killed, 159 wounded, and 25 missing for their morning's work. It wasn't surprising that they felt low. While the duke was there meeting with the general, a German shell came over. That morning in particular must have brought home to him how fortunate it was that Eddy was not in this morass, but safe in Paris, at least for now.

The day of departure for Canada finally arrived. On 4 November 1916, the duke spent the morning reading the papers and commenting on the headlines about the Great War in his diary: "The Italian news is good and Rumanians seem to be holding their own." At least that was something positive after all the setbacks the Allies had experienced in the last few months. Victor continued writing in his diary: "Lovely day. The place is looking very beautiful. Shame to leave it."[41]

At luncheon (he never used the word lunch), Victor met his estate managers for a last-minute discussion of details. These men would be responsible for his estates for the next five years. He was leaving in their care not only Chatsworth, but also the other houses that were part of the Devonshire holdings. Devonshire House in London, built in the mid-eighteenth century, was also participating in the war effort. It now housed both the offices of the British Red Cross Society and the Joint Women's Volunteer Aid Detachment (VAD), a department of the Order of Saint John. Later, in 1917, Victor would authorize the officers of the Women's Auxiliary Army Forces (WAAF) to share the accommodation with them. His estates also included two eighteenth-century houses – the Palladian villa Chiswick House in West London, and the Elizabethan-Jacobean country house, Compton Place, in Eastbourne – which were rented. An Elizabethan country house, Hardwick Hall, built by Bess of Hardwick in the sixteenth century, Bolton Abbey in the Yorkshire Dales, and Lismore Castle in Ireland completed the Devonshire estates. It was a heavy burden of responsibility for his estate managers.

The duke dressed in his travelling clothes – a Norfolk belted jacket with knickerbockers, spats, and a soft cap – and joined his wife, the duchess, who was attired in a warm fitted jacket, long skirt, and wide-brimmed hat. They said goodbye to the heads of staff at Chatsworth, but because their travelling date was kept secret for reasons of security, there was no ceremonial send-off. An article in the *Derbyshire Times*, including a picture of the duke and duchess as they left Chatsworth, described the community's regret at not having been given the opportunity to wish them Godspeed and bon voyage. The article appeared two weeks after their departure when they were safely in Ottawa.[42]

The whole family boarded the motors (they never used the word automobile) that would take them to the train at Chesterfield. On the station platform, the parents said an emotional goodbye to the four younger children. The duke and duchess were taking only their two eldest daughters on the voyage, having decided not to "put all their eggs in one basket."[43] Arriving in Liverpool, the party boarded HMS *Calgarian* and met the others who were to travel with them, the duke's aides-de-camp and his military secretary, who was accompanied by his wife and two children. The servants who would work for them in Ottawa – cooks, maids, valets, butlers, footmen, housekeepers, the duchess's secretary, and the comptroller – had been sent ahead two weeks before to prepare the house.[44] The duke's family and staff had the whole ship to themselves.

HMS *Calgarian*, built in Scotland for the Allan Line shipping company of Montreal, had launched as a luxury passenger liner just months before the Great War began. Needing more ships for the war effort, the

Royal Navy had commandeered her, removed interior fittings, and put her to service as an armed merchant cruiser working at neutral ports – Lisbon, and later New York – to prevent the escape of German liners. In 1916, the British government again refitted the ship with a few cabins in order to transport the Duke of Connaught back to England; as Queen Victoria's third son, the Duke of Connaught required a certain luxury. That mission accomplished, the ship was now ready to transport the new governor general and his entourage to Canada.

Captain Vivian Bulkeley-Johnson, one of the aides-de-camp (ADC) who joined them on the ship that day, wrote a diary and many letters to his parents during his two years in Canada. As a student at Oxford before the war, he had befriended a Canadian, Vincent Massey. Many years later, when Massey was the Canadian High Commissioner to Britain, Bulkeley-Johnson gave him the letters and diary he had written while an ADC to the Duke of Devonshire, requesting that they be placed

Figure 1.3 HMS *Calgarian*, launched in 1914 as a passenger ship, served the British navy during the war. It was refitted to carry the Duke of Connaught from Canada to England and to transport the Duke of Devonshire and his entourage to Halifax in 1916. The ship was sunk by four torpedoes in March 1918.

in the Canadian archives and opened only in the year 2000. During his time in Canada, Bulkeley-Johnson, affectionately known as BJ, developed a lifelong friendship with the family. His letters to his parents reveal details of family life both at Rideau Hall and during their travels.

Bulkeley-Johnson described his meeting with the family:

> We arrived on board an hour before the Duke and Rody [Rodolph Kenyon-Slaney, another aide-de-camp] and I were discussing what our first duty would be. He said that he was sure it would be to take the dogs onto the deck and entice them to do their duty thereon. We both began to talk very big about not being valets when their arrival was announced. After the ordinary how do you dos the duchess said "Oh, Captain Kenyon Slaney, I think after the train journey that perhaps the dogs may be a little weird and it might be as well to take them for a walk on the deck." So both of us, with a dog each, started our work. I led my dog to every pillar and every post without avail, then took him in where, in front of everyone, he at last found a spot to his liking. I caught the duchess's eye ... she was delighted.[45]

Bulkeley-Johnson went on to describe the officers: "This ship, which is something over 20,000 tons, is commanded by Captain Corbett of the Royal Navy. What this officer lacks in smartness of appearance he makes up by a loud voice, a bluff manner and a round red clean-shaven face surrounded by straight short hair. ... The second in command is ... short, thin, alert, and exceedingly talkative, being especially rich in racy stories." The crew included boys in training and "a few men of the Royal Navy and some veteran marines who manned the eight 6″ guns."[46]

Meals were served in a small dining room, its white walls decorated with sporting prints. When they were not sick on the rough voyage, they could use the comfortable chairs and sofas in the upper-deck drawing room. As soon as the sun set, the ship had to sail in complete darkness to avoid any lights drawing unwanted attention. When all the portholes were shut, the atmosphere of the whole ship became stuffy.[47]

Everyone knew of the danger at sea from German submarines. Just a week before, the Germans had torpedoed the civilian ship ss *Marina* off the southern coast of Ireland; six American civilians were killed, and the survivors told of being stranded in open lifeboats while the submarine sailors watched and offered no assistance.[48] At almost the same spot, in May 1915, German submarines sank RMS *Lusitania*, killing 1,200 civilians, including some Americans.[49] Despite those provocations, the United States had not yet entered the war. Victor soothed himself by thinking that the rough sea would be a bit too much for submarines.[50] He was undoubtedly right. Periscopes depended on visual information which huge waves would impede. His experience at the Admiralty gave him some knowledge of ships, and in 1916 neither sonar nor radar technologies had yet been invented.

The cautious Captain Corbett on HMS *Calgarian* steered the ship north from Liverpool, avoiding the rugged southern coast. Next morning they discovered that, in the dark of the rough Irish Sea, two of their four escort destroyers had collided with each other and were returning to England.[51] The three remaining ships began zigzagging on a dangerous course as they plied the North Channel between the rocky coast of Ireland and a minefield.[52] Since it was Sunday, the day began with a church service, offering a chance to pray for safe passage. As they moved out into the Atlantic, Victor went up to the bridge and saw the last of Ireland disappear into the fog. The storm grew worse, tossing everything around inside the ship – an ink bottle from a writing table shot across the room, a chair overturned, BJ's curry was tossed onto the floor.[53] The woodwork in the reinstalled cabins creaked and water dribbled in.[54] Most of the party disappeared into their cabins; only Victor and three of his staff appeared for dinner, but no one could eat much. Waves crashed against the ship, damaging one lifeboat, washing another overboard, and carrying off the aerial that brought the nightly wireless reports.[55]

A day later the storm had abated somewhat, and with a new aerial in place Victor could again indulge his passion for news. The presidential election in the United States was in progress. Supreme Court Justice Charles Evans Hughes, the Republican Party candidate, was ahead, but the results from California would take another day to come in. When all the votes were reported, Victor was not surprised that the news declared the Democratic Party candidate, Woodrow Wilson, had been narrowly re-elected. Wilson's slogan, "He kept us out of war," appealed to many American voters. However, some were speculating that a report that Germany intended to attack all ships making for England might just make the Americans change their minds.

Despite the stormy days, the intrepid Victor, whose Admiralty work had made him familiar with ships, wanted to see how the whole vessel worked. He visited the captain and officers on the bridge, "saw the gun control," which he found "extremely complicated," went down to the engine room to exchange a few shouted words with the chief engineer, and visited the officers in their mess. He pronounced the food good and never missed a meal. He invited Captain Corbett and his commander to dinner; Evie, who had been feeling the effects of the storm, emerged from her bedchamber to join them.[56]

Each night Captain Corbett turned the clock back a few minutes, so that by the time they reached Halifax the party had recovered from the five-hour time change.[57] Finally, after six days of rolling and pitching at sea, they met their escort ship, the armoured cruiser HMS *Carnarvon*, to be guided into Halifax Harbour. Zigzagging as they neared land, the two ships moved slowly into one of the largest natural harbours in the world, one to which the duke would return in 1917 under very different circumstances.

CHAPTER 2

Getting Settled in the Colony

At long last the stormy voyage to the New World was over. That day in November 1916 grey clouds hung low. Winter had shorn the trees of their leaves and the rocky hills looked barren. As they entered the calm harbour, the Duke and his entourage stood at the railing of the upper promenade deck, watching the scene unfold. Along the shore were factories – the Acadia sugar refinery, the Richmond printing company, the Hillis and Sons foundry, which made stoves and furnaces. Houses ranged in rows up the hill toward the Citadel at its peak.

Several huge ships lay in port that day, among them the Russian ship *Algol* on Pier 8, the British ship *Nagaristan* on Pier 9, and the British mail steamship *Caraquet* on Pier 3. *Matatua* from Ireland was in dry dock after a fire on board.[1] Halifax Harbour, which remained ice-free year-round, was large enough to hold a whole fleet of ships. From the outer harbour on past the Narrows of the inner harbour and into Bedford Basin was a distance of 17 miles (28 km). The harbour, used by the British from 1749, had reverted to Canadian control in 1906, but when the war began in 1914, the Dominion of Canada, still beholden to the British in matters of defence and foreign policy, returned it to British control.

At Pier 2, when HMS *Calgarian* docked no one knew exactly when the duke and his party would make an appearance, but people soon began to gather at dockside, waiting for a glimpse of the new governor general and his family. Customarily he would be met by the prime minister – Borden had met the Duke of Connaught in Quebec City in 1911 – but wartime security had trumped the seemingly inviolable rules of British protocol. Instead, Prime Minister Borden sent two letters of apology[2] and Sir Louis Davies, a justice of the Supreme Court of Canada, to bring greetings.

Halifax was a bustling boom town; almost fifty thousand people lived in the city with another thirty thousand in nearby towns and villages. Most people serviced the war: the Royal Navy and Royal Canadian Navy sailors and the soldiers of the Canadian Expeditionary Force shipped out from Halifax to Europe; some came back, many wounded. *Matériel* for the war also moved through the harbour.[3]

After luncheon, the duke, the duchess, and their party disembarked before an excited, cheering crowd. They made a colourful procession, the tall, round figure of His Excellency in his morning suit and black silk top hat, Her Excellency in a black sealskin coat, the two daughters, both with colourful suits and matching furs, followed by three young, handsome aides-de-camp and the military secretary, all in full dress uniform. "In spite of the rough trip, all had an excellent colour and were taking a keen interest in everything around them ... a western battalion was drilling nearby and the Ducal party seemed much interested in the manoeuvres," noted the Toronto *Globe*.[4] As they stepped ashore, the party was received by a guard of honour with a military salute from the 66th Regiment, Princess Louise Fusiliers.[5]

Khaki-clad troops – among them the 226th Battalion from Manitoba and the 246th Battalion, Nova Scotia Highlanders – and thousands of cheering citizens lined both sides of the street as the party proceeded to Province House.[6] Built in 1819, Province House had been the home of the Nova Scotia House of Assembly ever since. Although most of the ten British men who served as Canada's governors general sailed up the St Lawrence River to Quebec City for their installation, two were installed in Province House: the Marquess of Lorne in 1878 and Earl Grey in 1904. Usually the swearing-in of a new governor general occasioned ceremony: a luncheon or dinner, a large reception, and a twenty-one-gun salute;[7] however, in 1916, the king had directed that during the war "salutes shall not be fired,"[8] and the duke had requested a less lavish greeting than usual.[9] The swearing-in ceremony, though, was still a requirement.

At Province House, a detachment from the 63rd Halifax Rifles formed a guard of honour. In the entrance lobby with its four classical columns and delicate plasterwork, reminiscent of their own English homes, the duke and his party were met by Sir Louis Davies, gowned in scarlet and ermine. The party mounted the grand staircase, formed a procession with the duke and duchess at the end, and proceeded to the Council Chamber, where the assembled military, government, and church representatives rose in greeting.

Called the Red Chamber, with its red carpet and red upholstered chairs, the Council Chamber remained much the same as it was in 1819.[10] The heraldic badge of the Prince of Wales – three ostrich feather plumes – decorated the ceiling moulding. Large portraits of King George III and Queen Charlotte, who were on the throne in 1819, faced the assembly. Lord Dalhousie, then Lieutenant-Governor of Nova Scotia, had presented these portraits to Province House in 1820 to represent the authority of the British Empire.

Despite wartime restraint the people of Nova Scotia had brightened the chamber with white and yellow chrysanthemums, ferns, and palms. The Duke of Devonshire took his seat on the dais before the assembled guests; the duchess and her daughters sat on one side, the military and government officers on the other. Wives of dignitaries, representing the Dominion government and the Nova Scotia legislature, presented bouquets to the duchess. Lieutenant-Colonel Harold Henderson, the duke's military secretary, read the governor general's commission from the king. Sir Louis Davies placed the oath book on a table. The duke stepped down from the dais to swear the oath of office of Governor General and Commander-in-Chief of Canada; Davies signed the jurat, which certified that the oath had been administered. The secretary of state handed the Great Seal of Canada to the new governor general. It represented the power and authority of the Crown flowing from the sovereign to Canada's parliamentary government and, still today, is used on all official documents, such as proclamations and commissions.[11] For each new sovereign a new Great Seal is prepared; this one represented King George V. The governor general is the official keeper of the Great Seal and takes an oath to that effect, however, as was traditional, the new governor general handed the Great Seal back, saying, "I hand you the Great Seal of Canada for safekeeping." The Duke of Devonshire, Governor General and Commander-in-Chief of Canada, left the chamber, followed by those assembled in solemn procession. The duke and duchess stood at the bottom of the staircase to greet each guest. Then, while the band played "God Save the King," the duke inspected the guard of honour. That concluded the short ceremony.[12]

The duke and his party returned to Pier 2 to the special train that was waiting to take them to Quebec City and Ottawa. That evening, the duke sent a telegram informing Colonial Secretary Andrew Bonar Law that he had taken the oath and assumed the office of Governor General of Canada.[13]

For Canadians it was a remarkable day. In the midst of the uncertainty and sorrow of war, they were reminded "that the foundation of our imperial structure is an ancient, and impregnable Stone, the same yesterday, today and forever!" a reporter from the Halifax *Herald* waxed lyrically.[14] To the people of British heritage present at the swearing-in, to those lining the streets as the procession passed, to those who read the detailed descriptions of the ceremony, to the children of the nation in whose classrooms the world map showed in red the grand Empire on which the sun never set, the swearing-in of a new Governor General of Canada confirmed their vision of themselves as a proud part of the British Empire. They looked to the Duke and Duchess of Devonshire to uphold their vision and carry them through troubled times.[15]

The young Dominion of Canada that welcomed the duke and his family was experiencing the stresses of war, problems that would be felt with more force in the coming years of the governor general's term.

Figure 2.1 *Opposite*
Figure 2.1a The Great Seal of Canada representing King George V, who was sovereign in 1916 when the Duke of Devonshire was installed as Governor General of Canada. Canada creates a new Great Seal of Canada for each sovereign.

Figure 2.1b The Privy Seal of the Duke of Devonshire as Governor General of Canada. Each governor general has a unique privy seal. This one for the Duke of Devonshire depicts the arms of the duke in the centre. Around the edge are the words "His Grace Victor Christian William, Duke of Devonshire." The seal must have been created before the duke said he preferred to be addressed as "His Excellency."

One issue had already begun to rankle: the British considered Canadian soldiers to be simply part of their own army. Canada's politicians now sought greater recognition of the country's contribution to the war effort, and by extension an acknowledgment of Canada's growing independence as a nation. Canadians had enthusiastically volunteered to serve the Motherland and the Empire when the war began in the fall of 1914; after more than two years of war, that enthusiasm was waning. In his New Year's message at the beginning of 1916, Prime Minister Borden had doubled Canada's commitment from 250,000 to 500,000 soldiers, from a population of less than 8 million.[16] In the month of January 1916, just over 29,000 had signed up for the Canadian Expeditionary Force, but by October, recruits for the month had fallen to 5,500. Meanwhile, the attrition in deaths and wounds was huge. In September's week-long battle of Flers-Courcelette alone, Canadians suffered 24,029 casualties.[17] The country was in danger of falling behind on its commitment.[18]

The labour situation had changed dramatically as well. During the depression of 1914 many men had enlisted in order to have a job, but by 1916 the labour glut had turned into a shortage, with new essential jobs created in munitions factories, on farms, on streetcars and trains, and on assembly lines. Women were taking up much of this work, but still there were not enough men available for military service. The increasing cost of living was further fuelling discontent.[19] Between 1914 and 1916 the cost of food had risen by 12 per cent; wages had not kept pace, and the number of strikes and lockouts had almost doubled.[20]

Arguments between English Canada – mostly people of British origin – and French Canada simmered. French Canadians in Quebec, Ontario, and Manitoba still felt aggrieved by Ontario's 1912 Regulation 17, which limited French-language instruction in Ontario schools to the first two years. French speakers in Quebec and elsewhere in Canada believed that the Constitution, by which they meant the British North America Act, guaranteed equal rights for French and English throughout Canada and saw Ontario's new regulation as a further assault on

Figure 2.1c and 2.1d *Opposite* The two sides of the Governor General's Academic Medal of the Duke of Devonshire.

the rights of French Canadians, which were already being eroded. By 1916, the matter had reached the House of Commons. A motion by Wilfrid Laurier's Liberals proposing that Ontario children of French parentage be taught in their mother tongue was defeated. In late 1916, the British Judicial Committee of the Privy Council ruled that Regulation 17 was indeed within the jurisdiction of the Ontario government. French Canadians were not satisfied. As the duke would later learn, the passions aroused spilled over into the dispute over which community, French or English, recruited more soldiers for the war.[21]

However, basking in the adulation of the welcoming Canadians, the duke and his party enjoyed two days' travel on the luxurious train built by the Canadian Pacific Railway for the visit of King George V and Queen Mary, who had toured Canada in 1901 as the Duke and Duchess of Cornwall and York. In what a writer in 1902 called "a palace on wheels,"[22] young Lady Maud was so impressed at travelling "in great luxury with comfortable beds and real baths" that she remembered it many years later.[23] The group spent their waking hours in the large reception room of the day coach, *Cornwall*, decorated in Louis XV style, with walls of antique gold, walnut woodwork, and dark blue velvet draperies. A large sofa and armchairs, a table, a writing desk, and a piano of Canadian manufacture made it a comfortable sitting room. Although the coach opened onto the spacious observation platform at the end of the train, the chilly November weather kept them inside the sumptuous interior. The duchess wrote letters and prepared for dinner in a boudoir with light blue moiré silk window coverings, the walls decorated with soft Watteau-like paintings in frames touched with gold. The two girls could join her in the small room with its divan, gold-embossed table, and reading lamp.

The dining room, which could serve up to eight at a time—their party required two sittings—was lit by an electric chandelier, Green velvet draperies and warm brown velvet upholstery made it an intimate setting. Along the corridor they found the pantry, kitchen, and storeroom and then the night coach, the *York*, which had two bedrooms for the duke and duchess, each with a bed, wardrobe, dressing table, large mirror, and an ensuite bathroom. Adjoining rooms, meant for the valet and maid, were likely used by the ADCs, since the duke and duchess had sent their servants ahead. In the *York* were also two more staterooms, a general toilet, and a luggage room. Moving along they came to the *Canada* car with six additional staterooms and a smoking room, where the duke could enjoy a cigarette and a drink with his ADCs or update his diary at the large writing table.[24]

The train journey, which began on the afternoon of Saturday, 11 November, stopped briefly at Levy, across the St Lawrence River from Quebec City. There the Lieutenant-Governor of Quebec, Sir Pierre-Évariste Leblanc, welcomed them. Behind him appeared the familiar tall, willowy figure of the British ambassador to the United States, Sir Cecil Spring Rice, along with his wife, Lady Florence, who was the duke's first cousin. Sir Cecil's affectionate name among family and friends was "Springy." The Spring Rices had been on holiday in Canada during the presidential election in the United States. Although they'd known that Victor and Evie were on their way to take up their posting, like everyone else they had not known their exact schedule; they just happened to be in Quebec City on the right day. Victor and Evie were very pleased to see family and invited Springy and Florence to join them in Ottawa.[25]

The train arrived at Ottawa Central Station, across from the Château Laurier, at exactly 11:00 a.m. on Monday, 13 November. Union Jacks, bunting, and the royal coat of arms festooned the station. A large crowd spilled onto Besserer Street; onlookers waved white handkerchiefs in greeting and craned their necks, anxious to catch a glimpse of the new governor general and his family. Sir Robert Borden, the impeccably dressed prime minister, looking distinguished with his shock of white hair and erect posture, boarded the train accompanied by Lady Borden to bring greetings. Finally, the tall, broad-shouldered figure of the duke, clothed in a long black fur-trimmed overcoat and a silk top hat, emerged from the train. He inspected the Governor General's Foot Guards and charmed the assembled dignitaries with a short greeting to each as he shook hands. Journalists noted that the duchess and her daughters were plainly and warmly dressed against the cold.

The prime minister introduced members of the Dominion cabinet, the leader of the Opposition, Sir Wilfrid Laurier, and representatives of the city and clergy. When Borden called for "three cheers and a tiger,"[26] the crowd complied with such gusto that the rafters returned the echo.

Figure 2.2 The duke was relieved that a carriage would take them from Ottawa's Grand Trunk Railway Central Station to Rideau Hall, 13 November 1916. On the right is Colonel Henderson, the military secretary.

The tiger, an American custom, was a sort of growl or screech after the three cheers. It was commonly used at the time as a special demonstration of approbation. A band then played the national anthem.[27]

To the duke's relief, carriages awaited; their own, shipped earlier, had not yet arrived. The duke and duchess rode in one carriage accompanied by military secretary Henderson, the two daughters rode in another, and the staff rode in motors. The party proceeded down Sussex Street, which was lined with a guard of soldiers from the 10th Battalion, Canadian Expeditionary Force.[28]

The prime minister was pleased with the hearty reception. "I believe they will be very popular, and the Duchess of Devonshire is specially charming. She seems delighted to return to Canada once more," he wrote to the Canadian High Commissioner in London, Sir George Perley.[29]

Victor barely had time for luncheon and a short walk with Evie in the snow-laden garden before beginning his work as governor general.

Prime Minister Borden arrived for their first private meeting. Borden, then sixty-two years old, had been leader of the Conservative Party since 1901 and had defeated the Liberals under Sir Wilfrid Laurier in the 1911 election to become prime minister. He wanted to discuss his minister of Militia and Defence, Sir Sam Hughes.

The Duke of Connaught and Hughes had had a fractious relationship. Hughes had been argumentative and sometimes insulting to Connaught and had pestered him for a Victoria Cross for his Boer War service. Connaught, as a senior military man – he had risen to field marshal, the highest rank in the British army – thought Hughes incompetent as minister of Militia and Defence. Even before the war, Connaught had pressured Borden repeatedly to do something about the man, preferably dismiss him from his ministerial office. Borden had always put Connaught off, saying that while Hughes had been criticized, he had also received wide commendation, particularly for building the military training camp at Valcartier in 1914 where he had prepared more than 32,000 soldiers for transport to France in just eight weeks. This achievement had impressed Borden and others.

During the Connaught years, Borden's support of Hughes was based partly on their long-standing relationship – Hughes had always supported Borden loyally – and partly on the militia minister's enormous energy, both of which made it easy for Borden to overlook some of Hughes's eccentricities. When it turned out that the Ross rifle, manufactured in Canada and strongly recommended and supported by Hughes, jammed in the mud of Flanders to the extent that Canadian soldiers were throwing it away and taking up the Lee-Enfield rifle of fallen British soldiers, Borden did not remove Hughes from office. When the Shell Committee scandal broke in the spring of 1916, with accusations that Hughes's friends on the committee, formed in 1914 to purchase ammunition for the war, made huge profits, Borden appointed a commission to investigate the charges of profiteering; a few months later it exonerated Hughes, producing no evidence to justify dismissal. Hughes had created other embarrassing incidents, but Borden feared that removing him would undermine public confidence in the government and in the war effort.

However, shortly before the Duke of Devonshire's arrival, Borden had ordered Hughes, who was in England, to cable the changes he

Figure 2.3 Robert L. Borden, Canada's eighth prime minister, had been Conservative Party leader since 1901 and prime minister since 1911. He remained in office until 1920.

planned to make in the organization and command of the Canadian Corps so that they could be discussed and approved by the cabinet. Hughes had ignored the cable and formed a "Sub-Militia Council" to administer overseas forces. Reading this announcement in London papers infuriated Borden, who sent Hughes a reprimand. Hughes replied with a letter critical of Borden, which finally eroded the last of Borden's patience; he asked for Hughes's resignation. Hughes sent a letter resigning as minister on condition that their full correspondence on the issue be published. This was the situation the prime minister presented to the governor general: would the governor general read through the correspondence and give his opinion about whether it should all be published?[30]

One can almost hear Victor's sigh of relief on realizing that he would not be faced with this problem, which had plagued the full term of the Duke of Connaught. Victor did approve publication of the correspondence in its entirety. A short announcement of Hughes's resignation appeared in the press the next day. "On the whole the press [has] taken it very well," Victor reported in his diary.[31] The following day, the full correspondence, taking up several pages, was duly published.[32] A few days later, Borden came to Rideau Hall with Sir Edward Kemp, who was to be sworn in as the new minister of Militia and Defence.[33] Kemp, a businessman from Toronto, had been minister without portfolio in Borden's cabinet and had chaired the War Purchasing Commission.

On that first day as governor general, Victor was pleased with the results. His first collaboration with his prime minister had gone well, laying the foundation for a relationship that might survive any storms to come.

The next day, anxious to become familiar with the country and the issues he might face, Victor began meeting ministers at his office in the Parliament Buildings. With one or more of his ADCs, he would enter the central arched entrance of the East Block, over which a pointed pediment indicated the Office of the Governor General, a form of display that seems strange to our twenty-first-century desire for security and secrecy. The viceregal group would ascend the red-carpeted central stairway, which was used only by the governor general and his entourage. In deference to the royal representative, the other occupants of the second floor, the prime minister and cabinet ministers, used stairways at the end of the building.

These imposing Parliament Buildings with their Gothic architecture were faced with light-coloured Nepean sandstone quarried just a few miles away. Each window, with its arched frame like a raised eyebrow, peered down on the public below. Built in 1865, the whole suite of buildings perfectly expressed the unchanging Empire, its stability assured. The fact that the Centre Block had been demolished by fire just a few months earlier did not take away from that impression.

The governor general's office contained two outer rooms where the ADCs greeted each minister before introducing him to the governor general in his large inner office. As the guest entered, we can imagine the governor general leading him across the office to look out through those pointed-arch windows over the expanse of lawn. Opposite, he would see the West Block with the same Gothic design in the same sandstone, on his right the Centre Block, now under construction since the fire, and behind the construction site the elegant, castle-like Library of Parliament, which had survived the fire.

The duke might have motioned toward two lounge chairs near the windows where they could both sit and relax. Or the visiting minister might have taken one of two red leather chairs facing the governor general, who would have been seated in a red leather armchair at his massive desk, behind him a fireplace, which could be screened if the fire became too hot. The fireplace mantle, a length of light brown wood, supported a large gold-framed mirror that reached almost to the ceiling. On the other side of the room a long black tufted leather chesterfield looked dignified beside an expansive wooden bookcase, with leather-covered volumes peeking out from behind glass doors. Decorations along the top and bottom of the bookcase echoed the pointed arch of the windows. Portraits of King George V and Queen Mary probably hung above the chesterfield. A musty, pleasant odour of old leather, and traffic noises muted by the heavy stone walls, added to the calming atmosphere. The sound of the noonday gun, fired from nearby Nepean Point, penetrated the walls, alerting the men to set their watches. In this hushed and calm atmosphere, the governor and his minister would begin their acquaintance and the duke would gather information about Canada. He hoped he would get on well with his new colleagues.[34]

On his first day at the office, the new governor general again met his prime minister, who was thankful for his approval to publish the letters concerning Sam Hughes. He also met Sir Charles Fitzpatrick, chief justice of the Supreme Court, who had been acting as administrator during the short period between the departure of the Duke of Connaught and the Duke of Devonshire's arrival and swearing-in. Before joining the Supreme Court, Fitzpatrick had been a Quebec politician and minister of Justice in the government of Sir Wilfrid Laurier.

In the next few days the Duke of Devonshire entertained all the leading political figures at dinner or luncheon, met with leaders of the Roman

Catholic and Anglican churches, accepted the role of Chief Scout, a title the governor general traditionally held in the Boy Scouts of Canada,[35] and agreed to attend a dinner in Toronto with members of the Canadian Patriotic Fund, established to support the troops overseas.

While Victor was meeting his ministers, becoming familiar with Borden's government and with the Opposition members of Parliament, Evie tended to the children, the household, the staff, the servants, and the social functions. Though Evie talked over many things with her husband, it was clearly her responsibility to make a home for the family in what she viewed as "the colony." The first order of business was to put the household in order. Just two days after their arrival she wrote to her mother-in-law, Lady Edward Cavendish, whom she addressed as "Dearest Mummie": "We have got most of our things unpacked and feel much happier with our photographs and personal belongings about."[36]

Her next priority was the younger children left behind in England. They decided to send for them and have them make the hazardous trip across the Atlantic as soon as possible. Evie knew Lady Edward would be shocked that she was putting the children at risk, but she explained their reasoning: they thought, with some justification, that rough winter seas made it difficult for submarines to torpedo ships; everyone she spoke to thought that the calm spring weather would increase the submarine menace, so the time to send for them was now.[37] Later Evie told her own mother that they would not have risked it had they known that a heavily armed German steamship fitted with torpedo tubes was hovering in the North Atlantic steamship lanes at the time of the crossing. By the time that news came out, the children were already safe in Ottawa.[38]

Victor asked his friend Arthur Balfour to arrange passage for the children on the formerly luxurious RMS *Olympic*, a sister ship to the doomed *Titanic* and the fastest ship available. Originally a passenger liner, by 1916 it was in the service of the Canadian government carrying troops from Halifax, Nova Scotia, to Great Britain. Though this detail was never mentioned in any letters, the ship was also painted in

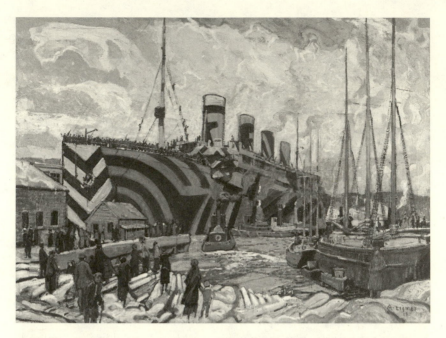

Figure 2.4 This painting, Olympic *with Returned Soldiers*, is by the celebrated Canadian artist Arthur Lismer. The duke and duchess's four children sailed on this vessel in 1916. During the war, many ships were painted in "dazzle" to make it difficult for German submarines to aim a torpedo accurately.

dazzle camouflage – bright colours and bold lines that made it more difficult for submarine observers to accurately estimate the ship's speed and heading when aiming a torpedo.[39]

In early December, the four children sailed with their governess, Miss Walton. Victor received a message from the Naval Department on 3 December that the ship had left port, though it had probably left a day or two earlier. On 7 December, a message said it had arrived in Halifax. Aboard the ship, sixteen-year-old Dorothy wrote to her grandmother: "It is extraordinary seeing magnificent rooms used as soldier's messes and storage for rifles. They can take 6,000 troops on board. There are only 600 passengers this time."[40]

On the night they arrived at Rideau Hall, before the luggage arrived, Evie put Anne to bed in one of her own vests and the little girl, just seven, was soon asleep. Then she looked for the other children – Dorothy, sixteen, Rachel, fourteen, and Charlie, eleven – and found

Figure 2.5 The Duke of Devonshire and his four youngest children at Rideau Hall. Left to right: (front row) Lord Charles and Lady Anne, with one of the many dogs; (back row) the Duke of Devonshire, Lady Dorothy, Lady Rachel.

them in the ballroom dancing to a gramophone.[41] Evie knew Victor would be a proud man next Sunday when all six children trooped into church behind him.[42]

The children had plenty of room to play. Rideau Hall had a floor space of about 90,000 square feet and the surrounding park was about 79 acres. Thomas MacKay, a wealthy stonemason, builder, and businessman, had built the house in 1838 using local limestone. In 1865, when Canada's capital was moving from Quebec City to Ottawa, the government rented the house for Lord Monck, then Governor General of British North America. Three years later, the government purchased the property to serve as Government House until a larger house could be built at Nepean Point, closer to Parliament Hill. In 1862, the government had gone so far as to hold a competition for the design of a new Government House, but financial strain delayed construction. As a stopgap, the MacKay house was expanded in 1865, and, over the years, additions were built in a rather haphazard manner. Fifty years later, with the changes made during the Duke of Connaught's tenure, the idea of a new house was finally abandoned and Rideau Hall became the official permanent residence of the governor general.[43]

Evie reported details of the house and grounds to her mother, who had lived there thirty years earlier. The Duke of Connaught had made many changes both inside and outside. "The Duke has stripped the grounds of all the 'cedars,'" Evie complained, "and has only planted a few fir trees, all the rest are hardwood trees which will be very nice 20 years hence. We are going to do a big thing in spruces and hemlock spruces for the sake of our successors."[44] Apparently the Duke of Connaught had personally marked many cedars in the entrance park for removal because he and his wife found them gloomy. Under his direction, they were replaced with six hundred maple, elm, oak, ash, and spruce trees, but of course, as Evie lamented, they would take time to grow.

The grounds of Rideau Hall followed the design concepts of an English country estate, rare in Canada for economic reasons, but also because the native wilderness often overwhelmed attempts to tame the environment. As early as 1902, underground electric wiring and limited fencing preserved the landscape's rural nature. The Duke of Connaught completed the transformation. To the north of the house were the services – laundry, stable, root cellar – and the winter sport facilities: the skating rink and toboggan run, with some land left for snowshoeing, and a curling rink, which Victor thought "a strange amusement and very chilly."[45] He occasionally watched competitive curling matches and handed out cups to the winners, but did not participate. To the east was a small farm which Victor would enjoy in summer. To the south, where they would get the most sun in the northern climate, a gentle series of descending plateaus featured the private gardens, and beyond them, the broad, sweeping lawns led to a cricket ground. To the west was the long, serpentine driveway entrance, widened by the Connaughts as the forest was replanted.[46]

The house, too, had come under the Connaughts' influence. They had overseen construction of a new, two-storey formal entrance to the home. "The larger built-out bit of dining room gets no sun as it is overshadowed by an awful clock room wing," Evie complained to her mother. "It was better to have a small dining room for ordinary dinners and to go to the ballroom for big ones. The main part of the drawing room is now only used on big occasions and is dark and dreary by daylight."[47] The smaller dining room served as a schoolroom. At the other end of a long hall, the "Minto Wing," built after her parents were in residence, Evie pronounced "hideous outside but convenient and sunny."[48]

Rachel, Anne, and Dorothy had the three front rooms, and Miss Walton, the governess, a back one, alongside a maid's bedroom, a workroom, and "a good bathroom." In the original 1838 Rideau Hall, builders had installed hot and cold running water, wine cellars, ample servants' quarters, and, according to the federal government's report, a hot-air furnace, but Evie said there were masses of radiators: if they were turned off they froze and if they were on the house became too hot.[49] Dorothy told her grandmother that "the house is awfully hot but apparently not as hot as most Canadian houses."[50] After Anne had suffered a bad cold, Evie complained that the heating system was far less healthy than the old stoves and fires. The older girls, Maud and Blanche, had bedrooms and a sitting room in the upstairs passage with nearby rooms for Miss Saunders, the duchess's private secretary, a maid, and a workroom. Charlie had a small room in the passage. Evie's room, at the round end of the passage above Victor's study, to her delight, was sunny all day.

Constrained by the war economy, they decided on only a few simple enhancements to the house. Dorothy told her grandmother, "We have got lovely sunny rooms. They are going to be done up as they are so untidy."[51] Vivian Bulkeley-Johnson, an ADC, described his room to his mother: "I have quite a nice little sitting room … My wall is papered with maps. I have got a good writing table, a large bookshelf and a comfortable armchair. The Duchess has lent me a couple of red table covers."[52]

Figure 2.6 Rideau Hall in winter.

The military secretary, Harold Henderson, his wife, Lady Violet, and children, Peggy, twelve, and Roderick, seven, lived at Rideau Cottage, a brick house on the estate, which had been built in 1866–67. Like Rideau Hall, the house had expanded to meet the needs of successive occupants. The term "cottage" was meant to evoke a sense of tranquility and rusticity rather than scale. By 1916, it was a two-storey building with verandahs on three sides and fourteen rooms, including a substantial kitchen. Located on the east side of the property near the farm, Rideau Cottage was not easily viewed from the public areas.[53]

To run the household, Evie had a small army of servants who had come by ship from England a month earlier – cooks, ladies' maids, parlour maids, butlers, footmen, chauffeurs, stableboys, and more. They were essentially invisible helpers, unacknowledged in her letters or Victor's diary, except occasionally when they created problems: both Maud and her maid fell when skiing and had to be seen by the doctor about possible knee injuries; Victor's valet became infatuated with Maud's maid, and neither could be sent away because the colonial secretary would not allow passage for English maids during the war. Later Evie told her mother that "Canadian maids won't stay – they say the work is too hard and they don't get as much time off as they require."[54] Such were the problems of a household manager, though the comptroller, Lord Richard Nevill, took most of the responsibility for servants.

A round building called "the gasometer," originally built in the 1870s to house gas cylinders so Rideau Hall could have its own supplies, was never used for its intended purpose and by 1916 had become female servants' quarters.[55] The male servants were, of course, housed elsewhere, perhaps in the basement near the kitchen, or possibly in the separate house now called "staff quarters" that was built in 1912 on the north section of the estate.

If the servants were invisible to the upstairs group, the staff – the ADCs, the military secretary and his family, the comptroller, the private secretaries, governesses, and the duke's clerk – became part of the family. They lived in close quarters, had meals together with the family, and Evie reported on their health, their quirks, their activities, and competence in her letters to her mother and her mother-in-law.

In the beginning there were the three ADCs who came from England with the family. Captain Angus Mackintosh, thirty-one, of the Royal Horse Guards (his regiment was nicknamed "the Blues" in honour of the colour of its uniform) had been shot in the chest at the Battle of Ypres and had only one working lung. He had served as ADC to the Duke of Connaught and Victor had asked him to stay on. A rather rotund Scot, he provided continuity and was very popular with Canadians. Evie thought him "very pleasant but not as interesting as the others." Maud and Blanche thought him fat and unattractive. Captain Vivian Bulkeley-Johnson (BJ), twenty-five, of the Rifle Brigade, had been wounded at the Battle of Neuve Chapelle in March 1915. He could still walk and dance, but his injured leg was shorter than the other and sometimes bothersome. He gave Evie the impression of being "high principled and straight" and she liked him right away. Captain Rodolph Kenyon-Slaney, twenty-four, of the Grenadier Guards, known as Rody, had been shot in the wrist and nearly died from a hemorrhage. He was very thin, had a patch on one lung, and, though he claimed to be healthy, Evie worried about his frequent cough.[56] In January 1917, they were joined by Lieutenant Mervyn Ridley, thirty-eight, of the Grenadier Guards Special Reserve, who had lost the use of his left shoulder and had a stiff ankle, but still managed to dance and skate.[57]

Figure 2.7 The aides-de-camp, 1917: Captain Rodolph Kenyon-Slaney, Captain Angus Mackintosh, Lieutenant Mervyn Ridley, Captain Vivian Bulkeley-Johnson.

The military secretary, Lieutenant Colonel Harold Henderson, thirty-one, was in the First Life Guards. Evie thought him slow at taking a hint, and tact was not his strong point. She and Victor both worried that his wife, Lady Violet, would be "silly" but in the early days she behaved well. The comptroller, Lord Richard Nevill, fifty-four, was "a good-looking old man with large blue eyes and a huge moustache. The children called him Prehistoric Peep (Peep for short) as his views were quite Victorian."[58] Later, even Evie occasionally referred to him as Peep.[59] Evie thought him "like a nice maiden aunt."[60] Two other Englishwomen were part of the extended family at Rideau Hall: the duchess's secretary, the beloved Miss Saunders, who had been with the family throughout much of the children's lives, and the children's governess, Miss Walton, an older, fussy woman who would later become a problem for Evie to resolve. As well, two Canadians who had worked at Government House for several years were of English background: Arthur Sladen, the duke's private secretary, who lived at 481 Slater Street in Ottawa, and the chief clerk, James Crowdy, who lived in the nearby village of Rockcliffe Park with his wife and family.[61] Their large household was thus entirely English from top to bottom. Evie would have it no other way.

In the first few weeks at Rideau Hall, Evie organized the children's lives. For Charlie, she told Lady Edward, "there is quite a good private school kept by an Englishman who was a clergyman, just outside the gates."[62] From early January 1917, Charlie attended this private boys' school, Ashbury College, just five blocks away, where he quickly made friends. The younger girls, Dorothy, Rachel, and Anne, were schooled at home by the governess, just as all the girls had been at Chatsworth. Evie became concerned about Miss Walton, who had been "most dreadfully fussing" on the ship and tried to keep the girls "entirely away from the staff which [was], of course, quite impossible with skating and tobogganing."[63] Evie hired a skating instructor and all the children could hardly wait for the skating rink to be ready. None had skated before, and it was Rachel who shone first on the rink and later made her mark in competitive figure skating. By the time she left Ottawa she was training at the Minto Skating Club and winning prizes in competitions.

Maud and Blanche took singing lessons and worked one day a week at the canteen of a Soldiers' Club run by the Imperial Order Daughters of the Empire (IODE). The IODE, founded in Montreal in 1900 to support Canadian troops leaving to fight in South Africa, had since expanded across the country. In 1916–17, its focus was on providing field comforts and hospital supplies for Canadian troops in France, and running canteens for returned soldiers in Canada. Maud and Blanche joined two chapters, one English and the other almost entirely French, which was good for their French-language skills. Maud's French was already passable and, as she would discover, the practice would soon come in handy on her solo visit to Washington in April 1917. Today, almost one hundred years later, the IODE is still an active women's organization.

Maud and Blanche also joined the May Court Club, Ottawa's first women's service club, founded in 1898 by Lady Aberdeen, wife of the Earl of Aberdeen, governor general from 1893 to 1898. Maud told her grandmother a story she had heard from Lord Richard Nevill: "He says that on the May Day when it was founded, Lord Aberdeen, with a wreath of flowers on his head, danced round the ballroom leading a cow! We imagine that is rather an exaggerated version." In 1916, the girls helped cut out clothes for the Red Cross and helped at a "Christmas tree" given by the May Court Club for the very poorest children in the city, "mostly French Canadian."[64]

By Christmas, the Rideau Hall toboggan run and skating rink were ready for use and the family was learning about Canadian winters, some of it the hard way with colds and flu. BJ described the duchess as a good skater and the duke as plodding round "puffing and blowing the while with the icicles hanging from his moustache."[65] The girls discovered cross-country skiing, which was more fun by moonlight. Even Victor skied, and Dorothy thought it very brave of him.[66] Maud described "ski-joring" to her grandmother. This involved a person on skis being dragged by a horse or sleigh, "sometimes with an ADC standing on the skis behind." Of course they fell. A year later they were more expert at it, riding along snowy roads behind a horse going at full gallop.[67]

For the Devonshires, far from home and family, 25 December did not feel like Christmas. Maud wrote to her grandmother, "Christmas seemed so strange out here ... It seemed so odd being only ourselves with no cousins."[68]

As BJ described it,

Xmas did not prove an exhilarating festival. We went solemnly to church in the morning ... Immediately after tea the Duchess gave presents to the servants, who were gathered somewhat lugubriously round the ball room, the only amusing part of it being to see Anne and Roderick, the Hendersons' little boy of seven, taking the presents round to certain of the servants who were their special friends. However, Richard Nevill (or "Peep" as we call him) rose to the occasion and, as soon as the presents were given and their Ex's [their Excellencies, the duke and duchess] disappeared, started the servants dancing, and it was not until about two hours later, he played "God Save the King" (which he does as if it was a polka) that they could be induced to withdraw. It was the first bit of real enjoyment during the day ... We had ... quite a cheery dinner party ... We danced after dinner, even the Duke taking the floor, the party ending off with Sir Roger de Coverley [an English country dance].[69]

The staff gave the Duchess a dark blue bowl with a little gold pattern on it, the choice of Peep, quite nice and the Duke the complete works of Stephen Leacock. The three "aides" gave the ladies Cavendish a large box of chocolates and Mackintosh and I joined in giving Charles a pair of skis. They are a curious, somewhat uncouth family of children. Lady Maud, herself a child in many ways, somewhat half-heartedly thanked us at breakfast, but not one word did any of us get from the others. The Duchess gave us each a very nice little silver bank note case which is exactly what I wanted ... [the weather] was the ideal Xmas day one sees on Xmas cards but never gets in England.[70]

BJ described the governor general's traditional New Year's Levee:

I don't think I have ever spent a more remarkable day than New Year's Day. We dressed up in our second best uniform and proceeded to Government Buildings where the Duke held his first levee. First the Ministers assembled in the ADCS' office where they took off their coats and "rubbers" and said "How do you do, Captain" an innumerable number of times to each of us ... They were then ushered in to shake hands with the Duke and wish him a happy new year, after which they took up their station behind him. Thereupon the doors were flung open and any man in Ottawa was free to enter by one door, shake hands, and go out by the other towards some lemonade which had been prepared for them. In spite of the fact that it was lemonade this year, some 800 people elected to take part in this ceremony, no Canadian ever missing an opportunity of shaking hands if he can help it. I stood in the anteroom in a tight tunic and gold aiguillettes – useless but ornamental – shaking hands with those I knew and smiling blandly upon those I didn't.

The rest of the day was also remarkable for BJ.

After a hurried lunch Rody and I got into our London clothes and our fur coats and armed with our card cases proceeded to call upon the Ministers' wives. In Canada all the men call on their friends' wives on New Year's Day. The wives "receive." However, Monsieur Casgrain, the Postmaster General, had just died and out of deference to his wife, a rather attractive Parisian lady of mature years, the wives were not receiving in their usual quantities.

Lady Laurier, however, was holding her salon in great state surrounded by a bevy of French Canadians in an early Victorian house. As she is somewhat deaf and completely blind, progress was difficult, but she beamed across her ample bosom upon her assembled guests. The French Canadian man servant ... was completely unable to come up [with our names] so that the Lady was completely in the dark as to our identity, but called us either Captain, or the "young men from Government House."[71]

With that, the extraordinary year that had seen so many changes for the Devonshires came to a close. The next year would challenge their view of themselves as aristocrats and viceroyalty.

✧

CHAPTER 3

Maintaining Imperial Standards

Evie felt keenly that it was her responsibility to maintain propriety at Government House. She kept a close eye on her four daughters and the four young men who served her husband as ADCs. They must all "help her in maintaining Government House as the acme of respectability," she told Captain Bulkeley-Johnson (BJ): "in a word, that we were to cultivate matrons who were old, or girls who were ugly, but turn a glassy eye upon the beauty of Ottawa."[1] Since Lord and Lady Dufferin had occupied the house in the 1870s, the governor general and his family had been the centre of Ottawa social life. The Connaughts, too, had entertained royally before the war. *The Globe* reported in January 1914 that a crowd of one thousand attended an event that they called a "drawing room," in the style of those once held by Queen Victoria: "Such an array of exquisite gowns, dazzling jewels and magnificent uniforms has seldom if ever been seen in the beautiful gold and crimson Senate Chamber."[2] But the war had put a damper on all social gatherings. Fancy dress balls and fashionable parties seemed frivolous when so many were serving in combat. Evie agreed that the young crowd could hold a few dancing parties, but for herself and her husband, Evie told Lady Edward, "We are advised to stick to the rule made by the Connaughts only to go to charity things during the war."[3] They did feel it was important to meet Ottawa's leading citizens, and they invited those with whom Victor would be working to dine with them at Rideau Hall. Their first dinners included Prime Minister and Lady Borden, Leader of the Opposition Sir Wilfrid and Lady Laurier, Chief Justice of the Supreme Court Sir Charles and Lady Fitzpatrick and their daughter. Evie thought the dinners especially dull for Maud and Blanche and decided to invite any daughters of similar age. Therein lay the first seeds of conflict with Evie's desire for strict propriety.

Prior to leaving England for Canada, Evie had heard about a group of young Ottawa women called "the Naughty Nine" and had been appalled at the stories describing their impropriety. "I hope that neither Rody nor BJ will get dragged into the cocktails-drinking fast set to which the 'naughty nine' belong," she told her mother, "but all the rest of the society here seems very dull for young men."[4] Unfortunately for Evie, the young men thought so too.

BJ wrote to his mother: "We had not been in the boat an hour on the day we sailed before she [the duchess] paced me round the deck and told me what she knew of them [the Naughty Nine], saying that Captain Mackintosh was obviously a lost soul, whom nothing could remedy, but that she hoped Captain Kenyon-Slaney and I would not fall, to too great an extent, into the snares which were doubtless being laid for us ... There is no doubt that she herself, though disapproving ... was keenly interested in the 'Naughty Nine' and that she would be extremely disappointed if the 'aides' proved not to take an interest."[5]

The "Naughty Nine" were young women who, in the absence of men their age, had channelled their high spirits into entertaining. The occasion that brought them to Evie's attention was probably a fundraising event held in the ballroom of Ottawa's Château Laurier in January 1916, where they danced before an audience of five hundred. "Cabaret de Vogue" was a benefit for the Duchess of Connaught's prisoners of war fund. "All the fashionable world was there."[6] Many of the men were in uniform, among them, at the viceregal table, Captain Angus Mackintosh.

As the cabaret evening wore on, the young dancers' costumes became increasingly skimpy, to the delight of the men and the distress of the conservative matrons of Ottawa. In some dances, half the group dressed as men. According to a newspaper report in *The Ottawa Citizen*, the grand finale began with "three immense bandboxes decorated with rose-colored ribbon gliding into the room, bumping into tables and chairs en route; then entered three charming pages dressed in black satin with knickerbockers, short black velvet capes and black velvet toques, who untied the ribbons, opened the boxes and drew forth three pretty young girls also attired in black with whom they danced."[7] General Willoughby

Gwatkin, Chief of General Staff of the Canadian Militia, whom the Devonshires would meet later, christened the girls "the Naughty Nine." Ottawa social life was never again the same staid, conventional place. Sandra Gwynn in *The Tapestry of War* called them "the first of the flappers, harbingers of the Jazz Age," the young women who bobbed their hair, danced the Charleston, and drank cocktails while most of the young men were on the battlefield.[8]

Ethel Chadwick, a woman in her mid-thirties who had frequented Government House parties and befriended the Connaughts, reported in her diary that after the cabaret, "for the sake of propriety," she and her sister refused all entertainments to which the Naughty Nine were invited. As Sandra Gwynn reported: "The young girls christened the sisters 'The Prudish Pickles' and when this got back to Ethel she responded with an affected shrug. 'I don't at all mind "Prudish,"' she wrote in her diary. 'But "Pickle" sounds too frivolous for us.'"[9]

At Government House in early December 1916, BJ wrote to his mother about the Naughty Nine:

Then the fatal day came. Not another dinner party must take place without asking Mr. Justice and Mrs. Anglin. Why had they not been asked before? Important people. Oh, they had a daughter? Oh, it would be nice if she came. The aide-in-waiting with furrowed brow and guileless heart had to explain that Miss Anglin *was* a nice girl; indeed she was more than that, she was a cheerful girl, but she was one of the Naughty Nine. Government House was shaken to its foundation – for the space of twenty-four hours. Then the invitation was issued, since it was finally resolved that the Empire wouldn't stand the shock of Mr. Justice Anglin being in any way offended.

Who was going to sit next to her? The duchess insisted that Angus Mackintosh should sit next to her, because she wanted to see how a "bird" and a "peach" behaved when in close proximity (Mackintosh has the reputation of being a great ladies man i.e., a "bird" in this country) besides which he was the idol of the Naughty Nine, hence a thrilling character to the inner soul of the duchess). However, Mackintosh sternly refused to be made the object of the ducal scrutiny, while it was known that Rody, who was aide-in-waiting, could and probably would, exert his undoubted prerogative of sitting next to her himself. Your son, however, also had ideas on the subject and had no intention of being placed next to a minister's wife without a struggle. Rody, if not a woman hater, is at least nervous of women; your son proceeded to work on these feelings of shyness, until Rody said, a few hours before dinner "I must alter the table. I can't talk to a girl I have never seen before." So, the object of every eye, I took Miss Anglin in to dinner. She may have been naughty ... she was not beautiful, but she was most certainly cheery and talkative, and instead of the usual conversation about whether I had been to Canada before, whether I liked Canada now, whether I would like it in the future, what I thought of "our winters," what I thought of Sir Sam Hughes, and other interesting topics, I found myself talking a great deal about congenial topics of nothing in particular. The duchess every now and then bent forward to see how we were getting on ... I think by the end of the evening the duchess had a strong suspicion that I had a few "birdie" qualities somewhere latent within me.[10]

While Ottawa society expected the governor general and his wife to uphold social standards, by the time the Devonshires arrived, Ottawa had become accustomed to the Naughty Nine and their antics. The daughter of Justice Anglin could arrive at Rideau Hall without censure from local society.

Despite twice-a-week dinners to meet the ministers and their wives, and often having what Evie called "stray people" to luncheon, Evie was bored. One unusual night, when all the ADCs and the girls had gone to a party, Evie wrote to Lady Edward that she and the duke had had a "Darby and Joan" dinner, home alone like a devoted old couple.[11] Today we would rely on radio and television to entertain ourselves, but for the Devonshires in 1916 there was not even radio broadcasting – it did not begin until the early 1920s. They usually made their own amusement with other people. After dinner, Victor would play bridge if there were enough people, and cribbage otherwise.[12] Even simple dinners with friends might have helped. Evie was used to being invited out frequently in London and being able to chat about politics and events of the day. The matrons of Ottawa probably did not like to invite the Devonshires to their homes, thinking they could not maintain the same standards as Government House. There is no evidence of the Devonshires ever being invited out to at-home parties in Ottawa, and as viceregals they "had no politics," so they could not discuss current events except between the two of them.[13] For Evie, social life in Ottawa was indeed dull.

They did keep up the Rideau Hall tradition of hosting skating parties, often on Saturday afternoon and sometimes midweek. Ethel Chadwick, friend of the Duke of Connaught, was an excellent dancer on skates. At one Saturday party in January 1917, she noted in her diary, after dancing on the ice she and her partner had to go into the rink-house to warm up at the stove, which "had a pan of hot water on top to wash skates in."[14] A month later Ethel had lovely fast waltzes with two different men and then went into the house to tidy up in Lady Maud's room. Dorothy and Rachel brought hot water for them to wash their hands, and then they all went down to the drawing room for luncheon. "The Governor General came in at the second or third course, we all had to rise, until he sat down. There were 23 at a long table: the Duke and Duchess, five daughters, Miss Saunders and Miss Walton, the children's governess, the aides and nine guests ... [The children's] numerous dogs came in and were fed from their plates ... There was one man at lunch, important in munitions they said, whom nobody met." It reminded Ethel of the scene in H.G. Wells's *Mr. Britling Sees It Through* in which no one is introduced to the American at an English party. Victor's guest would have been one of Evie's "stray people," someone who had come to see the governor general that morning. The duke was engrossed in his conversation with his guest, a man from the International Commission on War Supplies, whom he described in his diary as interesting not only on the present situation but also on future prospect of trade.[15]

One aspect of social life that Evie did enjoy was entertaining people from England. When the Devonshires first arrived in Ottawa, she had been happy to entertain Sir Cecil Spring Rice and his wife Florence. That visit was only the first in a parade of English people who arrived, some without notice, to talk with the governor general or to stay at Government House. Notable among them was Ian Hay Beith, who was on a lecture tour to publicize his recent book *The First Hundred Thousand*, a spoof of "Kitchener's Army."[16] The duke thought him a "rather odd but attractive man," and when Beith spoke to more than six hundred at the Canadian Club luncheon "his speech was admirable."[17]

In the midst of all this activity, Victor reported feeling shy, an experience unusual enough to rate a mention in his diary. In England he confidently moved among his aristocratic friends, his parliamentary colleagues, his university and church associates, as well as maintaining friendly relations with his working-class staff. In England his position among all of these was clear to him and to them. In Canada, his relationships with the people he met were important, and yet neither he nor they had a clear idea of how they should work together. In situations of social uncertainty, most of us look to others as models for our behaviour, but for Victor there were no exact models. He was at the top of the social ladder – others looked to him and to Evie to set the standards. It is a mark of Victor's sensitivity to others that he didn't just bluster his way through. Instead he watched, listened, and carefully considered how he should behave.

In October, he had written to Andrew Bonar Law, the colonial secretary, asking about his dress. While serving as governor general, the Duke of Connaught had always worn his military uniform, but he was both a top-level military man and a member of the royal family. Bonar Law wrote a handwritten, unofficial note replying to the Duke of Devonshire and saying that he believed the duke would be in a "more dignified position" if he stuck to civilian dress, a top hat and frock coat.[18] Still uncertain, ten days after he arrived, Victor, wearing a "high hat," joined the prime minister at the Château Laurier to watch the troops march to the train station across the road. Walking over to the station, Victor inspected the troops and said a few words to the officers. He noted that Sir Sam Hughes, despite his dismissal as minister, "appeared dressed in plain clothes and shook hands with everybody." Victor thought his own high hat seemed "incongruous."[19] He decided to talk to the prime minister about wearing a uniform instead. A few days later, when he had an opportunity to bring up the question with Borden, the prime minister concurred with Bonar Law in recommending civilian dress.

Just a month into his tenure, on his first trip to Montreal, the newspapers reported with some consternation that the new governor general dressed in civilian clothes as opposed to the field marshal's uniform always worn by the Duke of Connaught. By that time the duke was not even concerned enough to mention these reports in his diary. One newspaper article did note the duke's silk top hat, which must have pleased him since he had ordered his hats specially made in London.[20]

The question of his dress settled, the duke still had to get used to public speaking. His first speech from the stage at the Russell Theatre, during a meeting of the Ottawa branch of the Red Cross Society, again brought on the feeling of shyness. He was never a good speaker from the stage and suffered many times in the coming years about his speeches, but he got through that night. Two weeks later, Mackenzie King, the former Liberal Labour minister, attending a meeting of the Canadian Patriotic Fund, reported that the new governor general spoke very well in his few informal introductory remarks. Mackenzie King thought him "a man of force of character and ability, essentially practical and with a good business head."[21]

Once again, on his first visit to a French convent in Montreal, Victor noted in his diary, "Felt very shy, especially as my ideas of what we were going to see were not at all in accord with actualities."[22] Victor seems to have identified as the source of his shyness the fact that he did not know what to expect in Canada. Part of the discomfort was likely that the rules dictating his role as governor general covered only the most basic situations. These were contained in three documents given to him by King George V in August 1916 – his Commission, the Letters Patent, and the Instructions from the King sent in a letter from Andrew Bonar Law[23] – along with the principles outlined in the British North America Act of 1867, and various statutes.

The duke's Commission simply appointed the Duke of Devonshire Governor General and Commander-in-Chief of the Dominion of Canada. The Letters Patent, dated 15 June 1905, had served two previous governors general. They contained simple commands. The governor general had the authority to summon, prorogue, and dissolve Parliament; to appoint, and also to remove for cause, judges and other officers; to appoint deputies to assist him; and to read these Letters Patent at ceremonies. That reading had occurred at the swearing-in ceremony in Halifax. The Instructions document gave him a few more commands. He should communicate these instructions to Parliament; administer the oaths to those holding office; and assent to laws passed by both houses of Parliament. He had the power to grant pardons under certain conditions, and he must not quit the Dominion without the sovereign's assent.

As in British practice, there were unwritten rules, or conventions, as well. The three rights of the sovereign in a constitutional monarchy, as enumerated by nineteenth-century author Walter Bagehot – the right to be consulted, the right to encourage, and the right to warn – were thought to apply to the Governor General of the Dominion of Canada. And if this were in fact the complete list of Victor's duties, his position would be clearly analogous to that of Britain's king, who never interfered with decisions of Parliament; the sovereign, a neutral figure, remained above partisan politics. However, in 1916, the authority of the Governor General of Canada fell somewhere between the responsibilities of a full governor of pre-Confederation days and the ceremonial position with reserve powers that prevails today. While he had less authority than earlier governors general, he still held authority over Canada's foreign and defence policy and any decisions, broadly, that would have an impact on the Empire.[24]

Earlier governors general had exercised their considerable power in ways that the Duke of Devonshire would not, or could not, do. For example, in 1864, Viscount Charles Monck, Governor General of British North America, pressed his ministers to form a coalition to break a political deadlock between conservatives and reformers. Two leaders in Canada West, George Brown and John A. Macdonald, did Monck's bidding, working together with George-Étienne Cartier of Canada East to form what became the Great Coalition that paved the way for Confederation. Monck then continued to play an active role in preparing for Canada's Confederation in 1867.[25] But in 1917, the duke's attempt to bring two sides together during the conscription crisis did not succeed.

Post-Confederation, the governor general's role continued to diminish in authority. In 1874, the Earl of Dufferin as governor general became closely involved in a conflict between the government of British Columbia and the federal government over the slow progress in building the railway to the west coast, part of the terms under which British Columbia had joined Confederation in 1871. Dufferin acted almost as a minister of the Dominion, travelling to British Columbia to understand the situation for himself and encouraging the colonial secretary to arbitrate the dispute.[26] In contrast, the Duke of Devonshire was probably aware from the beginning of his tenure that in conflicts between the provinces and the federal government he could not intervene. Certainly by the time he faced the issue, he believed his intervention would bring on a constitutional crisis.

Though the Duke of Devonshire rightly viewed his role as carrying less authority than that of the earlier governors general, he was nevertheless aware that he still had authority in matters of Canada's foreign and defence policies. The rules governing the foreign policy aspect of Victor's duties were spelled out in another confidential letter from Andrew Bonar Law. Though the three formal documents made no mention of reserving bills – that is, not assenting to them until they had been submitted to His Majesty's government – in this letter Bonar Law reminded Victor that he had that authority, granted in the British North America Act of 1867.[27] Any bill that would affect the Empire should be reserved – thus, anything having to do with foreign or defence policy. However, Bonar Law also warned the governor general that it was important to avoid getting to the point of having to reserve a bill.

Only one governor general of Canada had reserved a bill since the colony had been granted responsible government in 1848, when the colonial government became responsible for their decisions to the people and not to the monarch. In 1867, Canada had been granted Dominion status, semi-independence, the right to run its own affairs except for foreign policy and matters that would affect the Empire. Reserving a bill, not assenting to it on the advice of ministers and sending it back to the king for his approval or disallowance, would put the Empire in a difficult position, probably creating a constitutional crisis.[28]

The duke's father-in-law, Lord Lansdowne, had come to the point of reserving a bill in the complex issue regarding the use of Canadian Atlantic waters for fishing. In 1883 the United States government abrogated the fishery articles of the Treaty of Washington of 1871, which had provided American fishermen access to the British North American harbours, not for fishing, but for taking on supplies and for shelter. By 1886, attempts to negotiate with the United States had failed. Fearing that Canadian fishermen might take matters into their own hands, in

May 1886 the minister of Marine and Fisheries, George Foster, intro-duced in the House of Commons a bill providing penalties for Amer-ican fishermen entering Canadian harbours or ports for purposes unrelated to supplies and shelter. Prime Minister John A. Macdonald be-lieved that the legislation simply improved procedures for enforcing what were, in fact, Canadian rights. He had a reasonable case. The British North America Act of 1867 had vested legislative control of the seacoast and inland fisheries in the Dominion Parliament. The bill passed easily in the House of Commons and the Senate. However, Lord Lansdowne, in the face of complaints from the U.S. secretary of state, and responding to a message from the colonial secretary in London, reserved the bill, sending it back to London for discussion. Lansdowne noted that the bill would not only antagonize the Americans but also put Canada "out of line" with the Mother Country, by which he seems to have meant that it was not Canada's role to deal with foreign poli-cy. After discussions in London – and after the conclusion of the 1886 fishing season – Queen Victoria gave assent to the act in November 1886.[29] By the Duke of Devonshire's time, reserving a bill in this way would almost surely have been unacceptable and would have created a constitutional crisis.

The other instruction in Bonar Law's letter was that the governor general must send all federal and provincial bills, and his own reports about the affairs of the Dominion, including some secret reports, to the Colonial Office in London.[30] These were the duties of a civil servant reporting to the colonial secretary. There was no British High Com-missioner to fulfill that function; not until 1928 was the first British High Commissioner to Canada appointed, after the 1926 Imperial Confer-ence had agreed that the Dominions had the right to make their own for-eign policy decisions. So in 1916, almost fifty years after Confederation, the governor general still functioned both as a sovereign with the power to reserve bills and as a civil servant reporting to the colonial secretary.

As well as these written rules, like the King in the Empire, the governor general's role hinged partly on convention; he could affect domestic policy by his personal influence. For Victor that meant that he must use his relationships with his ministers and the nation's leading citizens to ensure not only the smooth running of the country, but also the loyalty of the people to the Empire. Lord and Lady Dufferin, whose tenure had lasted from 1872 to 1878, had set the tone – and the pace – for governors general in Canada. The Dufferins became the centre of Ottawa social events and travelled throughout the country; they visited people in their own towns and cities and attended ceremonies; they distributed medals, received and made speeches, visited hospitals, schools, and other institutions.[31] After the Dufferins, these ceremonial duties became part of the unwritten code of the role.

Walter Bagehot wrote that there are two parts to England's constitution – those components that excite and preserve the reverence of the population, which he called the "dignified" parts, and those by which the constitution works and rules, the "efficient" parts. Every successful constitution, Bagehot wrote, "must first win the loyalty and confidence of mankind, and there employ that homage in the work of government."[32]

Victor had had extensive experience in the "efficient" part of government in Britain. He had been a member of Parliament for West Derbyshire from 1891 to 1908 before inheriting his peerage, after which he had become a member of the House of Lords. As a duke, he had also had plenty of experience winning the loyalty of staff and servants. He and the duchess had functioned in England in ways similar to what Bagehot called the "dignified" role: they had frequently been patrons of organizations, represented royalty, and participated in civil society. In Canada, perhaps Victor's most important duties concerned this "dignified" portion. No matter what the personal cost to the governor general, visits to local people in their own environment were an important part of keeping Canadians loyal to the British Empire during the Great War, in which Canada was spending its treasure in young men and in money.

Having come to grips with the superficial details and the formal written and unwritten rules of his role, the duke now had some freedom to be himself, to engage Canadians by showing his own personality and interests. Canadians would warm to this man with his unaffected manner and, especially, his knowledge of agriculture.

Two weeks after arriving in Ottawa, the duke and duchess began their first tours to meet the people of Canada in their own towns and cities, and to perform what Walter Bagehot called the "dignified" part of their work, to win the loyalty and confidence of the people.

Accompanied by Lady Maud and Lady Blanche, and with Captain Bulkeley-Johnson as ADC, they took their special train to Toronto and were met by Lieutenant-Governor Sir John Hendrie and his wife. Ontario's Government House was Chorley Park, a fourteen-acre estate in Toronto's luxurious Rosedale district, and Victor pronounced the house "a most magnificent affair but a trifle overdone ... everything most elaborate."[33] To Evie, Chorley Park reeked of confinement. They would always have to stay with the lieutenant-governor in Toronto and, although Sir John and Lady Hendrie were very nice people, she "found it tiring to be with them all day."[34] Sir John was an engineer and militia officer who had been a member of the provincial Parliament (1902–14), where he had served as minister without portfolio and chaired the legislature's Railways Committee. He was knighted in 1915 when he became lieutenant-governor.[35]

Evie had reason to be tired; Victor had arranged a heavy touring schedule. In one day the viceregal couple visited a huge technical school, a big military hospital, an officer's convalescent home, had luncheon at St Andrew's College – it was St Andrew's Day, there were prizes for the viceregal couple to give out – and in the evening they were guests of honour at a reception for three hundred guests at Government House. Victor appreciated Lady Hendrie's efforts at steering the right people to see him that evening,[36] but Evie found the reception "deadly dull," though she said "the girls managed to enjoy it."[37] One evening the Hendries' daughter took Maud and Blanche to the opulent Royal Alexandra Theatre where they saw a production of *Madama Butterfly* performed by the Boston National Grand Opera Company.[38] Blanche loved it, she wrote to her grandmother.[39] Evie and the girls continued their rounds of charities during the days and concerts, dinners, or receptions in the evenings.

Victor made a day trip to Guelph by train, "about 2 hours run," to visit the Agricultural College. Still feeling his way in this new country, Victor made sure to display his knowledge of agriculture and his interest in their work. *The Globe* reported on this visit: "It would have done the farmers of Canada good to see the way he judged a beast. Not a point was lost. Shorthorns at the college particularly interested him.

He himself is a well-known breeder of that favourite English show stock ... and has many a blue ribbon which his cattle have brought in." At one point, the writer noted, the duke "sidled into one of the stalls of the beef barns to almost caress" the college's prize bull, "Proud Diamond," and asked "the method of feeding, the cost of fodder, the market price and the progeny." Victor showed a similar interest in fowl, sheep, seed testing, and chrysanthemums. He told them at luncheon that they had a reputation in England for "their admirable and splendid work."[40] They were charmed.

Now that he was socially more at ease, Victor moved directly from the farming community to the city elite. He thought his after-dinner speech to the Toronto Club that evening was well received.[41] The previous evening he had addressed the Canadian Patriotic Fund's Toronto Branch, a government-established charity to help soldiers' dependents, this branch run by Toronto's wealthy businessmen. They asked him to take the Duke of Connaught's place as president, and Victor said he hoped to be more than a nominal incumbent.[42]

Back in Ottawa, the duchess recovered enough to continue entertaining ministers and their wives at Rideau Hall. She opened the first May Court Convalescent Home and became a patron of the May Court Club, the women's service club that Lady Aberdeen had founded in 1898.[43] That week, too, the duke met with his prime minister concerning their first difference of opinion – about British honours.

The following week, Victor and Evie left by train for Montreal, where the elite of the city greeted them. Prominent among those was the president of the Canadian Pacific Railway, Lord Shaughnessy, who had recently been elevated to a peerage by the king as Baron Shaughnessy in recognition of his strong support for the war effort. Born in Milwaukee, Wisconsin, Shaughnessy, fifty-three, had started his career at sixteen as a railway clerk; he moved to Montreal in 1882 to work with the Canadian Pacific Railway and in 1899 became president of the company. Also on the platform to greet the duke was the president of the Bank of Montreal, Sir H. Vincent Meredith, the first Canadian-born president. His bank essentially acted as Canada's national bank before the creation of the Bank of Canada in 1934. Both Shaughnessy and Meredith would become friends and advisers to the duke. During the week they also met newspaper publisher Sir Hugh Graham.

Sir H. Montagu Allan had offered the governor general and his entourage the use of his home, Ravenscrag, for their visit. From the house high up on Mount Royal, the Allans could see the black-white-and-red funnels of the Allan Line ships in the Port of Montreal. Sir Montagu had inherited the Allan Shipping Line from his father, Sir Hugh Allan. The Allans were not in Montreal that December but BJ felt their presence in Ravenscrag. Mrs Allan had been on the RMS *Lusitania* in 1915 when it was sunk by a German torpedo off the south coast of Ireland. She survived but lost her two little girls in the disaster. "Their photographs (the little girls) were the first thing which met our eyes," BJ told his mother. He found the house "oppressive."

"Every available space which is not filled up with a Victorian guilt [*sic*] mirror is painted with a fat cupid. The ceilings are adorned with Greek Gods and Goddesses from among whom hang glass chandeliers ... On a background of varnished wood paneling hangs the portrait of Sir Montagu Allan in hunting costume ... On to all of this add the fact that the architect thought windows superfluous, that the plumber thought that cold water coming through the neck and beak of a swan into one's bath preferable to hot water coming through an ordinary tap."[44]

As they had in Toronto, Victor thrived on a packed schedule while Evie found the week in Montreal draining. They hosted several luncheons and dinners at Ravenscrag, and the duchess and her daughters visited hospitals, convalescent homes, and the Red Cross offices. Their visits involved receiving bouquets of flowers and chatting with workers and patients, all under the watchful eyes of reporters. Lady Maud made her first solo appearance, though accompanied by the comptroller, Lord Richard Nevill, when visiting the Royal Victoria Hospital. In his position as commander-in-chief, the duke inspected troops soon to leave for the war and spoke at a Canadian Club luncheon

The duke was presented with an honorary degree at McGill University. In his reply to the welcome address he said, "Whatever the cost to this generation we are determined it shall be carried on until such a peace is secured that future generations may be proud and grateful of the part we are taking in it." That hopeful pledge would later be sullied by the next world war. But he also said, "There is a feeling that those distinctions and divisions which have separated classes and sections of the community will disappear to a large extent due to the common sacrifice."[45]

The duke also visited Laval University (later Université de Montréal) where he made a speech partly in French, something that always made him nervous. Before the event, Maud told her grandmother that her father was dreading his French speeches and rehearsed them to practise pronunciation.[46] "The entertainments at convents – when Victor had to answer the addresses of welcome in French," Evie told Lady Edward, "took years off my life."[47]

Victor was developing his own style as governor general, meeting people at all levels of society, taking the pulse of the nation. The Toronto and Montreal trips had begun his odyssey across Canada. In 1917, he would travel from coast to coast.

⚜

CHAPTER 4

Honours: The First Conflict

Less than a month after his arrival, the new governor general faced the first in a series of decisions about a thorny topic that would become a source of conflict and disagreement with his prime minister, and one that would threaten the duke's reputation with his colleagues in London. The subject was the granting of British honours to Canadians. The duke would come to call honours "a most unmitigated nuisance."[1]

Honours were British titles granted by the king to men (never to women) as a reward for work that served the British Empire. Twice each year, the king – on his birthday in June and at New Year's – would offer knighthoods and other honours to men in Britain, the Dominions, and the colonies. In Canada all the prime ministers, from Sir John A. Macdonald to Sir Robert Borden, had been knighted (with the exception of Alexander Mackenzie, prime minister from 1873 to 1878, who refused the honour when it was offered). Other men too had been knighted, and a few had received hereditary titles: baronet, or the higher title of baron, which also made the recipient a member of the British House of Lords. By the time the Duke of Devonshire arrived in Canada, Sir William Maxwell Aitken, a Canadian newspaper publisher, had been made a baronet (a short time later he would become Baron Beaverbrook), and Sir Thomas Shaughnessy, president of the Canadian Pacific Railway company, had been made the 1st Baron Shaughnessy. The king had higher titles to bestow – viscount, marquess, earl, duke – but none of these had yet been offered to men in Canada.

The procedure for advising the king regarding titles for Canadians was well set out. Twice each year the prime minister prepared a list of men recommended for titles and submitted the list for approval to the governor general, who in turn sent it to the colonial secretary for transmission to the king. Granting of honours was only and always the king's prerogative, but since 1902, it had been agreed that they would be granted only on the recommendation of Canadian prime ministers.[2]

Honours was to become one more issue in Borden's campaign to gain more independence from Britain without losing the benefits of membership in the British Empire. The large population of British men who had immigrated to Canada would not have stood for a break with the Motherland such as the United States had made 140 years earlier. Indeed, the memory of the American Civil War, only fifty years before, and the belief of many Americans in Manifest Destiny, a tenet holding that the entire continent would eventually come under American rule, was all too recent to allow Borden to move quickly on independence from the Imperial family. Instead, Borden trod carefully in trying to gain more independence in foreign policy, in relations with the United States, and with honours, without rocking the boat.

The honours story, which played out during the term of the Duke of Devonshire as Governor General of Canada, began in 1916 with Borden's attempt to gain approval for honours for some Canadians. Stymied, Borden then delayed preparing a list in 1917. In 1918, the story took a different turn with a proposal to abandon British honours altogether. By 1919, that proposal had been thoroughly discussed twice in Parliament, and Canada had rejected British honours for those living in Canada. However, since the Canadian government had no authority over the Crown, honours could still be recommended by a prime minister of Canada and granted by the king.

Thus, the Duke of Devonshire's entanglement with honours began in December 1916. Just three weeks after the duke's arrival, Prime Minister Robert Borden announced that he wanted a barony for Sir Hugh Graham, publisher of the *Montreal Star*. A barony, a hereditary title, would make Graham a peer in the British aristocracy and a member of the House of Lords. Borden had written the arguments based on information that Graham supplied,[3] and presented them verbally to the duke. Graham deserved the peerage, Borden said, because of his extensive service for Imperial interests. He had supported Canada's sending troops to the Boer War (1899–1902) and in 1914 had used his newspapers to promote Canada's entry into the Great War. Graham, Borden said, would be willing to move to Britain in order to take his seat in the House of Lords.

Born in 1848, Hugh Graham was raised in the small town of Athelstan in Canada East, and finished school at the age of fifteen. Beginning at the bottom in newspapers, by 1917 he owned several papers in Montreal and had made his fortune. Graham had generously supported the Conservative Party and had promoted Borden from the time of his election as leader in 1901. On the recommendation of the Liberal prime minister, Sir Wilfrid Laurier, Graham had been knighted in 1908 (apparently because Graham had refrained from criticizing Laurier during the election campaign of that year).[4] Once he became prime minister in 1911, Borden acknowledged a debt of "deep personal obligation for [Graham's] strong support" during his ten years as Opposition leader, as well as for the recent victory.[5]

As Borden and Graham both knew, the king published an honours list twice a year. The prime minister could recommend those he thought should be honoured and present his list to the governor general, who, if he agreed, forwarded it to the colonial secretary, who then brought it before the king. That was the formal channel. The duke understood from his conversation with the prime minister that day that Borden had tried to get this honour for Graham approved without going through the governor general. He was correct. The letter to Sir George Perley, the Canadian High Commissioner to London, about a peerage for Graham had been sent in October, a few days after Connaught's departure.[6] The duke was astonished and upset, and confided to his diary, "I do not think they have behaved well in trying to get some [honours] in during the interregnum."[7]

At their first meeting, the duke told Borden that he did not see any reason to grant Graham a peerage, but agreed to meet again the next day. The duke consulted Sir Joseph Pope, under-secretary of state for external affairs, who was "very much astonished at the proposal," and Sir Percy Sherwood, commissioner of the Dominion Police, who "did not think it was justifiable."[8] When he told Borden that he had decided not to put Graham's name forward for a barony, the duke noted in his diary that Borden "decided not to press and was really very nice and easy about it all. Great relief to me."[9]

But Borden was far from easy about it all. The same day, Borden cabled Sir George Perley about his meeting with the governor general: "I am intensely exasperated and bitterly disappointed at [the] outcome." He didn't blame the duke, who was "most kindly and considerate," he told Perley, "but I feel most strongly that this responsibility need not have been placed upon him."[10]

A day later, Borden met Sir Hugh Graham in Montreal. One can imagine the scene, these two powerful men seated in plush chairs, in the newly built and elegant Ritz-Carlton Hotel on Sherbrooke Street.[11] Borden described to Graham his difficulties with the new governor general, telling him that the duke apparently did not want to make a commitment until he knew Canada better. To Borden's astonishment, Sir Hugh "broke down and wept when told of difficulties." The newspaper magnate recovered enough to "pepper" Borden with notes and suggestions for solving the problem, even dictating what Borden should say in a new cable to Perley.[12] Borden's anger and stress flowed from his pen: "Have seen person mentioned in my secret telegram of yesterday. He is almost crushed by news and feels intensely humiliated as he was told that proposed honour would be conferred if suitable person was named." It was true that Graham had been led to expect the honour. The previous May, Borden had asked Perley to sound out Andrew Bonar Law, the colonial secretary, about whether a barony might be available for a suitable person.[13] Without knowing the name of the individual, Bonar Law had agreed; though the June list was final, it could be done at the New Year.[14] Under the direction of Sir Hugh Graham, Borden continued his cable to Perley. "Please take up the matter very earnestly and forcibly with Colonial Secretary and Prime Minister. I believe present situation is most unfortunate and even disastrous for all interests. No effort should be spared to change it and effort can only be made effectively at that end."[15]

Just as Borden was writing this note to Perley, the prime minister and colonial secretary changed in Britain. David Lloyd George replaced Herbert Asquith as prime minister and appointed a new colonial secretary, Walter Long. Perley could not approach the new colonial secretary until the dust settled.[16]

Ten days later, the duke heard about Perley's work. "Tiresome telegram from Walter Long about the peerage. I was in hope it was all over and settled, but someone has been making mischief. He [Long] said he had been privately told that the Prime Minister [Borden] was accused. Do not think there was a word of truth in it."[17] But there was. Perley, acting for Borden, had done his job well. Two days later, the duke received "a very long and tiresome cable from Walter Long about the Peerage case. Cannot understand it. He says the Prime Minister is much annoyed and thoroughly incensed. Also stated that two cables had been sent by the PM to the High Commissioner. It is evidently due to some pressure from him as I do not think Borden would have done this after having left me in the way he did without telling me. Walter's telegram was contradictory and silly."[18]

The duke cabled Borden, who was in Calgary on a western tour. Borden confided to his diary that he received the cable "asking if it is my confirmed opin[ion] that he should recommend it. I replied strongly in affirmative."[19]

The duke could no longer deny the fact that Borden had been working behind his back. He telegraphed Walter Long and reported to his diary: "Graham for Peerage. I am sure it is a mistake, but I cannot resist the PM and the Colonial office."[20] When Borden returned to Ottawa, the duke reported: "Saw the PM. We discussed the honours question and he was quite nice. At the same time I think he has not behaved well and I also think he knows it. It was significant that he said he had been in hopes that all would have been settled before I arrived."[21]

In the same interview that day, the duke told Borden about the invitation, which had just arrived in the governor general's office, for the prime minister to attend the Imperial War Conference in London.[22] Perhaps in an attempt to repair their relationship, the duke did not provide any advice about whether or not Borden should attend the meeting, which would begin in March. Three days later Borden informed the governor general that he had decided to attend, despite its meaning an absence of about three months in the difficult political conditions. The duke told him he "thought he had done right in accepting the invitation."[23]

This dispute about the Graham peerage could have discredited the duke in the eyes of his government colleagues in Britain, especially since Prime Minister Lloyd George supported the honour. The duchess wrote to her father, Lord Lansdowne, who replied that he had heard about the issue in London, and "Walter Long evidently realized that Victor had not been fairly treated."[24] The issue could also have soured the relationship between these two powerful men, the duke and his prime minister, who had to work closely together. To the credit of both, their relationship survived and they eventually became firm friends.[25]

It is not clear why it was so important to Borden to make his friend and supporter Sir Hugh Graham a baron and peer of Britain, or why it would have been "disastrous for all interests" if the peerage were denied.[26] However, a series of events that occurred before the Duke of Devonshire's arrival apparently made Borden believe he could make an honour happen without the governor general's permission. In May 1916, Andrew Bonar Law, the colonial secretary, had written a personal note to Borden asking that Sir Max Aitken, a Canadian living in London, be proposed for a baronetcy from the Canadian honours list. He argued that Aitken's services had "all been Canadian and if I recommend him it will be considered as due entirely to personal friendship,"[27] which of course it was. This was not following the rules. Borden said he agreed and would support the proposal but steered Bonar Law back to protocol by asking him to go through the governor general, then the Duke of Connaught.[28] Borden also wrote to inform the governor general.[29]

Sir Max Aitken's baronetcy did go through, but from the British list. It was announced in the London *Gazette* on 7 November 1916, when the Duke of Devonshire was on the high seas. Sir Max Aitken became the 1st Baronet Aitken. Then, on 17 December 1916, Victor wrote in his diary: "Heard by telephone that Sir Max Aitken had been given a peerage. Afraid it will have a bad effect here."[30] Sir Max Aitken became the 1st Baron Beaverbrook, of Beaverbrook in the province of New Brunswick. This was a quick rise from baronet, a title that was hereditary but did not bestow a peerage, to baron, which was both. All of this had been done from London, apparently promoted by Lloyd George.[31] Bonar Law had been successful in moving Aitken to the British list, though he was Canadian.

The duke's prediction was correct – the appointment did prove to be unpopular in Canada.[32] Max Aitken had departed from Canada in 1910 under a cloud of suspicion after creating a merger of several cement companies, a deal that brought him great wealth along with many enemies – and there were some who still remembered.[33] He had, however, become a member of the House of Commons in Britain and made many friends.

Also in May 1916, Borden had tried out this system of bypassing the governor general by asking Bonar Law to see that his friend, long-serving Conservative member of Parliament and cabinet minister Sir George Foster, be made a British privy counsellor.[34] The approach was successful. Foster received a letter from the Duke of Connaught congratulating him on having that honour conferred on him by the king.[35] From these events, Borden had learned that the honours rules could be flouted. However, his attempt to do the same for Graham had been frustrated at every turn. Borden was known to have a short fuse.[36] Perhaps his words "disastrous to all interests" were just an explosion of temper.

The new peerage was announced 13 February 1917.[37] Sir Hugh Graham became the 1st Baron Atholstan of Huntingdon, in the Province of Quebec in the Dominion of Canada, and of the City of Edinburgh.[38] Borden might have thought he had completed his work for Lord Atholstan, but the new peer was not finished yet. As he had no male heir, Lord Atholstan wanted his title to be inherited by his daughter on his death. Borden tried to make that happen, writing at least two letters to Walter Long. Although females had inherited titles in Britain and in Canada – Lord Strathcona had, by special remainder to his peerage, left his barony to his daughter on his death in 1914, and Lord Atholstan was undoubtedly aware of that – Borden's effort was in vain.[39] Sir Hugh Graham became the first and last Lord Atholstan as the title extinguished at his death.

Reaction in Canada to the Atholstan peerage was slow in coming. On 17 January 1917, an article in the *Montreal Standard*, one of Sir Hugh Graham's own newspapers, was complimentary about Graham deserving a peerage.[40] But by August 1917, a *Globe* editorial was decrying hereditary honours for Canada.[41]

Borden and the governor general might have returned to the normal routine of two honours lists a year, commendations by the prime minister, signed by the governor general, which then went to the king. Instead, the Graham affair seemed to be the beginning of something new. In his cables to Perley, Borden had railed that "if the opinion of the Prime Minister of Canada is not sufficient for the British Government on such a matter, honours had better be eliminated altogether as far as Canada is concerned."[42] He added, "[Bonar] Law asked me by cable last spring to recommend Aitken for Canadian honour without reference to then Governor. If British Government was prepared to accept my recommendation in that case, why do they hesitate now."[43] Borden's anger would lead to the next stage in Canada's wrangle with British honours, which began a year later.

✤

CHAPTER 5

The Blossoming of Lady Maud

If 1916 had proved a turbulent year for the family, sending them in a new direction, 1917 would nudge and sometimes elbow them toward even more unexpected experiences. Events early in the year brought into focus how far they had come from their home and from all that was familiar.

First, a cable from Eddy, the eldest son of the duke and duchess, announced that he was engaged to Lady Mary Alice Gascoyne-Cecil, daughter of the 4th Marquess of Salisbury.[1] Everyone called her "Moucher," after the character Miss Moucher in Charles Dickens's *David Copperfield*.[2] "Must we always call her by this name?" Evie complained to her mother,[3] but the nickname stuck. Everyone in the family knew Eddy had hoped to marry Moucher and they were all delighted at the news. Maud wanted to return to London to represent the family at the ceremony. Her parents contemplated the idea,[4] but in February the Germans announced their policy of unrestricted submarine warfare on ships entering English or French waters; Victor and Evie decided it was too risky for Maud to travel.[5]

Evie had another family wedding to organize that spring, which helped to distract her from missing Eddy and Moucher's ceremony. In early February, Rody Kenyon-Slaney, one of the ADCs, announced that he was engaged to Evie's cousin, Lady Mary Cecilia Rhodesia Hamilton. Evie had time to arrange the wedding before Lady Mary sailed in May from England, accompanied by Prime Minister Borden, who was returning from the Imperial War Conference. To avoid extravagance, Evie helped make the bridesmaids' dresses at Government House.[6]

Figure 5.1 Visit of the Duke of Devonshire to Deer Lodge Military Convalescent Hospital, Winnipeg, 3 March 1917. Maud's "disagreeable" experience was in a different hospital.

In late February, the family began their first trip, a visit to western Canada, elegantly accommodated in the luxury train in which they had travelled from Halifax to Ottawa. After a few days in Toronto, with the usual round of hospital visits, dinners, and speeches by the duke, they travelled north to Sudbury before turning west along the beautiful northern shore of Lake Superior. At major towns, and some smaller ones, the duke and duchess would stand on the small platform at the back of the train to receive a welcome address and cheers from the assembled crowd;[7] the duke would say a few words and they would move on.[8] Blanche stayed behind in Toronto because she was ill, but the party included Maud, the ADCs, and the military secretary. In snow-clad Winnipeg, they stayed at Government House with Lieutenant-Governor Sir James and Lady Aikins. Sir James was a lawyer and former Conservative member of Parliament. In contrast to Ontario's Government House, the duke pronounced the thirty-five-year-old Victorian structure "a nice old fashioned building and … most comfortable."[9]

One cold winter day, the duke and duchess, with Lady Maud, all dressed in their furs, visited Deer Lodge Convalescent Hospital, a hotel that had been converted the year before to treat injured returning soldiers. BJ reported to his mother on the hospital visits: "We rather overdid hospitals. At a children's hospital one poor little boy, who had just arrived there, took hold of the duchess's hand and begged her to take him back to his home. Nothing would induce him to leave go of her and she had to wait and talk to him for some ten minutes."[10]

After two heavy days of visits, receptions, luncheons, and dinners, BJ wrote to his mother, "The amount we had to do and see soon knocked the Duchess up." She was tired out and suffering from lumbago. Maud took on her functions. BJ continued:

The duchess generally stayed in bed during the mornings. This was particularly unfortunate in one instance. We were to visit a hospital run by the Salvation Army [the Grace Hospital]. The Duke asked me to find out whether there were any returned soldiers in it. I telephoned to Coleman, the Lieutenant Governor's Secretary and put the question to him. "No," he said decisively. I said "Oh a sort of General hospital?" "Yes" he said doubtfully.

So, in happy innocence, the Duke, Lady Maud, and myself started out. We arrived. We walked down the first passage. Lines of children arose from the lower regions of the building. I walked into the first ward … It was a small room with one lady in bed. Before I had gone another yard, signs and tokens of what at any rate this part of the hospital was for were not wanting.

I whispered to the Salvation Army Colonel who was walking beside me "This is a maternity Branch?" "Yes," he replied with great unction. "We run through more maternity cases in this Hospital than any other hospital in Winnipeg." I expressed my interest and admiration and retired into the darkest recess. A few minutes after we passed a closed door and I heard the same gentleman telling Lady Maud exactly why it was closed. I heaved a sigh of relief when he at last said "Now, Sir, we will go to our other wing." "Ah," I said jauntily, "I suppose you have every sort of patient." "Yes," he said "in this wing we have the women we have retained off the streets." … The finishing touch was when the Colonel led Lady Maud and me up to a photograph and said "These are the triplets we had last month. The mother got over it very well."[11]

The duke was incensed. "A most unfortunate event occurred," he wrote. "We found that it was a maternity and rescue home only. It did not matter about me but was dreadful for Maud. Really we ought to be told things."[12] His attitude is hard to credit in today's world, but in 1917, an unmarried aristocratic daughter, even at twenty, was apparently protected from any and all information with respect to pregnancy and childbirth. Her parents were raised as Victorians who did not discuss sex or what brought about childbirth or any of its physiology with their children. Evie wrote about the incident to her mother-in-law:

There was rather a contretemps yesterday. She [Maud] went to a Salvation Army hospital. We thought it was a general hospital, but it was for maternity and rescue work. Victor had not the presence of mind to send her home so she inspected the mothers, babies, confinement rooms and heard all the details of management. Captain BJ was in-waiting and was horribly embarrassed and dreadfully distressed about it. He effaced himself as much as possible but Maud said every door was propped open, and women in dressing gowns with huge figures were walking about. Luckily a half-breed Indian with a beautiful team of dogs took her for a drive directly after which cleared away the disagreeable impressions![13]

Maud, writing the same day to her grandmother, Lady Edward, did not mention the hospital visit at all, but she did describe her ride in a dog-pulled sleigh with the Indian half-breed. "He is a most amusing boy," she wrote. "He won the race from Winnipeg to St. Paul, 500 miles in 10 days. He guides his dogs entirely by word. Chuck means left and Gee means right." Maud, who was perhaps not quite as prudish as her parents assumed, was also rather amused that in Winnipeg one could not use the word "leg." Referring to her own sprained leg from a skiing accident a month earlier, she said, "here we have to call it 'limb' as leg is supposed to be indelicate! One even says the limb of a piano!"[14]

Evie mused to her mother about seeing Maud and BJ together on the western trip. "BJ was in-waiting so the little flirtation went on happily though with great decorum. I hope it's not serious … We are going to try and send him to the Washington embassy for a bit."[15]

Shortly after their return to Ottawa, Sir Cecil and Florence Spring Rice arrived for a holiday. While they were there, on 17 March, the duke noted in his diary, "Russian news is most dramatic. The Romanoff dynasty is at an end and the revolution appears to have been peacefully carried out."[16] Both the duke and the ambassador, buoyed by the German retreat, were hopeful that the new government in Russia would help in the war effort.[17] Springy was in a difficult position in Washington, trying to maintain cordial relations between Britain, which was fully engaged in the war, and the United States, still neutral. He told BJ: "[President Woodrow] Wilson wants to fight and so do most of the cabinet, but the mass of the people don't and Wilson is educating them into it."[18] Toward the end of the two-week visit, the duke noted that Springy seemed "nervous and hysterical."[19] BJ elaborated to his mother: "He [Springy] solemnly warned General White [an American visiting Ottawa] not to remain at the Ritz[-Carlton] Hotel in Montreal as one of the foreign waiters might poison his coffee; and at the last moment he was very averse to taking Lady Maud to Washington in case the Embassy should be blown up. He quite earnestly believes that one of our leading officials here is in German pay."[20]

When the Spring Rices returned to Washington, Maud did go with them, accompanied by Captain Angus Mackintosh as ADC; BJ joined them a few weeks later.[21]

Left behind in Ottawa, Evie found many things to try her patience. In addition to the usual practice of observing Lent by holding fewer dinners, the king had decreed a period of mourning for the Duchess of Connaught, wife of the previous governor general, who had died in mid-March.[22] Her husband, the Duke of Connaught, was an uncle of the king, and so she was included as a member of the royal family. Even the regular dinner parties were cancelled until after Easter.[23] Evie complained to her mother, "There is still nothing to do here." Despite living on a seventy-five-acre estate, she went on, " I am very sick of this suburban life – one never gets away from tramlines and asphalt motor roads."[24] She complained to Lady Edward that Ottawa was noisy, with train bells ringing all day.[25] By April, no doubt she was thinking of an English spring and did not appreciate Ottawa's version of that season: "At present this place is odious, slush everywhere and fresh falls of snow from time to time just when the roads are drying up."[26] Evie was also distressed because Eddy and Moucher were married on 21 April and she could not be there. Soon the letters began to arrive describing the ceremony and celebrations they had missed.

Evie did attend Red Cross meetings – she had been founder and president of the Derbyshire branch of the Red Cross in England – and some women's conferences and organizations.[27] It was at one such event that Evie's nervousness about making speeches came to the fore. In Winnipeg, Victor reported, "Eve and Maud went to Women's Canadian Club. Evie had to say a few words. We must make a rule that she should not be called upon to speak."[28] Apparently this affliction lasted all her life. In her memoir, *Wait for Me!*, the Dowager Duchess of Devonshire, Deborah Cavendish, who knew Evie many years later as her husband's grandmother, described Evie's nervousness before an opening of a fête or bazaar: "For two days beforehand Granny Evie was fidgety and unhappy, and sometimes took to her bed. Once the ordeal was over, she was a different person." The dowager duchess noted that it didn't matter that the audience was friendly, or that she had raised seven children and been chatelaine of four great houses and a castle in Ireland, she was nervous at the prospect of appearing before an audience.[29] Later, Evie did rise to the occasion to make what her husband termed "an admirable little speech" at a Red Cross meeting in Toronto and another in Chatham, Ontario, at an IODE visit, events unusual enough to rate a comment in his diary.[30]

Over Easter in April 1917, the Canadians won a victory at Vimy Ridge, an event that made those at home very proud. At the cost of 3,598 dead and 7,004 wounded, and against tremendous German forces, the four Canadian divisions, working together for the first time, took the ridge on Easter Monday, a feat that had eluded other Allied armies.[31] Walter Long, the colonial secretary, sent a note of congratulations to the governor general.[32] BJ made no mention of it in his letters, but Victor reported to his mother that "we are all much elated at the news of the last few days and the success of the Canadian troops."[33] Evie's acerbic comment to her mother was, "The Canadians think they have won the war on the Vimy Ridge."[34] Someone had told Evie that Canada's four divisions were a very small proportion of the army, and she thought the Canadians "ignorant and conceited."[35] Later she told Lady Edward, "A good many people have lost relations at Vimy, but the country is so prosperous and the proportion of soldiers so small that the bulk of the people don't really feel the war. Of course, the better class English speaking people do as their sons have mostly gone."[36] Evie's prejudices about Canadians were in full bloom already with four more years to go in their viceregal term.

The events at Vimy were only a footnote to the family at Rideau Hall that Easter. During his visit, Springy had told Victor he thought "the United States will not declare war, but will find itself at war in due course." Ambassador Spring Rice wrote to Mr Balfour, the British foreign secretary, that he thought the Americans were drifting into war, and though the United States did not want war, their hand had been forced by Germany after the sinking of the United States merchant ship *Algonquin* on 14 March 1917. The Germans had refused to help the crew who were all in lifeboats, and who then took twenty-seven hours to row to the English shore. No one died, but the public was outraged by the newspaper accounts of the event. Spring Rice continued, "The President, according to all indications, will not declare war on Germany ... but merely assert that a state of war has existed between the United States and Germany since ... the sinking of the Algonquin. Great hopes are entertained that Germany will herself ... declare war."[37]

The duke wrote to his mother, "The Americans certainly are peculiar in their methods."[38] Within days of Maud's arrival in Washington she was to witness the historical events that would prove Springy wrong.

In contrast to her mother in Ottawa, Maud was in her element in Washington. She had a seat in the Diplomatic Gallery on 2 April while the two houses of Congress waited to hear President Woodrow Wilson's historic speech about the United States and the European war. Maud wrote to her parents from the British ambassador's home:

We have just come back from Congress but the President has not been able to speak yet as the election of various officers is not yet finished ... There is wild excitement here today – especially as train after train of pacifists arrive – they are waiting in their thousands about the steps of the Capitol, all wearing armlets or sashes with "we don't want war" written on them ... We passed the White House this morning and saw a number of suffragists waiting for the President.[39]

After the evening session of the joint houses of Congress she wrote:

We went back again at about seven and the President came in at about 8:30. He had a tremendous reception – there was dead silence in the house till he came to the word "submission" when the whole place shrieked.[40]

Maud knew that her parents would know what she meant because the full text of his speech had been reported in the press.[41] President Wilson gave details of the unrestricted submarine warfare that Germany had declared on February first and its effect on shipping and use of the seas. He said, "we will not choose the path of submission and suffer the most sacred rights of our Nation and our people to be ignored or violated."

Maud continued:

After that, almost every sentence was cheered. He spoke very clearly and distinctly, one could hear every word. In the middle of his speech there was a noise overhead like several people running, everyone thought a pane of glass in the roof would be broken and a bomb dropped. Mrs. Wilson was sitting two places away from us and was terribly nervous ... we were surrounded by pro-Germans in the gallery and the Pacifist members were sitting just below us, and they looked more and more sulky as the evening wore on.

On 6 April 1917, the United States formally declared war against Germany.

Maud's stay at the British embassy included shopping, riding, luncheons, and dinners – in the company of an ADC, either Captain Mackintosh or Captain Bulkeley-Johnson – and a "Rubber Neck" tour of Washington in a charabanc, an open-topped vehicle that seated a crowd.[42] She met politicians, diplomats, and industrial magnates. One day she lunched with Mrs Marshall Field, whose husband ran the family's department store empire. Another evening she dined at the White House, and President Wilson talked to her after dinner, "which I believe he rarely condescends to do, so I feel very honoured! He compared American men to English men, very favourably for the latter I thought."[43] She charmed the U.S. diplomats and was invited to an after-the-war cruise on a U.S. destroyer.[44]

Understandably, Maud was reluctant to leave the social whirl of Washington and go back to her dull life in Ottawa. With an invitation from Springy and Florence, and with her parents' consent, she extended her stay through the month of April. Springy declared that "Maud is quite a politician and has been most useful ... People like her so much."[45] Florence and Springy called her "the lobbyist" because of the amount of information she picked up at the Capitol from senators and others.[46] Lady Spring Rice wrote to Lady Edward, her aunt and Maud's grandmother: "she charmed everyone young and old and her looks, intelligence and absolute want of self-consciousness was much commented on."[47]

On 22 April, the British mission arrived in Washington. The mission, led by Arthur Balfour, Britain's foreign secretary, included twenty-five men, leaders in British military and intelligence positions as well as those responsible for shipping and munitions, a group that had been assembled to help coordinate the war efforts of Britain and the United States. Maud reported: "There were great rejoicings here on Mr. Balfour's arrival ... the house which has been lent to him must be two miles from the [train] station and there was a good crowd all the way ... Mr. Balfour had a most perfect photographic smile all the way and has pleased everyone very much!"[48] Maud and cousin Florence were out on the streets with the crowd. Later that evening they had a quiet dinner with Balfour.[49]

A week later Maud described her experiences with the British mission. "This last week has been so extraordinarily interesting. I think they all seem satisfied. The big reception here [on 25 April] was a great success. Cousin Florence seems to have successfully avoided the pushing and the ultra-rich! ... Our little dinner up at the 'Mission House,' as it is called, was delightful. There were only two of Mr. Balfour's people and Lord Eustace, the Lyons, Miss Fitzpatrick and me. After dinner a footman appeared and played the electric organ."[50] Lord Eustace Percy

(1st Baron Percy of Newcastle) was a British diplomat, the Lyons were John Herbert Bowes-Lyon – whose sister Elizabeth would become queen on the ascension of King George VI and later queen mother to Elizabeth II – and his wife, Frenella.

On 25 April, the French mission arrived headed by René Viviani, minister of Justice and Public Information, and Marshal Joseph Joffre, hero of the Battle of the Marne. They, too, were greeted by wildly enthusiastic crowds. It was here that Maud's fluency in French proved useful. She told her father, "it is rather trying for the French mission that not one of the administration speaks a word of French."[51] The French ambassador to the United States, Jean-Jules Jusserand, invited Maud to a dinner he hosted for the men of the French mission. Maud had expected to attend the dinner in the company of Vice-Admiral Sir Montague Browning, British commander-in-chief, North America and West Indies station, a section of the Royal Navy.[52] She had been amused by Browning at a dinner at the Italian embassy a few days before. However, he was called to his flagship, HMS *Leviathan*, and she was the only English person at the dinner.[53] Earlier that day she had visited Annapolis where the French cruiser *Jeanne d'Arc* lay offshore, and she told her father "we were invited to go on board and the Admiral's quarters were placed at our disposal!"[54] The French officers, she said, "were so amused at a regiment of French Canadians which they met in Bermuda. They say their French is exactly as it is spoken today by the country people in Normandy."[55]

While Evie worried about the flirtation between Maud and BJ, others began to see something between Maud and Angus. BJ was startled and did not believe what he was hearing. He wrote to his mother, "Who on earth has spread such an absurd rumour about Angus and Lady Maud. Pigs might fly and Angus might fall in love with Lady Maud in the far distant future ... but I have never known two people further from it at present."[56] But BJ, at twenty-five, did not know much about love.

Maud's Washington sojourn finally came to an end and she returned to her family in Ottawa on 7 May. To her father's disgust she brought a planchette board (more commonly known as a Ouija board).[57] More than two years later, in 1919, William Lyon Mackenzie King, who himself had an avid interest in spiritualism, reported in his diary a story that the Duchess of Devonshire had told him about an incident that must have occurred in 1917. One evening, the duchess told him, she, Maud, Angus, and one or two others were amusing themselves with the planchette board. "They asked who Angus Mackintosh was to marry ... it spelled out 'sweet Maud Cavendish.' ... Next someone asked who is to be the next premier & the reply – to use the Duchess's own words 'the thing read out Mackenzie King.' She laughed quite heartily about it."[58]

Evie's period of discontent was to last a few more months. First there was a problem about a tour to Hamilton and Niagara. It had been arranged for mid-May before the wedding of Mary Hamilton and Rody Kenyon-Slaney, just a few days in southern Ontario and then back to Ottawa in good time for the ceremony. Although Evie had recovered from the Winnipeg trip, she dreaded this one. On the day of departure, she and Victor had an argument and she decided not to go. "I had a bad headache on Friday," she explained to Lady Edward, "and was quite unable to face the night journey followed by 11 functions on Saturday. Victor has a positive mania for these overfilled days. It has never been done before and I must try and cure him of this habit."[59] By the next day she apparently felt some guilt. Victor, writing on Sunday, mentioned a letter from her that had just arrived, perhaps to apologize.[60] He described all that had happened in Hamilton and tried to patch up things between them. He missed her very much indeed, he said, and "we must have no more worries. I know that I am more irritable but I will really try."[61]

Maud handled the Hamilton ceremonies with aplomb, receiving addresses, jewellery, and bouquets, going to luncheon with Lady Hendrie, the lieutenant-governor's wife; she seemed to be enjoying herself and did not seem a bit tired, her father noted.[62] "She is certainly excellent on these occasions,"[63] Victor told Evie. Maud also wrote to her mother saying that "the program was not half so tiring as it looked," and she had received for Evie "a hideous piece of jewelry from the Council of Women, their badge in sapphire and turquoise."[64]

While Maud could handle the pace of events with ease, especially after her experience in Washington, she was also much younger than her mother. Evie, then forty-seven, was apparently experiencing menopause. Victor had noted in the spring of 1916 that the nursery was coming to an end and then a few months later "horrid to think that the nursery is over."[65] Evie admitted to her mother later that fall that she "felt disinclined to face functions, 'temps de la vie' no doubt!"[66] Undoubtedly the physiological and emotional effects of menopause brought her an extra level of discomfort.

Through all her discontent that spring, Evie charmed her dinner guests, something at which she excelled. William Lyon Mackenzie King, who had already been part of the society group invited to Rideau Hall,[67] described an event in April 1917. At a formal dinner he "was given Her Excellency, the Duchess to take in," an honour that would have been bestowed by the duke.[68] According to formal English protocol, when the butler announced dinner, the host would lead the way, taking the most senior lady present. The guests would follow in descending order of the ladies' precedence, except the hostess, who would go in last with the senior man present.[69] Mackenzie King, who had lost his parliamentary seat in the 1911 election, was employed as a consultant on labour issues, and was not as high ranking as Prime Minister Borden, who was also attending. Though Canadians were concerned about precedence in some formal public events,[70] the duke did not always follow strict English social rules in Canada. Mackenzie King would have offered his right arm for the duchess as they entered the dining room to a table set for twenty. They were seated beside each other and discussed Russia – no doubt the recent revolution and the rumours of Russia moving toward making a separate peace with Germany – and the 1902 Anglo-Japanese Alliance, for which the duchess's father, Lord Lansdowne, had been responsible when he was British foreign minister. The duchess was likely aware that Mackenzie King had been concerned, while labour minister in the Laurier government, about Japanese immigration to Canada.[71] They spoke about the recently published book *The Broken Road*, a novel about an Indian prince educated in Britain who wanted to marry an Englishwoman.[72] The duchess, King reported, spoke of the book "as a true representat[io]n & of the mistake the Eng[lish] made in bringing Indian students to Eng[land] & Indian soldiers to Europe to fight. Beneath all was the question of inter-marriage of the races."[73] Evie's prejudices were showing, and there's little doubt that she would not have welcomed a

Figure 5.2 The Right Honourable Arthur Balfour, British foreign secretary (left), during his visit in May 1917, with the Duke of Devonshire and Sir Cecil Spring Rice, British ambassador to the United States. Balfour came to Washington to discuss war strategy after the United States had joined the Allied forces.

mixed-race marriage for her daughters. However, her attitude was in step with the times. In Canada, from the early days of the war, recruiting officers faced a plethora of volunteers from whom they selected recruits; one of the selection criteria was race.[74] Mackenzie King does not record what he thought about interracial marriage but opposition to it was not uncommon in 1917.

Figure 5.3 This picture was taken in front of Rideau Hall during Arthur Balfour's visit in May 1917. Balfour (front row, fifth from left) sits between the duke and duchess; Sir Cecil Spring Rice is third from the left in the front row. The duchess was relieved to have an Englishman to talk to.

Finally, with the weather improving, Evie's mood began to lift. Several hundred guests attended the simple wedding of Mary and Rody on 24 May at Christ Church Cathedral. The whole party returned to Rideau Hall for the reception: afternoon tea in the Blue Room decorated with a few flowers from the Government House garden, and no wedding favours.[75]

When Arthur Balfour and his mission colleagues arrived in Ottawa following their Washington sojourn, Evie wrote to Lady Edward, "it *was* nice to have some Englishmen to talk to."[76] In the Devonshire household Arthur Balfour was known as AJB, a family friend and Charlie's godfather.[77] It was Balfour who had arranged transport to Canada for the younger children just a few months before.

Balfour spoke to a joint session of the two houses of Parliament. "Standing on the flag-bedecked rostrum of the House of Commons," *The Globe* enthused, before a thronged Chamber, the Right Honourable Arthur J. Balfour, foreign secretary of Great Britain, delivered his message to Parliament. When the applause finally died down, he began his speech in French, at which the French Canadians in the crowd "sprang to their feet and renewed their cheering."[78] He called this world war "the struggle between democracy and autocracy," and expressed "profound appreciation of the patriotic part played by the self-governing Dominions" of the British Empire, rousing the audience to heights of patriotism and idealism by his oratory. The duchess and her daughters and the ADCs were enthralled. By tradition, the governor general does not enter Parliament except for the Speech from the Throne and to prorogue Parliament, so he did not go. Evie reported that "Mr. Balfour's speaking is utterly unlike the flowery clap trap [sic] the people here generally indulge in." She did admit, however, "They fully realized the difference and were clever enough to appreciate it."[79]

After a formal dinner in Balfour's honour the duke worried that it was not formal enough, but he thought everyone enjoyed themselves.[80] He was already relaxing into Canada's less formal social life. Three busy days later, the visitors had all departed for home and Government House returned to its normal quiet routine. However, life didn't stay quiet for long. In early June, the family left for their first visit to Quebec City.

CHAPTER 6

Summer Adventures, 1917

After seven months in office, it was high time for the duke to make a visit to the governor general's other official residence, in Quebec City. In early June, the family, including the ADCs, travelled by their special train, arriving at the newly constructed, chateau-style Gare du Palais. On the platform to greet them were Lieutenant-Governor Sir Pierre-Évariste Leblanc and Mrs Leblanc, the premier of Quebec, Lomer Gouin, and Lady Gouin, along with other dignitaries. (The duke almost always called heads of provinces "prime minister" rather than the more modern title "premier.") The duke inspected the guard of honour, who were in full dress uniform, and they proceeded in motors to the Citadel, Quebec's old fort high on the promontory called Cap Diamant overlooking the St Lawrence River. The star-shaped fort was built between 1820 and 1850 to protect British soldiers while they defended the city from the expected invasion by Americans, but the fort was never threatened and never saw action. Although the duchess had been there before when her father was governor general, for the rest of the party it was their first glimpse of the fort and the adjoining Plains of Abraham, where British forces in 1758 under General Wolfe defeated General Montcalm's French army to claim the territory for Great Britain.

On a warm, overcast spring evening, the duke and his party alighted at the governor general's quarters within the fort, a grey-stone two-storey building, originally built in 1831 as the officers' barracks. Sentry stations guarded each side of the white porticoed entrance.[1] Victor found the house comfortable and charming, with its picturesque view of boats far below on the St Lawrence River.[2] Evie reported the house

Figure 6.1 View down the St Lawrence River from the Citadel, Quebec City.

had not changed much since her mother's time, thirty years before, but on the terrace, a room had been built using "tin and wood on the outside and lined with awning stuff to look like a tent."[3] She thought the Citadel a delightful place, but it lacked something to her artistic eye. "It could be made charming with a little trouble, if we could have a bonfire of existing chintzes and carpets," she wrote to her mother, ". . . and there is quite a good garden patch below the terrace. All this could be made really pretty with a few tub plants and some rock garden. Perhaps when the war is over, I shall be able to get it started – it would just be getting nice when we leave."[4]

During their ten days in Quebec City, once again Evie found the pace gruelling, while Victor thrived on it. They fit in several sightseeing tours around the capital between the luncheons and formal dinners that they hosted at the Citadel. One evening the duke received a degree from Laval University, where he spoke in French with only a few words of English and "got through much more easily" than he had expected.[5]

He noted, "Lots of young men of military age at the proceedings."[6] Lieutenant-Governor Leblanc invited them to dinner at Spencerwood, the official residence, a grand estate and luxurious villa overlooking the St Lawrence.[7]

The duke began to meet the important figures of Quebec society and had private conversations to discuss the current political situation. A year earlier Canada's military force had been at about 300,000, and recruitment since then had slowed. The country was in danger of falling behind on Prime Minister Borden's commitment to build Canada's military to half a million men.[8] Some were calling for a more organized and compulsory recruitment – in other words, conscription. Borden and his government had previously said they would not impose conscription unless it was necessary. Nevertheless, in late 1916, the government had begun a voluntary national registration to find out how many men were available. By May 1917, it was clear that there were at least 150,000 available men who were not engaged in agriculture or industries necessary to the war.[9]

Recruitment efforts began to inflame tensions between English and French Canada. Many believed French Canadians were not volunteering in the same proportion as English Canadians. Statistics indicated whether volunteer recruits were Canadian-born, British-born, or foreign-born, but the language of recruits was not recorded, so there was no way to be sure how many francophones versus anglophones were signing up, and rumours circulated unchecked. Apologists listed possible reasons for these supposedly lower recruitment numbers: French Canadians had little connection to either Britain or France, and in the largely rural population of French Canada young men married early and had families and farms to look after. In contrast, English-speakers who had volunteered were largely single, city-dwelling men who had recently immigrated from Britain. It didn't help that English Canada counted those British-born or foreign-born volunteers as part of their numbers; French Canada thought a fair comparison would include on their side Frenchmen or Belgians who were residents of Canada but went to Europe and enlisted in their native lands.[10] It didn't help that the army continually broke up French-Canadian units, sending the men to serve in predominantly English-speaking units. Only the Royal 22e Régiment (nicknamed the Van Doos), established in October 1914 after lobbying by wealthy and politically influential French Canadians, survived as a regiment serving in the French language.[11] It didn't help that the English-language press in Canada was especially insulting about the allegedly lower recruitment numbers from French Canada.[12] Old language-related fights were revived. The Manitoba Schools Question of the 1890s, when Manitoba had eliminated public funding for Catholic schools – most French Canadians were Catholic – had left a stain on relations between what was then called "the races," French and English, as did Ontario's opposition to French-language instruction in schools.[13] By the end of May, the press was calling attention to a divide between the English and French in Canada and calling the conscription issue a political crisis.[14] The duke too worried that the results of Borden's and Sifton's negotiations with Liberals would "accentuate racial feeling."[15]

During his time in London at the Imperial War Conference, Prime Minister Borden had discussed the war and strategy with his British counterparts, visited the fighting fields in France just as the duke had done, spoken to wounded Canadian soldiers being treated in hospitals, and come to believe that conscription was necessary. What he saw and heard convinced him that Canada's contribution to the fighting was critical, and voluntary enlistment was not bringing in enough men to maintain the four Canadian divisions at full strength. On his return to Ottawa, Borden had informed the governor general, on 17 May 1917, that he intended to implement conscription. He spoke to his cabinet that day and to Parliament the next day.

A week later, Borden began a series of meetings with Sir Wilfrid Laurier, the Opposition leader, to whom he described the conditions he had seen in France. Borden asked Laurier to join a coalition government in which there would be equal numbers of Liberal and Conservative cabinet ministers, under Borden as prime minister. He also asked for Laurier's agreement to delay the election until the war was over, arguing that a stable government would be less disruptive to the war effort. Laurier resented the fact that he had not been asked to join the coalition before the announcement was made in Parliament. He opposed conscription and believed it would be difficult to enforce in Quebec, unless support for it were established by a referendum or a general election. Laurier met with his Quebec friends, in particular Premier Sir Lomer Gouin, and then discussed with Borden the possible makeup of a coalition cabinet. On 6 June, Laurier asked Borden whether bringing in conscription was the sole basis of the coalition, and when Borden said that it was, Laurier replied that he could not join the coalition on the terms proposed.[16] Laurier also refused to extend the life of the Parliament. He had agreed in 1916 to an extension for one year, but now, with the conscription issue, Laurier believed that an election was necessary.[17]

Borden apparently began almost immediately to attempt to bring into his cabinet individual Liberals, men who supported his policy of conscription, with a view to supporting his government's chances of winning the election. Eventually, this group of Conservative, Liberal, and some independent cabinet members became known as a Union government. For several weeks, the duke was unaware of these negotiations with individuals.

Evie confided her own views on the matter to her mother: "Sir Robert has invariably done the right thing at the wrong time and in the wrong way. He made a good speech at the introduction of the conscription bill, but it was folly not to consult the Liberals as soon as he got home."[18] To Lady Edward she expressed herself in a little more detail. "Sir Robert means very well, but he does not seem to manage the opposition at all cleverly and they are in any case slippery people to deal with, these Canadian politicians, particularly the R.C.s."[19] While Victor never expressed such a definite opinion in his letters or his diary, undoubtedly he and Evie had discussed it together and it is likely that he shared her opinions. Just before leaving for the Quebec City visit, the duke had heard from Borden that Esioff-Léon Patenaude, a Quebec member of Parliament, secretary of state, and minister of Mines, had resigned in protest against Borden's decision to implement conscription. "Afraid that will mean Quebec is ruled up in line against the rest of Canada. Most deplorable," the duke wrote in his diary.[20] The tension was rising.

In Quebec, the duke began to do what he could to resolve this impasse by consulting the French Canadians. He met with Sir Lomer Gouin, who believed that an election was the only way out of the confusion. He talked as well with the influential Sir George Garneau, whom he pronounced a "moderate, quiet, strong man, Roman Catholic but tolerant."[21] Garneau, a businessman, was chairman of the National Battlefields Commission, which looked after the Plains of Abraham, and he was also

Quebec chairman of the Bonne Entente, a movement originated by a few Ontario businessmen who invited their counterparts from Quebec to join them in an effort to promote "racial goodwill" between the English in Ontario and French in Quebec.[22] The duke also spent some time with Henri Bourassa, editor of the Montreal newspaper *Le Devoir*. At the outset of war, in August 1914, Bourassa had supported Canada's participation, saying that it was "Canada's duty to contribute ... to the combined efforts of France and England."[23] By 1916, Bourassa had taken the position that Canada, a small nation, had done enough, had spent more lives and money than other nations in proportion to its population, and should look after its own interests at home.[24] In June 1917, Bourassa was running a campaign opposing not only conscription but any participation in the war in Europe. The duke listened to Bourassa's view that Canada was a nation by itself, independent of Britain or France, that only the Canadian nation was worth fighting and dying for, that Canada would not exist except as a bilingual, bi-ethnic voluntary partnership.[25] It is unlikely that the duke, with his English background and sentiment, understood Bourassa's arguments. His diary records that Bourassa seemed "obsessed with the Canadians in a nation idea."[26] However, from his consultations the duke must have learned more about the differences between various English and French Canadians' views of their country.

In late June, Victor left Quebec City and the conscription crisis for a fishing trip. He travelled north by train with two ADCs, BJ and Mervyn Ridley, to meet their host, Mr Amyot, who guided them to fishing grounds. To Victor's delight, they paddled by canoe through a succession of lakes connected by little rivers. When they encountered waterfalls, they landed and carried everything – canoes and all – overland. "These are called portages," Victor recorded.[27] He was unconcerned that his exposed skin was covered in blood from insect bites, apparently from blackflies, the scourge of Canadian Shield country, which take a chunk of flesh from both humans and animals, leaving a bloody, itchy wound. After a good dinner Victor declared himself comfortable.

Mervyn was comfortable too, but BJ was swollen from bites. They fished in a stream, caught little fish called gudgeon and cut a bit off the back to bait their hooks, "a very effective method," Victor thought. In three days, they caught over one hundred small trout in the one- to three-pound range, but "no great skill is required."[28] This trout fishing definitely did not match Victor's expectations for Canadian back-country travels.

While Victor was fishing, Evie took the children and Angus Mackintosh aboard the yacht *Lady Grey* down the St Lawrence River.[29] She had decided not to take maids as they would only be in the way, so they had only the ship's steward to wait on all of them – a company of eight.[30] Angus Mackintosh took up the slack. He made the children's beds and served as assistant steward. "It really was very funny to see this very smart Guardsman making up temporary beds in the saloon, tucking Charlie and Rachel into them," Evie told her mother.[31]

They stopped first at Tadoussac, a small north shore village at the confluence of the Saguenay River and the St Lawrence. Evie looked over some cottages as possible summer places to take the children but made no decisions. She knew that Lord Dufferin had built a house there when he was governor general (1872–78).[32]

The cruise continued up the Saguenay, which appeared more like a fjord than a river with its steep granite cliffs, splashing waterfalls, and pine trees growing in seemingly impossible places. Charlie pronounced it "perfectly wonderful"[33] and Evie thought it one of the most beautiful places in Canada. She told Lady Edward that she was happy being away from noisy trains and chattering servants.[34]

Victor and his family had been given fishing rights for salmon on the river by Sir William Price, a wealthy lumber and paper merchant whose company, Price Brothers, owned much of the Saguenay region. Price himself was in France that summer with the Canadian Grenadier Guards. He had been instrumental in the construction of the military camp at Valcartier in 1914, for which he had been rewarded with a knighthood by King George V in 1915.[35] The little group on the *Lady Grey* spent three happy days and nights enjoying sunrise and sunset, fishing for the abundant salmon, and watching the northern lights dance over the sky.

Evie's party returned to Quebec City to meet Victor, back from his fishing trip, but the governor general was required in Ottawa for the nation's fiftieth anniversary celebrations.

Throughout the Dominion of Canada, celebrations of the fiftieth anniversary of Canadian Confederation were held on 2 July 1917 – the actual anniversary was 1 July, but that was a Sunday, and it would not do to celebrate on a Sunday, the day reserved for prayer and intercession for the war.[36] In Ottawa, promptly at noon, before a throng of thousands, the duke was received on Parliament Hill with military honours; a band played the national anthem and a chorus sang "Rule Britannia." On a dais festooned with the flags of Britain, France, the United States, and other allies, the duke addressed the crowd and unveiled a memorial plaque to be placed on the central pillar of the new Centre Block of the Parliament Buildings, then under construction, dedicating the building to the Fathers of Confederation and to the valour of those serving at the front. Sir Robert Borden spoke of the Canadian men "holding our battle line beyond the seas," and Sir Wilfrid Laurier spoke of the potential for rejoicing being muted by war. A military march past included troops quartered in Ottawa, returned soldiers, Boy Scouts, and Girl Guides. That was it. The ceremony was all over within the hour. The duke thought it "quite dignified and appropriate to the occasion in wartime."[37]

In London, England, also on 2 July, Westminster Abbey was the scene of another service in commemoration of the fiftieth anniversary of Canadian Confederation. King George V and Queen Mary graced the occasion along with the Duke of Connaught, other members of the royal family, and representatives of Allied nations. Sir George Perley, Canadian high commissioner, represented Canada.

While Victor was back in Ottawa, from Quebec City Evie took a small crew aboard the *Lady Grey* to continue their adventures on the St Lawrence River. This time BJ travelled with Evie[38] and wrote a full description to his mother.

The yacht, he wrote, was "a handsome looking boat of some 500 tons painted white with a yellow funnel." On the top deck were two bedrooms with a sitting room and bathroom attached, which were assigned to the duchess and Lady Maud. The lower deck had two large cabins with beds and two smaller ones with berths. BJ, in consideration of his war wound, had one of the large cabins, "so as to fit my leg into the big bed"; Dorothy and Rachel shared a large cabin, and Angus and Charlie had the remaining two.[39] They headed for Matane on the south shore of the St Lawrence River – the northern coast of the Gaspé Peninsula – where they expected to stop to pick up Victor before going on to their final destination farther east at the Magdalen River. Before they reached Matane, the captain announced that the storm had freshened and they could not find shelter or a safe docking at any of the ports on the northern coast of the peninsula. The options were to travel on to Gaspé Bay, well beyond their destination, which would take another sixteen hours in the rough sea, or to head for the north shore of the St Lawrence, a mere three hours away. They opted for the shorter route.

On this voyage Angus began to distinguish himself as a resourceful, helpful individual. He rescued Dorothy when she got her head stuck under Maud's bed in the rolling ship, helped to wait at table, and looked after those who were seasick "most attentively," Evie wrote to Lady Edward.[40]

The *Lady Grey* found shelter from the storm in an isolated bay near the Pointe-des-Monts lighthouse. Immediately Dorothy's little dog, Kitchener, had to be attended to. BJ was detailed to stage a special landing party on the wet rocks, where Kitchener did his duty and was transported back to the ship under BJ's coat. Next morning, Evie stayed near the sea to escape the blackflies, which she said devoured the others. "Their bite is a very messy one, as they take a small piece right out and leave a trickle of blood. They creep up one's sleeves and down one's collar and are in every way worse than mosquitoes," she wrote to Lady Edward.[41]

BJ described the scene differently:

We all went ashore. There was a thick mist which came up from the sea and then lifted as suddenly. The coast was at first apparently uninhabited. Great rocks shelved over the sea and above them were forest-clad hills. In spite of the cold, the shore was covered with every sort of flower, wild iris, bog ayaliath, calmia, wild gooseberry,[42] all of which grew in profusion to the rock's edge. There was a strong smell of young spruce in the air. We had walked a few hundred yards when behind a point of rock we found two men rowing in an old boat ... They turned out to be French-Canadian fishermen and they had three live salmon in the bottom of the boat which they had netted. We knew there was a lighthouse in the vicinity so Lady Maud, Charles and I asked them to take us to it, which they assented to. It was almost impossible to comprehend their French ... The guardian of the lighthouse was a M. Fafard who had lived in the promontory of [Pointe] des Monts all his life and who is, I believe, rather a well-known character.[43] We found him tinkering with his light at the top of the tower. He was very excited to find out that Lady Maud was the daughter of the Governor-General, immediately ran down and put on his best clothes and then told his daughter to get a glass of milk for each of us. No one connected with the Governor General had been to his lighthouse since Lord Lorne [Governor General 1878–83], and in honour of the occasion he sent his son to the ice-house and produced a large salmon for us to take back to the yacht as a present to the Duchess.[44]

They moved the next morning to the neighbouring bay, Godbout, where they found Napoléon Alexandre Comeau, Guardian of the Godbout River. Comeau, then sixty-nine, was a self-taught expert naturalist, hunter, fisher, and swimmer. BJ described the adventure that the old man obviously recounted with great pleasure to his attentive audience: "His chief exploit [it happened in 1886] was crossing the St. Lawrence in the middle of winter in a canoe with the ice breaking and wedging all around him to save two men in another canoe who had been cut off from the Northern shore. It was not only a very brave action, but a great test of endurance."[45] Comeau also told them about his book *Life and Sport on the North Shore of the Lower St. Lawrence.*[46] BJ was obviously very impressed. While M. Comeau showed the younger generation where they could find some sea trout, Evie had biscuits and tea with Mme Comeau and visited a Montagnais Indian family who lived in a little settlement behind the Comeau family's house.[47] The town of Baie Comeau, established in 1936, was named after this man.

Finally the storm relented and they were able to cross the river to their destination, the harbour of the Magdalen River on the north shore of the Gaspé Peninsula.[48] The Magdalen River and the territory around it had been a seigneury. In early colonial days, under the feudal system, land in Quebec was divided into long, narrow strips, each with waterfront rights on the St Lawrence River. They were known as seigneuries and granted to seigneurs (lords) for their use. After the feudal system was abolished in 1854, the land could be purchased. Mr Frank Ross, "a small wiry little man just turning grey,"[49] had made his money in lumber and owned the property including the Magdalen River. In the summer of 1917, he offered his small house of seven rooms and his fishing rights in the river to the Devonshire family. His wife could not join him at his river home that year as she was pregnant, so the house was available, but he and his friend, Dr Chipman (possibly Shipman)[50] stayed in a little cabin nearby, guiding the visitors and indulging in their own passion for fishing.

The Magdalen River was reputed to be one of the best salmon rivers anywhere and, on his first day, BJ experienced the thrill of catching his first salmon:

> I had had only two days salmon fishing before at Lismore and had then caught nothing. I had with me the Doctor who gave me a few hints. I had not cast more than eight flies when I had a fish on. He did not run out much line. Just stayed there like a log without my being able to move him an inch nearer the boat. I played him for an hour and a half and by that time we realized I had a big fish on. My arm was full of cramps and pains. At last we landed him into the boat – a huge floundering monster. The scales we had with us were too small to weigh him. We took him back home and found he weighed 48 lbs. a record for the river and my first salmon.[51]

After that feat, no fishing expedition reached quite the same level of excitement for BJ.

Although Evie felt guilty about enjoying the peace and quiet of a remote cottage in the middle of the war,[52] she was in her element. All formality had been left behind, along with most of the household help.

A housemaid, kitchen maid, and footman had arrived separately,[53] but Evie had left behind her personal maid, Stiles, who was in disgrace because she had been indiscreet with the duke's valet, Taylor.[54] "We all feel sure they are living together. It is a bad example in the house even if the worst has not happened," Evie wrote to her mother. "I don't know what we shall end by doing about it."[55] Evie even contemplated living with no maid at all. She told BJ, "I would soon get into the way of it. Stiles has really had nothing to do for the last two months and it seems to me I have made all my own shirts and Anne's frock. But Stiles does do my hair beautifully."[56] Evie was being unrealistic as she probably could not have lived without a maid. In any case, even if they could have arranged passage to England for the problematic pair, they could hardly send servants across the dangerous Atlantic, and servants, especially English servants, could not be replaced. As far as we know, both Stiles and Taylor stayed on.

Evie spent her mornings sewing. There was no electricity and she does not mention a treadle machine; she probably did all her sewing by hand. The village store provided fabrics and she made children's clothes and bathing suits for BJ and Mervyn.[57] As luck would have it, the water was uncomfortably cold for "bathing" – by which she would have meant swimming, though it was not clear that any of them could swim – in the sea. Maud said they did bathe early every morning, but BJ said it was only for a few minutes.

"This is the most glorious place," Dorothy wrote to her grandmother. "We have all caught some salmon. I was nearly pulled in by mine! ... It is so nice always being close to the sea. It is very funny that there is nothing nice on the beach at all, no shells or perrywinkles [sic] or sea anemones – but it is delicious all the same ... just off the beach everything is covered with iris. And there are the most lovely wild strawberries."[58] Evie described the place from her perspective for her mother: "The house is just above high water in a lovely harbour with a shingle beach. The river starts just behind it and goes up for miles through lovely hills. There are four canoes and Mr. Ross generally sends two people out in each one. Some go to an upper reach where there is a tiny camp and a beautiful waterfall."[59]

BJ loved the place too. He wrote to his mother from Cape Magdalen: "The duties of Governor General do not sit too lightly on the shoulders of the Duke," nor, he said do the duties of ADCs sit lightly on their shoulders. "You can therefore imagine the happiness of us all in this wild spot far away from railway or even a good road with little communication with the outside world except by sea. All formality has been left behind … Rachel's dog has just eaten Dorothy's jersey which means a row between Dorothy and Rachel. The duchess is deploring the fact that she must buy a new one and wondering whether she can't put a stitch into the garment somewhere. Dorothy's dog has thrown a fit. Tea is now ready, which may relieve the situation."[60]

Having presided over the fiftieth anniversary celebrations, Victor decided he could take a little more time away from the conscription crisis to join the family. He travelled by train from Ottawa all the way to Gaspé Bay at the end of the peninsula, where the *Lady Grey* picked him up for the ten-hour voyage back to Cape Magdalen. Lord Lansdowne had described fishing in the Gaspé region thirty years before, and Victor had fished for salmon near his Irish home, Lismore Castle, but he was excited to have a Canadian experience of this exhilarating sport. He arrived at 6:00 a.m. on 5 July, briefly checked on the family, and then headed out to the river. He caught four fish that first morning and six more in the afternoon. "Really a wonderful day. Ten fish 252 lbs. average 25. Fish are quick to hook if they are on the take."[61] He meant that the salmon were taking the flies he angled out to them that day. Other days he complained, "Lot of fish about, but they did not take."[62] That first day set the standard for his time in Canada. BJ reported, "The Duke is in the seventh heaven of delight. He is out all day fishing and grunts and groans as he plays his fish. Besides which he does not get quite so much good drink and good food as he is used to and he has had in consequence only the slightest twinge of gout."[63] Victor did suffer from gout occasionally, but he never let the pain keep him from a good fishing river.

Carefully typed records of the catches for everyone in the family, including the ADCs, are in the records kept at the Chatsworth archives. Together they caught 125 fish, a total of 2,543 pounds with an average weight of 20.3 pounds. They reeled in more and heavier fish in a shorter time than they had done at Lismore, which made it all the more satisfying. Victor wrote the news to Lord Lansdowne, who shared his passion for fishing. "Your fishing report made my mouth water," Lansdowne replied.[64] What they did with all that fish is a mystery and did not concern them enough to mention in diary or letters, though on another expedition the duke mentioned sending some back to Evie.

Victor fished thirteen of his sixteen days at the Magdalen River. He would have been on the water every day, but by tradition no one fished on Sundays. And he was also away for a day, on a trip to Anticosti Island, in the middle of the Gulf of St Lawrence, about sixty miles from Cape Magdalen. On the evening of 10 July, Victor and his party boarded the *Lady Grey*. Evie and the ADC, Mervyn Ridley, stayed at Cape Magdalen, Evie for fear of seasickness, Mervyn to take the opportunity to fish in the best pools, which were usually reserved for the duke. The rest of the family, along with Angus, BJ, Mr Ross, and his friend Dr. Shipman, went along for the overnight trip. By the time the *Lady Grey* sailed from Cape Magdalen at 3:00 a.m. they were all comfortably asleep, and they awoke to find they were anchoring at Ellis Bay, Anticosti Island.[65]

At 140 miles long by 35 miles at its widest, a total of almost 3,100 square miles, Anticosti is larger than Prince Edward Island. Ringed by reefs that stretch two miles into the gulf, and assailed by strong currents and treacherous winds, the island had been the scene of many shipwrecks.[66] Anticosti was owned by a Frenchman, M. Henri Menier, who had made his fortune in chocolate, and paid $125,000 in 1895 for the whole of the island to use for his own pleasure, with future business development also in mind.

Victor undoubtedly knew that Anticosti was owned entirely by one man. As Duke of Devonshire, Victor controlled, within the limits of British law, land amounting to almost 200,000 acres in England and Ireland[67] – much smaller than this wild island in the sea – while Henri Menier controlled nearly two million acres on Anticosti. Victor must have wanted to see how such a large private land holding was managed compared to his own property. What he saw and heard astonished and astounded him.

No news of their intended visit had reached the island, and BJ told his mother their story:

On rowing ashore at about 10 o'clock we were met by the Customs Officer, a short bearded French Canadian in a knickerbocker suit and a Homburg hat, and a man who bore in his cap the words Chef de Police. We afterwards discovered that the latter official was the only policeman on the island; that he was also the head and only porter; and that he works the electric launch. We were first ushered into his bureau which was completely empty save for 8 old rifles ... and three largely printed laws threatening dire penalties to anyone who committed trespass. We asked him if he often had to take people up. He said "No," he had never had to do so. If anyone was troublesome M. Menier's Secretary, the viceregent of the colony, just turned him off the island. He added that a small cottage was being turned into a prison – as a preventative rather than a corrective.[68]

They were then introduced to the head of the Forestry department, "a very nice looking and stalwart American," and the Chief of the Administration, M. Malouin, "a very fat man with a red clean-shaven face, garbed in a knickerbocker suit of a French cut, a pair of gaiters, and a yachting cap, smoking a long cigar. He is a French Canadian ... a J.P. [Justice of the Peace] and the official representative of the Government. He had a hearty, fat chuckle and whenever he had anything of importance to point out to the Duke, took him by the arm. Until he heard one of us talk of him as his Excellency he addressed him with great deference as 'Mister.'"

BJ related what they were told of the history of the island:

On arrival Monsieur Menier hoisted the French flag which nobody took very much notice of; but when he began to allow French goods of all sorts to enter the island and be sold free of charge, the Canadian Government stepped in and sent a Custom's [sic] official to Ellis Bay. So Monsieur Menier was constrained to hoist the Union Jack. But in all other respects he is, or rather was, absolute King of the Island. He died shortly before the outbreak of war and his brother [Gaston Menier] succeeded him. Since the war he has not been near the island and apparently does not take so much interest in it as the old gentleman, leaving everything in the hands of the latter's secretary.[69]

The "secretary" was M. Martin-Zédé, whom they would meet.

When Henri Menier bought the island, it was inhabited by a few fishermen who lived more from what they could collect from shipwrecks than from the fish they caught. As BJ told the story: "What people there were on the island ... he either bought out or employed in his own interest, so that every inhabitant of the island is a paid employee. He attempted to settle Frenchmen [on the island], but the latter did not relish the somewhat lonely life and, though they did not generally return to France, settled elsewhere in Canada." Obviously their informants did not mention to the duke's party that the people of Fox Bay, who had fought to remain on the island, were expelled in 1900 by the Government of Canada, which transported these fisher people to an uncertain future as farmers in Manitoba.[70]

BJ continued:

The island is covered with dense virgin forest. Menier's first concern was to erect a lumber mill at Ellis Bay, which at once attracted a number of labourers to the island. These were all French Canadians as were the original inhabitants who remained – with the exception of the overseer of the Forests, the General Manager of the Mills, and the chief Engineer who are Yankees – a certain amount of American capital being employed in the mills. Doing nothing by halves, Menier built a huge pier with every facility for shipping lumber, a railway from the head of the pier 35 miles inland, a road nine miles long to the original settlement of island at English Bay, which he completely rebuilt, a village at Ellis Bay by the Mills with a hotel, a slaughter house, a bakery (excellent bread some of which we bought) a store well stocked with everything imaginable and a village green, a chateau for himself, and a model farm. He stocked the island with game – deer, which have done extremely well, moose which have done rather badly, foxes and hares. Bears are indigenous and then there are 27 excellent salmon rivers. Above all, he has completely obliterated the fly from the face of the island, which was renowned for its flies.[71]

It was Georges Martin-Zédé, Henri Menier's friend, who found a method for getting rid of flies. He built a contraption with a wire mesh box mounted on a tripod and placed it over a bath of water and lime. He then inserted sheep's heads into the box. Flies laid their eggs on the heads and when the maggots hatched they dropped into the bath below and died. In this fashion, he apparently erased flies from the island.[72]

The duke and his party were then led round the various institutions of the settlement: the bakery and the store, "where we helped Menier to carry on the good work by buying some of his chocolate, and a mouth-organ, 'made in Germany.'" At the lumber mill they saw that the trees were cut into cylindrical unbaked logs to be shipped for the manufacture of pulp and then paper.

They were told that, before he died, Henri Menier used to spend two months on the island every summer fishing, shooting, and working out his plans. BJ asked what M. Gaston Menier's plans were now and was told that he had no wish for settlement to any great extent on the land, that he wished to keep the whole island as his personal estate under his own direction, that he hoped the lumber business would increase, that after the war he hoped to turn the wood into pulp on the island and perhaps institute a paper mill, that he hoped the fur production from his foxes would increase and that parts of the island would be let out for sporting purposes.

They returned to the yacht for lunch and, BJ remarked, had "a most divine bathe – the water in the bay being most beautifully warm." After lunch they again went ashore and:

> were motored to English Bay or "Baie Ste. Clair" as the French call it, along the 9 miles of road.[73] It was the only motor on the Island – an old Simplex which grunted and growled and shook and had to be refilled with cold water from a kettle carried for the purpose whenever we passed a stream. As we passed we saw some children running across a field towards the road and the chauffeur – one of the overseers at the Mill – said, "It's the first time they've seen a motor." On either side of the road the trees had been cleared of the space of some 50 yards to enable the sun to melt the ice quickly at the end of the winter. We saw several deer as we passed.
>
> Baie St. Clair was originally a fishing village with a few shacks to it, but it has been completely rebuilt by Menier, who employs

most of the inhabitants in one way or another. It boasts a good store, a little church, a curé, a hospital, and a doctor and a "Governor's House," the Governor being Monsieur Malouin whom we had met in the morning and whose wife we found sitting in the verandah. The Duke saw the only patient in the Hospital. The Doctor was out, but we just walked in and found the patient, an old man, sitting up by the side of his bed. We then paid a formal visit to the Madame Malouin. The Duke speaks very little French and she spoke very little English. But they sat in a large well-furnished and darkened room and looked at each other, which seemed to afford great gratification to Madame. When we met the old gentleman in the evening and told him we had called on his wife, he said with some pride "Ah, she loves to show off her English."

We returned to Ellis Bay at 5:30. Throughout the day all the worthies of the village had been telling us how sorry Monsieur Martin, Menier's Secretary, would be to miss us; that our arrival was absolutely unknown to any of them, that Monsieur Martin was away fishing.

On coming back we were told that Menier's steamer was in sight with Monsieur Martin on it. So we sat down on the wharf and waited. In a few minutes the little open trolley came down the pier and drew up alongside the wooden platform. The ends of fishing rods protruded from various corners. Our friend, the Chef de Police, had donned a magnificent garment which combined the uniforms of a policeman and a train guard. Out of the trolley stepped a man some 6 ft. 2 inches in height with a massive frame and a red face adorned by a small grey pointed beard. He wore a smart looking dark grey London overcoat, gaiters, and a yachting cap ... Behind him came Monsieur Turgeon and Monsieur Taché, Ministers in the Quebec parliament, whom we had frequently met at Quebec and who could tell M. Martin who we were directly they saw us.

The huge frame of Monsieur Martin advanced towards us. There was hand-shaking, and apologies and greetings and expostulations and gesticulations. Has His Excellency seen this and has he been told that and had everyone done everything they could for him? He hoped so. He brought up the people of the island to be polite … To make up for his absence he would entreat His Excellency and everyone else to dine with him at the Chateau. "It will not be like dining at Monsieur Menier's Hotel at Paris; but what we can do we will." The Duke had meanwhile been unable to get in a word edgeways. When he did, he said that he, Lady Maud and myself would be delighted to dine.

The M. Martin they met was Georges Martin-Zédé, Henri Menier's friend and agent in Anticosti. Martin-Zédé called himself Director General and essentially ruled the island. Mr Menier spent a month or two each summer fishing and hunting, but Martin-Zédé was there much longer each year, though he too usually returned to France for the winter.

BJ continued: "We were fetched off the yacht at 7:30 by the Chef de Police – this time in a blue nautical jacket as driver of the motor boat. Monsieur Martin was on the quay to meet us with the trolley. We soon found out that he had served 25 months in Gallipoli and Salonika as Captain in the Artillery and that he was just returned from France. He must be at least 58 years old." (He was fifty-three.)

They were transported to the Chateau, "a large house of dark painted wood with bay windows, jutting corners, and gables, surrounded by short fir trees." BJ noted that the chief room contained "a very good Persian carpet, a lovely old Dutch cupboard and table, and some Italian renaissance objects." Dinner consisted of "beautifully cooked cod, eggs on mince, a perfect piece of meat and wild strawberries. The wine was equally good, Sherry (iced!) Pommery and Cognac … Monsieur Martin offered many excuses for the want of elegance on the part of his servants. The Duke said it was the best dinner he had ever eaten, and, far from the eye of the Duchess, ate and drank everything – entirely forgetful of his gout."[74]

After dinner, they returned to the yacht to talk over their experiences. BJ wrote: "To think of a large island and its inhabitants just within the gates of the New World, completely in the hands of a Frenchman. And in this wild place a chateau such as a rich Frenchman might have to spend two months in the summer. It was quite a different atmosphere to anything else in Canada."[75] Victor too was astounded by the feudal rules and private ownership of this island within Canada. He told his mother, "It is the most remarkable mixture of highly organised modern ideas and absolute primitive conditions that I have ever heard of and I certainly would not have believed in it if I had not seen it." He noted some of the rules: "No dogs, guns or spirits are allowed on the island; if anyone is troublesome he is sent off to the mainland."[76] In his diary Victor wrote: "Everyone on his island is in M. Menier's service. The heads of departments live in an excellent hotel. Somehow one cannot realize it all. A strange mixture of modern civilization and practically a controlled land."[77]

Anticosti Island is no longer a private domain. In 1926, Gaston Menier sold it to a logging company. Subsequently it changed hands several times from one company to another trying to make a profitable lumber business, until the Depression of the 1930s further diminished this prospect. Finally, in 1974, the Quebec government bought out the last of these companies and turned the island into a Quebec national park.[78]

What is surprising in our modern day is not that an owner controlled what happened on his private property, but that the whole island of Anticosti was privately owned well into the twentieth century. Although much of Canada had been developed by private interests, the Hudson's Bay Company being a prime example, by 1900 the amount of private ownership in Canada had been greatly reduced. However, in 1917, private ownership and control of lands and fishing rivers still remained in Canada; the family had already discovered some of them: on the Saguenay and at the seigneury in Cape Magdalen. The duke would soon discover even more private rivers full of fish, at least one of which remains private today.

After only two weeks, Victor left the Magdalen River to return to Ottawa and the conscription crisis. Evie decided to enjoy this remote cottage until the end of July, treasuring the peaceful, quiet life. To her regret, it didn't remain peaceful for long; she soon faced a family crisis of major proportions.

Two days after his departure from Cape Magdalen, Evie reported to Victor:

> We have had the most agitating time since you left. When we went upstairs that evening Maud told me that Angus had proposed to her in the afternoon. She had not accepted him but thought she would probably do so. Next morning I talked to Angus. He was too nice about it all, said he had believed that she was engaged to Ralph,[79] so for months he tried not to think about her. Finally he got desperate and could not keep out of her way any longer. He was full of confidence and I thought Maud had practically made up her mind as she had allowed him to kiss her and had not at all minded his doing so! In the afternoon some change came over her. She is now in a regular funk, feels she has behaved atrociously to Angus and is not really fond enough of him to marry him. He was *so* happy and is now in an awful state … I wish you were here – though we can do no good. Your own Evie.[80]

Evie was not entirely unprepared for this event. Lord Richard Nevill had warned her months before that Angus was fond of Maud. She had paid little attention, until Maud got a fly hook deep into her finger while they were at the Magdalen River cottage. "It had to be pulled through and the barb cut off by a doctor who is staying here, and he [Angus] was much whiter than she was when it was done."[81] BJ, too, noticed their growing attachment. He wrote to his mother, "Do you remember saying you heard a rumour she was engaged to Angus Mackintosh. I answered you that pigs might fly. Well, perhaps they might."[82]

Evie had begun to notice Angus's good qualities. Though he was reserved and diffident, he was unselfish, thoughtful, keen about politics, and, she thought, "very warm hearted and emotional under a rather prosaic exterior."[83] She knew that Angus's lung was a problem. He had only one functioning lung, having been injured in the other at Ypres in 1914. He tired easily and was getting fat because he could not exercise enough. Though he could swim and walk quite a long way and ride a certain amount, he could not exert himself violently and she feared that the damp English winters would affect his damaged lung.[84] Evie wrote to her mother, "I think she [Maud] feels – as I do – that he is not exactly the right sort of man for her."[85]

For Maud, the conflict must have included thoughts of her recent triumph in Washington, where she had mingled with the elite and felt an important part of society. Angus had no position in England or in America that would afford her the kinds of experiences she had enjoyed during those weeks in the American capital. She must also have wondered, too, what her grandmother and friends in England would think of her marrying one of her father's ADCs.

Before leaving England, Evie had anticipated the problem of ADCs around her daughters. She had written to Aunt Lucy: "The nicest available men are mostly quite penniless and with so many daughters the risk is great!"[86] While Angus Mackintosh, Captain of the Royal Horse Guards and ADC, was not what they might have anticipated for their first son-in-law, as BJ noted, "his ancestors were potentates in Scotland before the Cavendishes were heard of."[87] His father was The Mackintosh of Moy, 28th Chief of the clan, which dated back at least to the thirteenth century.

Evie still worried. After the proposal, as yet not accepted, Maud and Angus continued to spend their time together. Evie expressed her displeasure to Victor. They "bathed together this morning ... Somehow there is, to me, something rather indelicate in this 'mixed' bathing since the crisis. I don't like to see them rowing about in wet clothes together if they are not going to marry."[88]

Evie determined to take the whole party back to Quebec City next time the *Lady Grey* docked at Cape Magdalen. Angus and Maud had agreed to stay apart and "leave it open" for a month.[89] Angus would go to the Royal Victoria Hospital in Montreal "to have his lung overhauled and reported on."[90] Maud would go to visit Baron Shaughnessy, the duke's friend, president of the Canadian Pacific Railway, and his wife at their summer home in St Andrews by-the-Sea, New Brunswick, accompanied by Blanche, Charlie, and Anne. In the quiet there, Evie hoped Maud could make up her mind. "One does not want her to run the risk of mistaking pity and friendship for anything else."[91]

Victor travelled from Ottawa to meet the party when they arrived in Quebec City. Victor had always liked Angus and thought he "would make her a very good husband."[92] He was pleased that Evie had also come around to liking him. For Evie, though, accepting him was conditional on his lung report and on Maud's feelings. At least for both Evie and Victor their first conditions were met – he was an aristocrat and his family would likely settle on him enough that he would be able to support Maud in an acceptable manner.

Victor had only one day in Quebec City before he hurried back to Ottawa and the government problems. Maud's crisis seems to have brought up Evie's feelings about her own marriage and the stresses she and Victor had experienced recently. She wrote to Victor, on 30 July 1917, their silver wedding anniversary. As usual she began her letter with "My own Darling," and she continued:

> I do hate spending today away from you ... I am no good at saying grateful things but I *am* grateful to you darling for these 25 years of happiness. I don't know why lately we seem to have grown rather frightened of each other ... I simply can't exist without talking over everything with you and perhaps that has been the cause of the troubles. I think you know how proud I am of you and how tremendously anxious I am that everything you do or say should be the very best possible. I know I am a fool to criticize, but it is just owing to that great wish to arrive at the very best and if you could remember that you would not feel so irritated with me. God bless you my darling.

She signed off, as usual, "Your own Evie."[93]

For the month of August, the family was scattered. Maud and Blanche stayed two weeks in St Andrews and then took the train to Boston to be met by Lady Spring Rice, who took them by motor to their cottage in Woods Hole, Massachusetts. Victor was in Ottawa worrying about the conscription crisis. Evie returned to Ottawa and took the train north into the Gatineau Hills of Quebec, accompanied by Dorothy and Rachel. There they discovered the pleasures of Blue Sea Lake and awaited word from Maud about what would happen next.

CHAPTER 7

Crises of State

When the duke returned to Ottawa on 23 July, he found the conscription crisis had solidified into a stalemate. While Borden still wanted to extend Parliament's mandate without an election in order to establish a coalition government with the Liberal Opposition party, and institute conscription, Laurier remained adamant that he could not approve either an extension of Parliament or a coalition government as long as the conscription issue was on the table. Laurier believed that bringing in conscription by a coalition government would divide the country because Quebec, under the influence of Henri Bourassa, was against the measure, and he "dreaded very serious difficulties if a conscription law was passed by the present parliament." He insisted that such a decision would require either a referendum or an election. Borden then offered to hold off on the actual implementation of conscription until after an election, but Laurier still refused to join a coalition that would go into an election in which conscription was the major policy.[1] Later, after the conscription bill passed, Sir Wilfrid told the duke that enforcing conscription would certainly lead to passive resistance, and he feared "disorders."[2]

The duke's secretary, Arthur Sladen, informed him that while he was away, someone – the records do not make it clear who – had criticized the governor general for not doing enough during this period of crisis.[3] A letter had also arrived from someone named Shane Leslie, who addressed the duke as "Dear Cousin," and who had a similar complaint.[4] Stung by these criticisms, the duke met with the prime minister nine times over the next month. At their first meeting, on 24 July, he found the prime minister "tired, worried and quite at sea."[5] The duke discussed the situation with the under-secretary of state for external affairs, Sir Joseph Pope,[6] and with Lord Shaughnessy of the CPR.[7] They both agreed that Borden seemed almost paralyzed with indecision.

The duke made up his mind to embark on an unusual project for a governor general – he called a meeting of both parties. He began by asking the prime minister to participate. Borden agreed as long as he could invite Sir Clifford Sifton, publisher of the *Winnipeg Free Press*. Throughout his career, Sifton had changed his political affiliations, depending on whether those in power agreed with him. As a cabinet minister in Laurier's government, he had broken with the Liberals in 1911 over reciprocity, a form of free trade with the United States.[8] After the reciprocity policy failed with the Liberal defeat in 1911, Sifton never joined the Conservatives. His behaviour had not endeared him to his contemporaries, east or west. He worked mostly behind the scenes and stayed out of the limelight,[9] but in July 1917 he published an open letter in which he urged Canadians "to stand by our men at the front," which, he said, could only be done by a "Union War Government."[10]

The duke suggested the meeting should include Lord Shaughnessy and Quebec premier Sir Lomer Gouin, men that the duke believed "would be of material assistance" to the meeting. The duke had conferred with Lord Shaughnessy, who considered the situation in the country to be very serious, especially in relation to Quebec. Both these men were very willing to attend but not at all pleased about having Sifton there.[11] The duke wanted to hold the meeting straight away, but Sifton was out west. Borden insisted Sifton be present and also wanted to wait for the outcome of the Western Liberal convention to be held in Winnipeg in early August, where both conscription and Laurier's leadership were under review. The date for the governor general's meeting was finally set for 9 August. George Graham, a prominent Liberal, and Sir George Foster, minister of Trade and Commerce, were also invited.

Meanwhile, the conscription bill – called the Military Service Act – passed third reading in the House of Commons and went on to the Senate. Borden told the duke he might appoint additional senators to be sure it passed in the Liberal-dominated body, which the duke thought was "a strange and exasperating thing to do."[12]

On 9 August, everything was set for the meeting at Government House. The duke did not expect anything major to occur, but he thought the meeting would clear the air and could do no harm. He understood that it was an unusual procedure for a governor general to be so involved in Canada's political affairs, and he spent some time thinking through what he would say and how he would handle the meeting.[13] Sir Wilfrid was buoyed by the results of the Western Liberal convention, which had voted to sidestep the issue of conscription and to support his leadership.[14]

The participants arrived at Government House at 12:30 and settled themselves around the table.[15] Meeting Sifton for the first time that day, the duke reported that he was more impressed than he had expected.[16] Gouin described how they arranged the seating to accommodate the newspaper publisher, who had a hearing deficit. Sifton used a hearing tube or trumpet; the speaker put one end to his mouth while Sifton put the other to his ear. Sifton, Graham, and Shaughnessy sat on one side of the table, with Borden, Foster, and Laurier opposite them, and Gouin at one end. The duke entered and sat opposite Gouin, close to Sifton and Borden. When Borden was ready to speak, Sir George Foster would change seats with Sifton so that Sifton sat beside the prime minister, who could then speak into the tube. Later, the duke reported to Walter Long, the colonial secretary, "it is an intolerable nuisance to have to conduct a conversation when the speaking-tube has to be passed round and one has to speak into the mouthpiece as well as to the rest of the room." Undoubtedly this procedure contributed to a rather stultified meeting with each person speaking in turn rather than having a spontaneous conversation.[17]

The duke opened the meeting by telling the group that "my excuse for any departure I might have made from strictly constitutional practice was my anxiety to preserve as far as possible national unity and to see if any means could be devised to avoid plunging the country into a General Election at so critical a period of the War."[18] He noted that the military power of Germany was far from being broken and, although the United States had entered the war, that did not relieve Canada of her responsibilities. He appealed for a full, frank, and open discussion, and then proposed that he retire from the room. Sir Wilfrid declared that he did not see why the governor general could not remain at the conference. The others agreed, and the duke consented to stay.

Borden reviewed the necessity for more troops at the front and more money to aid Britain, and he spoke of the necessity to restore harmony among the population of Canada. He repeated his offer of a coalition government. The Liberals – Laurier, Gouin, and Graham – said that a general election was necessary, and as soon as possible. Sifton and Shaughnessy thought an election should be delayed and an effort made to recruit the 100,000 men needed by voluntary enlistment, before conscription was implemented. A program of National Service registration had yielded over 100,000 men still available for military duty. Foster spoke of the bitter feeling and racial animosity and delays that would occur in terms of troop training and deployment if an election were insisted upon. Borden offered to suspend the conscription law for six months if Parliament were prolonged, but Laurier and Gouin were firm in believing an election was required before conscription could be law, and the Military Service Act had yet to be ratified by the Senate and signed by the governor general. Laurier told the governor general that "even after a General Election the enforcement of the Conscription bill would be met with passive resistance in the Province of Quebec."[19]

These were the same positions each had held for at least a month. Although nothing changed in the stalemate as a result of this conference, the duke thought "no harm was done and the atmosphere may to some extent be cleared."[20] Apparently he was still uncertain about the wisdom of holding this meeting, as he wrote to Lord Lansdowne, who replied, "Your conference has, I'm afraid, failed to produce the desired result. I am sure you were right to convene it. If the G.G. is to be precluded from such unofficial efforts he ought not to be there at all. But they were not an easy crowd to handle."[21] In fact, Victor was simply too late. Had he thought about it in June, he might have been able to make some progress, but by late July, the positions had solidified and the situation was at an impasse. On the other hand, he could not have held the meeting in June because the situation was not yet desperate enough to justify his intervention.

After the meeting, though he seldom made negative comments in his diary or letters, he did tell Walter Long that he thought Borden "had failed to make the best of his opportunities," especially in "not taking Laurier into his confidence."[22] And, he continued, "I do not see from what quarter the Prime Minister will be able to gain much strength in any reconstruction of his cabinet." The duke thought that Borden had anticipated a split in the Liberal party at the Winnipeg convention. "Instead of cursing Sir Wilfrid, the convention blessed him," the duke wrote to Walter Long. Though he admitted that things change rapidly, he believed that "at this moment it seems that if a General Election were to take place now the Cabinet would be beaten." What the duke probably did not understand in the early days of August – Borden had only told him in the vaguest terms – was that Borden had been negotiating since June with conscriptionist provincial Liberals to join a Union government. Borden himself had met with Newton Rowell, leader of the Liberal Opposition in Ontario, who was considering lending assistance to the project, and Sir Clifford Sifton was actively negotiating with several western Liberals.

In the two weeks following the duke's meeting, the political situation did change rapidly, as the duke had anticipated. On 17 August, Borden asked to see the duke. He had received a letter from Robert Rogers, minister of Public Works, who, the duke wrote, "for bad taste and narrowness is the worst I find I ever saw ... Rogers tendered his resignation on the ground [of] the slackness and inactivity of the Govt. Borden's reply was quite good. I gave permission for the publication of the letter and I wish the PM had chucked him out instead of his resigning."[23] Rogers's resignation alleviated some of the resistance of the western Liberals who did not want to work with him in a Union government.

A few days later, Borden brought the duke into his confidence about Sifton's efforts to secure western Liberal support.[24] Shortly afterward, some western Liberals sent a telegram saying they agreed to join a Union government but only on the condition they found a new leader. Borden took this telegram to his caucus and, though he offered to step aside, they unanimously insisted that he must stay on as leader.[25] They all thought that Union was dead.

On 27 August, when a wild melee erupted in Parliament about the government's takeover of the Canadian Northern Railway, the incident hit the front page of the Toronto *Globe*, under the headline "Union

Declared Dead as Wild Scene in Commons Nearly Ends in a Riot." The duke, who was in Toronto, noted calmly in his diary: "There seems to be some trouble with Ottawa over the Railway Bill and also the Western Liberals are said to have refused to come in to the Govt but this is not authenticated."[26] Other than the title, the article said nothing about Union government; the whole report was about the railway bill.[27] The press, however, may have heard about the telegram from the western Liberals and their demand for a new leader. Meanwhile, the Railway Bill passed after closure of the debate. It nationalized the almost bankrupt Canadian Northern Railway, which eventually incorporated four other railways and became the Canadian National Railway we know today.[28]

On 29 August, the duke, still in Toronto, gave his assent to the Military Service Bill. In the end, Borden had not needed to make additional appointments for the bill to be passed in the Senate. While in most of Canada the measure was accepted, in Montreal that night and the next the anti-conscription demonstrations turned violent.[29] Earlier in August, Lord Atholstan's home in Cartierville, north of Montreal, had been bombed. Atholstan, the former Sir Hugh Graham, owner of the *Montreal Star,* had advocated conscription. No one was hurt in the incident, but it sent a message that the anti-conscriptionists were serious.[30]

After his 9 August meeting, the duke was anxious to get back to his family and his holiday, and to arrange a western tour, but he needed to stay close to Ottawa until Parliament was prorogued. Borden said he planned to be ready to prorogue by the middle of August, but the duke thought Borden's assessment "sanguine"[31] since Parliament still had to deal with an income tax bill, a railway bill, and a franchise bill.[32] Borden did move quickly to put through these measures, which he thought necessary to the prosecution of the war and winning the election.

There were two franchise bills. The Military Voters Act gave the vote to all soldiers, even those on active duty in the theatre of war. The Wartime Elections Act disfranchised citizens of enemy alien birth naturalized after 31 March 1902, except when such citizens had a son, grandson, or brother on active duty. It also granted the vote to the wives, mothers, and sisters of serving soldiers, as well as women serving in the armed forces.[33] This was the first time that women were allowed to vote in a federal election.[34] The government also passed the Income

War Tax Act, which was considered a form of conscription of wealth. This was Canada's first income tax and was expected to last only until the war was over.

On 20 September, the duke prorogued Parliament, but he was not yet free to travel far, as there might still be Liberals to swear in to Borden's cabinet. By this time, Borden's and Sifton's negotiations had brought in several Liberals who would join the Union cabinet with Borden as leader. Some of the Conservatives in cabinet had resigned and others were asked to leave, creating space for the Liberals. The duke did manage a six-day trip to Halifax while Borden prepared a cabinet for his Union government. Not until 23 October did Borden complete the finishing touches and have all the new cabinet ministers sworn in by the governor general. Borden's cabinet was well balanced with ten Liberals and twelve Conservatives, and coverage across the country in both parties.[35] The election writ was issued on 1 November and the election called for 17 December .

During the conscription crisis, Victor wrote to Evie that he had received "a rather mysterious telegram from Walter Long saying: 'Accept heartiest congratulations for deeds ... of gallant Canadian troops'"[36] Though he read several newspapers every day, he knew nothing about a battle that would have prompted the telegram. "Ld Richard asked at the *Citizen* office if anything had come in but there is nothing so far. The Editor said ... often ... that telegrams of congratulations mean heavy losses." This turned out to be true. The Canadians had taken Hill 70 as part of the battle for Lens in northern France, and had suffered heavy losses in hand-to-hand fighting. It is surprising that the duke did not understand that this battle was crucial in the defence of France and that Canadians had acquitted themselves with great bravery. In his defence, perhaps he was used to reading about Canadian strength and courage and was waiting for an actual victory, such as the takeover of Lens.

As if conscription and Union government were not creating enough turmoil, there was another issue, which came to fruition in October 1917, an issue that put the governor general in the position of negotiator between the Canadian and British governments.

Borden, as he later wrote in his memoirs, "chafed under the control and domination which Downing Street had arrogated to itself in determining the scope and destiny of foreign policy."[37] The Dominions, although independent on matters of domestic policy, were still subject to Great Britain in matters of foreign policy. Borden wanted something more for Canada, while still maintaining the nation's status within the Empire. Canadians in English Canada, especially those of British origin, felt themselves to be an important part of the Empire and wanted to belong as a full partner.[38]

During his three months in London at the Imperial War Conference – February to May 1917 – Borden had sought out General Smuts, prime minister of South Africa, then also a Dominion. Smuts, too, wanted more independence for his nation with respect to foreign policy. They approached representatives of the other Dominions – Australia, New Zealand, and Newfoundland – and finally brought in India. India at that time was still a British colony and not yet a Dominion, but had been invited to the conference. Together they drafted what became Resolution IX, which Borden presented to the conference and Smuts seconded. The resolution asked that a special conference be convened after the war to readjust constitutional relations to "recognize the right of the Dominions and India to an adequate voice in foreign policy and in foreign relations."[39] Resolution IX passed unanimously, to Borden's satisfaction. He was to revisit this issue just over a year later, but meanwhile, Canada's participation in the war effort supported his position.

In October, Borden tested the idea of more independence by requesting a Canadian representative in Washington. While in London, he had discussed the idea with Walter Long, who had taken it to the British cabinet. Borden had also discussed the idea with Lord Northcliffe, Director of Propaganda for the British government and head of the British War Mission to Washington, when Northcliffe had stayed in Ottawa at Rideau Hall in early October. On 13 October, Borden wrote to Sir George Perley, Canada's high commissioner in London, to say that he intended to appoint John Douglas Hazen, who had been Borden's minister of Marine and Fisheries and minister of Naval Services, as Canada's representative in Washington, with a title similar to high commissioner.[40] Perley replied that Walter Long suggested Hazen be attached to the British embassy but completely under control of the Canadian government.[41] A message from Walter Long reached the governor general's office in Ottawa while the duke was away on his short trip to Halifax.[42] Long wrote as if the duke had been fully briefed about this issue. The duke's staff sent a reply after consulting with the prime minister, but without contacting the duke.[43]

The first time the duke heard about all this was when he returned to Ottawa. In his diary for 20 October, he recorded his umbrage at being ignored – he was, after all, responsible for foreign relations: "Afraid the PM has been rather sharp about Hazen's appointment to Washington. It is nothing more than a political job. Saw him for a few minutes and told him I hope in future I could be told about these appointments before they went to England to the High Commissioner."[44]

This issue had the potential to discredit the duke with British officials, who might see him as incompetent for not having known about it and not appreciating the problems it could bring to the Empire. He explained in a private telegram to Walter Long that the first he had seen of the issue was Long's cypher (encoded) telegram when he returned from Halifax, that he thought any Canadian representative should be attached to the British embassy, and that he did not consider Hazen qualified for the post.[45]

Meanwhile, Hazen was awaiting the results of these negotiations between Canada and Britain. At Borden's request, Hazen had been "sacrificed" from his cabinet position to make space in the Union cabinet for Liberal members.[46] Hazen didn't mind; he had three possible jobs awaiting him: lieutenant-governor of New Brunswick, chief justice of New Brunswick, and high commissioner in Washington.[47] Though he thought the Washington job preferable, he wanted to be sure that the title and salary would be suitable, and that he would definitely be independent of the British embassy on "questions of Canadian interests."[48]

That was the sticking point. Walter Long's reply to the governor general arrived on 26 October . If Borden was proposing that the representative be independent of the embassy, he wrote, that was incompatible with the unity of the British Empire. Any political unit could have only one embassy at a foreign capital. If Canada got such a representative, the other Dominions would want one too, which would be equivalent to a breakup of the Empire. He thought something could be worked out, and suggested Borden speak to the ambassador, Sir Cecil Spring Rice. Long also asked Borden to send "an exact statement of what he proposed both as to the status of his representative and the mode of accrediting him to Government of United States."[49]

The duke showed the telegram to Borden and recorded that Borden took it very well and said he wanted to think about it. Although he was busy and exhausted, Borden did prepare a reply, but it fell short of giving Long what he had asked for. It simply reiterated the need for someone in Washington who would have a suitable and dignified status.[50] Once again a stalemate was reached, this time with the British government.

Just in time, fortune worked in the duke's favour: Spring Rice, who was in Ottawa, gave them a face-saving way out of the impasse. He told them that housing was difficult to secure and expensive in Washington.[51] The duke noted in his diary, "Got Springy in who managed in his most dexterous manner to throw buckets of cold water on the whole proposal both in regard the appointment itself and the individual occupant."[52] On 6 November, the duke notified the Colonial Office that Borden had given up, for now.

In the aftermath, Hazen took the job of chief justice in New Brunswick, the duke could finally forget the whole thing, and Borden was short a man in Washington. They did revisit the issue after the election and, in February 1918, a Canadian War Mission at Washington was established to handle Canadian communication with the U.S. government for the rest of the war.[53] Borden did not let go of this issue. In April 1920, he achieved his aim of the British Parliament accepting the appointment of a Canadian diplomatic representative in Washington, but the first appointment was not made until 1927.[54]

CHAPTER 8

A Most Notable Wedding

While Victor dealt with the conscription crisis, Evie had her heart set on finding a place in the country for the summer where the children could play, where she could relax away from the noisy city, and where Victor could join the family when he had time. She remembered spending time as a young girl with her family on the Cascapedia River in Quebec, where her father had built a summer home in 1884. She had explored the idea of a cottage at Tadoussac on the Saguenay River, but with the conscription crisis keeping Victor in Ottawa, she preferred something closer to home. The whole family explored the lakes around Ottawa: there were excursions to what they called Meach's Lake, a short distance from Ottawa, where their military secretary, Colonel Henderson, had taken a cottage; there were picnic expeditions "by motor" over terrible roads to McGregor Lake farther north; they visited Admiral Sir Charles Kingsmill and his family on the Rideau Lakes west of Ottawa. None of these suited.

When told of a place for rent at Blue Sea Lake, Evie didn't hesitate. As soon as she returned from Quebec City in August, she took Dorothy, Rachel, Miss Walton, Mervyn Ridley, and Charlie onto the train to check out the property. Before seeing it, she told her mother, "There are two or three bedrooms in the house and everyone else will be in tents. I shall be quite happy doing nothing and there is bathing and bass fishing for the others."[1] After the inspection tour, she gave it her full approval and stayed on, telling Victor "the house is comical but quite roomy and very clean."[2] "The tiny house," she told her mother, was "supplemented by tents, last night. Victor joins us for Sunday."[3] The party also included a dog and probably a cook and a footman. As usual, she didn't mention servants.

One hundred years later, Blue Sea Lake is still spectacularly beautiful, with dark-green forested hills on both sides, a winding shoreline, and small islands dotting its surface. Its spring-fed water is clear, cool, and inviting in summer. The quiet that Evie craved is still there, shattered only by the laughter of children and the mournful evening call of the loon, or the occasional squawking of a blue heron disturbed by human interlopers. The lake is now an easy one-and-a-half-hour drive from Ottawa, but in 1917 it was a three- to four-hour trip by the Canadian Pacific train that ran regularly from Ottawa and stopped at Burbidge Station on the east side of the lake.[4] The property they rented was on the west side, accessible only by boat.

On that first weekend, Victor and BJ went up by train to join the others, "a journey of three hours through a nice country," Victor noted in his diary. "An excellent motor boat has been lent to us and we got across to the house in half an hour. Really very attractive place but it is no more than an enlarged shack."[5]

Ethel Chadwick, an Ottawa diarist and sometime journalist, then thirty-three, was also on the train that Saturday, 18 August 1917. She had been a friend of the Duke and Duchess of Connaught and their daughter Princess Patricia during their tenure at Rideau Hall and must have missed the Government House social life when they left. She had been invited by the Devonshires to skating parties and followed their activities when she could find information. In her diary that weekend she noted: "The Gatineau train, which usually takes about four hours to Burbidge Station, seemed to go faster, perhaps owing to the fact that the Governor General's car was attached, as the Duke of Devonshire and Captain Bulkeley-Johnson, went too. They got off at a flag station, where Percy Sherwood's launch met them. One can see the Carliers' house across the lake which the Devonshires have rented. People on the train were pointing it out, greatly excited apparently, at the event."[6] Ethel's diary makes it clear that the members of Ottawa's elite who had cottages on Blue Sea Lake paid close attention to the governor general's activities there. Two weeks later, Ethel reported staying with her friend Pauline Lemoine, whose father was sergeant-at-arms for the Senate. Mr and Mrs Lemoine had a magnificent cottage with five hundred feet of shoreline on the lake. Ethel wrote: "Pauline and I paddled Mrs. Lemoine across the lake to see the place where the Devonshires are living. A small house, two bedrooms. The Duke sleeps in the maid's room, the girls, aide-de-camps [*sic*] and servants in tents about the grounds."[7] It wasn't long before the community wanted closer connection with the viceregal family. Lady Maud commented to her grandmother, "Our idea of the simple life is very different from our Canadian neighbours. I hear they call in their best clothes and find the others bare-legged and Mervyn and BJ in their shirt sleeves."[8]

The Blue Sea Lake community of 1917 reads like a Who's Who of Ottawa. On the east side of the lake was "Fairview Point," the large cottage of D'Arcy Scott, a former mayor of Ottawa, who was on the Board of Railway Commissioners. When Victor and Evie were invited to the Scott cottage that first weekend, the duke pronounced it "Much the most I have seen yet. Light air and room."[9] Next door were the Sherwoods. Colonel Sir Percy Sherwood was commissioner of the Dominion Police.[10] The Lemoines' "Hilltop Cottage" was also close to Burbidge Station. On the opposite shore, near the Devonshires, was the home of Napoléon-Antoine Belcourt, a senator. Close by was the Right Honourable Frances Anglin, a justice in the Supreme Court of Canada, who had a boy Charlie's age.

The Keefer and Crowdy family also had children for Charlie to play with. It was probably James Crowdy, the duke's clerk, who had mentioned the rental property near his own cottage. Crowdy's brother-in-law, Allan Keefer, a well-known Ottawa architect, had designed many homes in Rockcliffe Park, and it was Allan Keefer's grandfather, Thomas Keefer, who had laid out plans for the Village of Rockcliffe Park.[11] Like the other old, established families around Blue Sea Lake, the Keefer and Crowdy family was pleased to have the Duke of Devonshire as a neighbour.

Evie described the house for Lady Edward:

I am writing this in the verandah of a very funny little house we have taken for the rest of the summer. When the political crisis made touring impossible we settled to take something for the children and ourselves and a friend told us of this. The house, which is quite roughly built of planks inside and wooden tiles outside, consists of a living room, kitchen and two bedrooms downstairs and two bedrooms upstairs. Tents are dotted about all round and we have all our meals on the verandah so we manage very well.[12]

For BJ it was an idyll.

I have seldom enjoyed anything more, an absolutely free and easy life (except when broken by some wild letter from Lady Maud) ... We have got a tiny little house in which at present only the Duchess and Miss Walton live in. Dorothy sleeps under an awning, Rachel, Charles and myself in tents. We have our meals in the verandah. I live in an old pair of flannel trousers and my shirt-sleeves. The children go about without stockings. Just below is a little wharf, where our two canoes and a motor launch which has been lent us, are tied. We have fixed up a springboard to dive from. We bathe three times a day starting before breakfast. Rachel [she was 15], who always says "I can't" and always ends in doing everything beautifully, is the best of us at swimming which she has only just learnt. She is the soundest, sturdiest most capable child I have ever come across. We are in a very secluded bay of the lake, surrounded by forest. Little islands stretch in front of us. The only objection is that the lake is considerably populated. But after paying one or two calls on the more important people which generally meant a bathe and a tea as well, we have managed to choke off any attempts at social intercourse, and from where we are there is not a house to be seen. It is not altogether unpleasant to have Crowdy, the Duke's clerk, to go fishing with and to be able to take the children over to his shack to bathe. He is the best friend I have made in Canada, but then he is English and was at Harrow.

BJ continued:

One afternoon, we all went over to bathe and have tea with Judge Anglin. After tea I hurried back and about 6:30 in the evening started off by canoe, with the old French Canadian habitant who works on the place, to Minnow Lake. You have to paddle across the lake which takes about 45 minutes, then walk along the railway line for about a mile and a half. By the time we had set our minnow traps (minnows are the best bait for bass fishing) it was nearly dark. We trudged back to Burbidge where we drank a glass of beer and then paddled back home. By that time it was completely dark save for the Northern lights. Two huge arcs spread across the sky from which long streams of light flashed like shifting searchlights. Before we had paddled far, the whole sky, east west south north, was a mass of flickering light as if sprays of water were being thrown across it. It was quite unlike anything I had seen before and made a most weird effect as we threaded our way across the lake among the wooded islands.

The next morning I was up again at 4:30 and paddled myself back across the lake (I am quite an expert paddler now) to fetch in the traps again. The sun was just rising when I started. Peggy Henderson and Rachel and Dorothy emerged from their tents in their pyjamas, strange fleeting figures in the dim light, to see me off. I walked through the village and the neighbouring farms where the animals were just beginning to show signs of life. The Minnow Lake was hidden in mist, the tops of the trees being just touched by the growing sun. I was back by 7:30 woke up the children again and we all bathed. Breakfast at 8:15. Then put our boat on an old cart and followed it to Lake Morissette about three miles from the house along a sandy track among the woods. It was one of those calm hot misty days ... We fished all the morning.

The Duchess and Lady Violet [Henderson] joined us at lunch which we cooked ourselves, fried cutlets and potatoes the best you have ever tasted. We slept all the afternoon, bathed again before tea (it was a beastly lake to bathe in, but Rachel would have it) and then a tramp back singing as we went ... Then dinner and more Northern lights and so to bed very tired and very well pleased.[13]

Evie, too, loved this place, and especially enjoyed the children's antics. "What they all love is paddling about in canoes in their bathing clothes."[14] Dorothy, then seventeen, told her grandmother: "We have had such fun bathing. At first we used to bathe three times a day and sometimes stay in for nearly an hour at a time, but it is getting cold now [early September] ... All the children here are just like fish in the water. They all learn to swim almost as soon as they can walk. This is such a lovely place. The house is quite close to the water and we get a lovely view of the lake."[15] Charlie, too, in a rare letter to his grandmother, showed his enthusiasm. "Yesterday I went up to a place called Mannaworkie [Maniwaki] there is a big Indian colony up there and they can't talk a word of any other language. You can get birch bark canoes and all other sort of thing there."[16]

One weekend at the camp, Victor paddled a canoe to a nearby point and thought about building a house there. He wrote to his mother, "it would be very convenient for us to have a 'camp' there. That would mean a wooden house with a big verandah and a few bedrooms. We should also have tents."[17] Though Victor preferred the comforts of Rideau Hall, even in the summer heat, he was more than willing to provide for the needs of his wife and children. For him, there was the compensation of indulging his passion for fishing in the lakes nearby. On his second day at the Blue Sea Lake camp, he had driven over rough, steep roads to Whitefish Lake where a small group fished all day. He didn't record the catch for the day, which could not have matched the Magdalen experience, but the day was a success.[18]

Evie spent the month of August writing letters and worrying. To her mother-in-law she painted a blissful picture of the time, but to her own mother she was free with her complaints. She worried that Angus might have tuberculosis (he did not).[19] She worried about Maud and what would happen to Angus should Maud refuse him.[20] She worried about Victor letting himself go to pieces from want of regular exercise,[21] but she qualified her criticism of Victor during the conscription crisis: "Just now, he is of course horribly worried into the bargain." She worried about the trays of port wine and whisky and soda that went into the smoking room in a "dry" province,[22] though it was Ontario that was dry, not yet Quebec.

That August, Maud had a wonderful two weeks at St Andrews by-the-Sea, New Brunswick, on the protected Passamaquoddy Bay, an inlet of the Bay of Fundy and the Atlantic Ocean. She enjoyed swimming, sailing, playing tennis, riding, and going out to dinner. All the activity took her mind off her troubles. But when she and her sister Blanche went on to visit the Spring Rices in mid-August, her anxiety returned in the quiet atmosphere. She told her mother that she still felt quite uncertain[23] and "I change with the wind all the time … One just thinks it up and down over and over again."[24] As Victor's cousin and Evie's friend Blanche Egerton, wrote, "it isn't all our fancy painted for Maud."[25] Before the war, Maud's social circle had included the Prince of Wales, so probably Angus was not what Maud's fancy had painted for herself, either.

As the month of their agreed separation drew to a close and Angus was released from hospital, both Angus and Maud asked Evie's permission to meet away from family, who knew all about everything – "on neutral ground," as Angus termed it. Angus wrote to Evie declaring his devotion to Maud – "She is the only person in the wide world for me" – and asking her permission to meet Maud in Boston on her way back to Ottawa.[26] Of course, her sister Blanche would be with her. As soon as Evie's telegram arrived giving her permission, Angus boarded a train; from Boston, he wrote to thank Evie and to say that he was still distraught about not having seen Maud yet.[27] The next day the two young people met in a hotel sitting room. The separation had done its work; they had missed each other. At last it was quickly settled. They dispatched a telegram to Evie.[28]

The only post office at Blue Sea Lake was at Burbidge, across the lake from the Devonshires. Mail would be delivered after the train arrived. "Everybody on the lake steams, paddles, or rows in to meet it," BJ wrote. "There is a crowd on the platform in the twilight, some to meet new arrivals, others to find stores, most from mere curiosity. When the train has been unloaded of passengers and goods, the crowd moves off to the post office. One D'Arcy Scott, who has constituted himself as laird of the lake, acts as postmaster, jumps over the counter, and reads out the names on the letters. Meanwhile everyone gossips about their day's doings." Then, on 29 August, "the station-master hurried out of his office and passed a telegram into my hand, saying in a knowing way 'I think Her Excellency will find this of interest.' ... We sped across the lake. The Duchess tore open the telegram 'Engaged: Maud and Angus.' ... The Duchess seems quite delighted."[29]

This news spread quickly. Ethel Chadwick's diary for 30 August records: "Walked to the mail tonight, for exercise, with Pauline. The Duchess of Devonshire was there to meet Lady Blanche Cavendish. They say she announced the engagement of her eldest daughter, Lady Maud, to Captain Angus MacKintosh [*sic*], son of the MacKintosh. Great excitement! The Anglins, Scotts, Sherwoods, and Mrs. Crowdy were all at the station. Lady Rachel was in bare legs and a wild Blue Sea costume. She is very good looking. They are all 'roughing it in the Colonies.'"[30] And two days later, Ethel wrote, "In the Burbidge Post office, we met Lady Maud and Captain MacKintosh, in rough and tumble attire and congratulated them."[31]

The newly engaged couple returned from Boston flushed with happiness. They bought an engagement ring in Ottawa, and continued on to Blue Sea Lake camp. Victor did not come to Blue Sea that weekend – he was in Ottawa with a "sore toe." Evie longed for a talk about wedding arrangements,[32] but she really needed him only to agree to the date, the church, and probably the guest list. She could do the rest.

The few weeks at Blue Sea Lake were enough to whet the family's appetite for their own summer place on Blue Sea Lake, and in early 1918 they began to make plans for the following summer.

By early September the family was back in Ottawa, and the wedding was set for 3 November at Christ Church, the Anglican cathedral on Sparks Street in Ottawa. An announcement of the upcoming wedding went out to the family. There was surprisingly little negative reaction, in Canada or England, to news that the eldest daughter of one of England's leading aristocratic families was marrying an aide-de-camp. Evie had warmed to Angus over the summer days, when she saw him as an efficient nursemaid and adept sailor. And Victor liked him. Besides, as BJ told his mother, the Mackintosh family predated the Dukes of Devonshire in the aristocracy. The Mackintosh of Mackintosh, Angus's father, declared himself to be delighted with the engagement and offered congratulations.[33] Evie did not need to worry further about a penniless ADC marrying her daughter; the ensuing negotiations over the marriage settlement were reassuring. Evie told her mother, "Angus is to get 4000 pounds a year, Maud 1000 pounds from Victor, so they ought to manage all right [£5,000 in 1917 would be equivalent to more than $500,000 Canadian today].[34] Later he expects to have a small property with the rents and a nice house near Moy [in Scotland] made over to him."[35]

Only Victor's mother responded with the traditional sentiment – she was not enthused about her eldest granddaughter marrying a man she considered below her class – but she did not make her views known to Victor or Evie. The telegram they sent to her said: "Maud engaged to Captain Mackintosh. Most satisfactory, we are delighted," so she knew how the duke and duchess felt.[36] Evie followed that message up with a letter relating that "the whole thing was settled in the hotel sitting room."[37] Her letter sounded very casual, as usual, and she was obviously not expecting a negative reaction from her mother-in-law. Evie did hear from Blanche Egerton that Lady Edward "was a little flat about it," but Blanche had persuaded the old lady that it wasn't a vital matter "that we should know all 'his sisters and his cousins and his aunts.'"[38]

Victor was consumed with the political situation and with travel. He also had a steady stream of visitors. Lord Northcliffe, the newspaper magnate, came alone in early September. Evie, still at Blue Sea, was pleased to avoid the man whose newspapers had been critical of her father. When Evie returned to Ottawa, they managed to squeeze in a ten-day tour of northern Ontario with Dorothy, Rachel, and Charlie. Victor thought the tour a good education for the children and worth interrupting their lessons. Evie wrote to Lady Edward, "We have been down gold mines and silver mines, over pulp and paper works, to Indian settlements and returned soldiers' training farms besides receiving a great many addresses at railways and listening to a great many school children singing 'God Save the King, and 'Oh Canada' [sic], a tiresome little song which is becoming their national anthem."[39] The day after their return, Lord Northcliffe was back, this time with members of the British War Mission to the United States, including Lord Reading, Lord Chief Justice, and two men who would soon figure in a dispute about honours, Campbell Stuart and Sir Charles Gordon, accompanied by

Lady Gordon. They all stayed at Rideau Hall and were entertained at official dinners. After the mission's departure, Victor visited Brantford, Ontario, where he unveiled a memorial to Alexander Graham Bell.[40] Bell himself, then seventy, also spoke at the ceremony and presented the duke with a silver telephone.[41] Victor also made a trip to Montreal to visit the shipyards of Canadian Vickers Limited,[42] and a five-day visit to Halifax, all before the arrival of wedding guests. In between trips he swore in new Liberal cabinet ministers as they were appointed, and dealt with several important government issues, among them the possibility of a Canadian representative in Washington and disputes concerning the honours list. It is unlikely he had any more than a few minutes to listen to the wedding arrangements.

Wedding preparations included a visit to the doctor, who reported to Evie that Maud had a spot on her lung – tuberculosis.[43] Evie and Victor decided to keep this information a secret from both Maud and Angus. Blanche Egerton, still in England, took exception to this secrecy and wrote, "wouldn't it really be better to tell her as she is so sensible?"[44] One hundred years later it seems inconceivable that a twenty-one-year-old woman about to be married would not be told she had a spot on her lung, but as far as we know Maud was not told (and she lived to a ripe old age).

Evie began preparing Maud's trousseau. Angus gave her a silver fox fur for her neck and Evie and Victor a matching muff, so "she will be well dressed whatever else she wears." Victor had a row of pearls, which they had bought for the younger girls, added to Maud's existing row of pearls – he could replace them some day for Rachel, Evie decided. Trying to be economical, Evie told Lady Edward, "I only got her one good dinner frock and one good tea gown besides – and two nice afternoon frocks, one 'taupe' and one black chiffon velvet. Also a white frock for California." Evie noted that it was an "all Canadian trousseau" and "the shops which made her frocks are giving themselves terrific airs." The wedding dresses were also prepared with economy in mind. Maud's gown was of silver tissue which could be dyed later. Evie had a workwoman to help her make the bridesmaids' dresses of lemon-yellow georgette over white, with fur trimming at the neck and wrist.[45]

Excitement about the wedding began to build. Invitations went out and presents arrived. The people of Ottawa contributed to give Maud a diamond and platinum maple leaf brooch, and the Rideau Hall staff gave her a silver breakfast set in a Georgian pattern. Before the wedding, Evie had worried about the presents – "I am afraid there will be a shower of ugly things." After the wedding she told Lady Edward, "People have been very generous – the presents are really very nice indeed – some of them quite lovely."[46] The full guest list, with the presents and their donors, was published in *The Ottawa Evening Journal* just after the wedding.[47]

As the wedding day approached, guests began to arrive. Staying at Rideau Hall were the Spring Rices from Washington and three lieutenant-governors and their wives: Sir John Hendrie of Ontario, Sir James Aikins of Manitoba, and Sir Pierre-Évariste Leblanc of Quebec.[48] All of Ottawa's elite attended, including Prime Minister Sir Robert and Lady Borden and Opposition leader Sir Wilfrid and Lady Laurier.[49] "Maud and Angus' friends trooped over from Montreal and Toronto and even a few from Quebec."[50]

Finally the preparations were ready for what was to be a simple wedding, in deference to the war. And it was relatively simple. On the morning of the wedding the girls made wreaths of silver ribbon for the bridesmaids to wear in their hair. Evie "felt very proud of the little group of pale yellow frocks and copper coloured chrysanthemums" that she had helped make.[51] The bride wore a wreath and veil sent by her sister-in-law, Eddy's wife Moucher, and, in lieu of a bouquet, carried a "white vellum Bible," a gift from her aunt, Lady Moyra Cavendish. *The Globe* mentioned her "magnificent rope of pearls" given by her father, and the diamond and turquoise ring from Lord Richard Nevill. There was no mention of a wedding ring. About 1,700 guests were invited[52] representing every province in Canada and including the consuls general from many lands and all Canadian notables in official circles.[53] In Toronto, *The Globe* reported that over one thousand had accepted to attend what it called "one of the most notable weddings ever witnessed in Canada, Lady Maud Cavendish being the first daughter of a ruling Governor-General to be married in the Capital."[54] The cathedral, which could accommodate about eight hundred in a pinch,[55] was crowded by 1:00 p.m. for the service that began at 2:30 p.m.[56] William Lyon Mackenzie King arrived late, but it seems he got into the church. "There was the wedding of the Govr. General's daughter at 2:30. I decided not to trouble about that," he wrote in his diary. He was working on the

Figure 8.1 Captain Angus Mackintosh and Lady Maud Cavendish were married at Christ Church Cathedral, Ottawa, on 3 November 1917. Captain Mervyn Ridley stands to Maud's left. In front are Rachel, Dorothy, Anne, Roddy Henderson, Peggy Henderson, and Blanche.

Liberal policy about conscription. He "left for the wedding at 2:30 arriving at the Church in time just to see the end of the ceremony,"[57] so perhaps everyone was able to squeeze in. After the hour-long service, reported to be simple and reverent, with a white-robed choir leading the hymns, the bride and groom left the church to the strains of the "Wedding March" from *Lohengrin* and walked to their motor under an arch of crossed swords as a piper played.[58]

The reception at Rideau Hall was also kept simple, and "Owing to the war, no favors were distributed."[59] But it was a "crush" according to Miss Walton, the governess, who wrote to Lady Edward, "The wedding cake was made in the house and had on the top orange blossoms grown here and white heather sent from Scotland."[60] Guests were received in the Blue Gallery, where Maud and Angus shook hands with

Figure 8.2 A group picture of guests at the wedding party of Lady Maud Cavendish and Captain Angus Mackintosh.

everyone. A simple wartime tea was served in the ballroom, where tables were decorated with yellow chrysanthemums.[61] Both the wedding and the reception went off perfectly. Evie wrote to Lady Edward about the "wonderful friendly feeling that pervaded the whole thing and touched us very much."[62]

At about 5:00 p.m., the couple departed for a few days' honeymoon at Colonel Henderson's cottage on Meach's Lake[63] before making a trip to California. Evie was pleased to see them so happy. "Angus has been a perfect dear about everything. I have never seen a more happy and absolutely contented face than his when he came to fetch her after she had changed into her going away dress."[64] Victor too was pleased. "They looked as happy as possible when they left about ten minutes to five."[65] (Victor liked to record exact times in his diary.) Dorothy and Rachel cried as Maud left.[66]

Once the wedding was over, Evie breathed a sigh of relief and decided not to accompany Victor on his western tour. She told Lady Edward that she was a little rundown,[67] but admitted to her mother that she was probably feeling the effects of menopause.[68] Instead of the long and tedious tour, she and Blanche would accompany the Spring Rices to Washington. There she could motor out daily to "Chateau Tosh" – the little house that Angus had rented at Chevy Chase outside of Washington – to see to curtains and upholstery.[69] Angus was to work at the British embassy as assistant military attaché, a position that provided an entrée to Washington's social life for both of them. Lady Spring Rice told Lady Edward, "Maud had such a success in Washington and everyone is delighted at the idea having her back."[70]

Victor was at last free to take his first trip to the west coast. It was late in the year, past the harvest on the Prairies, and with the danger of very cold weather, but Victor was happy to be going about his business of meeting the people of Canada.

CHAPTER 9

Travels from Coast to Coast

Victor had wanted to see the grain harvest on the Prairies, but events in Ottawa had kept him close to home. After the wedding, with the last of the Union cabinet members sworn in and the election campaign underway, the politicians did not need him and he could contemplate travel. However, though the political situation was quiet for the moment, Victor still worried about reactions to conscription. Laurier had published his manifesto for the election, still opposing conscription without a referendum;[1] his opposition had quieted Quebec for now, but Sir Percy Sherwood, commissioner of the Dominion Police, told the duke he too was worried.[2]

Victor also worried about the war. The situation in Europe was dire. The French and British armies had failed in their summer offensives, suffering heavy casualties, many of them Canadian. The Italian army had been defeated at Caporetto, and the Russians were rumoured to be negotiating a three-month armistice with Germany. "The Russian news following so quickly on the Italian disaster is most depressing," Victor wrote to his mother, "but we must hope for the best."[3]

The last of the wedding guests, the Spring Rices, left Ottawa on 9 November, and on the night of 10 November, Victor, BJ, Henderson, and Lord Richard Nevill, the comptroller, boarded the viceregal train, the special CPR cars that had transported the family from Halifax to Ottawa just a year before. Heading west, they arranged to travel back across the country in daylight in sections where it would be dark on the way out. The prairie harvest was over, but they would travel all the way to the West Coast.

The duke's itinerary reads like a train station announcement. The train stopped at Port Arthur, Saskatoon, Edmonton, and Vancouver. A trip by boat took them to Victoria, then they began again by train up Vancouver Island to Duncan, Ladysmith, Qualicum, and Nanaimo, and many small towns in between. On the way home, they stopped at Vancouver, Kamloops, Revelstoke, Banff, Calgary, Lethbridge, Medicine Hat, Moose Jaw, Regina, Winnipeg, and then Ottawa. Everywhere people were excited to see the governor general. In a scene that was repeated across the county, in little Chapleau in northern Ontario, population 2,000, there were 150 people waiting to greet him when the train stopped for ten minutes. He spoke briefly to the assembled crowd from the back of the train.[4] The duke was pleased that everywhere he found "the same genuine expression of loyalty and devotion."[5]

The duke did not make many gaffes, but at a luncheon in Saskatoon, trying to explain why the duchess was not with him, he gave the impression that she was about to add an eighth child to the Cavendish family. Though the duke didn't tell her about the incident,[6] she heard about it from Colonel Henderson and was "much amused."[7] By dinnertime that same day in Saskatoon, the duke had recovered his aplomb. BJ reported: "under the pleasing influence of the Mayor, he warmed up and in spite of some ten speeches delivered during the day he made one of his happiest during dinner." BJ was surprised that the evening ended in one of the speakers calling him "'Our beloved governor general,' and that after a prohibition dinner."[8]

Moving on to Battleford, Saskatchewan, the former capital of the North-West Territories, the duke was driven to the old Parliament buildings, an inauspicious structure that he thought should be preserved for its historical importance. He was distressed to learn that it was now let to the "Seventh Day Adventists ... sect composed of vegetarians, conscientious objectors and other peculiar people." Addressing the children there, he told them that "the war was being fought to preserve the laws of God and man, and in defence of humanity and justice, and left them to draw their own conclusions."[9]

At the major centres, ceremonies began with an address of welcome from local officials to which the duke replied. He inspected guards of honour (soldiers or Boy Scouts), visited hospitals and convalescent homes full of wounded soldiers returned from the front, reviewed troops getting ready to ship out to Europe, presented decorations to soldiers or – what was more trying – to the wives and mothers of those who had been killed. He visited schools where he asked for a holiday for the children, something he had found popular, and called for three cheers for the King. He also toured major industrial sites. In the evenings, there were formal receptions and dinners at which he would meet the local "worthies," as BJ called them. In Edmonton, Victoria, Regina, and Winnipeg, the whole party stayed at what were then opulent Government Houses, homes of the lieutenant-governors.[10]

In Edmonton, they went everywhere in a carriage, escorted by the Royal North-West Mounted Police. The duke thought the men were exceedingly smart, though he observed that the horses were not up to much.[11] At the University of Alberta, a well-organized ceremony at which the duke was presented with an honorary degree was very pleasing to him. Of the people he met in Edmonton he wrote, "Their determination in everything connected with the war and their unbounded faith in the future of the country are the two outstanding facts which I shall always associate with my first visit."[12]

The train then took them south to Calgary, and without stopping they turned west, travelling through the mountains. The duke wrote: "The scenery became more and more beautiful but I cannot attempt to describe the Rocky Mountains. All I can say is that nothing which I have ever seen in books or pictures conveys anything like the true impression."[13] He told his mother that the Rockies were "far more wonderful than anything I have ever seen."[14] At Banff, they "drove round the place, saw the hotels and the sulphur baths, but compared to the scenery they were uninteresting." The party stopped at Lake Louise and the duke pronounced the view "magnificent." At the Great Divide, where the watersheds of the continent flow both west to the Pacific Ocean and east and north to the Atlantic or Arctic Oceans, and which also defines the border between Alberta and British Columbia, the duke had his picture taken with one foot in each province. But, he told Evie, "the Yoho valley is the bit I like best."[15]

While he was travelling, Victor received letters from Evie about her life in Washington. "I am asked about [meaning she was asked out] a good deal," she told Victor, "but am going to refuse all invitations except from officials." But when an invitation came to attend a concert with Mrs Wilson, the president's wife, she quickly accepted.[16]

Arriving at Vancouver, Victor and his party embarked on the CPR steamer *Princess Alice* for the overnight trip to Victoria. Victor got up early but it was so damp and misty he could not see much. When they arrived in Victoria, the governor general was cheered lustily in the streets. Both Victor and BJ remarked on the Britishness of this city – hearing English "accents," driving in the rain and mist, seeing cockpheasants by the side of the road, and the fact that drivers kept to the left (drivers in British Columbia drove on the left until 1920).[17] There was also more formality than elsewhere in Canada. "Women would curtsey when withdrawing from the room," BJ said, "something not done everywhere outside Ottawa."[18]

The duke made what BJ termed "one of his best speeches" at a Canadian Club luncheon in Victoria when he spoke of the Empire in the war and impressed upon an audience of six hundred that wartime efficiency must be maintained after the return of peace.[19] In Victoria, he was invited to a formal ball in aid of the Victory Loan, a campaign to sell small-denomination bonds to aid the war effort.[20] Tickets to the ball cost four dollars, of which three dollars went to the Red Cross Society in the form of Victory Loan bonds. The duke thought it a strange way of raising money. And though he agreed in general with the loan campaign, he found the event itself repugnant, seemingly because it was an entertainment in wartime, and he did not "understand or admire" the modern dancing.[21] For the ball, the duke wore his Order of the Garter insignia, the sash and medal that denoted the highest honour of chivalry in Britain. BJ thought these insignia impressed the visiting American officers and was pleased that, as the duke entered and the band played "God Save the King," the Americans stood at attention.[22]

The party took a day trip up Vancouver Island to Duncan, Ladysmith, Qualicum, and Nanaimo. The duke noted the enthusiasm and the lack of young men of military age. At Nanaimo, however, "the centre of a coal-mining district," there were among the group who greeted him "a number of aliens ... who looked unpleasant and sulky." He spoke of the importance of production but thought he did not make any impression on these men. The rest of the crowd was as enthusiastic as elsewhere.

Throughout his travels, the duke often came across people who had come from Chatsworth or the county of Derbyshire.[23] He especially enjoyed having tea with the Butcharts and viewing their quarry garden, north of Victoria, where he found the gardener had worked at Chatsworth. Butchart Gardens began development about 1906 when Robert Butchart's quarry ran out of limestone. His enterprising wife, Jennie, decided to transform the quarry into a sunken garden. In 1917, despite the rain and the winter season, the duke enjoyed going round the garden. Still family-owned in the twenty-first century, the famous Butchart Gardens now play host to as many as a million visitors each year.

On their return journey, the duke enjoyed the different atmosphere he found in the Prairie provinces. He loved the "enterprise and go-aheadness"[24] there and later called it the "driving power and public spirit." He was impressed by the people's "determination in everything connected with the war and their unbounded faith in the future of the country."[25] In Calgary, he bought fifty-dollar bonds for his and for the Henderson children, and then he bought the last of the Victory Loan bonds to donate to the Red Cross. These government bonds, intended to support the government and the war, paid 5.5 per cent per annum. Evie told Lady Edward that she hoped the Victory Loan campaign would be a success, but "the [Canadian] people are naturally very extravagant and disinclined to save so it takes a lot to rub into them any idea of economy."[26] In fact, the Victory Loan campaign that fall was well subscribed, raising over $350 million in loans to the government.[27]

The duke also enjoyed the more casual atmosphere he found on the Prairies, but for BJ it was formality that spoke of respect and loyalty. He approved of the welcome in Regina, at the provincial Legislative Building, where the duke was received at an imposing and dignified ceremony with everyone in evening dress.[28] In Winnipeg, BJ was frustrated by the informality at Government House. Before each dinner or luncheon, it was his job to give the duke "a miniature dinner plan with notes about each on it." In Winnipeg, the lieutenant-governor did not know until the last minute who would attend; sometimes people would arrive when luncheon was half finished. Since everyone else warmly welcomed late-comers, the duke probably took this in his stride.

In both Regina and Winnipeg they encountered the severe cold that is characteristic of winter on the Prairies. The temperature fell to thir-ty-three degrees below zero, and for the first time the duke saw "sun dogs," the halo on either side of the sun that is evident only in the cold-est weather.[29] During the journey home, the train sitting room could not be warmed in the intense cold and the duke became chilled. He returned to Ottawa with a raging cold and went to bed.

The duchess told her mother that the duke's trip was an immense success. "He had an excellent reception everywhere – made about 120 speeches and attended endless functions. It is lucky I did not go as it would have knocked me up altogether. But of course I shall never quite make up for having missed his first visit to so many places."[30]

Two other events occurred toward the end of the duke's journey, events that would have consequences for the viceregal family: Lord Lansdowne published his famous letter, and there was "the most appalling explo-sion in Halifax."

While Evie was in Washington with the Spring Rices fixing up Maud's house and Victor was on his first tour to the West Coast, Evie's father, Lord Lansdowne, published a letter in which he proposed clarifying the war aims of the Allied countries, including Britain, and their new partner, the United States. The letter appeared in the London *Daily Tele-graph*, 29 November 1917, after it had been refused publication by Lord Northcliffe's *Times*. Lansdowne wrote in the letter that he thought the German people had been misled about the Allied war aims. He believed that Germany might be ready for a negotiated peace if the German pop-ulation understood that their foes had no desire to occupy their coun-try, to impose a government, or to ruin their commerce. Civilization, he wrote, was threatened if the war continued for many more years. Security among nations must be the primary aim of the war. He believed that instituting the universal association of nations proposed by Presi-dent Wilson of the United States would allow nations to settle disputes by arbitration and secure peace. The moral position was to do everything possible to "prevent the same curse falling upon our children."[31] Since Lansdowne had been a respected foreign secretary in the British government, his opinions could not be ignored.

Lansdowne's letter was essentially a restatement of the "peace letter" President Wilson had sent to the belligerent and neutral nations on 18 December 1916. From the perspective of the twenty-first century, Lansdowne's arguments seem reasonable. The United States had entered the war in April 1917, though their troops were not yet in Europe. The Allied summer and fall offensive in Passchendaele had failed to produce victory and had resulted in extensive losses. As Lansdowne stated, the war was in its fourth year, and "the killed alone can be counted in the million, while the total number of men engaged amounts to nearly 24 millions."[32] In Russia, the new Bolshevik leader, Vladimir Lenin, fresh from his successful coup in which he had overthrown the Russian Provisional Government of Alexander Kerensky, had just begun a three-month armistice with the Central Powers (Germany, Austria-Hungary, the Ottoman Empire, and Bulgaria).[33] Freed from their eastern war front against Russia, German troops were already moving to the Western Front. Some statements by the German leaders suggested that they might be willing to talk with the remaining Allies.

When he received "a telegraphic summary of Lord Lansdowne's letter" on 30 November 1917, the duke was travelling east out of Revelstoke, British Columbia, aboard the viceregal train.[34] He wrote to Evie in Washington: "Without the full context it is difficult to express an opinion. I don't think he would have published it without the knowledge of the government."[35] But the duke appeared to be wrong; in Britain, the government denied they had discussed this position with Lansdowne. A review of Lansdowne's own notes after his death revealed, however, that he had indeed written to and spoken openly to the foreign secretary, Arthur Balfour, and the permanent under-secretary, Lord Hardinge, before publishing the letter.[36] Lansdowne took their censure and that of the press without revealing that he had indeed consulted the government.

Negotiation was not such a far-fetched and unpatriotic idea as the newspapers made it seem. A year before, in late 1916, some in British Prime Minister Herbert Asquith's coalition government were uncertain whether they could win the war by traditional means – their military strategy had not produced results over the previous three summers of fighting – but they were not about to tell the public that.[37] Others, especially David Lloyd George, minister of Munitions in Asquith's government, were holding out for a "knock-out blow" to the Central Powers. In December 1916, Lloyd George collaborated with the Conservatives to oust Asquith and become prime minister. By late 1917, when victory was still not in sight, Lansdowne must have thought that the voice of reason might prevail.

Reaction to the letter in Britain, the United States, and Canada was swift and intense. Most of the press reviled Lansdowne, calling him a pacifist without courage or patriotism, saying the letter could not have been published at a more inopportune time, and accusing him of being an appeaser, wanting "peace by compromise."[38] In Washington, Evie wrote, "I feel sure he did not mean it as a suggestion of a bad peace, but as it has been taken in that way, it is a good thing that the press, both here and at home, have jumped on it."[39] Indeed the *New York Times* review of the press reaction in England and America showed that most were vehemently opposed to the import of the letter. However, the British paper *The Sun* and, inevitably, the German-American *New Yorker Staats-Zeitung* both supported the demand for a restatement of war aims.[40] The *Manchester Guardian,* too, approved of a clearer statement of war aims "to fortify the spirit and resolution of our people," noting, accurately, that Lansdowne had not intended it to mean abandoning the war.[41]

From England, Evie's friend Blanche Egerton wrote on 2 December, "The excitement your Father's letter has caused is intense. Personally ... it did not seem to be very unlike what many people think ... but it has raised an awful storm."[42] She wrote again on 9 December that, in her opinion, "in the months hence we shall look back to the letter as the first start of a real move ... But things are looking very black just now."[43] Victor's friend Lord Sandhurst wrote that "Lansdowne has electrified us," and, while he thought it courageous, he saw it as "ill-timed."[44]

The Canadian press did not seem to have an independent opinion on foreign policy matters, but the Toronto *Globe* did give an even-handed review of the opposing opinions expressed in the British press.[45] Prime Minister Borden was in the middle of the election campaign, with conscription as the major issue, so Lansdowne's letter could not have been welcome. Since Canada did not have an independent foreign policy, Borden did not have to comment; in any case, he had already made his position clear, with his conscription policy seen as a means to implement Lloyd George's "knock-out blow." Laurier, leader of the Opposition, was also busy campaigning, and nothing in his biography suggests that he expressed an opinion.[46]

By 2 December, Evie, who was still in Washington, was mildly upset.

> The commotion caused by Father's unfortunate letter seems to be growing. It is really awkward for me when people who drop in to tea or sit next to me at luncheon start off about it. I have to hurriedly explain that Ld L is my father and I feel certain that he takes it for granted that we must win before we think of making terms … I do hope it won't do harm in Canada, one does not know what use the Liberals will make of it. Poor Springy has to see reporters, and tries to point out the fact that there is no question of immediate peace or peace at any price in any part of the letter.

She feared the controversy would make her mother ill. She thought the whole thing must be very awkward for Victor and asked him what line he was taking, noting that it was difficult to ignore what everyone was talking about.[47]

Evie wrote to her mother that Springy had done all he could to keep people from discussing the letter in front of her:

> The pro-ally people were in a great state about the effect the letter might have. In a country full of pacifists and Germans, anything that checks enthusiasm about the war is serious. It has been so difficult to bring Congress up to the scratch, and even now they might slacken their efforts if an anti-war wave erupts over this country. If they did that I imagine that our chances of a decent peace would be smaller. One can hardly expect the President to care if we do have to give up all that we have gained in the East and Africa. Neither can we really blame him for wishing to spare

his country part of what we have suffered. One can only be thankful that the US came in to the war at all.

Then she revealed her own rather conflicted position: "Personally, although I agree with Father, I am thankful that all the soldiers don't. After all, every single man who thinks we are not going to win weakens the morale of the army which we hear is not by any means what it was."[48]

Victor, for his part, was puzzled since he knew his father-in-law well to be a reasonable man. He noted in his diary on 1 December, "Lord Lansdowne has published a letter which may have important results. The telegram says it was without the knowledge of the Government. If that is so it is probably mischievous. Very strange of him to do so, especially as the Allied Conference is meeting at the moment in Paris."[49] The Paris conference was the first Allied gathering since the United States had entered the war. The next day, Victor confided to his diary, "Lord Lansdowne's letter seems to have caused considerable annoyance. Bonar Law strongly repudiated it ... Cannot understand why Lord Lansdowne has done it."[50]

Victor's remaining letters to Evie in early December reveal his interest in the prairie communities he was visiting and nothing about the Lansdowne letter. He did ask Evie, however, if she had heard President Wilson's address to Congress delivered 4 December. *The New York Times* had reported that everyone was waiting to hear that speech to see which the president would support: Lloyd George's "knock-out blow" policy, or Lansdowne's attempt to make peace soon.[51] Wilson, without saying so, did respond to Lansdowne's letter in his speech. He asked "When shall we consider the war won?" and proceeded to make it clear that there would be no negotiations until Germany's leadership was defeated, though he stressed that the quarrel was not with the German people. He also made it clear there would be "no annexation, no contributions, no punitive indemnities," a slogan that had been discussed between the Allies and the Russian Bolsheviks in an attempt to keep Russia from surrendering to Germany.[52]

By mid-January, public reaction to the letter was beginning to grate at Rideau Hall. Victor confided to his diary, "Eve had letters from her father and the King about the interminable letter. It would be a relief if they would leave the thing alone."[53] Although it is unlikely that anyone would have openly stated it, no doubt both Victor and Evie felt the censure of those around them. If Lord Lansdowne, father of the duchess and a former governor general, could be so unpatriotic as to suggest talking to the enemy, how staunch and loyal were they?

By the end of January both were upset. The duke wrote in his diary: "Notice appeared in the evening paper that Lord Lansdowne was to receive a deputation about his peace letter. What a nuisance he is. Evie got very excited and hysterical and I sent a telegram asking him to be less emphatic than the President and Lloyd George."[54] Two days later he added, "Longer reports of Lord Lansdowne's speech. Seems alright, but hope he will hold his tongue now ... Had a cable from him saying 'Thanks for the useful hint.'"[55]

When Lansdowne's second letter appeared in the *Daily Telegraph* on 5 March 1918, the duke was aggravated once again. "Lord Lansdowne has written another letter to the *Daily Telegraph*. Think it is a pity that he should do so."[56] This time *The Globe* reported that an article in the French press was decidedly cool to the proposal for peace talks. The article pointed out that the terms achieved by Russia were well known. Russia had by then signed the humiliating Treaty of Brest-Litovsk in which they had ceded territory three times the size of Germany, containing a quarter of Russia's population and industrial resources and a third of its agricultural land.[57] *The New York Times* again stood against Lansdowne's proposal, saying that, during negotiations, Germany would expect to be recognized as victor and that the United States could not accept.[58]

We know now that the Paris Peace Conference of 1919 dealt with many of the issues being discussed by Lord Lansdowne, but it took another year of war for both sides to come to the negotiating table. Germany was not invaded, the German people chose their own government, and commerce continued. The League of Nations embodied Lansdowne's and Wilson's call for an international organization. And we know that, even after the war, many of the German people did not accept the idea that they had been defeated.[59] But in December 1917, Lord Lansdowne's ideas stood alone against the prevailing desire for a "knock-out blow."

On his return journey from the West Coast and the Prairies, the duke wrote to Evie from Regina on 6 December: "There has been a most appalling explosion at Halifax with serious loss of life and immense destruction of property."[60] The duchess, who was in Washington, wrote to him the next day, "The details are still so vague we don't know whether the dockyards are safe."[61] And the following day she sent a telegram saying she thought they should go to Halifax.[62]

However, when the duke reached Ottawa he had caught a cold and was too sick to travel. In any case, he awaited the election results, which might mean swearing in new ministers. During his week of recovery, the election results came in; though the soldiers' vote had still to be counted, the result was clear: the Unionists under Sir Robert Borden were returned with a majority. They won three seats in Quebec, three in Ontario, and the rest in the west. The duke feared trouble in Quebec, but at least he did not have to swear in a new cabinet.

The explosion occurred on a bright, cold morning in Halifax Harbour when two ships collided at 8:40 a.m. in the Narrows between the harbour proper and Bedford Basin. The ss *Imo*, under charter to the Belgian Relief Committee, was leaving the inner harbour carrying relief supplies. The ss *Mont Blanc*, a French ship, contained a full load of explosives destined for Bordeaux, France. Under Canadian rules, a munitions ship would not have been allowed in the inner harbour, but the British Admiralty had taken control of the harbour during the war. A few minutes after the collision, a fire on the *Mont Blanc* began to set off some live shells. The noise, flames, and smoke brought people to their windows and sailors to the decks to watch the show. Just before 9:05 a.m. the *Mont Blanc* exploded. It was said to be the biggest non-nuclear explosion ever. The *Mont Blanc* disintegrated entirely; the barrel of one of its guns landed three and a half miles away, and its anchor, weighing 1,140 pounds, flew more than two miles. The ship was next to Pier 6 at the northern end of the inner harbour. Pier 6 was gone.[63] A whole section of the north end of Halifax was flattened and people were either killed, or blinded by minute shards of glass when their windows blew in, or injured by falling buildings. More than 1,600 people died instantly and more than 9,000 were wounded, some of whom died later. A tidal wave killed more on the Dartmouth coast across the harbour. Some 20,000 people were made homeless by the explosion. No windows remained in any of the buildings and, to add insult to injury, a storm that night dumped knee-deep snow onto the wreckage.

The news affected people in Ottawa along with the rest of the country and farther afield. Miss Walton, the governess, wrote to Lady Edward from Ottawa about the catastrophe, "So many Ottawa people have boys there [in Halifax]."[64] Charlie, twelve, also wrote to Lady Edward, about boys he knew from his school. "A lot of my boy friends were hurt. One boy ... who was at the Royal Naval College was very bad and the relief parties ... found him and they took him for dead and put him in a morgue which was absolutely crowded and he was not dead at all, he recovered consciousness and to find himself there must have been awful and he was there for three-quarters of an hour."[65]

The duke left Ottawa with the duchess on the evening of 19 December, accompanied by Captain Kenyon-Slaney and Miss Saunders. Colonel Henderson had gone ahead to make arrangements. On 21 December, they were met by Lieutenant-Governor Grant MacCallum of Nova Scotia and other dignitaries and moved quickly to visit the various hospitals and relief centres. The Toronto *Globe* reported:

> The party brought with them from Ottawa great boxes of chrysanthemums, carnations, hyacinths, lilies of the valley and other flowers, which the duchess presented to the patients in the various hospitals. She was particularly solicitous regarding the children ... At Camp Hill [hospital] her Excellency gave a five-year-old tot, who was amusing himself with a toy frog, a big chrysanthemum. The little fellow was much pleased, and looking at the big bunch of flowers in the Duchess's hand he asked: "Can I have one for the froggie too?" Froggie got the chrysanthemum.[66]

The Globe noted, "The Governor General and his wife tried to exchange a word and a handshake with every one of the patients in the various hospitals." And the *Halifax Morning Chronicle* reported that duke thanked the medical and nursing staff at two centres. "The work you have achieved will go down through history and the bravery you have shown in your nursing service ... I am more than pleased with the way the work was organised and managed." He made a point of thanking those from Boston, Massachusetts, who had arrived so quickly bringing their expertise and supplies to set up a hospital at St Mary's College, as well as a group from Rhode Island who were working at Bellevue Military Hospital.[67]

After luncheon at Government House, they continued the tour. The duke wrote to his mother, "In what is called the 'devastated area' only a few twisted remains of houses are left and all the rest is absolutely powdered to dust." *The Globe* described a scene there. "Out in the vicinity of Richmond the party came upon a ruined home. In the centre of the ruins was a child's cot and near it a baby carriage. Beside the wrecked house someone had stood up several dolls. It was a pathetic sight which moved the Duchess to tears."[68]

At the docks, the entire scene was dramatically different from the one they had encountered the year before on their arrival in Halifax. Not far from Pier 2, where they had landed, the Acadia Sugar Refinery was flattened, and the Hillis and Sons Foundry and Richmond Printing Company were completely destroyed, all with considerable loss of life. The Wellington Barracks were badly damaged. On Pier 2 itself, the Casualty Depot had been flattened.[69]

The duke and his party boarded the train late that afternoon for the return journey. He wrote in his diary: "Impossible to imagine how terrible the whole thing must have been till we saw it. Broken glass and destroyed buildings, but the worst is the wounded and especially the blind. Think the people were pleased that we came and especially with Evie who distributed flowers in the hospitals."

The devastation and loss of life affected the whole party. When they returned to Ottawa it was Christmastime. No one felt like celebrating.

CHAPTER 10

A Troubled Winter, 1918

After the horrors of the Halifax Explosion, a feeling of gloom settled over the household in Ottawa. No one could find the Christmas spirit, not even the limited gaiety of the year before, especially without Maud to lighten the atmosphere – she and Angus were still on their honeymoon in California. BJ described receiving presents in their rooms: "Mervyn and I each had our stockings early this morning made up by the children and brought in by the footmen with our tea – the head of a woolly bear … sticking out of the top of each."[1] No one mentioned any other Christmas celebrations.

The war, too, weighed them down. In Europe, the Allied war effort was at a low ebb. Although the United States had declared war on Germany eight months earlier, the U.S. military was still organizing and training and had only 183,000 troops in France.[2] The French army was still recovering from the failure of the Nivelle Offensive on Chemin des Dames ridge, and during the summer French soldiers had refused to return to the trenches.[3] The British army was reeling from the defeat it suffered at Passchendaele, where the Canadian army lost more than 15,000 soldiers, killed and wounded.[4] The Bolsheviks had signed an armistice with Germany in mid-December, which later became the Treaty of Brest-Litovsk, enabling the Germans to transfer the best of their eastern army to the Western Front.[5]

In Canada, where the newly elected Union government was moving forward with its policy of conscription, there were fears of more reaction in Quebec. Sir Charles Fitzpatrick, the chief justice, whose role it was to stand in for the governor general while he was away, said that if anything could be done about Quebec, the governor general was the only one who could do it.[6] It was not clear what he expected him to do, but the responsibility lay heavily on the duke's shoulders.

To add to all the gloom, Prohibition had reared its head. Victor told his mother in January, "The government have taken drastic steps about the prohibition of alcohol. After today no more, except what is already ordered, is to be brought into Canada and the manufacture is shortly to be stopped also." He thought, "on the whole the proposal is well supported. We shall have to follow suit here and go 'dry.'"[7] The wine cellars at Government House were locked until the end of the war.

The demand for Prohibition had been slowly growing in Canada. Much of the pressure to ban alcohol came from evangelical movements in western Canada. The Woman's Christian Temperance Union (WCTU), with its outspoken member Nellie McClung, had focused its considerable energies on creating a better world for women. Having achieved the goal of women's suffrage in the western provinces, the WCTU reinvigorated its campaign to "ban the bar," and by 1916 all provinces west of Quebec had passed Prohibition legislation. Ontario had been "dry" since 1916. In Quebec, though several municipalities went dry earlier, the provincial government resisted the demands of this movement until 1919; even then, the ban was not well enforced and lasted only two years. BJ noted in December 1916 that the Country Club, just across the river in Quebec, was "exceedingly popular"[8] with his male friends from Ontario.

The new federal regulations banned the transport into Canada, and the manufacture of, "intoxicating liquor," which was defined as that containing more than 2.5 per cent alcohol. The newly elected Union government said that all of the country's energies must be devoted to the war, and this measure was necessary to achieve victory. Though the governor general was not bound by any of the regulations, Victor thought it "best to act in accordance with the Spirit of the new rules."[9]

Everyone at Government House found the new custom difficult. Formal dinners now included only four courses and no alcohol.[10] Evie told her mother, "The poor men felt it a lot at first but they can get drinks in other people's houses if they like (Col. Henderson distributes cocktails and whisky to all comers). Lord Richard is the only one I am anxious about. He drinks a lot normally and has looked very blue lately.

Mervyn Ridley felt it at first as he has been very ill with his poisoned arm but now he has got used to it. BJ drinks very little at any time. I have felt very tired lately but shall probably also learn to do without my glass of claret in the future. We have only been 'dry' for two months and one is bound to miss it at first."

Evie doesn't mention Victor's reaction except to say that "Victor thought – as did I – that it would be a good thing as the legislation was Federal," and "as the feeling in the country is decidedly in favour of tea totalism [sic], I am sure we were right." She also noted that most of the ministers were horrified at the governor general having a "dry" house and they (the ministers) "have filled their cellars extra full, as one can't buy drinks in the clubs."[11]

Over the Christmas season, Victor and Evie were both preoccupied with a trip to Washington and New York that was looming ahead of them. Victor told his mother he was "absolutely terrified" about the speech he was to give to the New York Bar Association.[12] Evie was apprehensive about meeting the president because of what he had obliquely said about her father's letter – that he did not want a premature peace, and anyone who wanted one could "go elsewhere with their suggestions."[13] Victor, Evie, Henderson, Mervyn, and BJ left for Washington on 8 January. The children stayed at home.

The visit to Washington was a courtesy call on the President of the United States by the Governor General of Canada. On the day of their departure, President Wilson delivered his historic speech to Congress outlining his Fourteen Points to ensure national security and world peace, points that would later form the backbone of the negotiations to end the war. He also urged the establishment of an international governing body that would later form the basis for the League of Nations. Two days later, the duke, addressing the National Press Club, described the president's points as the "Magna Carta of Peace." He reiterated that Canada supported and would stand behind the war effort "through thick and thin." Though he was careful not to mention it, overhanging his visit was the Lansdowne letter, which many had interpreted as a bid for a negotiated peace rather than the "knock-out blow" they preferred.

In Washington, their first outing was to see the president. BJ described it for his mother:

At 11:45 the President's cars called for us at the Embassy and drove us to the White House. It was certainly one of the things I will never forget … think of a man, who is commonly thought not to have a real friend in the world, a lonely figure in the White House, a man standing under the portrait of Lincoln, the light behind him so that you could hardly see his face, and on either side of him an ADC, one naval, one military, both immobile … The Duke shook hands and was welcomed in the name of the people of the U.S.A.; he said that in the name of Canada he wished to thank the President and his people for what they had done and were doing; that he wished to thank the President for his speech delivered yesterday before Congress in which he endorsed the peace demands of Lloyd George. The President replied that he meant his speech to show the unity of the Allies, that he meant it to penetrate into Germany, and that it showed the American nation was determined. It was absolutely formal, absolutely simple … Then the President shook hands with Henderson, then with myself, then with Mervyn; then, preceded by two of his staff, we bowed and left – leaving him standing in the half-light, his two ADCs immobile on either side of him.[14]

BJ left out the fact that Ambassador Spring Rice also attended this meeting and formally presented the governor general, who then presented his staff.[15] No one mentioned whether the president presented his ADCs.

Later that day, President and Mrs Wilson entertained the duke and duchess along with Ambassador and Lady Spring Rice at an "informal" luncheon with two of the president's daughters, "with no one but his own family assisting."[16] Spring Rice reported to A.J. Balfour, the foreign secretary, that the president spoke "with great frankness on many subjects, finally turning to the political situation which he discussed at length with the Duke."[17] The duke reported to his mother that "the President was extremely pleasant and talked very freely."[18]

At the British ambassador's residence, Sir Cecil gave two formal, men-only dinners, one for the cabinet and other government people and one for diplomats, "so that Victor saw everyone he ought to have seen," Evie reported.[19] Victor confided to his mother, "Everywhere I found the greatest enthusiasm – in words – for the war, but I was in hopes that I would have found more had been accomplished in action."[20] While the men had their dinners, Evie and Florence dined with Maud and Angus, who had just arrived back from their honeymoon.[21] Later, Victor had a chance to visit them too and to see their little house, which he thought "quite nice."[22]

In New York, before an audience of nine hundred members of the New York Bar Association, the duke spoke for half an hour, thanking the United States for its quick contribution of aid to the Halifax disaster and for taking part in the war as "comrades in arms." He pointed out that "we in Canada are in to the finish," no doubt to head off any potential criticism stemming from Lord Lansdowne's letter. He also made reference to the contribution of women to the war effort, and to the potential for preventing "such an outrage" as this threat to democracy from happening again.[23] The French and Italian ambassadors also spoke briefly, and the major speeches that evening were made by Secretary of State Robert Lansing, who praised Canada for its splendid record in the war, and by Elihu Root, a former secretary of state, who roused the audience to such heights of enthusiasm that they jumped to their feet, shouting and applauding.[24] The duke observed wryly, "The audience have a tiresome habit of standing up when they applaud."[25] After all his worry, the duke thought his own speech was well received and was pleased that *The New York Times* called his address "eloquent."[26]

Their stay at the embassy in Washington was overshadowed by the fact that the Spring Rices, their cousins, were moving. The ambassador had received a telegram from the foreign secretary recalling him to London. Sir Cecil was to be replaced as ambassador by Lord Reading, Lord Chief Justice in the British government, who would also head the British War Mission in the United States. *The New York Times* quoted the ambassador as having asked for relief of his duties when British Foreign Secretary Arthur Balfour had visited in April.[27] The Duke and Duchess of Devonshire, however, thought there was more to it than that. Evie told her mother-in-law, "we are both furious at the way Springy has been treated but it is better not to talk and to hope that the lack of courtesy on the part of our Govt was due to hurry and stupidity."[28] Victor thought that it could easily have been done in a kinder manner.[29] It appeared to Victor and Evie that he had been ousted on purpose in order to install Lord Reading, who would coordinate the diplomatic, financial, and military aspects of the British Mission. They suspected that the hated Lord Northcliffe, owner of the *Daily Mail*, had also had a hand in it.[30] Springy himself was surprised and more than a little upset by the telegram, which made no mention of another post. Presumably he was to retire.

Sir Cecil Spring Rice had been British ambassador to the United States since 1913. He was credited with keeping the channels of communication open between the two countries during the neutral period, despite the hostility that still existed in the United States toward the British. As a diplomat he was known to be capable, accomplished, and charming. Springy had a facility for friendship. He had met Theodore Roosevelt when they were both young and the two men had become close friends. Cecil was Roosevelt's best man at his wedding in London and spent time with the family during his several work terms in the United States. He also became close friends with Henry Cabot Lodge, a Republican senator and adversary of President Wilson, but without alienating Wilson. The consummate diplomat, he was an astute observer and analyst of nations and peoples, and a brilliant writer whose written reports on countries as diverse as Russia and Japan, Sweden and Persia, earned him recognition from his political superiors. Springy had been knighted by the king in 1906 for his work in St Petersburg during the civil disturbances that had rocked Russia in the previous months.

Once he'd received Balfour's telegram, Springy then had the added worry of how to support his family. No one had mentioned a pension, which was not an automatic benefit. In 1904, at the age of forty-five, he had married Florence Lascelles, Victor Cavendish's first cousin, and the daughter of the ambassador under whom he'd served in Germany. Springy and Florence had two children, Betty and Anthony, who, in early 1918, were eleven and nine. Following the duke's visit to Washington and New York, Springy and the children came to stay in Ottawa, leaving Florence behind to pack up the house; she followed in late January. Both Victor and Evie understood that Springy was deeply unhappy about his ouster from the diplomatic service. They assumed he would return to England after a rest at Rideau Hall, and that Florence would remain with them until the seas were safe for travel.

It is difficult to paint a clear picture of what was happening to Sir Cecil Spring Rice that brought about his removal from the ambassador's office. As early as December 1916, Evie had confided to her mother that "Springy has got the jumps badly. Between ourselves we are miserable about his being at Washington just now in his present unbalanced state ... He is in terror of being murdered and altogether he is not maintaining the dignity of England."[31] BJ described Springy as "very highly strung and there was never a rumour or a spy scare in the truth of which he was not ready implicitly to believe."[32] There may have been some reality to these worries as there was considerable anti-British feeling in the United States, and Springy had received threatening letters more than once.[33]

Though he had previously suffered from Graves' disease, a type of hyperthyroidism, which may have accounted for his earlier jumpiness, he seemed to have recovered. In May 1917, when he and Lady Spring Rice accompanied the Balfour mission to Ottawa, the duke thought Springy was much better and in excellent spirits. Much of the tension related to his position must have been reduced since the United States had entered the war. But in 1918, BJ had no doubt that it was for the best that the ambassador be succeeded by someone else, though they had removed him in "a most ungenerous way ... Having served his country in the diplomatic service for some fifty years he was given a fortnight's notice to quit Washington."[34]

In January 1918, while at Rideau Hall after his recall, Sir Cecil continued thinking as an ambassador. He spoke to the Ottawa Canadian Club about the diplomatic aspects of the war.[35] He prepared a memo describing how Canadian business was transacted in Washington in the absence of a Canadian ambassador and forwarded it to Sir Joseph Pope, under-secretary of state for external affairs in Borden's government.[36] He had a luncheon with the U.S. consul general.[37] He seemed unable to come to terms with his dismissal.

At the same time, the atmosphere at Government House in Ottawa was not conducive to his relaxing and being distracted from his troubles. As BJ wrote:

We had our breakfast "hate" of Northcliffe, our luncheon "hate" of Reading. FE Smith [the British Attorney General] supplied our meal of hate at the dinner hour. Lady Spring Rice would sit a silent hating mass. The Duchess would work herself up to a sort of hysterical screeching hate. Northcliffe had called her father an "idle octogenarian." Reading was a Jew, Lady Reading was having a lift put up in the Embassy while the Spring Rices were unable even to have their rooms freshly papered; FE was worst of all. He had no pretentions of being a gentleman ... No one escaped. Conversation was reduced to one long hymn of hate.[38]

BJ's letter suggests this "hymn of hate" was just among the three of them, that the duke did not participate in these conversations. BJ himself tried at one point to intervene and was resoundingly told that he was only a young man.

Sir Cecil did try to recover. He skied daily with the children. On 13 February, when he appeared to be feeling better, he and Victor attended the Ash Wednesday service at church in the morning, and Springy skied with Anthony and Anne in the afternoon while Victor came along on snowshoes – Victor couldn't manage skis. That night, from the next room, Florence heard him moaning and went in to find him unconscious. He died early on the morning of 14 February, apparently of a heart attack, though a doctor in Washington had recently found him to be fit. His good friend Senator Henry Cabot Lodge wrote that he believed Springy's spirit was completely bound up in his work and he had died of a broken heart.[39]

Victor and Evie arranged his funeral, which was held at their little church, St Bartholomew's, in nearby New Edinburgh followed by burial in Ottawa's Beechwood Cemetery. Angus Mackintosh, along with a representative of President Wilson and some of the embassy people, came from Washington. At the same time, a memorial service was held in Washington, which was attended by the president.[40]

There was another side to Springy's character that was not well known during his life, a rich inner life of spirituality, almost of mysticism. After serving in Tehran, where he hired a language tutor and learned Persian, he translated and published two books of Persian poetry and legend that his Persian Mirza, or teacher, had read aloud to him.[41] He continued to write poetry but seldom published his work, perhaps fearing it would interfere with his diplomatic career.[42] In his final days, he sent a poem to a friend, "I Vow to Thee My Country," which was set to music by Gustav Holst in 1921 and became a well-known hymn in the Anglican Church. This hymn was sung at the funeral for the Princess of Wales in 1997, and was apparently one of her favourites.

> I vow to thee, my country, all earthly things above,
> Entire and whole and perfect, the service of my love;
> The love that asks no question, the love that stands the test,
> That lays upon the altar the dearest and the best;
> The love that never falters, the love that pays the price,
> The love that makes undaunted the final sacrifice.
>
> I heard my country calling, away across the sea,
> Across the waste of waters, she calls and calls to me.
> Her sword is girded at her side, her helmet on her head,
> And round her feet are lying the dying and the dead;
> I hear the noise of battle, the thunder of her guns;
> I haste to thee, my mother, a son among thy sons.
>
> And there's another country, I've heard of long ago,
> Most dear to them that love her, most great to them that know –
> We may not count her armies, we may not see her King;
> Her fortress is a faithful heart, her pride is suffering;
> And soul by soul and silently her shining bounds increase,
> And her ways are ways of gentleness, and all her paths are peace.

For a short time after Springy's funeral, life at Rideau Hall took on a sense of calm. Florence Spring Rice seemed to be getting better; her children played with the Devonshires', and all enjoyed skiing and skating parties. Blanche, Rachel, BJ, and Lord Richard Nevill sang in the choir at St Bartholomew's, the little stone church on MacKay Street across from Rideau Hall. Governors general have been attending this church since it was built in 1866. Since that time, a pew has been reserved at the front of the church for the viceregal family. The duke often read the lesson on a Sunday,[43] and the family often stayed for the second of the two services offered in the morning.

Figure 10.1 Sir Cecil Spring Rice, British ambassador to the United States from 1913 until 1918.

Far away from the conflict, the family worried about their relatives in England. One letter from Blanche Egerton, Evie's friend and Victor's cousin, who often stayed in London with Victor's mother, her Aunt Emma, was particularly graphic. On 16 February 1918, she wrote just as they were experiencing an air raid: "It began just as we ought to have been going to bed, so here we are sitting in the icy dining room on very hard chairs with a very poor light and a miserable newly lit fire. If we are to sit up five hours I shall end as a pacifist … It is too boring for words." She wrote about the death of Sir Cecil Spring Rice and poor cousin Florence. Then, "as the chill of the dining room strikes deeper, the guns boom." Blanche thought of her own home at Weybridge, far away from the German bombs then raining on London. When there were no bombs for ten minutes, she awaited "the blessed bugle" signalling that the raid was over. She ended the letter by saying,

"I do believe owing to air raids I've not mentioned food! It is still as absorbing a topic."[44]

With all the talk about food, Evie tried to be economical. "We feel quite guilty at having enough of everything, but people are trying now to save the foods that can be exported."[45] At Government House, they reduced meals to four courses with no alcohol and did not have dessert except fruit.[46] And by March, "We have reduced beef to once a week and cut off bacon altogether. Up to now we had it twice a week and one does need fat food in the very cold weather. We have two 'meatless days' always but as fish and chicken are allowed that is no privation."[47] She did miss white bread – she could only have bread and cakes made with rye, corn, or potato flour. She wrote to her mother, "I do hope you got the white bread ration. The others must be bad for you."[48]

The message of thrift in food was reinforced at a Women's Conference in Ottawa at the end of February. For the first time in Canada – and this was said to be a first for the British Empire – representatives from women's organizations across the country were called to meet with the government and to offer suggestions. Sir George Foster, minister of Trade and Commerce, spoke of the need for thrift and the elimination of waste. He counted on Canada's 150,000 housewives to solve these problems. The governor general opened the proceedings and *The Globe* noted that the Duchess of Devonshire was there, not only as the wife of the governor general but as president of two organizations: the Canadian Red Cross and the Victorian Order of Nurses. The duke and duchess entertained the women at tea in the afternoon.[49]

About the Women's Conference, Evie told her mother:

> The war cabinet invited the principal women of all the big women's organizations of Canada to come and confer about the Registration Bill and other matters. There were about 90 women … It was very satisfactory to notice that many of the most efficient members were English-born ones. The deputy from Saskatchewan was an English housemaid and only came over 8 years ago. She … is a born leader. Of course the socialist women were down on everything and the Temperance women wanted all the whisky converted into trade alcohol for motor work but on the whole they were most reasonable.[50]

Among the influential women at the conference was Nellie McClung, the noted Prohibitionist from Alberta, who presented a rousing speech expressing the loyalty of Canadian women to Great Britain and the Empire, and her belief that the elimination of alcohol from the Empire would be one of the reforms resulting from the war. Several speakers emphasized that women's lives needed to be simple and frugal so that they would be able to send money and food to soldiers, and especially that women's fashions were an unnecessary luxury. The conference unanimously supported equal pay to women for equal work, a notion that took another sixty years to become part of Canada's Human Rights Act.[51]

It was at this conference that Sir George Foster announced the government would pass a bill authorizing Daylight Saving, something new for Canada, though it was already the practice in the United States and other countries. The idea was to save energy during the war, so dusk was postponed for an hour by putting the clocks forward. When Daylight Saving began on 14 April, the duke, who seems to have found the clock-turning confusing, noted, "Got the advantage of the extra morning hour." And later that day "The extra hour of light is a wonderful boon."[52] Daylight Saving was allowed to lapse after the clocks were turned back in the fall. The next year, it became controversial because the farmers did not like it, but the railways and big companies adopted it in line with the United States. In March 1919, the federal government rescinded it. The duke thought that was a mistake because it would put Canada on a different timetable than the United States and would cause confusion.[53]

Evie's work with women continued. She attended meetings of the Council of Women, the Victorian Order of Nurses, and the St John Ambulance, but she found herself unable to settle down to any definite work. One day, she told her mother, "I had to present badges on behalf of the IODE (Imperial Order Daughters of the Empire) to about 20 Ottawa women (ladies) who had sons serving and 9 had already lost theirs. I don't know how I got through the ceremony but the mothers were wonderful."[54] And later, "Blanche is fairly busy with the Red Cross and other things. There is not much that I can do except visit committees and work rooms which I HATE. Lots of women are working splendidly but hardly any except the English-born realize what is going on and the vast majority don't care."[55]

However, BJ, and perhaps others, thought that the duchess could be doing much more. He told his mother what he had heard from Mrs Massey, wife of his friend Lieutenant Colonel Vincent Massey of Toronto (later Canada's first Canadian-born governor general): "The Duchess of Devonshire does nothing, her family do less. Instead of knitting socks she makes curtains etc. for Maud's house at Washington. Mrs. Massey, a great friend of mine, who is in touch with every branch of women's work, hinted to me yesterday that there was criticism among the women of Toronto to the effect that the Duchess had not come up to their expectations. The Duchess of Connaught was loved throughout out the length and breadth of Canada and she was untiring in her war work."[56]

The duke was busy with a series of visitors. His favourite was the Archbishop of York, the Most Reverend Cosmo Gordon Lang, a man he had known in London. He found him "very much altered ... such hair as he has yet is quite white."[57] The duke was impressed that this gentle man had crossed the ocean in dangerous times to plead with the Americans, as *The Globe* reported about his speech in Toronto, to "throw their whole might into smashing of the Molch [sic] of Potsdam."[58] In Ottawa, speaking at a Canadian Club luncheon, the archbishop praised the glorious victory of the Canadian troops at Vimy, which he believed had been a turning point on the Western Front, and he said the contribution of the women of Canada had been one of the finest things the war had produced.[59] The duke, at the head table for that luncheon,[60] was impressed with the archbishop's speech.[61] The next day, a Sunday, after preaching at Christ Church Cathedral on Sparks Street, the archbishop met an enthusiastic crowd of men at the Russell Theatre at the corner of Queen and Elgin Streets, now Ottawa's Confederation Square.[62] The duke presided, and this time he pronounced the Archbishop's speech "really quite magnificent," high praise indeed from the usually reticent duke.[63]

In April 1918, the archbishop's visit was opportune. The Germans had begun an offensive on 21 March; many thought the war would go on for another year or two, and morale was flagging. Though everyone was tired of war and death, they knew that they had to fight on. The archbishop seemed to have a wonderful way of rousing his audiences to find the moral courage to continue until the job was done. The duke was sorry to see the last of this charismatic man.

At the end of March, Chief Justice Sir Charles Fitzpatrick's prediction that there would be consequences from the conscription bill came true. Riots began in Quebec City on Thursday, 28 March, the day before the Easter weekend. It started when a man, thought to be avoiding military service, was taken into custody by the Dominion Police. He claimed to be exempt but was not carrying his exemption papers, as he was required to do. When the papers were finally retrieved from his home, he was released, but by that time a small crowd had gathered to protest his detention. They stormed the police station, beating down doors and injuring the three policemen responsible for the arrest. The duke thought the Riot Act had been read, but later the newspapers reported that this was not the case.[64]

The next evening, Good Friday, a mob of rioters attacked the offices of two newspapers that had supported the Military Service Act[65] and vandalized another building containing registration records, though they did not succeed in destroying the records. That night, after the city police appeared powerless to stop the mob, the mayor was reluctant to read the Riot Act but called out the military from a local garrison. After several were injured by the mob's weapons of choice – bricks, ice, and stones – the soldiers succeeded in quelling the riot. The third night, Saturday, the rioters broke into hardware stores and seized guns and ammunition; three civilians were injured. The local military asked for reinforcements. Prime Minister Borden sent in English-speaking infantry and cavalry from Toronto. Though they were commanded by a French Canadian, Major-General François-Louis Lessard from Halifax, the presence of English-speaking troops, who charged the unruly crowd with bayonets, further increased the tension. On Easter Sunday rioting continued all day. Three civilians were injured by gunfire. Still the mayor did not read the Riot Act, and no one was arrested.

On Easter Monday, still a holiday, rioters opened fire, troops returned fire, cavalry charged the mob with drawn swords, and infantry picked off snipers who were firing from behind snowbanks and from housetops and doorways. Several soldiers were injured and four civilians killed. Finally, several were arrested and, as the military gained control, many injured rioters were spirited away by their friends under the cover of an enveloping fog. Even though the Riot Act had not been read, soldiers detained pedestrians, searching them for weapons. A 9:00 p.m. curfew was declared – people were expected to be off the streets; suburban trains and ferry service were halted at that hour.

By Tuesday, when most of the population went back to work, the streets were quiet. During the weekend of rioting, four civilians had been killed, five soldiers and many citizens injured, and over sixty arrested. Sir Robert Borden proclaimed that the Military Service Act law would be enforced. Laurier agreed with him, saying that because it was the law, it must be obeyed, even by those who disagreed with it. On 4 April, the government passed an Order in Council under the War Measures Act suspending *habeas corpus* for those arrested and stating that any male obstructing implementation of the Military Service Act or demonstrating against the Act would be conscripted immediately and would no longer be eligible for any exemption.

Many thought that Henri Bourassa, in his newspaper *Le Devoir*, had fomented the rebellious feelings and believed he should be arrested. Bourassa, however, wrote about the riots and counselled coolness and avoidance of violence, insisting that the Military Service Act must be enforced equitably throughout the country. The prime minister told those who called for Bourassa's arrest that he would be more influential in prison than free. Sir Charles Fitzpatrick told the duke that arresting Bourassa would be a fatal mistake at that time. Bourassa remained free.

In the aftermath of the riots, each side viewed the events from the perspective of their own prejudices. In Quebec, the federal government was blamed for clumsy and punitive measures used to enforce the act, and for inciting anger by bringing in English-speaking troops from outside the province. English Canada blamed the people of Quebec for resisting participation in the war, and pointed a finger at the Quebec civil authorities for not calling the troops in earlier and for not stopping the riot themselves – some thought the police were in sympathy with the rioters. To ensure that events did not get out of hand again, on 5 April, Prime Minister Borden brought an order-in-council for the governor general to sign that empowered the governor general to call out the troops without a request from the civil authorities if riots occurred. Chief Justice Sir Charles Fitzpatrick must have approved this measure, believing the governor general to be the only one who could act effectively if riots occurred again.

Evie worried about her husband. She told her mother, "Victor is very much worried over the Quebec riots. No one knows whether they were more or less accidental – or timed and organized from outside. It is bad luck on him that he should not have one single man to talk freely to, except Sir Joseph Pope who is old and tired and who has been away a lot."[66]

During the crisis, the duke had gathered information from the prime minister and the Opposition leader, Sir Wilfrid Laurier, as well as from General Willoughby Gwatkin, chief of the Canadian Militia. It was Chief Justice Sir Charles Fitzpatrick who gave him the most detailed account. Fitzpatrick had been in Quebec at the time of the outbreak. He blamed the municipal authorities for allowing the attack on the registration office, the provincial authorities for not making arrests, and the clergy for not taking more active steps to support the Military Service Act. He remained apprehensive about the future, and thought the duke should speak to the clergy and point out to them their duty. In the end, most believed, as Fitzpatrick seemed to, that the riots were not the result of outside interference but a series of misfortunes and incompetent responses.[67]

The long winter of 1918 began to warm into spring, but relief from the doldrums would wait for better news from the war front. As the Rideau Hall group endured cold, rainy, and only occasional sunny days interspersed with sprinkles of snow, their depression increased. In mid-April, Victor wrote, "Evie and the staff very gloomy and depressing. It certainly makes it very difficult to keep one's end up." He took out his frustrations on clearing stones from a bit of ploughed land and planning its renewal with the gardener. As usual, the duke liked to have his hands in the soil when he could.[68]

The governor general had his work to occupy his mind. A steady stream of visitors brought information about conditions elsewhere: the Archbishop of Regina paid a short visit; Mackenzie King brought John

D. Rockefeller, Jr, the noted American philanthropist, to luncheon;[69] Prime Minister Borden and Sir Joseph Pope discussed affairs of state. There were luncheons with MPs and senators. Correspondence between England and Canada all passed through the duke's office. He read the newspapers and kept abreast of events in Canada, England, and Ireland, and the war in France.

The Quebec riots at Easter reminded the duke of the troubles in Ireland, and he thought about his own property, Lismore Castle, in County Waterford. The Irish Easter Rising of 1916 had been confined to Dublin and had not affected Lismore Castle, but it had resulted in executions, turning the leaders into heroes and reigniting a movement for Home Rule. The Quebec riots of 1918, also at Easter, were not aimed at taking over the government, as the Irish rebels had tried to do, but they were unsettling because they represented a rebuke to the current government and its policy of conscription. The British government had recently imposed conscription on the Irish, and the duke worried it would lead to further trouble there.[70] In May, when Sir John French, former commander-in-chief of the British Expeditionary Force, was appointed Viceroy of Ireland,[71] the duke began to feel more relaxed about that situation. Just two weeks later, however, he was astonished at the revelation that some Irish were co-operating with Germany in a treasonous plot.[72] Lord French issued a proclamation calling on the Irish to volunteer for military service so that the government would not have to resort to compulsion,[73] and the following day saw the arrest of several Sinn Fein leaders. Sinn Fein, a political party committed to establishing an Irish Republic independent of Britain, was accused of fomenting violence in its cause. Lord French's proclamation seemed to settle the Irish situation – for the time being.

Communication between the Canadian and Imperial governments sometimes created trouble for the governor general, who defended Canadian interests and sensibilities. Like Borden, who was lobbying for more independence on foreign policy, the provinces were sensitive about their independence with respect to certain issues within the Canadian federation. In one incident, two requests from provinces reached London asking for Imperial legislation, requests that had made their way from the provinces to the Canadian secretary of state, through the governor general's office, and on to the Colonial Office. Quebec was asking for a royal charter for a college, and British Columbia was looking for validation of provincial legislation that had been passed by the legislature and assented to by the lieutenant-governor but amid procedural irregularities. In both cases, Walter Long, the colonial secretary, wrote to the governor general asking for the view of the Dominion government, and eventually received the response from the government that such Imperial legislation was unnecessary.[74] The duke's British colleagues in London discussed among themselves the governor general's decision to relay these messages to London rather than referring them directly to the Dominion government, and their assessment was critical of the duke. Walter Long wrote, "This view of the Governor General as a post office commissioned to transmit papers is entirely wrong ... There are no doubt many people who think that a Governor General is an ornamental and useless figurehead."[75] Long sent some of these sentiments to the duke in a watered-down version, to which the duke responded,[76] pointing out that he had sent all the information available concerning these requests to the Imperial government. On the issue of the charter for a Quebec college, the duke said, the information he had forwarded to the colonial office was "the expression of opinion of the highest authority in the Dominion competent to deal with a question concerning education, the province of Quebec."[77] He further stressed that the provinces "have the right of direct appeal in matters of this sort to the Imperial Govt ... Should the Imperial Govt see fit to ask for the opinion of the Federal Govt ... that opinion is of course given, but it is still within the discretion of the Imperial Govt to treat the request of the province in its merits. I am informed the provinces are extremely sensitive to any interference with their rights by the Federal Government and that forwarding a request from a province with a comment from the Federal Government which would be prejudicial to that request would be very strongly resented."[78]

The duke also believed that he could only forward information that was received from the government, and he could not generally ask for further information. "Any insistence on his [the Governor General's] part would be regarded as an interference with the political liberty of the Dominion and would undoubtedly cause friction among Ministers and in the end would have the old cry of the autonomy of the Dominions raised again."[79] And he noted that he, as governor general, "can see and does see that unfair legislation is not passed and that impossible requests are not made to the Colonial Office, but he can only prevent such things happening by personal influence."[80]

The duke did use his personal influence. He had regular interviews with the prime minister and with Sir Joseph Pope, among others, and, with his gentle, firm hand, he was able to direct the Canadian government officials without alienating them. He knew he could not act like a British authoritarian without creating tension. In his diary he expressed his frustration: "They seem to know nothing about Canada at the Colonial office."[81]

Another issue brought out the differences of opinion between the Canadian and Imperial governments, putting the governor general in an uncomfortable middle position. Borden had been asking London for information about the war effort, but not receiving much. In 1915, when the Duke of Connaught was governor general, Borden and Sir George Perley, Canada's high commissioner to Britain, had asked that all communication between the Colonial Office and the governor general be copied to Perley at the high commissioner's office in London. Bonar Law, then colonial secretary, had agreed, since Perley was a cabinet minister. For a time these despatches were forwarded, but after Perley decided not to run in the December 1917 election, he was instead appointed high commissioner as a public servant. When he and Borden asked again to receive the despatches, Long at first refused to forward such confidential information to someone not in government.[82] Finally, after entreaties from Borden, Long acquiesced.[83]

All this discussion about how the war information was to be communicated went through the governor general's office, and at first the duke did not have to intervene, simply relaying messages.[84] But Borden and Perley also wanted war information that could be released for public consumption. Again a flurry of cables attempted to sort it out. This time the governor general had to act. In January 1918, he sent a cable asking for a weekly statement that the Canadian government could share with the public, a statement issued under the authority of the War Cabinet that would detail the progress of the war, including the military, economic, shipping, and food supply situation. The object was to encourage interest and sustain the spirit of the people.[85] In February, Walter Long replied that it was being considered.[86] In

March, Long said the colonial office had agreed and would begin sending information almost immediately;[87] he began sending messages to all of the Dominions.

At last Borden was getting some information. Perley was receiving the despatches sent to the governor general, except those of a confidential nature, and the weekly cable was supplied for public consumption, but the information was seldom up to the minute. By May, the South African government had rejected the weekly cable as not as good as the Reuters news service,[88] and Lord Reading, ambassador to the United States, said that one of the cables contained errors and was an embarrassment. Long said he was not responsible for errors because the new Ministry of Information, with Lord Beaverbrook as cabinet minister, had taken over.[89] That prompted the duke to reply that the request had been for a weekly cable to be issued under the authority of the War Cabinet, not the Ministry of Information.[90] Responding to the upset over Lord Reading's complaint, Maurice Hankey, secretary of the War Cabinet, noted that the Ministry of Information had to take "a middle line between any excess of optimism, which would tend to check recruiting, and a pessimism, which would give the impression that we are panicky and would be an encouragement to the enemy."[91]

In mid-April, the duke asked that private information he had received as governor general be released for a secret session of Parliament planned by Borden to discuss the threatening war situation.[92] This time they received up-to-date information quickly.[93]

During these difficult months, even the usually optimistic duke began to feel the depression. He recorded his views in his diary on 22 March: "Very heavy fighting, but not clear yet if it is the beginning of the offensive. Although the Germans have punctuated a few outposts our reports are very confident." On 23 March: "The fighting has been terrific but the report says our losses are not out of proportion. Our line appears to have been bent in places but not broken." On 24 March: "Press cables indicate that the fighting still continues very severe, but as far as one can judge the Germans have not broken through. The shelling of Paris still continues."

By 3 April, things seemed to have settled down. "Although there is no definite or pronounced news the general reports from France are more optimistic. The German losses must be very heavy." He was right, the German losses were very heavy, but so were the Allied losses. By 17 April, his optimism was fading: "The Germans have practical possession of Messines Ridge. Afraid position is very critical." Messines Ridge was the high ground in Flanders that the Allies had captured in June 1917 after blowing up the German positions from underground, a massive explosion that was heard even in London. After retaking Messines, the Germans continued and took Mount Kemmel, the highest point of all. Indeed, this was a critical position for the British and French defenders. The stalemate was broken; German forces were on the move with their lighter rifles. Airplane technology had improved so they could identify Allied gun positions. Only a few divisions of Allied soldiers stood between the German army and a clear path to the channel ports.

But then the forward movement stopped. Essentially the Germans were running out of men. So were the British and French, but the Americans were finally ready to fill the gap for the Allies. The fighting continued for a time, but on 24 April, the duke read in the papers about the naval raid on the German U-boat base at the port of Zeebrugge, Belgium. He began to hope again. When the fighting resumed, the Allied position seemed to have improved. The German offensive appeared to be held off by the French and American troops. But it wasn't until mid-July, when the duke returned from a fishing trip on the Restigouche, that things began to look really satisfactory.[94]

As the war news improved, and spring in Ottawa turned into summer, depression in the household began to lift. The duke did some hoeing and planted potatoes and corn in the garden, with the help of eight-year-old Anne. As usual he took in many events. One night he recorded in his diary, "Soldiers Club entertainment for the Tank Battalion, Cheery and worthwhile." Ottawa diarist Ethel Chadwick, attending the same event, wrote, "The Duke stopped to thank [the organizer] for asking him to come. He's certainly nice, simple, kindly and unaffected in manner."[95] The viceregal couple entertained Sir Lomer Gouin, premier of Quebec, and Lady Gouin at Rideau Hall for a weekend. The duke and duchess gave photographs of themselves to Sir Wilfrid and Lady Laurier, who were celebrating their golden wedding anniversary. Life began to feel more normal.

In late May, after Parliament finally prorogued, leaving the duke and duchess free to travel, they embarked on a tour of southern Ontario with Blanche and Dorothy, accompanied by Mervyn Ridley as ADC. Evie, who hated these tours, especially in the heat of summer, may have been acting with an awareness that her reputation was slipping. In any case, Evie didn't have an excuse this time for not going. In Toronto, she reported to Lady Edward, "I rather hated the race meeting though it was all for charities and there was only one race, the King's Cup."[96] Victor wrote in his diary, "If it had not been wartime it could have been a very nice meeting, as it was it was quite enjoyable."[97] In Hamilton, it was Victor's fiftieth birthday. Evie reported, "He looked very elderly hobbling through our functions in a felt boot."[98] Victor did not mention the gout in his diary, though later he said it had been hanging about. Instead he enjoyed the trip with its very busy days.

Next stop, Niagara. Evie wrote to Lady Edward, "We have got an off day after a very strenuous one lasting from 10-5 o'clock without a break. The usual round – civic address and reception (open air), hospitals, schools. Red + [Cross]. civic luncheon. munition works, cotton works, presentation of diplomas to nurses. long drive over bumpy road there and back. Tomorrow the same thing at a place called St. Catherines [sic]."[99] The duke's description of the same day began, "At 10:30 we met all the children at the Collegiate Institute. The Mayor came with us. The children looked nice and keen, sang songs and waved flags. I asked for a holiday." His diary goes on in that vein; he enjoyed the crowds and felt he was doing important work for King and Empire.[100]

The routine was similar as they visited the small towns and cities of southern Ontario: St Thomas, Chatham, Windsor, Sarnia, London, Woodstock, Stratford, Kitchener, Waterloo, Galt, Guelph, then north to Hepworth, Owen Sound, Collingwood, Orillia, Gravenhurst, and back to Ottawa four weeks later. Blanche Egerton wrote with sympathy to Evie from London, "How exhausting it does sound ... to have to move about and do so much."[101] Evie soldiered on, but was tired much of the time and took an afternoon or evening off here and there. Even her patient husband complained to his diary, "Afraid Evie was very tired, but it is quite impossible to arrange anything which appears to suit. Makes everything very difficult."[102]

Figure 10.2a and 10.2b
The Duke and Duchess of
Devonshire. Almost certainly
these are the photographs they
gave to Sir Wilfrid and Lady
Laurier, who were celebrating
their fiftieth wedding anniversary on 13 May 1918.

Victor described the district to his mother:

Everywhere the reception has been excellent and most enthusiastic and the general tone as good as possible. The War has hit this part of the country very hard and at every place there is a long roll of men who have been killed ... At Windsor I met Mr. Ford, the celebrated motor manufacturer ... they are turning out 200 cars a day. We saw a car made from the beginning. It is on a continuous moving plane and as it passes each man does his particular bit of work and in about six minutes the car is complete and a man jumps in. The engine is automatically started and he drives it away into a crate where it is ready to be sent to any part of the world. It is a wonderful organization.[103]

From Windsor to Sarnia, they travelled by boat through Lake St Clair and the St Clair River. "I thoroughly enjoyed it," he reported, "but some others felt sick. It was quite rough for a few minutes."[104] In London, he met Sir Adam and Lady Beck. Beck was the champion of publicly owned electricity, the first chairman of the Hydro-Electric Power Commission of Ontario and a Conservative member of the Ontario legislature. In Kitchener, "the Mayor and Mayoress were pleasant but German, and spoke with quite an accent. They both had been here for all their lives."[105] Rachel and Charlie joined the family after their lessons were over for the summer. In Collingwood, Rachel launched a new trawler in Georgian Bay, and the children and staff bathed and fished in Lake Simcoe.[106] Back in Ottawa, Victor reported to his mother that he had made eighty-nine speeches, "but most of them were painfully similar."[107]

Because of the war, there were still no formal social events at Government House and no celebration of the king's birthday, as there would be after the war. Instead, the duke and duchess, having done what they could, moved on to their private lives, Evie to Blue Sea Lake, Victor to fishing. In mid-May, when Sir Lomer and Lady Gouin were at Rideau Hall, Victor "spoke to him about a salmon river."[108] By the end of May a letter had arrived from Gouin containing an invitation to fish with the Restigouche Salmon Club. He fixed the date for July first.

CHAPTER 11

⚜

Honours: The "Unmitigated Nuisance" Returns

The honours issue – the granting of British knighthoods and peerages to Canadians – that the governor general and the prime minister had dealt with in December 1916 could have returned to the normal twice-a-year list of recommendations. The prime minister could have prepared his next list for June 1917. However, the issue was not to be put to rest so easily. In April 1917, the king announced a new honour called the Order of the British Empire.[1] Canada was granted a total of 363 of these in five classes, two of which carried knighthoods.[2] Borden did not reply at once to the request for a list of recommendations for this new honour, or for the June list, and finally, in November, he asked that the whole matter be delayed.[3]

Shortly afterwards, a problem arose that seriously antagonized both the governor general and the prime minister. In December 1917, Borden received a letter from Lord Northcliffe, then head of the British War Mission in America, recommending that two Canadians be honoured: Campbell Stuart, a wealthy Montrealer, who in 1915–16 had raised in Quebec an Irish-Canadian battalion to fight in France,[4] and Sir Charles Gordon, a wealthy Montreal businessman, co-founder and president of Dominion Textile Company, and a member of the Imperial Munitions Board. Both Stuart and Gordon were working for Lord Northcliffe in Washington, and in October the duke had entertained them both along with Northcliffe at Rideau Hall. Borden discussed the request with the governor general. Both were incensed. The duke confided to his diary: "Northcliffe has no business to butt in."[5] Borden wrote to the Canadian ambassador to Britain, Sir George Perley, that these honours were for imperial services and should not limit the Canadian list.[6] Each Dominion and Britain had its own list, and each list had a limit. When Campbell Stuart's knighthood went through without the knowledge or approval of either the governor general or the prime minister, Borden wrote to Northcliffe with barely contained anger: "From the standpoint of public opinion in this country the recent bestowal of the honour to which you refer was most unfortunate and embarrassing. It is not easy to state this with adequate emphasis. However impressive the services of Sir Campbell Stuart may have been, the general public have in mind hundreds, if not thousands, of men whose services have been more conspicuous and have been rendered at the daily risk of the supreme sacrifice."[7]

Campbell Stuart had, however, received his knighthood on the British list, not the Canadian one. Walter Long later admitted that "a mistake occurred ... owing to the fact that the Honour was offered to Colonel Stuart under the impression that he was an Irishman, and not a Canadian" and, once offered, the knighthood could not be rescinded.[8] Later, Sir Charles Gordon would petition Borden for the honour Northcliffe had recommended and Gordon felt he deserved.[9] Borden dismissed his request with the reply that the practice under which "recommendations affecting Canadians are sometimes submitted by Imperial authorities produces additional embarrassing complications in Canada. I shall, however, keep in mind what you have said."[10] However, despite Borden's opposition, Gordon received the Order of the British Empire from the British list in 1917 and was promoted to the Knight Grand Cross the following year.[11]

Borden had been brooding over Canadian independence for the past year. Canada did not have independence in granting honours, just as it had no independence in foreign policy. Not only had Borden delayed preparation of a list for the new Order of the British Empire,[12] he had also refused a new honour that had been proposed for himself and for Sir George Foster. Perhaps Borden also felt some guilt, or at least distaste, for having tried to go behind the backs of two governors general in 1916, especially after being caught. Certainly he knew that public opinion in Canada was "in a somewhat disturbed condition in regard to the bestowal of honours."[13] He was particularly opposed to the granting to Canadians of hereditary honours, such as peerages. *Saturday*

Night magazine agreed: "They [hereditary honours] are entirely foreign to the social fabric of Canada. An hereditary system which carried the honour forward to future generations strikes at the very roots of Canadian democracy."[14] They worried that the end of the war would bring a host of hereditary honours and create a class system similar to that in Britain.

To his credit, Borden wanted to move the argument away from particular individuals and toward a broader level of principle. He contemplated changing the rules and removing British honours from Canada altogether. He knew it had implications for the rest of the Empire and for the British constitution, especially with respect to the House of Lords. Fully aware of the delicacy of this issue, he trod carefully.

In February 1918, and again in March, in their private conversations Borden told the duke he was afraid that the honours issue would come up in the spring session of Parliament.[15] He may have been aware that Mr W.F. Nickle, MP for Kingston, intended to bring forward a bill about honours for discussion. Before the debate, Borden prepared an order-in-council outlining his thinking about honours in Canada and asked the governor general for his advice. The recommendations, he said, touched on "questions of constitutional relations."[16] The duke listened carefully. Borden recommended that only on the advice of the Prime Minister of Canada should the king confer honours on people "ordinarily resident in Canada." (It was necessary to use the term "ordinarily resident in Canada" because there was no Canadian citizenship at that time. All those living in Canada were British subjects of the Dominion, which was part of the British Empire. Citizenship in Canada was enacted only thirty years later.) Borden also recommended that titles should not be hereditary, and that those hereditary titles already in place should be rescinded.

When the recitation was finished, the duke noted in his diary: "In the circumstances I do not think it is as bad as might have been the case."[17] Borden urged that the document be sent in its present form to England. The duke complied and tried to soften the blow that he knew would be felt in His Majesty's Government. "Such an assumption of control by the Government of Canada," he wrote in his despatch, "follows the natural course of constitutional development in this country, as the tendency has invariably been in the direction of complete control of every function of government." He further explained that the prime minister believed "creating or continuance of hereditary titles in Canada is derogatory, incompatible with ideals of democracy as they have developed in this country."[18]

Before he received a reaction from London, the duke struggled to further explain Borden's proposal.[19] "I wish to emphasize in the most emphatic manner that the Royal Prerogative is unquestioned and I am fully convinced that nothing is further from the wish of the Prime Minister and his colleagues that anything contained in the Order should be construed to imply any reflection or doubt as to the Royal Prerogative or the manner in which it has been exercised."[20] In other words, the king could do as he liked. Walter Long replied that "the settled policy of His Majesty's Government with regard to persons ordinarily resident in Canada as in other Dominions has been and is to follow precisely the recommendations of the Governor General made on the advice of his Prime Minister"[21] and the Colonial Office and the king would adhere to the request for no more honours at present, but the last proposal – hereditary titles already in place not being passed on – was a problem, and they would discuss it with Borden when he arrived in England later that spring. Long again admitted that the baronetcy to Campbell Stuart had been offered without notice to Borden and that it had been a mistake because they had thought he was Irish. The other baronetcy recently offered, to Sir Joseph Flavelle, had been approved by Borden and presented in June 1917.[22]

On 4 April 1918, the duke gave his assent to Borden's order-in-council about honours.[23] On 8 April 1918, the House of Commons began discussing a resolution presented by Mr W.F. Nickle, who proposed that they ask His Majesty to refrain from conferring any hereditary titles upon his subjects domiciled or living in Canada. Most of his argument centred on Canada rewarding service to the country – military service – but not giving hereditary titles to those who had been safely in Canada while others risked their lives on the battlefield.

After a recess for dinner, Mr Richardson, MP for Springfield, Manitoba, moved an amendment that would remove the word "hereditary," so that the resolution would ask His Majesty to refrain from conferring any titles on those domiciled in Canada. This motion was warmly applauded, but the prime minister pointed out that such a resolution would deny the awarding of military honours. He knew it would also negate his carefully constructed – and governor general–approved – order-in-council. Near midnight, Borden moved to adjourn the discussion and agreed to resume debate at a later date.[24]

On 21 May 1918, the honours debate continued. Prime Minister Borden took up the challenge of defeating the amendment. Many MPs were strongly against titles; feelings ran high. Once again, the House debated until nearly midnight.

As the duke explained to the colonial secretary:

> The government was within an ace of being defeated on this question which rather suddenly developed in a quite unexpected direction. The resolution of Mr. Richardson, had it been adopted, would have entirely overridden the policy of the Government as set forth in the Order in Council ... and it would also have put the Government in the very ridiculous position of settling definitely a question which they had avowed their intention of discussing at future date with His Majesty's government.
>
> When the Government tried to impress the view on the Opposition and the members of their own Party, with a view of closing the question, they found that if the matter came to a division, the Government would not have a majority. Sir Robert therefore took the somewhat drastic step of stating that he would regard the passing of the amendment as a vote of no confidence in the Government and would resign. Mr. Richardson offered to withdraw his amendment but the House would not permit him to do so and in the event the Govt was sustained by a majority of thirty-three.[25]

The resolution that was adopted by the House on 21 May 1918, was the original one proposed by Mr Nickle that asked the king to refrain from bestowing hereditary titles to those domiciled in Canada. Borden's order-in-council had gone further, expressly noting that military honours were not included in the proposed ban on honours, and asking that hereditary honours now in place be rescinded.

Two days later, when the prime minister was leaving for the War Cabinet meetings in London, the duke reported to his diary: "He [Borden] was more annoyed than I ever knew him about the honours debate."[26] Borden's anger stemmed from Nickle's behaviour in Parliament. Borden had left the House during a portion of the evening, and when he returned he found that Nickle had been circulating among members the erroneous statement that there was to be a free vote.[27] In order to preserve his position on the issue, Borden had threatened to resign. Though Borden usually kept his temper under tight control,[28] after two days he was still simmering. Borden had prepared an original order-in-council and had it approved by the governor general and forwarded to Britain before Mr Nickle brought his resolution to the House of Commons, yet Borden was upstaged by Nickle.

Borden received personal endorsements of the resolution from many groups of citizens,[29] and the press was generally supportive of the idea of ridding Canada of hereditary titles. However, a *Globe* editorial said the vote actually taken was not the real view of Parliament or the public, that the people wanted to "put an end to the title-mongering business in this Dominion," and the issue would resurface in the next Parliament.[30] They were right.

Opinion was not unanimous, however. Some Canadians supported honours, including hereditary titles.[31] Borden also received entreaties for honours to be awarded to particular persons, some even asking for an honour for themselves.[32] To each of these he replied, saying that he could not recommend awards in view of the resolution of the Canadian government, that honours were not popular in Canada, and that Canadian democracy was impatient of such distinctions. As for the Order of the British Empire, the resolution did simplify his work; he said there would be no orders for the year.

For His Majesty's Government in London – now forced to pay close attention to the arguments – Canada's proposals created a storm. The ministers agreed to follow the standard practice of taking the advice of the Canadian prime minister in granting honours, and they understood that the recent deviations from this practice (they meant the Campbell Stuart honour) had occasioned the debate in Canada. But they felt that to avoid hereditary titles altogether and then to put a time limit on those titles already granted presented grave problems. George Fiddes, permanent secretary of the Colonial Office, thought that for hereditary titles "the Canadian Government are not really entitled" to object, since the honours are a gift of the king.[33] The lord chancellor, Viscount Finlay, thought the proposal about extinguishing the hereditary titles granted to those ordinarily resident in Canada would create great difficulty. "The Empire is one, and when an hereditary honour is conferred, hitherto it has always been operative all over the Empire."[34] He thought an Act of the Imperial Parliament would be required to make any such modifications, but one proposed would not carry in the British Parliament. They decided to send the matter to Lord Stamfordham, the king's private secretary, who would inform the king of the proposed changes for Canada.[35] For George Curzon, leader of the House of Lords, the situation was a conundrum. "As to legislation prescribing a time limit, after which a hereditary title should cease to be hereditary ... the House of Lords, as at present constituted, could give no countenance to such a project for it would be an abrupt denial, not merely of the prerogative of the Sovereign, but of the entire basis on which the House of Lords, indeed the hereditary aristocracy of the UK, exists."[36]

They did not tell the Duke of Devonshire or Prime Minister Borden of these concerns but agreed to wait until Borden reached London that summer to discuss it further. And there the matter rested – for a while.

Borden left for England on 24 May 1918, to attend meetings of the Imperial War Conference and Imperial War Cabinet. He did discuss the honours issue with Prime Minister Lloyd George and some of the ministers in England, but nothing further happened that summer.[37]

The honours issue did subside for a time; however, as *The Globe* had predicted, it would return a year later.

⁕

CHAPTER 12

Blue Sea Lake and Other Summer Pleasures, 1918

Taking up the invitation that came from Sir Lomer Gouin, Victor and his new ADC, Tommy Clive, reached the Restigouche Salmon Club's stately wooden mansion at Matapedia, Quebec, on 1 July 1918. On that first day, he reported to Evie that they "got to work without delay ... Tommy got four and I got two."[1] The club limit was eight fish per person per day.[2] Because Victor caught only a small number of fish that first day, the secretary was worried, as he had been given the best pool, but Victor excused him: "the wind was so bad it was almost impossible to make much of it."[3] They still had two weeks to improve their score.

The Restigouche River arises in western New Brunswick and flows for over one hundred miles north and east into the Bay of Chaleur before reaching the Atlantic Ocean. Part of this river forms the border between Quebec and New Brunswick. Along the whole length of the river, which is mostly shallow with some deep pools, there are no falls to impede a canoe, though the rapids make it an exciting ride.[4] The fast-flowing water is crystal clear, and in spring, when the salmon are returning from their ocean voyage, it can be a brawling torrent.[5] Victor wrote to his mother, "The river is very beautiful – fast and broad with steep banks wooded down to the water." He recounted too that they had seen moose and deer as well as wild ducks, and there had been great excitement at one time when a bear appeared.[6] The trees he saw were mostly evergreen (spruce and fir) interspersed with some maple and yellow birch. There was very little pine so it didn't have the characteristic smell he would later experience in the West Coast forests.

Figure 12.1 The Restigouche Salmon Club at Matapedia, Quebec. The duke liked the simplicity of the surroundings.

Nine wealthy men from New York, familiar with the delights of salmon fishing in the area, had incorporated the Restigouche Salmon Club in Quebec in 1880. They bought a farm at Matapedia on the Quebec side and, in 1884, obtained the right to purchase land on the opposite side of the river in New Brunswick. Ownership of land on the river shore gave the club riparian rights, a concept with its origins in English common law. The word riparian is derived from the Latin *ripa*, meaning the strip of land closest to the river. Property owners whose land touched surface water had riparian rights, which gave them exclusive use of that shoreline and the water up to halfway across the stream. Rights were limited to domestic purposes, which meant that the landowner could not sell the water to a manufacturing business and had to allow for reasonable transportation on the water by others. By purchasing land in New Brunswick opposite their Quebec holdings, the club secured exclusive fishing rights to a whole section of the river. Over the years, the club acquired property upriver from Matapedia and, by 1918, had built nine small clubhouses, which they called "stations."

Among the founding members of the club were William K. Vanderbilt, a railroad millionaire, and Chester Arthur, who served as the twen-

ty-first president of the United States, from 1881 to 1885, and president
of the Restigouche Salmon Club from 1885 until his death in 1886.[7]
From its inception, membership in the Restigouche Salmon Club was
available only to men. After the club grew to about forty members,
a prospective member had to buy a share from someone else or from a
deceased member's estate, then be nominated by a member and elected to membership. Ladies could occupy club lodges only after the first
of August, as guests of members.[8]

Each member was allowed to bring one male guest, but each member could have only one rod, so that the member and his guest must
share one rod and fish from the same canoe. In this way, the number
of men fishing at any one time was controlled. A member could own two
shares and have two rods, but no member could own more than two
shares. Each guest had to be "passed on" by the executive committee.[9]
Both Victor and Tommy had rods, and when they arrived there were five
other rods at the club.[10]

Victor fit easily into this world. He met the club members present
and found them all interesting men and keen fishermen, with "no swag-
ger or bluster about them." Though the clubhouse was large enough to
accommodate all club members, Victor saw it as plain and simple, with
no luxuries.[11]

Within a few days, the members invited him to go to some of the
upriver stations. He described the first one for Evie. Called Chamberlain Shoals, it was about twenty miles from the Matapedia clubhouse
and was reached by the canoe "being towed by a horse" that walked
along the bank, or waded in the shallow edge of the river. Chamberlain Shoals was a double station, meaning there was room for two fishing parties of two rods each. The station itself consisted of a living room
about forty feet long by twenty, with a kitchen and pantry behind and
a verandah about twenty feet long leading to the four bedrooms. There
was "a hut some little way off for the men,"[12] who included two cooks,
two guides for each boat, and a man-of-all-work.[13]

Victor reported to Evie:

Everything is done by towing. Each party – i.e. two rods with
a canoe apiece tied together – is towed up by a man on a horse
which remains with the party all through the trip. The station

is about the middle of the beat and the horse is used to tow the canoe to the up-stream place in the morning and then comes back [later in the day] to tow the down-stream man back again ... The fish do not run nearly as big on the average as the Magdalen, but the extent of the fishing is of course far bigger. Private servants are not allowed so I did not bring Taylor [his valet] in the first instance but when the gout appeared I sent for him. There is a regular mail boat organisation and he came up with that. The mail boat is a canoe with a horse and leaves Matapedia every morning.[14]

Victor explained that each mail boat went farther upriver to other "stations" before turning back again, and that the "service" consisted of three boats so that mail arrived every day. He had already told Evie that "in case of urgency, I can be got at by a man on a horse."[15]

Fishing began after breakfast each morning punctually at 7:00 a.m. when their canoes were towed to the assigned fishing pool.[16] They returned to the clubhouse for lunch and a rest, then went out again to a different pool in the late afternoon when the sun, if it was out, had left the water and the fish were more likely to rise.[17] Most days the river yielded their limit of eight fish. Returning for dinner, they would spend a pleasant evening recording the day's catches, recounting their stories, reading the newspapers and letters just delivered, writing of their adventures, then at last to bed to be ready for another day.

On the water, each fisherman sat in a chair in the middle of the twenty-six-foot canoe with the guides paddling at the bow and stern. Because of Victor's gout, he wrote: "the boatmen are most careful with me and in their excess of zeal to save me from bending my knee they almost lift me into the canoe, the result being that the canoe nearly upsets ... After much thought one of them suddenly volunteered that one of the members of the Club who was fishing up river was a 'regular dandy doc,' in other words he is a fashionable New York doctor. They suggest that I should ask him to 'put me right' as we shall meet him on our way up today."[18]

Victor did meet the "dandy doc" as they travelled up to Indian House station, though he does not mention consulting him about his gout. They called on Dr Morris, a member of the club. "He lives in a houseboat or a scow with his wife and children. Must be really nice way of doing it," Victor recorded in his diary.[19] The scow was a flat-bottomed boat about ten feet by fifty with a draft of about eight inches. A portion of the deck held a cabin in which the family lived for the summer. A huge wooden rudder curved over the stern of the boat, and power was provided by the usual horses to transport the scow upriver. Apparently it was acceptable to have family members on the club's river as long as they were on a scow.[20]

One day, Victor experienced a little Canadian patriotism: around a bend in the river two horses appeared towing a large scow that was flying a Union Jack. It turned out to be a fishing boat taking salmon fry from the hatchery to deposit upriver. "I thought the Union Jack might be for my benefit," Victor was obviously amused to tell Evie, "but with a good deal of winking my boat men explained that the Union Jack was very popular and that it was good for the gentlemen from New York to see it."[21]

From Chamberlain Shoals their canoes travelled a distance of fifteen miles toward Indian House, reputed to be the most beautiful of the upriver stations.[22] Victor was beginning to feel hemmed in by the riverbanks lined with evergreen trees. When they arrived and found a clearing, about fifty yards square, he told his mother, "It was quite a relief."[23] At Indian Head the house stands on a knob at the river bend, which gives a good view in both directions. "A certain amount of clearing has been done and there are two acres of grass which keeps a cow for the use of the Club."[24] Apparently the place had the usual untended look of Canadian backcountry. Victor, with his Englishman's eye, told Evie, "it could be made really beautiful with cutting paths out and a lot of clearing."[25]

Victor enjoyed the meals, especially the salmon. "We have been given pickled salmon and also what is called 'planked' salmon. Both are excellent and I have asked for the recipe. The planked salmon is done on [sic] by pinning the fish to a board which is cut from fresh fir and gets the taste of the wood."[26]

For Victor's gout, Taylor brought up some medicine, and it was a "great relief to get a bandage on."[27] Later, he wrote that, to his surprise and delight, "The gout has disappeared and I can get about quite well again."[28] Although BJ knew that excessive eating had something to do with gout, Victor seemed unaware of the effect of food, or perhaps he just denied it. He considered going to Banff, Alberta, for a cure in the sulphur baths, but was unsure it would work and never went. In 1918, it seems no one knew what brought on gout and which foods to avoid. The meals at the fishing camps seemed to contribute to his recovery.

They were towed again upriver to Red Bank Station, forty-one miles from Matapedia, a camp for two rods. Here, despite the restriction on private servants staying in the house, Taylor and the cook were also accommodated within the lodge. With his valet there, Victor confided to his diary, "It is certainly a relief to have someone to pack one's things."[29] The rain had let up, so one can imagine he went out onto the verandah to watch the fireflies, "a wonderful sight,"[30] but the mosquitoes and the cold soon drove him inside to the warmth of the big open fireplace.[31]

Victor's letters have given us more access to his thoughts in this setting than in some others. He wrote seven letters to Evie during his two weeks at the Restigouche, many more than the two he managed to write to her during his ten days on the Cascapedia River a year later. On the Restigouche, he had plenty of free time in the stations and little company. He and Tommy had only Taylor and the cook for company at Indian House and Red Bank. Used to a much more active social life, the uproar of his family, the ADCs, his work colleagues, and a constant stream of visitors, Victor may have been lonely. Tommy did not seem to play the part of companion, which was expected of an ADC. Victor reported to Evie that "Tommy is a very nice companion and is enjoying himself immensely," however, he went on to say, "at the precise moment he has got the fidgets and will not sit still for more than two minutes at a time."[32] In another letter, he wrote, "Tommy's capacity for fidgeting is marvelous, but he is really nice and most useful."[33] Tommy's fidgets seemed to rule out cribbage or long chats, which Victor enjoyed in other settings – there is no mention of such activity on the Restigouche – but Tommy was "desperately keen" about fishing, and that was what mattered most.[34]

The war, still raging in Europe, invaded his pleasure a few times. As was his custom, he read the papers that were delivered daily along with the mail, though sometimes their lateness irritated him – he reported receiving Monday's papers on Thursday.[35] He mentioned the torpedoing of a Canadian hospital ship – the *Llandovery Castle*, sunk off the south coast of Ireland with extensive loss of life. "The only thing I can see that can be done is to arm them [the hospital ships] and tell the Germans so."[36] And he mentioned the murder on 6 July of the German ambassador in Russia, and wondered if it would lead to any developments.[37] With those exceptions, he was free to think about fishing and how much Evie would have liked the setting.

When the two weeks came to a close, the travel that had required so many hours, pulled upriver by horses, was accomplished in only eight hours; it was an easy ride down, including a visit with the New York doctor on his scow at Pine Island and luncheon at Chamberlain Shoals.

In total, Victor "killed"[38] 58 fish for a total weight of 937 pounds, an average of 16.1 pounds.[39] His biggest fish, caught at Red Bank, was 32 pounds, "the ugliest salmon I have ever seen, more like an alligator than a fish."[40] Tommy's catch was 57 fish over the fortnight.[41] The Restigouche Salmon Club records show that for the whole summer of 1917, club members killed 1,525 salmon for a total weight of 28,250 pounds. In 1918, the club's catch totalled 1,272 fish, a total weight of 22,238 pounds, including Victor's and Tommy's catch.[42]

Victor was so happy with his fishing holiday that he wished he could have another. And his wish came true when he was invited to another salmon river the following year.

Finally, Evie, too, had time for summer recreation. On their return to Ottawa, when Victor left for his Restigouche fishing adventure, Evie took the train to Blue Sea Lake with the girls and Charlie. At Burbidge, on the lake's eastern shore, Judge Anglin met them and took them by boat across the lake. Victor had rented an attractive bit of shoreline with a little peninsula jutting into the lake. A small shack provided some protection from the elements. Evie loved the place and wrote that first day to Victor, "The wharf is not up yet. So we landed from the motor boat with some difficulty in a deluge of rain by getting into a row boat in the bay. I had a waterproof but the others were soaked to the skin." She found the place "even more attractive than I thought" and "we had better start negotiations for purchase at once." Victor agreed, and within days it was done.[43] He purchased ninety-two acres on the western shore of Blue Sea Lake for $3,000.[44]

At Blue Sea, Evie was happy again. During their recent tour, she told Lady Edward, "talking and smiling all day and every day for over a month is quite a strain when one is really thinking about the war all the time."[45] To her mother, she wrote, "It really is a wonderful rest after having to be civil to people for such a long time."[46] At Blue Sea, she did not have to face people other than family and servants.

In some ways, her life at the lake was similar to that of any cottager. There were the usual problems. The boat engine worked only sporadically, and without boats they were cut off from the world (there was no telephone, only telegraph facilities at Burbidge on the other side of the lake). The weather was cold, rainy, and thundery at first, then very hot. The WCs (bathroom facilities) were nonexistent and the bushes were cold and wet. The roof leaked at night. Evie seemed to delight in these problems and gradually got them fixed. She, however, had an advantage over present-day cottagers. She had live-in servants: a carpenter to build the outdoor WCs and repair the leaking roof; a groom to tend the horses and build a shed for them; a cook to prepare meals and arrange for a full larder. She wrote to Victor, "We had a shock yesterday when our half a sheep, the best part of a lamb and a huge piece of beef arrived, also 4 loaves. As this was supposed to be our half weekly stores, one understands why the books are always so high." They also had the salmon that Victor had sent from the Restigouche. Evie was concerned that they should not waste food, but probably little went to waste with such a large and active crew to feed.[47]

As she had the previous year, Evie enjoyed her quiet retreat away from the heat of Ottawa, the children had a place to play, and Victor could come whenever he had time. Victor liked his comforts at Rideau Hall. However, he admitted to his mother in a letter written one July night, "I am trying to write in my dressing room at 1:30 a.m. with the thermometer standing at 82 [F]. I like this heat but it is inconvenient as the ink won't run and the blotting paper won't work. Hence the blots."[48]

As life at Blue Sea Lake became more organized, Evie wrote to Lady Edward from the camp, which she named New Lismore, after their Irish home.

Here is it so peaceful that one almost feels as if the war must be an impossible nightmare. From my little room I look straight into the eastern side of the lake. At bed time the fireflies dart about everywhere and in the morning the pink reflections of the sunrise in the water are wonderful. We have not had any northern lights yet. Last year they were like great search lights over the hills ... At present we have got a funny little house made of thin boards – which was there already. It consists of two rooms one of which we use as a living room. The other is Frederick's [the cook] pantry and store room. There are also two small lofts where food is stored. Then we brought with us a ready-made house of two rooms for Victor and me which is much nicer than living in a tent for long. It would go easily into the lower dining room at DH [Devonshire House in London]. The rest of the party are in tents – ten of them altogether.[49]

Eventually they had a marquee tent to use as a dining/sitting room. They whitewashed the shack walls and made blue-and-white-checked gingham curtains to hang at the windows. Evie did watercolour sketches of the scenery to decorate the walls.[50]

Dorothy wrote to her grandmother, "It is right away from all the other people and we've got the most wonderful view of the lake as we are on a point of land and can see for miles in every direction."[51] The camp was set on a peninsula, now named Presqu'ile Lismore, one of the most beautiful sites on Blue Sea Lake.

As the weather warmed, Evie enjoyed watching the children cavort in the water. "The great joke is to paddle the canoe out a little way and then upset. It is most difficult to get in again as the canoe turns over at the slightest provocation and the result is an absurd scramble."[52] Rachel was by far the best swimmer, and little Anne was learning too. The duke "bathed" occasionally but he wrote that he had "procured an odd shaped garment which I am told is a bathing dress. I tried to get into it before dinner but could neither get into it or out of it and got very hot."[53] One day, Dorothy, Rachel, and Mervyn went off in the skiff to Burbidge where they met Tommy, the ADC, but the storm was so bad they could not get back without help and had to be towed back by friendly neighbours.[54]

A large group of children often gathered. The Spring Rices were across the lake, where Florence had rented a property for the summer. The Hendersons' two children stayed for a while. The Crowdys – Jim Crowdy was a clerk at Rideau Hall – who had a cottage on the same side of the lake, had a young daughter, and Judge Anglin's boy was near Charlie's age. Only one ADC, Mervyn Ridley, was with them the whole time at Blue Sea, which worried Evie – she was concerned he would get too fond of Dorothy.[55] Unfortunately, BJ was in a Montreal hospital having surgery to remove bone fragments from his injured leg. When he finally had a few days' rest at Blue Sea Lake, his leg was still draining and he didn't enjoy camp life. He did write to his mother one cold rainy day and told her, "The Duchess is at her very best – chatty, genuine, and thoughtful. You would not know her for the same woman as at Ottawa in the winter."[56]

When the Duke of Connaught dropped by in late August on his way back from a mission to Japan, Victor told his mother it was "a great change and relief to see some English people again. Everyone is as nice as possible but they are not quite the same thing as one's English friends."[57] The Duke of Connaught was headed home, and BJ, whose leg, even after surgery, was still bothering him, took the opportunity to return to England. They were sorry to lose him, as he had become part of the family.

Evie wrote to her mother about Victor. "Victor has got over his gout and a doctor who has lately overhauled him says his general health, blood pressure etc. are excellent. All the same I can't think that he is really in good condition as his nerves seem decidedly bad and he is very sleepy and apathetic at home, though all right about political business. He gets on very well with all the ministers which makes a lot of difference just now when so many things are in the melting pot. They think him very 'democratic' (how tired one gets of the word) so he can say some things more easily than, for instance, the Duke of Connaught. They like to feel that he was an MP and also a mayor."[58]

Victor made only a few short trips to the lake that summer. On Sundays, when he was there, they attended the little church across the lake, St George's-by-the-Lake, where he read the lesson.[59] He took in a bit of fishing and planned for the new house they would build on the prop-

Figure 12.2 Prince Arthur of Connaught's visit to Rideau Hall, August 1918.

erty. They employed Mrs Crowdy's brother, the well-known Ottawa architect Allan Keefer, to design something modest. Evie believed that "we should not lose by building a small bungalow and selling it at the end of our time."[60] While Evie planned the house, Victor planned a water system and a new road. By fall, the plans were finished and construction could begin.

In late August, Evie changed her original plans, cutting out several rooms and a part of the roofing in order to keep the cost down. She had agreed that Keefer could proceed, on the understanding that the cost would not exceed $10,000.[61] Within a few days she heard that the estimate was down to $8,700.[62] However, by early October Evie was livid: "That wretch Keefer sent me the blue prints of the house 3 days ago with various disastrous alterations."[63] She met Keefer, who revealed that the alterations had already been built, and tearing them down would only add to the cost. She decided to grin and bear it. Victor was obviously leaving the decision-making to Evie on this house as it was her pet project. The household accounts for the duke's time in Canada show that the building and equipment costs from 1918 to 1921 reached only about $10,700, so Keefer did stick closely to his original estimates.[64]

Amid his visits to Blue Sea Lake that summer, Victor had to deal with some concerns of state. One that occasioned only a small entry in his diary was Canada's commitment of troops for the Allied expedition to Siberia. The issue of a Siberian expedition had been brewing among the Allies for some time. In March 1917,[65] when the Russian Revolution began, the duke noted, "Russian news is most dramatic. The Romanoff dynasty is at an end and the revolution appears to have been peacefully carried out."[66] The Allied forces waited to see whether Russia would carry on with the war, and at first it seemed they would, but then the Russian situation became more "perplexing and unsatisfactory."[67] In July 1917, the duke noted, "July 3: Very good news from Russia. [They have taken] over 10,000 prisoners. Good news if it is correct." But on 23 July he wrote, "afraid the Russians show signs of falling to pieces again." And on 4 September, "Russians have abandoned Riga and afraid it may mean the fall of Petrograd." But the Germans did not get to Petrograd, now St Petersburg. Alexander Kerensky's shaky government was finally deposed in November 1917 by the Bolsheviks, led by Vladimir Lenin, and it was they who seized Petrograd.

The Bolsheviks signed an armistice with the Central Powers on 2 December 1917, but in order to avoid ceding territory, the Bolsheviks delayed signing a treaty for several months. Finally, in March 1918, they concluded the Treaty of Brest-Litovsk. The Russians lost control of Estonia, Latvia, Lithuania, Finland, Belarus, and also Ukraine, which became independent. For the Allied powers, it meant that the Germans could send many of their troops to the Western Front, an ominous sign since the American forces were not yet fully engaged in Europe. At the same time, the Allies feared German troops would head east toward Archangel and Murmansk, which were stocked with Allied supplies, and the Germans would have access to the "food basket" of Russia. The Allies, including Britain, France, the United States, and Japan, decided on a Siberian expedition. Canada was not included as a separate player but Borden knew about these discussions.

On Saturday, 20 July, when the cable arrived from Walter Long, Victor was at Blue Sea Lake enjoying a weekend of fishing. He returned to a sweltering Ottawa to deal with Long's cable containing "proposals," which were really requests, "for the concurrence of the Dominion government."[68] Long proposed that Canada send an Expeditionary Force to Vladivostok. The cable outlined a command structure under the War Office in London and asked when the troops could be ready to sail. Long asked that Canada's response be cabled as soon as possible. Apparently this cable angered Borden. Once again, the prime minister had been overlooked as communication was sent through the governor general. For Borden, this action did not adequately recognize Canadian independence, so hard-won on the battlefields of France. He cabled Sir Thomas White, acting prime minister while Borden was in London for the War Cabinet meetings, that "no reply shall be sent to the British Government's message except through me."[69]

The Allies entered Russia to contain the Bolshevik revolution, acting in support of the White Russians. In October 1918 a Canadian advance party was sent, and the rest followed in December. Borden, in London preparing for the Peace Conference, wrote to Sir Thomas White, "It is not anticipated that our troops will be called upon to engage in active warfare except perhaps to quell some local disturbances. They will assist in stabilizing conditions and in giving needed aid to the newly organized formations of Russian troops."[70] The Privy Council of Canada approved a force of 5,000 troops for the Canadian Expeditionary Force Siberia (CEFS).[71] Ultimately 4,210 Canadian troops from across Canada deployed from Victoria for Vladivostok, 1,653 of them conscripts. There was unrest among the CEFS troops, especially after the armistice in November 1918. Some questioned whether it was legitimate to send conscripts, since they had been conscripted for the war that was now over, but they were sent anyway.[72] The 21 December departure resulted in an attempt at mutiny by those who did not want to go to Siberia and they were marched aboard, escorted by other soldiers armed with rifles and fixed bayonets.[73] While in Russia, the Canadian troops did not leave Vladivostok, except for a small contingent of fifty-five sent to Omsk to provide administrative support to the British.[74] Borden ordered them home in the spring of 1919, and the last of them were shipped home in June that year. Other troops from Britain, France, Italy, and Japan left later. The Allied expedition to Siberia was a failure: it did not stop the Bolsheviks.

CHAPTER 13

Influenza, Armistice, and Aftermath

Information about an influenza epidemic was first published in the spring of 1918 in neutral Spain, so it became known as the Spanish influenza, though later evidence showed that it probably arose in the United States, where it spread rapidly through the military camps. Because the warring nations did not want to damage morale, news of an epidemic was not shared in the press. By late summer, the Devonshire family, along with the rest of the populace, was still unaware of the looming threat.

A pregnant Lady Maud arrived in Ottawa from Washington in early August 1918, ready for her "confinement," the last two months of her pregnancy during which, by tradition, an aristocratic woman would withdraw from public life, not wanting her pregnancy to draw attention to her sexuality, and to be free to dress without the constraint of her corsets. It also allowed her a period of rest before the birth. Victor had arranged for Maud, along with her mother, to spend her confinement at Elmwood, in Cartierville near Montreal, the home of Lord Atholstan, the former Sir Hugh Graham. Sir Hugh, the subject of the first contretemps between the governor general and Prime Minister Borden in December 1916, had become Baron Atholstan at the stroke of the governor general's pen. Victor's diary does not record any previous contact with Atholstan, except a visit to Elmwood on his way to the Restigouche River in June 1918 to check out the home that Atholstan had offered for his daughter's use. This was the same home that had been bombed on 9 August 1917 by anti-conscriptionists who were angry that Lord Atholstan had used his newspaper, the *Montreal Star*, to support conscription.

By the time of the duke's visit in 1918, the house had been completely restored and the rioting about conscription had subsided.

Evie and Maud arrived on 31 August, but "the road was awful," Evie wrote from Elmwood. Though there was a paved road, it could not be used because "the bridges are not yet built over the railroad."[1] The Montreal hospital was twelve miles away so they decided to be firm with the doctor and insist that Maud have the baby at Elmwood. Lord Richard Nevill, the comptroller, and Colonel Henderson, the military secretary, came with them. As usual, no one mentioned cooks, house-keepers, and maids, but presumably they were part of the household. The house itself was perfect, right on the river, with a lovely garden. Evie arranged an office on the upper floor for Victor, a place where he could write, away from the noise downstairs, whenever he was able to visit. Angus arrived and went to see a specialist about his lungs, who told him that there was nothing seriously wrong, just asthma. "Maud is fond of him. It is nice to see them together," Evie wrote to Victor.[2] Only the anxiety of waiting for the baby to arrive marred this scene of domestic bliss.

The rest of the family was scattered. Rachel and Anne were at the Citadel in Quebec City with Victor; Charlie was in Ottawa, still at school at Ashbury College; Blanche and Dorothy were closing up the camp at Blue Sea Lake. Dorothy, in her ebullient style, wrote to her mother about a last fishing trip: "At first it was so rough we could hardly get the boats to move and then there was an awful downpour. We had tea in the middle of that and succeeded in making a lovely fire. In the end it cleared up and the fish started biting. By that time it was nearly dark which was very sad. I caught one quite nice fish, the only one we got. It was very exciting as Blinky [a dog] had sat on the rod and there was only a piece of it left."[3] Some of the ADCs were at Blue Sea with the girls. BJ had sailed home to England with the Duke of Connaught. Victor had only one ADC with him.

Finally, the duke felt he could fit in a two-week tour of Manitoba and Saskatchewan before the baby arrived. He wanted to see the grain harvest that he had missed the year before. His love of excursions made it a busy, happy time; he visited the farms and little towns, received welcomes, made speeches, shook hands, visited returned soldiers in hospitals, and made trying visits of condolence to women whose men had been killed in the war. Writing to Evie about a visit to a Mennonite farm

Figure 13.1 Harvest time: the Duke of Devonshire driving a binder with a new stooking machine attached, near Brandon, Manitoba, in 1918.

in Manitoba, he told her they were "a curious looking lot and in most ways very backward according to our ideas, but they are certainly wonderful farmers." Though his visit was unannounced, "I do not think I have ever seen cleaner or fresher looking places."[4] At Dauphin, Manitoba, he and Premier Tobias Norris each rode a binder around a field. "He [Norris] was much pleased and said he will always claim that he and I had harvested in the same field."[5] Near Brandon, the duke drove a binder with a new stooking machine attached.[6]

So many men had left for war that labour was in short supply. New machines helped, but the harvesting process still required much manual labour. A binder cut and bundled the grain into sheaves tied with binder twine. Men then stooked the sheaves – they set four or more sheaves together standing upright. Grain in the stooks was then left to dry and mature until it could be threshed using another machine. Men would use a pitchfork to lift the stooks into a wagon to be taken to the thresher. The duke saw a new machine that loaded stooks onto a wagon, but he did not think it would be very useful because it scattered the grain.[7] These were long and tiring days of visiting and observing, but he revelled in it all.

Seen through his English eyes, the flat, treeless Prairies were not appealing to the duke. He told Evie several times "I would not want to live on the prairies." He thought it a bore to wake in the morning, look out the window, and know that you were not going to see anything else all day. A prairie person would say that he had not noticed the beauty of the changing sky and waving fields of grain. Farmers constantly monitored the sky to predict the weather, much as the duke often used his "glass" or barometer as his predictor. For the duke, trees were the saving grace of the prairies. He most appreciated the hilly and partly wooded landscape of the Prince Albert area in Saskatchewan, though he understood that the flat prairies were much more fertile and conducive to making fortunes. He also enjoyed the change of scene in southern Saskatchewan when he entered the Qu'Appelle Valley with its hills and trees. "It is a strange place and one comes on it without warning," he wrote, "a great change and contrast to the prairie."[8] It was also home to the Provincial Sanatorium for Consumption (tuberculosis), parts of which were still under construction to meet the growing need for treatment of this disease. He visited all the military patients there.

The duke was amazed at the size of the prairie farms. He saw one field being cultivated that was four miles by one mile. He calculated the economics of farming on these very large properties. One farmer with 480 acres told him about sowing seed in April, having it blown away in May, replanting by 4 June, and harvesting by 4 September, expecting a yield of thirty bushels an acre. Victor did the figures, and at $2.20 a bushel came up with a startling total yield of $32,256, or, by his calculation, £6,451 (about $500,000 Canadian today[9]), of which less than 25 per cent would amply cover expenses. "The fertility and recuperative powers of this soil are wonderful, but the optimism of the inhabitants is far more so."[10]

For two full weeks, Victor was steeped in prairie conversations that focused on the weather and the expected yield of the grain crops of wheat and oats. He was astonished that the authorities expected 90 million bushels of wheat in Saskatchewan alone, despite a period of drought and wind, before the summer rains had put new life into the crops.[11] As a farmer himself, he understood the concerns and loved the experience.

When Victor arrived back in Cartierville in mid-September, he was receiving mixed messages about the war. Lord Lansdowne wrote to Evie that he expected the Allies were still a long way from "the knockout," and "if we are to fight on until Germany is ready to let us strip the shirt off her back we must look forward to many weary stages in this horrible struggle."[12] The Duke of Connaught wrote, "Some people are beginning to imagine that we will finish the war this year," but he did not think it would be over before the new year.[13] On a more optimistic note, Borden, who had recently returned from England, shared news he had received from British Prime Minister Lloyd George. Germany was running out of reserves. Prisoners reported that boys of the class of 1920 were appearing in German field depots (they would have been about sixteen). Lloyd George warned that, though it was not time yet, he might ask Borden to return to England as the war situation changed.[14]

Meanwhile, Maud was comfortable at Elmwood with two nurses, her mother, and Angus in attendance. Evie wrote to her mother about Maud and Angus, "I still think him quite uninteresting but they adore each other and his thought and care for her are wonderful."[15] Finally the awaited baby began to arrive. Evie wrote to her mother about the baby's delivery on 24 September. "The doctor found that the head was not getting through so he asked for leave to use instruments. It appears that he had an awful job. The head is round like a bullet and large and very hard, no give in the middle like most babies. He did not know which was the front and which the back as it was the same size all round. And was afraid of injuring it by pulling the wrong way. Maud was pretty badly torn."[16]

Despite the difficult birth, both Maud and the baby, a girl, were fine. The baby weighed seven pounds, twelve ounces. Evie thought she looked the image of Angus with her big round head and "hair which I think will be curly like his and rather big eyes."[17] Angus and Maud were thrilled. Angus tried to amuse the baby with strange faces, not realizing she could not yet see.[18] Victor and Angus played a celebratory round of golf.[19]

The baby often screamed and Evie realized she was not getting enough food. When she told Victor, he asked, trying to be helpful, if Maud could take porter, a dark beer, which he and many others believed was of assistance in such circumstances.[20] Instead of porter for Maud, they gave the baby a bottle after each nursing,[21] keeping up for Maud the fiction that she alone was feeding the child.[22]

Evie described for Lady Edward the new flat that Maud and Angus had taken at the edge of Washington. Their little house in Chevy Chase was now too small, the roof leaked, the furnace was bad, and it was a long way out of town. For the new flat, Maud planned to buy cheap furniture and have it painted since they didn't expect to stay long in Washington. Until she recovered, Maud would stay in Canada, travelling to Ottawa for the christening of the baby.[23] Everything was perfect.

However, storm clouds were gathering. On 25 September, Evie wrote to her mother, "We are getting rather fussed about the Spanish Influenza. It is raging at Quebec and several people have died. They have got it in all the [military] camps here and in the US. Victor joins the rest of the family at Quebec on Monday and was naturally going to all the camps ... It would be dreadful to bring the germ back, particularly to ... this baby."[24]

Despite the influenza, Victor and Evie continued with their social engagements. Evie attended the Women's Canadian Club luncheon while Victor went to the Men's Canadian Club. Victor launched the ship *War Faith* at Canadian Vickers Shipyard in the east end of Montreal.[25] Then he returned to Quebec City, visited a silver fox farm, and went to Spencerwood to confer with the lieutenant-governor of Quebec.[26]

On 3 October, Angus left to return to work in Washington. On 4 October, in response to the influenza epidemic, Washington was declared a "sanitary zone" by the Public Health Service. This meant that theatres, moving picture houses, dance halls, and schools were closed until further notice; government office opening hours were staggered in order to avoid congestion on streetcars. Most of the influenza cases were in the military camps where, in close confinement, it spread quickly.[27] The news reports suggested that this influenza could be controlled. The surgeon general issued a bulletin telling people to sneeze into a handkerchief and to go to bed at the first sign of the disease. Doctors knew that the incubation period – that period when the disease can be spread before the patient becomes ill – was one to four days. People were told to avoid crowded places. The malady was compared to "grippe," not dangerous unless neglected, when it could turn into pneumonia. Doctors believed it was caused by the influenza bacillus, which had been identified and named by a German scientist, Richard Pfeiffer, a quarter century earlier.[28] Later it was determined that the infectious stage lasted only a few days, and that bacterial pneumonia was usually the cause of death for those who survived the first few days.[29] Little had been published about the incidence of influenza earlier that spring; by fall, it was impossible to contain the information that influenza was sweeping North America and Europe and extending around the world.

On 9 October, Victor wrote to Evie: "There are said to be 10,000 cases of flu or colds in Quebec – 10% of the population. I have put off all my engagements."[30] But he hadn't. That same day he went to the Huron Village of Lorette outside Quebec City for a ceremony that made him honourary chief of the tribe, with the name "SALOĀTRASI (L'Ami des Arts)."[31] He continued to have guests for luncheon at the Citadel, and to visit those who would accept him. He implored the ladies of the IODE and the Red Cross to accept his visits; how could they refuse the governor general's direct request, even during an influenza epidemic?[32] Evie upbraided him for going about so much.[33] "I do think it is wrong that you should do all that you are doing. It is most unfair on the children and a bad example, besides being hard on the other Citadel people who are in strict quarantine."[34] To top off Victor's isolation, a series of visiting Englishmen had to bypass him because they hadn't allowed enough time for their North American travels.[35] He complained to his mother that they thought this continent was the same size as England.[36]

On Sunday, 6 October, Angus wrote to Maud saying that he was in bed with the Spanish flu. The letter arrived on Tuesday, 8 October, and as they heard nothing more from him and their anxiety mounted they sent telegrams asking for information. Finally, on 10 October, they received two satisfactory telegrams saying that Angus had a patch on the base of his lung, but while his condition was still serious the worst of the attack was over. He was in a big military hospital, and his boss, Major General James D. McLachlan, military attaché to the British Embassy in Washington, had been to see him. Since Angus seemed to be getting better, the little group at Elmwood had cocktails before luncheon "as a preventative of the flue."[37]

On 12 October, another telegram "gave a very bad account indeed of Angus."[38] Evie called Victor by long-distance telephone and they agreed she should go to Angus. Evie told Maud about the telegram; then, accompanied by Miss Saunders, she took the night train to Washington. Though Evie herself was terrified of the disease and even more terrified of bringing it to her family, she knew it was her role to go to Angus in Maud's place. She reported to Victor: "I am thankful I came. Thank God he was conscious when I arrived." She gave him messages from Maud and the family. He asked after Maud and the baby. Then, "It was something to hold his hand at the last."[39] It was 13 October. He had been ill for eight days. "I am half dazed by it all," Evie wrote to Victor. "I have written to Maud. Give her the letter if she is fit to have it." And, "I strongly advise you not to come."[40]

Victor travelled by train from Quebec City to Cartierville to be with Maud at Elmwood. He waited until the doctor came before he told her the news. "Oh it can't be true," she wailed. "We were so happy."[41] Though she cried, Maud was not hysterical and did not collapse.

Two days later, Evie and Miss Saunders returned to Elmwood. Evie was very tired and overwrought.[42] She must have worried for a week or more about getting influenza herself or bringing it to her family, though she never mentioned that in her letters. Evie was concerned about the three cases in the nearby village of Cartierville, but thought that the family at Elmwood was fairly safe since they saw so few people.[43]

Angus, with his one good lung, had little chance against this disease. As a young, healthy man he was in the susceptible age group. This influenza was different from others that each year attack mostly the very young and the very old. In fact, what was called the Spanish influenza was a viral disease more lethal than any previous flu. It was later identified as a particularly virulent strain of H1N1, the most common type of influenza. A similar strain arose in 2009 creating a pandemic that killed more than 18,000 worldwide. However, the 1918 Spanish influenza was much more lethal, infecting most of a region's population and killing about 2.5 per cent of those infected. A normal flu season will result in the deaths of about 250,000 to 500,000 people worldwide, about 0.1 per cent of those infected.[44] Although statistics were not kept accurately at the height of the disaster, it has been estimated that between 20 and 100 million died worldwide. In Canada, 30,000 to 50,000 succumbed.[45] The virus made its way to most countries and, in a ten-week period from mid-September on, created havoc, especially among healthy youth. In Philadelphia, where the epidemic reached mammoth proportions, there was nowhere to dispose of the dead, so people kept them in their homes where they themselves were ill, or just put them outside the door to be picked up by policemen in surgical masks driving trucks or horse-drawn wagons.[46]

For Maud, Angus's death was a disaster. In one blow she had lost her adoring husband, her little home in Washington, and her social position among the Washington elite. Her only consolation was her healthy baby, just three weeks old. However, she was now the widowed mother of the granddaughter of the Mackintosh of Mackintosh. The family at Elmwood did not know whether Maud's baby would become the heir. If she did, Maud might be expected to live at their ancestral home, Moy Hall, in the sparsely populated Scottish highlands, which she had never visited, with Scottish in-laws she had never met.[47] Maud was bereft, but took comfort from her child. She did express the wish that she could have had a boy "just like him" to take back to his parents. Angus, she said, wanted a girl like her. Instead the baby girl looked like Angus.[48]

Maud was too weak to go to her husband's funeral in Washington. Angus was buried with full military honours in Arlington National Cemetery.[49] Lord Richard Nevill and Mervyn Ridley attended for the family. Evie reflected on Angus to her mother: "His great devotion to her had brought out all that was finest in his character. He had always been very popular but as you know I thought he had rather a shallow nature. This however proved to be quite wrong. The other two ADCs, M Ridley and BJ, always said Maud would develop his character and he certainly had got rid of a lot of the lacks of confidence in his own judgement and had begun to think much more about all sorts of things. His unselfishness and tenderness to Maud was wonderful."[50]

Evie was impressed by the condolences sent to the family. She continued to her mother: "You can't think how kind both Canadians and American friends have been. Every sort and kind of person turned up at his funeral and Maud has had the nicest letters from Ministers and others about the good works he did in helping to cement the friendship between the two nations. He took so much trouble about that that it has pleased her to feel he was appreciated."[51] Someone brought a widow's bonnet for Maud. Evie thought "Maud's poor little white face looks too pathetic in it."[52]

While the influenza continued to rage in Quebec and in Ottawa, Victor was at the Citadel with Rachel, Charlie (his school in Ottawa had closed because of the flu), Anne, and Larry Minto, an ADC. Evie suggested to Victor that he spray his throat frequently.[53] Victor appeared to be following Evie's advice. "This afternoon I took the children out for a walk on the plains. We carefully avoided our fellow creatures and I applied the spray before and after."[54] There is no mention in the letters of the family wearing masks, but those attending the sick in the United States were advised to wear them to prevent spread of the disease.[55] In Toronto, the medical officer of health recommended walking, rather than taking streetcars, as a precaution.[56] Ever the optimist, Victor thought the infection could be avoided. But the number of cases continued to increase, with deaths being reported daily. The authorities finally took steps to try to contain the epidemic. In Ottawa and Quebec City, schools, theatres, and churches were closed, shops closed early, and railway cars and streetcars were regularly disinfected.[57]

In Montreal, the epidemic peaked on 21 October with 201 deaths; the following day, 1,058 new cases were registered. It then began to recede, but the final death toll in that city was more than 3,000 by the time this plague was over in 1919.[58] In Ottawa the epidemic peaked in October with 440 deaths, but then it receded there, too.[59] Though the disease was pandemic, rampant throughout the world, there is no evidence that the family understood its extent. The war took precedence in their thoughts. And yet, until recent years, not much was ever made of the fact that this disease killed more people than the war, and in fact more than both world wars together.

In late October, with the influenza epidemic slowly fading, Evie was anxious to get back to Ottawa where she could settle Maud and have the baby christened. On 1 November, the party from Quebec City took the special Canadian Pacific train and picked up the Cartierville group in Montreal. Evie wrote about the trip to her mother: "You know the kind of cheery party we always are when we make a big move. Children, dogs, parcels of all sorts, a pony etc. It makes ones heart ache to see Maud's little white face and the tiny baby in the middle of it all."[60]

Meanwhile the war news they were receiving by cable and from the press was increasingly hopeful. Bulgaria's application for an armistice had already been accepted, and Turkey's surrender was reported on 30

October.[61] Lloyd George warned Borden to be ready to start "without delay" for London to be part of the peace talks if Germany signed an armistice.[62] Evie began to plan her trip to take Maud and the baby back to England.

For weeks there were rumours of Germany collapsing, and then signs of revolution within the country. Prime Minister Borden received the expected call from Lloyd George to come to London. He left on 8 November, just as the rumours of Germany capitulating were said to be a hoax. The next day news came that the German emperor had abdicated. Still, there was a treaty to negotiate and that was expected to take time.

In Ottawa, Victor decided to inspect the construction at Blue Sea Lake. Dorothy and Blanche were already there, camping in the nearly completed house with Miss Saunders. Victor took the special train on 9 November with Rachel, Charlie, and an ADC. He and his party stayed overnight on the train parked at Blue Sea Station. (Though Blue Sea would not become an official name for the town until 1921, the Canadian Pacific Railway already used the name for its station.[63]) In the morning, they travelled the three miles to the house, presumably by horse and buggy. Victor found the house "certainly very nice but rather on a bigger scale than I had expected."[64] He and Charlie walked down to the point, noticing how different the lake looked without leaves on the trees. They took less than an hour to hike back to the train. At the end of this pleasant day, they took the three-hour train trip back to Ottawa, arriving at 9:30 that evening to news that revolution in Germany was continuing "but so far without excesses or much bloodshed."[65] They still did not expect the armistice.

They had scarcely had a few hours' sleep before Ottawa erupted in pandemonium. Ethel Chadwick, the Ottawa woman who had been a friend of the family of the Duke of Connaught when he was resident at Government House, described the scene in her diary: "A few minutes after three this morning, I ... saw the light in the hall go out three times – the signal given us when peace was declared ... It was a moment of intense excitement, mingled with sadness. Then hundreds of whistles began to blow."[66] Like many Ottawa citizens who had been expecting the armistice declaration, Ethel had left lights on so she would notice them dip. *The Citizen* had pre-arranged with the Ottawa electricity companies that they would dip their lights, and the *Ottawa Journal* had asked industrial plants to blow whistles as soon as they received news that the armistice was signed.[67] The actual signing took place at 6:00 a.m. Paris time (1:00 a.m. in Ottawa). It took until 3:00 a.m. for this news to reach the Ottawa news desk by telegraph from Washington. The armistice was to go into effect five hours after the signing – 11:00 a.m. Paris time.

Ethel and many Ottawa citizens made their way downtown, waving flags, blowing whistles, ringing bells, and yelling wildly. Firecrackers and rockets went off. People used pots and pans as drums, anything to make a noise. Church bells rang out, a band played, revellers on Sparks Street sang "God Save the King," "O Canada," and "The Maple Leaf Forever." Ethel and her friends stayed out until nearly 5:00 a.m.; the party continued for nearly twenty-four hours. As dawn tinged the sky, the Sparks Street crowd billowed onto Parliament Hill where bands set themselves up on the steps of the new Centre Block building. The company sang in unison the "Old Hundredth" hymn using the words "Praise God from whom all blessings flow." Both the music and words were familiar and comforting to those raised in the British tradition.

Just after 2:00 p.m., a formal ceremony began on the Hill. Some ten thousand people crowded in front of the new Centre Block building, where the speakers were flanked by veterans and representatives of the Allied nations acting as standard bearers for the flags of their nations. The Duke and Duchess of Devonshire and their staff took their places along with Lady Borden and the Honourable N.W. Rowell, president of the Privy Council, acting for the prime minister. Rowell opened the ceremony, and the duke praised Canada's war effort and noted that "we have laid the foundation for a long peace." When Rowell read the principal terms of the peace, the crowd cheered. Prayers and hymns of thanksgiving, followed by a rousing version of "Rule Britannia," closed the formalities.

The sudden armistice changed everything at Rideau Hall. For Evie, the armistice meant the seas were now open and she could escape to England, as she had been planning in her mind since Angus's death. Her plans went into overdrive. She applied for passage. She would leave her daughter, Blanche, to act as her father's hostess – Blanche needed the experience of having to think for herself. However, civilian passage on ships was difficult to find and Evie had to wait.

They could finally arrange the infant's christening, which was held on 12 November at St Bartholomew's Anglican Church. The baby had not been named in letters or the duke's diary until the christening. Probably because of the recent peace, for which they had waited so long, they named the baby Anne Peace Arabella.[68] Later they called her Arabella, or Arbell for short. Evie wrote to Lady Edward, "I can't tell you how trying the christening was. The little tartan sash and Angus' robes which the Mackintosh so hoped would be worn by a baby boy, made it worse."[69]

Victor planned a trip to the Maritime provinces, but he could not begin until he knew Evie's plans. With little to do in the uncertain atmosphere, he entertained himself playing golf with the staff and began to resume discussing affairs with politicians, receiving visitors, and attending events.

Finally, they heard that Evie and her company had berths leaving Halifax on 8 December on RMS *Aquitania*, the Cunard Company luxury liner, sister ship to the *Lusitania*, which had been torpedoed and sunk in 1915. On 2 December, Victor resumed his travels, taking the train to Fredericton, New Brunswick. As usual, he travelled to as many cities and small towns as he could, a total of eighteen venues by the end of the tour. In each place, crowds gathered to greet him, and he would offer a few words of praise for their war effort. He visited factories, hospitals, schools – where he fell back on a tried-and-true crowd-pleaser and asked for a holiday for the children – and convents, which, he once remarked to his diary, "have an absolutely paralyzing effect on me."[70] He did not understand or appreciate the Roman Catholic faith. At one time he told his diary, "I wish the RCs would not pain me as they do."[71] And on a visit to an Ursuline convent: "the cloister system seems more objectionable every time I see it. I'm sure they would teach the children better if they knew more about the world."[72]

On all his visits, the duke was well received. The official visit of the governor general to Fredericton was eagerly awaited.[73] He received an honorary degree from the University of New Brunswick and spoke at a dinner given by the government.[74] When he was required to make a formal speech in Sydney, Nova Scotia, he was worried that it was not good enough, but was pleasantly surprised when the report in the paper the next morning was complimentary.[75] He visited the Amherst

Internment Camp in Amherst, Nova Scotia, the one where Leon Trotsky, the Russian revolutionary, had been detained for a month in April 1917. Trotsky had been on his way to Russia to support the Bolshevik revolution led by Vladimir Lenin when he was imprisoned.[76] "About 800 prisoners there," the duke said in 1918. "They were well lodged and their food excellent – far too good for them."[77] Trotsky's view had been quite the opposite.[78]

Victor managed to be in Halifax to see Evie on the morning she was to sail for England. Evie's party included Maud, baby Arbell, Dorothy, and ADCs Mervyn Ridley, Tommy Clive, and Rody Kenyon-Slaney, along with Rody's wife Mary and their baby. These ADCs had finished their assignment in Canada. The party also included nurses for the babies but, in her usual fashion, Evie mentioned the servants only when they were sick and left her to look after the babies.[79]

Victor was aware that the postwar period might be difficult as the soldiers returned to civilian life. On his Maritime province tour he kept track of the "tone" of each gathering and everywhere found it excellent; people were enthusiastic and progressive and not at all interested in revolution. In Halifax he visited the area devastated by the explosion just twelve months before and was impressed with the rebuilding work already completed.[80] In Sydney, Nova Scotia, a mining town, home of the Dominion Iron and Steel Company, he made special note that the place was thriving and the tone excellent. "No sign of Bolshevism."[81] No doubt he had already read the report by Charles Cahan, whom Borden had appointed in May 1918 to head a special inquiry into the extent of radicalism in Canada. Cahan reported in September that much of the labour unrest in the country was the result of propaganda issued by "Bolsheviki" organizations that were "advocating the destruction of all state authority, the subversion of religion and the obliteration of all property rights."[82] In response, the government passed orders-in-council prohibiting publications in an "enemy language" and banning some political and labour organizations, including the Industrial Workers of the World (IWW).[83] The duke took these fears with his usual calm; nevertheless, he was on the lookout for resentment. He found instead an enormous welcome from the people of all the little towns and villages. He was, after all, the representative of the British sovereign, an important personage in the Dominion. The armistice had changed everything, the postwar period was upon them, but for now the Canadian colony remained calm.

With Evie and her party away, the duke's household in Ottawa now consisted of Blanche, the two younger girls, Rachel and Anne, and Charlie, who stayed only until just after Christmas when he was shipped off to school in England, travelling with Florence Spring Rice and her children. Rachel, seventeen, was becoming an accomplished figure skater. Since she had only started skating when they arrived in Canada three years before, the duke was pleased when she came second in competition after a girl who had been skating all her life. Anne, nine, skied, tobogganed, and skated, and occasionally spent time in the classroom with Miss Walton, the governess.[84]

Now that the war was over, going out for entertainment was acceptable. "Went to the play. It was a novel sensation for me to be at the play again and I thoroughly enjoyed it," Victor noted.[85] Government House could also entertain as much as they wished. The military secretary, Colonel Henderson, told Evie that they were "working off a large number of 'officials and socials' with dinner parties,"[86] entertaining almost two hundred in January. "The cellar is unlocked, it does help with the large dinners," he wrote.[87] Anne hosted children's parties. At one of her parties they showed a Charlie Chaplin movie to the shrieking delight of over two hundred children.[88] Each Saturday they held skating parties, for which people registered to receive invitations. One Saturday there were over 550 skaters on the Rideau Hall rink.[89]

A series of overnight visitors helped to keep up spirits in those months with Evie absent. The duke enjoyed the visit of U.S. War Secretary Newton Baker, but was disappointed when he could not stay for the dinner party planned for him.[90] Sir Arthur Pearson, founder of the *Daily Express* in Britain, who had gone completely blind from glaucoma, proved an interesting companion.[91] The whole household was also entranced by the visit of Captain Alfred Carpenter, who had received the Victoria Cross as commander of HMS *Vindictive* during the attempt to blockade the German U-boat harbour at the port of Zeebrugge, Belgium, in April 1918. Carpenter gave a public lecture at Ottawa's Russell Theatre and, as Miss Walton wrote to Evie, gave "His Ex a piece of the Mole [the harbour breakwater] that they shot away at Zeebrugge."[92]

Despite the renewed social life, the house seemed quiet and empty without Evie and the older girls. Lord Richard Nevill, the duke's faithful comptroller, managed the household smoothly – most of the time. Rachel had singing lessons from an opera singer. One morning, the duke reported to Evie, he heard a great crash. "All the dogs barked. I … went to see what it was all about and found it was merely the lady singing."[93]

Social activity was interrupted for a week in January when Prince John, the youngest son of King George V and Queen Mary, died at Sandringham, the royal estate in Norfolk. He was thirteen and had suffered from epilepsy for many years. The duke received word from London: "the King commands there should be no official parties for a week."[94] He had to cancel some dinner parties, his plans to travel to Montreal and Toronto, and Rachel's birthday party.

The family took another trip to Blue Sea Lake to see the new house. Once again, the Duke and his ADCs slept in the train, and travelled to the house by sleigh. The girls and Miss Saunders camped in the empty rooms heated by wood-burning stoves.[95] Rachel, according to Blanche, looked "too peculiar for words" when she went to bed with all her ordinary clothes under her pyjamas.[96]

Life in Ottawa and in Canada was very quiet. The duke wrote to his mother, "It only shows how uneventful our existence is at present that a violent controversy has arisen over some gargoyles on the new Parliament buildings in which the Architect has introduced a number of likenesses – the Duke of Connaught and myself among them."[97] *The Globe* reported that Mr Newlands, supervisor of art in the public schools, called the gargoyles "jokes in stone." He thought the "caricature of the Duke of Devonshire makes one think of a childish attempt to produce a replica of a death mask of Falstaff."[98]

Later that spring, the duke took an interest in "the flying man" whose feat of daring was reported in the newspapers. He was referring to two Australian airmen, pilot Harry Hawker and navigator Mackenzie Grieve, who left St John's, Newfoundland, on 19 May in a Sopwith Camel biplane for what *The Globe* called "the most perilous airplane flight in history."[99] They were competing for a $50,000 prize offered by the London *Daily Mail* for the first transatlantic flight to be completed within seventy-two hours. Their two-seater British biplane could reach speeds of over one hundred miles an hour. They were expected to reach the Irish coast the next morning, but the plane did not arrive. "Afraid there is no news of Hawker," the duke noted in his diary.[100] The two men were thought to be lost at sea. A week after their departure, the press jubilantly reported that they were safe, having been picked up by a Danish steamer after landing on the ocean midway on their journey. They returned triumphantly to Britain, even though they had not won the prize.[101]

In early February, an event occurred that shattered the quiet of Ottawa. Opposition Leader Sir Wilfrid Laurier died at the age of seventy-eight. On 16 February, he had attended the Canadian Club dinner and gone from there to his office, where he apparently suffered a slight stroke, but made his own way home. The next day, he had another stroke, this time fatal. Laurier was heralded as a great Canadian figure in the press of the day. *The Globe* called him Canada's most distinguished son.[102] Parliament was supposed to open on 20 February with a reception and a state dinner, but in deference to Laurier's death, the government decided to continue with the opening but to cancel the social occasions.[103] His body lay in state in the House of Commons immediately after the opening of Parliament. The duke laid a wreath on the coffin, and then, for two days, immense numbers of people streamed past.

For the state funeral on Saturday, 22 February, the duke timed his departure from Government House to arrive at Parliament – temporarily housed in the Victoria Museum on Metcalfe Street[104] – just as the coffin was brought out. He followed in his sleigh to St Patrick's Basilica on Sussex Street.[105] Describing the unfamiliar Catholic service, he wrote to Evie:

> The Laurier funeral was a tremendous pageant ... The service was very fine but I, of course, did not know what to do and had to watch Sir Charles Fitzpatrick to know when to kneel or stand. On one occasion we were all kneeling and he suddenly stood up, so I did so too, but he only took his great-coat off. The service was very long and we had two long sermons, one in French by the Archbishop of Regina and the other in English by Father Burke of Toronto. I was rather confused as they continually introduced "Your Excellency" and at one moment Burke said

Figure 13.2 Sir Wilfrid Laurier. Laurier had served as leader of
the federal Liberal Party from 1887. He was Prime Minister
of Canada from 1896 to 1911 and leader of the Opposition
until his death in 1919.

when "Your Excellency prayed for the Living." I was unconscious of having done anything of the sort, but suddenly [it] occurred to me that the Apostolic Delegate is also "Excellency"
so my mind was relieved.[106]

After Laurier's funeral, the duke wondered what the Liberal Party
would do for a leader. "It's hard to see whether they can find a first rate
man who would be acceptable to both the English and French members of the party," he wrote to his mother.[107] However, in August, when
the party elected William Lyon Mackenzie King, the duke thought "he
ought to do very well."[108]

CHAPTER 14

Parliament Rejects British Hereditary Honours – Again

To the governor general's distress, Canada was not yet finished with the honours issue. After Borden's March 1918 order-in-council and the parliamentary vote in May asking that the king refrain from presenting hereditary honours to people in Canada, the resulting petition from Parliament was laid before the king. That summer, Borden discussed it with government officials in London, who agreed not to present any recommendations for honours to the king except those sent by the prime minister of Canada. Since the honours were a gift from the king, the British could not tell the king what to do, so that was the best they could offer. However, the issue did not subside.

Even while he was in Paris at the Peace Conference of 1919, Borden received fervent appeals for honours for those who had worked in civilian organizations during the war – the Red Cross, Canadian Forestry, Nursing Sisters working in military hospitals, munitions workers, and others.[1] Sir George Perley, the Canadian high commissioner, who lived in London, appealed passionately for recognition of civilians who had worked in England all during the war, and for some representation of Canadians among those receiving the Order of the British Empire to match those honoured in other Dominions. Perley said he was expressing the opinion of the Canadians living in England.[2] Even Lord Alfred Milner, the new colonial secretary, agitated for civilian honours,[3] and Sir Edward Kemp, minister of the overseas military forces, asked for military honours for those who served in the British Isles as well as those who entered the theatre of war.[4]

Borden suggested to the acting prime minister, Sir Thomas White, that the question of honours, including civilian honours for war services, might be submitted to a committee of the House of Commons in the coming session of Parliament.[5] Borden tried to define carefully what was meant by civilian versus military services, since military honours were still approved under the order-in-council passed in 1918.[6] The difficulty with civilian honours, as Borden saw it, was that "the selection will be not only arbitrary but invidious as it will not be possible to obtain that full knowledge of relative service which will be essential. On the other hand if such service is not recognized ... then Canadians will feel a sense of injustice and discrimination."[7] He was aware that other Dominions were recognizing civilian service. It was this issue of honours for civilian service that Borden thought would be sent to a committee of the House. Instead, the issue became much broader.

On 14 April 1919, Mr W.F. Nickle brought forward another resolution to ask His Majesty "to refrain from conferring any titles upon your subjects domiciled or living in Canada," except for "professional or vocational appellations" issued to persons in military or naval service of Canada or to persons engaged in the administration of justice. This was essentially the resolution of 1918 with the word "hereditary" left out.[8] During the long debate that day, which lasted from mid-afternoon until near midnight, Sir Thomas White presented an amendment that the issue be sent to a special committee of the House to review and report on the question of conferring honours, titular distinctions, and decorations. This was accepted, and a committee of twenty-five MPS was constituted with Mr Nickle as chair.

When the committee reported, it recommended asking His Majesty to agree to the same two points discussed before: to refrain from conferring any titles on subjects domiciled or ordinarily resident in Canada; and to act to extinguish, on the death of the holder, the hereditary titles already conferred. The committee also added a third recommendation: that no title from a foreign ruler should be accepted. Once again, these restrictions did not apply to military or naval decorations.[9]

In the ensuing lengthy debate on the report (22 May 1919) almost everyone appeared to be in favour of abolishing hereditary titles in Canada. However, a few brought arguments supporting honours. Mr G.B. Nicholson, MP for Algoma East, moved an amendment that the report be sent back to the committee for revision – it should contain restrictions for hereditary titles only; other titles should be allowed. Several put forward the idea that recognition in the form of honours was a strong incentive, and the value of a man to society should be measured in more than his wealth. The House seemed to think only of the largely despised British honours; the idea of Canada having its own honours system did not arise.[10] When the vote was taken, the amendment was defeated; the report carried.

The duke was not impressed. "Last night the HofC adopted the report of the Committee on honours. Think it is unfortunate but the whole business has been badly bungled."[11] He probably anticipated that he would be blamed by his colleagues in London. He was correct. In memos within the British civil service, they railed against him: "The matter could easily have been put right at an earlier stage and the Gov Gen is greatly to blame for not seeing to it then."[12] And, "The Gov Gen and the Govt of Canada have made a terrible mess of this."[13] However, they did not send these ideas to Canada's governor general, who, having agreed to Borden's order-in-council in March 1918, had little authority to interfere in 1919. In any case, it was his view that he should not interfere.

The issue began to subside in Canada, though during much of 1919 the duke was still receiving requests for honours. Someone wrote to him concerning honours for the Order of the Hospital of St John of Jerusalem.[14] He sent the inquiry to Borden, who consulted the Department of Justice and concluded that these honours came within the meaning of the resolution and must be denied.[15] By this time the issue did not make the duke's diary. He knew what to do.

Mr Nickle had moved that an address be forwarded to the governor general asking him to forward the address to the king to "be laid at the foot of the throne."[16] The address was duly engrossed,[17] dated 23 May 1919, and laid before the king on 2 August 1919 by the colonial secretary, Lord Milner,[18] who informed the duke that the king "was pleased to receive it very graciously and that His Majesty will take it into consideration and will in due course intimate his pleasure with regard to the matters of which it treats."[19]

The document requested two things: that the king refrain from conferring honours or titular distinctions upon those living in Canada, and that he do something to extinguish on the death of the holder those that had been granted. But for the king's ministers, what to actually do about these requests from Canadians was a conundrum. One writer noted: "A popular assembly usually has no right to tell the King to refrain from exercising his right. The form was not only wrong but the blunder was unnecessary. All Canada had to do is to get recognition of the principle that Can honours should be given out on the advice of the Can PM and this has been fully conceded."[20]

Another wrote, "The address really involved an absurdity. How is the King to bind his successor? Or indeed himself if next year the Canadian PM presses a recommendation for KCMG?" As for the second request, "it is not clear how the desired result can be attained unless Canada legislates to impose a penalty, on e.g. Lord Beaverbrook's successor in the peerage, if and when he shows his face in Canada."[21]

Milner brought the issue to the War Cabinet, which recommended that the issue be laid before the king (it had already gone to the king) and that Milner consult the law officers of the Crown with regard to the second proposal.[22] The law officers' response was that the second proposal could be carried out only by legislation, but that it might extinguish the rights of persons who have never been in Canada and have no intention of going there.[23] This was not very helpful. Lord Birkenhead, who as lord chancellor presided over the House of Lords, then suggested that he chair a committee to consider the issue.[24]

A thorough scouring of the Colonial Office records reveals no evidence that the lord chancellor's committee ever met. Aside from a few more inquiries about whether military honours were acceptable, the record runs dry in late 1919 and 1920. There was not much they could do in Britain. They had already decided that legislation was not possible; it would contravene the British constitution and, in any case, would never pass. The king had agreed not to bestow any more titles or honours except with the recommendation of the Canadian prime minister.

Despite the Nickle Resolution, as far as the king was concerned, the prime minister of Canada could still recommend honours and the king could still grant them. R.B. Bennett, during his tenure as prime minister (1930–35), took advantage of this power and recommended knighthoods for some of the most deserving Canadians, including Sir Frederick Banting, the co-discoverer of insulin. Bennett focused mostly on nonpolitical awards and, for the first time, recommended women be honoured, but only for the lower orders, not for knighthoods.[25]

Mackenzie King, in his second term as prime minister (1935–48), allowed non-titular honours, but was not interested in recommending knighthoods. It was not until the 1960s that the Nickle Resolution came into focus again with a proposed peerage for Roy Thomson, a Canadian who owned a string of newspapers on both sides of the Atlantic. Both prime ministers involved in the issue, John Diefenbaker and Lester B. Pearson, refused to recommend him for the peerage he wanted, so he abandoned his Canadian citizenship, became a British citizen, and was raised to the peerage in 1964 as the 1st Baron Thomson of Fleet.[26] More recently, another newspaper magnate, Conrad Black, followed the same course when Prime Minister Jean Chrétien refused to recommend him for a peerage, citing the Nickle Resolution. Black took Chrétien to court for his refusal and lost. The court said it was up to Parliament and the people to decide.[27] Black then renounced his Canadian citizenship, became a British citizen, and, in 2001, became Baron Black of Crossharbour.[28]

Except for Bennett's proposed knighthoods, bestowed in the 1930s, Canada has continued to spurn British knighthoods and peerages, as well as honours by foreign governments.[29] The feelings evident in the 1918 and 1919 debates in the House of Commons did represent the feelings of the Canadian people, and those feelings, though somewhat tempered, have not subsided. Canada solved the problem in 1967 under the government of Lester B. Pearson by creating its own made-in-Canada honour, the Order of Canada, which preserved both its independence from Britain and its democratic philosophy. Citizens recommend persons for the Order of Canada to an advisory committee, which remains at arm's length from the government of the day.

Though Nickle is often either credited or reviled for his resolution, it was Borden who began the process with his order-in-council in March 1918. The Duke of Devonshire, although the process aggravated him in the extreme, understood Canadians' desire for independence and kept a smooth hand on the process during the purging of the British honours system from Canada. In the end, it did not affect the duke's standing with his colleagues in London.

CHAPTER 15

Evie in England, 1919

Though peacetime was welcome, it came with its own irritations, and worse. Evie had been anxious to get back to England after three years in Canada, but once there she found it was not an easy transition. She had many things to accomplish, but she complained to Victor that "plans are difficult when one never knows whether one can get a taxi and it rains continually."[1] She and Dorothy, with Maud and baby Arbell, were staying with Victor's mother, Lady Edward Cavendish, at Carlos Place, London. The old lady, now eighty, wanted to know everything, but became bewildered by the telephone ringing all day and the constant stream of visitors. One of Evie's first visitors was BJ, the aide-de-camp who had returned to England in August. "We had a long gossip up in my bedroom where I was resting," Evie wrote to Victor. "It shows what roots one has struck in Canada that one really enjoyed the talk with him more than with our own relations."[2]

Evie had many people to see, but wanted to get on with her real work. Her most important task was to see Maud settled with the baby. On their arrival in London, Maud's in-laws, the Mackintoshes, along with Evie's parents, the Lansdownes, met them at Euston Station. The Mackintoshes offered Maud their house in South Wales, called Cottrell, and were generous in offering their London home for Evie and Dorothy to use during their time in England. Evie found the London house "a tempting offer but we ought to entertain and we don't like the feeling of using their house to dance in," she told Victor.[3] She solved that problem by arranging to use the London home of Victor's brother, Lord

Richard Cavendish (known to the family as Dick), for entertaining guests, which meant they could stay at the Mackintosh home.

Maud and the Mackintoshes spent Christmas at Cottrell, not far from the city of Cardiff, Wales, while Evie and Dorothy went to Bowood, the Lansdownes' country home in Wiltshire. For the New Year's celebrations, Evie and Dorothy joined the group at Cottrell, where they found that Maud had taken a great fancy to her father-in-law, The Mackintosh, who loved baby Arbell, sometimes called Anne Peace.[4] Maud did not, however, find common ground with her mother-in-law. Evie reported to Victor that Mrs Mackintosh "does not care for or understand small babies and thinks Anne Peace must be ill if she cries."[5] Mrs Mackintosh was "very kind but very very narrow-minded and old-fashioned."[6] Evie wrote that Maud hated the house she was living in, "lumbered up with bad pictures and masses of china ornaments. Dorothy has promised Maud to break one each time she comes to stay!"[7]

Maud's affairs were "rather in a muddle" because Angus had not left a will.[8] Neither Victor nor his solicitors had thought to ask Angus to make one as part of the marriage settlement the year before. Now, The Mackintosh had no intention of giving up Angus's insurance money. At Cottrell, with the Mackintoshes, Maud was "filled with horror to think that this was to be her home until Arbell was 21."[9] At Evie's entreaty, the Mackintoshes agreed that Maud and Arbell could live in London; however, they did not offer to help pay for a house there. Evie was not deterred. As soon as she was back in London, she began to look for a suitable and inexpensive house for Maud. By February, she had found a small house in Clarendon Place, still quite central but much less expensive than Mayfair. She wrote to Victor, "Have I broken to you that you are buying a house for Maud!!"[10] By March, the house situation was all settled and Maud's new home was set up with furniture from Devonshire House to supplement the little that Maud found in Angus's London flat.[11] Eventually, The Mackintosh conceded the argument about insurance, though he took out payment for the premiums and funeral expenses before handing it over. Maud got one third and Arbell two thirds of the remainder.[12] Apparently this left Maud with sufficient income to live in London.

As soon as Evie could arrange for servants and linen, she and Dorothy settled into the Mackintoshes' residence in Hill Street, Mayfair.[13] Evie could then take up her other duties. One of these was to inspect and report on their various properties. In London, their traditional residence, Devonshire House, was up for sale. It had been occupied by two organizations for women's work during the war.[14] Now that they had closed their offices, the house, if it were to be a residence again, was in need of refurbishment. Instead, the duke, on the advice of his administrators, had put the house on the market.[15] They had received an offer of £500,000 (more than £23 million, or $39 million Canadian today), but Evie found out that the potential buyer was German-born and she did not want to sell to him. Victor agreed. They decided to hold out for a higher price. The house finally sold in August 1919 for £750,000 (£34 million, or more than $59 million Canadian today).[16]

Evie visited their house at Chiswick, a grand villa and large garden built in the eighteenth century. Evie and Victor considered moving there when they returned to England, but the place was leased, and they thought breaking the agreement might be too expensive. Evie also thought it too far from London: "25 minutes to shop in the morning – 25 minutes back for luncheon. The same in the afternoon and again in the evening. Practically 3 hours a day in the motor. Also a great expense to friends who want to see one."[17] So they abandoned the idea.

Evie and Dorothy spent a few days at Compton Place, Eastbourne, another grand estate built in the eighteenth century, which came into the family when it was inherited by the 7th Duke. A tall and healthy thirteen-year-old Charlie joined them there. He had been sent home in December with Florence Spring Rice and her children, and was enrolled at St Cyprian's School, Eastbourne, prior to entering Eton. Evie liked Compton Place but suggested selling the estate as she thought they would not want to move constantly from place to place again. However, the idea of selling never took root.

Managing the enormous Chatsworth property in Derbyshire presented many problems, but Evie loved the place. After Blanche arrived – she had stayed in Ottawa to be hostess for Victor – Evie took her and Dorothy to Chatsworth. "The girls are so happy," Evie reported, "picking snowdrops and looking over old treasures ... Even with long grass and paths all over weeds, the views from the windows remain lovely."[18] She definitely wanted to live at Chatsworth when they returned from Canada.

In March, Evie managed to organize a delightful month at Lismore Castle in Ireland with a large party of family and friends. Again, Charlie joined them, as did BJ and his new fiancée. BJ was looking for a permanent position, a necessity before he married. Later they heard that because his job search was unsuccessful, this marriage was called off.[19] About Lismore, Evie wrote to Victor, "I am afraid opening this place will have been quite expensive," but she and her guests enjoyed it thoroughly, despite rainy weather.[20]

As well as checking out their properties, Evie was in search of new ADCs for Ottawa. In December, when Evie left Rideau Hall, Victor had two ADCs, and though they could both do the paperwork, they were socially awkward. "They can neither dance, play bridge or skate," Victor complained.[21] Victor described one of them to Evie: George Fortescue, a timid young man. "It is most pathetic but at the same time most inconvenient to be watched as he watches me. On at least two occasions my moustache has been singed by my unexpectedly finding a match applied to a cigarette which I was about to light myself."[22]

The difficulty in finding men to come to Ottawa as ADCs was that the single men were all young, and the older, more experienced men were not tempted by a salary of £230 a year.[23] Evie wrote to Victor, "It is all very well to think we must have experienced men, but those that have not been killed are all Generals! ... Did you know that 40,000 British officers have been killed?"[24] It is possible that Victor did not know, because the military had been less than forthcoming about the gruesome details of the war.

Evie was concerned that the Canadian government would try to foist a Canadian ADC on the governor general, so it was urgent that she find some suitable single, young Englishmen with good manners.[25] However, there was another major criterion for suitability. One young man who was suggested to her "would have been excellent on your staff," she told Victor, "but we thought him too attractive for a very penniless young man."[26] She did find Harold Macmillan, a publisher's son, very suitable, since the Macmillan book publishing firm was well established and profitable. She wrote to Victor in January about Harold. "He is tall, extremely good looking, clever, three times wounded" (it was five times[27]). She added, "Should you mind if B[lanche] fell in love with him? Mother would be horrified. He is rather honey-tongued but would I am sure be the perfect ADC."[28] Dorothy, though she did not take a special interest in any of her partners at the parties, thoroughly approved of Harold Macmillan as an ADC.[29] Through her friends, Evie also found Harry Cator, Lord Hugh Molyneux, and Lord George Haddington (known to the family as Geordie), all of whom met her criteria and eventually came to Ottawa.

One of Evie's most cherished desires was to see her girls, Dorothy and Blanche, taste some of English social life. It was not easy to accomplish. Evie complained to Victor, "It is rather despairing work to try to start a girl just now. Only the ones who are already great friends of the men know when they come home on leave and by the time one sees them anywhere they are engaged for every night."[30] It was a new twist to the social life that everything was done on the telephone, so you had to know who to ring up.[31] Still, Evie and Dorothy planned as many dinners with plays or dancing as they could cram in. They continued to use Victor's brother's house as their entertainment base.

Blanche arrived in early February, just in time for a big dinner-and-dance party. Less than a month later, Evie wrote to Victor that Ivan Cobbold had proposed to Blanche, who had not yet agreed to the marriage. Evie investigated Ivan, asking her friends about his character. She found out that the family had money – they were in the brewing business – and she interviewed Ivan himself. She thought him a nice boy, but rather immature. However, Ivan had been in the army, and as his father wrote to Evie, "boys of 22 today ... who have stared death in the face are much older than their years."[32] Evie finally agreed that Ivan was a nice, clean, thoughtful boy. Mervyn Ridley, one of the former ADCs, thought that Ivan would marry Dorothy and that Blanche would not be enough of a companion for him, but Evie wrote to Victor that she was "sure she will be, if only she takes the trouble to read the papers and continues to talk over what is going on in the world. At present she merely looks very pretty and talks only about the most obvious things."[33] Indeed, Blanche's letters reveal her to have a rather pedestrian mind compared to the spark of intellect evident in Dorothy's and Maud's letters. But when Evie suggested a longer engagement, and that Blanche could come back to Canada with her, "there was a wail from both of them."[34] So the wedding was arranged.

Since May weddings were supposed to be unlucky, the wedding was planned for 30 April. It did not leave much time for the negotiations about a marriage settlement, but with a few letters and cables that was arranged, this time with Ivan providing a proper will. Before the wedding, Evie took a party to Lismore Castle, where Blanche and Ivan could spend some time together. But Evie did not mean them to be too close. She told Victor, "I have just caught him [Ivan] coming away from Blanche's room – very naughty of him."[35] For the honeymoon, the young couple planned to take a train to Scotland. Evie "had a rather embarrassing talk with Ivan … and made sure that he does not mean anything to take place on the train," but she was not sure he would stick to this resolution.[36] "One can only hope the marriage won't be 'consummated' in the night mail to Scotland. I can't imagine anything more disagreeable!"[37]

Blanche was serenely happy. "Those two go about holding each other's hands in the most barefaced way," Evie wrote to Victor.[38] Blanche's few weeks acting as Victor's hostess, without her sisters to take on the social duties, seemed to have brought her out of her shell. Evie told Lady Edward, "We have had the nicest letters from Canada about Blanche; she had become very popular."[39] She was indeed very pretty. "Her happiness gives her just the something that she lacked before," Evie told Victor.[40]

Ivan's father came to see Evie about the marriage settlement. The senior Cobbold proposed to give the couple one of his Scottish lodges on Loch Rannoch[41] and a house in London. He proposed "to take Ivan into the firm as a paid partner, giving him £4000 [more than $300,000 Canadian today] a year as a salary for doing nothing as he wishes him to stop on in the Guards for the present. Then he said he would settle £20,000 [£931,000 or about $1.5 million Canadian today] on him and I think the same on Blanche." Evie discussed with Mr Cobbold making arrangement for children should Ivan predecease him, in order to avoid Maud's problem. "Altogether," she added, "it looks very comfortable and promising and the boy is really very attractive."[42]

Blanche and Ivan were married on 30 April 1919 at the Guards Chapel, Wellington Barracks in St James's Park, Westminster. Bridesmaids included Dorothy, Ivan's sister Pamela Cobbold, and two others. Eddy, Moucher, and Maud attended, and Victor's mother was escorted by her niece, Blanche Egerton. A choir preceded the bride up the aisle, singing the "Old Hundredth." Lord Richard Nevill, who as usher escorted people to their pews, including Sir George and Lady Perley, reported that "a page lost his shoe and had to hoble [sic] down the aisle after the Bride and Bridegroom."[43] Lord Lansdowne reported, "There was a wondrous show of presents. I did not know the world contained so many coffee cups."[44] A reception followed at Lansdowne House in London.[45] In Ottawa, Victor celebrated the event with a dinner and dance for seventy-four at Rideau Hall.[46]

Evie was ambivalent about going back to Ottawa; she toyed with the idea of not going back at all. She wrote to Victor from Lismore Castle: "Dorothy groaned at the thought of going back to Canada. I nearly sent you a cable to say I could not come back!"[47] But that would not have been Evie, who knew her duty and valued her reputation. She knew her engagement with Canada had slipped a little. She had said to Victor in 1917, when he was out west after Maud's wedding, "I still feel that it is a pity I did not do the tour with you."[48] Evie knew she should take part in a western tour. "It will seriously affect my popularity not to have been there [the west] in the first three years."[49] As well, there had been talk in Ottawa when she and her party left so shortly after the armistice.[50] As Victor put it, "I gather that there is a certain amount of disappointment in Ottawa that immediately peace came there was such a clearance."[51]

Evie and Dorothy left England aboard the HMS *Olympia* and arrived in Ottawa on 18 May. When he met them at the station, Victor was surprised to find that Evie was very fit and well, not at all tired.[52] Though it had been a busy five months, Evie had accomplished her goals and more. Evie had been in her element.

☙

CHAPTER 16

The Winnipeg General Strike

While Evie was in England, early in 1919, she wrote to Victor that she found England beset by striking workers and restless people. "Over here even the most optimistic feel that we are living on the edge of a volcano and that all expense must be kept down."[1] And later: "The strikes are very serious – and the general tone of London to my mind rather disquieting. There is an absolute craze for amusement – quite natural and harmless – but not really wholesome … People say: 'How shall we live in our country places again.' which *is* a horrid conundrum – but it won't be solved by people shutting up shop and coming to dance in London."[2] And later still: "Some people think we shall be at war again in a few weeks, others that there will be a real revolution."[3]

Victor also read about strikes in Glasgow and Belfast, and was concerned that all the unrest might spill over into Canada.[4] He knew that fitting returning soldiers into a peacetime economy created the potential for labour unrest. In February, he told his mother that, so far, the labour difficulties experienced in England had not been transported to Canada. "If we can get through the next six or seven weeks without trouble we ought to be fairly safe."[5]

In December 1918, at a meeting at the Walker Theatre in Winnipeg, speakers expressed concern about the government still running the Dominion of Canada as if it were at war: orders-in-council under the War Measures Act, military intervention in Russia, the incarceration of political prisoners. Co-sponsors of the meeting were the Winnipeg Trades and Labor Council and the Socialist Party of Canada. A labour conference, held in Calgary in March 1919, including some of the same people, discussed reorganizing workers into One Big Union (OBU) rather than in craft groups of workers with particular skills. The resolution for the OBU went to a steering committee with instructions to prepare propaganda and draft a referendum to see whether members agreed with the concept.[6]

In February 1919, amid considerable labour unrest in the United States, Seattle shipyard workers demanded increased wages after two years of wartime restraint. When they were denied, they called for other unions to join them in a general strike. It lasted only five days. The strike committee organized to maintain essential services, but the government called in federal troops to keep the peace, and several unions just went back to work. Although no violence occurred during the strike and no one found any evidence of its leaders planning to establish a Seattle Soviet, many believed it was inspired by Bolshevism. They blamed the Industrial Workers of the World (IWW, also called the "Wobblies") for fomenting revolution, believing the union intended to take over the state.[7] The press was full of these fears. Toronto's *Saturday Night* magazine took a stern view of the Seattle strike, saying: "Prompt action to assert governmental authority is absolutely necessary; redress of grievances, if they exist, can come later. Toleration of Bolshevism even in its most incipient stages bears incalculable consequence."[8]

The duke's response to these fears was a watch-and-wait attitude. He did write to Evie about the speaker of the House of Commons, the Honourable Edgar Rhodes, who was very emphatic that the governor general ought not to be far away during the coming parliamentary session. "He told me I had a distinctly moderating influence here and both Ministers and MPs had confidence and reliance on me. I hope it is so."[9]

The six to seven weeks after mid-February that the duke had hoped would complete the country's transition to peacetime work passed without incident in Canada. The storm finally broke on 15 May. "Afraid there is a very critical state in Winnipeg with a general strike on," the duke noted in his diary.[10] He saw Sir Thomas White, the acting prime minister, who was glad to report that Sir Robert Borden would soon be starting back from the Peace Conference in Europe. Both men thought the country would be calmer with Borden at the helm. White told the duke that he thought the strike would have to run its course.

On day four of the strike, the duke invited Senator Gideon Robertson, minister of Labour in the Union government, to luncheon. Robertson, with his labour background, had managed to settle the Winnipeg Strike of 1918, which had involved 14,000 workers.[11] The strikers felt that the settlement had favoured their unions.[12] Robertson was again called into service in 1919, travelling to Winnipeg with Arthur Meighen, who was acting for the Justice minister, Charles Doherty.[13]

In Winnipeg, a Citizens' Committee of One Thousand was formed to rally opposition to the strike. Membership was secret – no list of members was ever made public, no records kept of its meetings. Even today there is little evidence to suggest that it had more than a few members. The committee, apparently run by prominent Winnipeg men, published its own newspaper and organized volunteers to maintain emergency services, such as fire, water pumps, gasoline pumps, and telephone.[14] Labour, too, had its own newspaper, the *Western Labour News*, and a strike committee of five leaders.

Though the tension between labour and employers had been building for weeks, the spark for the general strike was the employers' refusal to negotiate with the newly organized Metal Trades Council, an industry-wide umbrella organization. Although not yet the OBU, the Metal Trades Council was seen as a move in that direction. Workers demanded shorter working hours (fifty-five hours a week was usual), higher wages to make up for wartime inflation, which had cut purchasing power in half,[15] and the right to collective bargaining rather than separate negotiations for each craft union. Thousands of unionized and non-unionized workers joined the strike. Telephone, railway, postal, streetcar, and movie theatre workers stopped work, along with elevator operators and firemen. Police wanted to join the strike, but strike leaders asked them to remain on the job, fearing the government would use their absence as a pretext to impose martial law.[16]

The government, the Citizens' Committee, and the press thought that the strike had been fomented by "aliens," by which they meant foreigners. The returned soldiers also resented these "aliens" because they had not served in the war. They were especially resentful of those who came from enemy countries. Even the duke, who tended to think the best of people, was influenced by what he read. He wrote to his mother on 11 May, when there were walkouts in Winnipeg but the

Winnipeg General Strike was still a few days away: "The unrest is showing signs of increasing and we have had one or two quite unjustifiable strikes. It is very difficult to get any definite proof but there appears to be a secret influence at work. At one time I did not think any such movement would make much headway, but I am afraid there must be something."[17]

The duke kept careful track of developments in the strike; his diary comments followed the information in the press. At first, he thought the strike would be settled within a week (18 May), but when it dragged on, he worried about sympathetic strikes elsewhere in Canada (24 May). When such strikes began in Edmonton and Calgary, the duke met with Sir Edward Kemp, minister of Militia and Defence – "he didn't have much to say" – and Major General Gwatkin, chief of staff of the Canadian Militia, who "seemed easy in his mind as far as military conditions in the west were concerned" (27 May). This was the duke's opportunity to exercise his rights as governor general: the right to be informed, the right to advise, the right to warn. He must also have felt responsible for the civil order because he had been given the power to call out the troops without civilian request after the Quebec City riots a year earlier, though that power had been granted only for disturbances against the Military Service Act.[18]

The information coming out of Winnipeg was sparse, however, because the strike committee had closed down the press, telephone, and telegraph. Postal workers and railway mail clerks left their jobs in sympathetic strikes. Life in Winnipeg became fraught with problems. Food was difficult to obtain because bread and milk truck drivers had walked out, and bakeries and restaurants were closed by the strikers; ice was hard to get, and water pressure was low. Moving around the city was also a problem since streetcar drivers and elevator operators had walked out; gas for automobiles was sold only to farmers, doctors, and members of the strike committee. The city, with a population of about 150,000, came to a standstill with 30,000 workers off the job.

There were some attempts at mediation between the industrial employers and the Metal Trades Council, but these finally failed. The strikers stuck to their demands, especially for collective bargaining. They might have compromised on hours of work, but the employers and the governments, city and federal, insisted that the sympathetic strikes must be called off by the Central Strike Committee before they would nego-tiate further. On that demand, they could not agree.

When a general strike was called in Toronto in sympathy with the Winnipeg strikers, the duke met at his office on 30 May with Arthur Meighen, minister of the Interior, who told him that "the strike was broken in Winnipeg but would last for some time owing to the sym-pathetic strikes elsewhere."[19] The Winnipeg strikers began a new tactic, parading each day from Market Square to the Legislative Build-ing to ask Premier Tobias Norris to either resign or enact legislation favourable to the strikers' demands. Predictably, Norris would do nei-ther. Also predictably, the parades began to get out of hand. The city swore in additional special policemen, most of them returned soldiers, because some policemen were still not back at work.[20] On 11 June, a man was injured in a fight between the special police and strikers at Portage and Main, Winnipeg's iconic town centre. "It so happened he had a V.C. [Victoria Cross] and will probably stir up considerable sym-pathy," the duke wrote.[21] The mayor threatened to call in the militia if there was any further rioting, and the next day four foreigners involved in the rioting were arrested.

In Ottawa, Parliament rushed through legislation that empowered it to deport revolutionists, anarchists, rioters, and agitators, including British subjects. Senator Robertson travelled again to Winnipeg. On the morning of 18 June, the duke recorded what he read in the papers: "Drastic steps have been taken in Winnipeg by arresting many leaders." Ten strike leaders had been arrested under the Criminal Code for sedi-tious conspiracy (inciting the police force to neglect of duty), and war-rants were issued for the arrest of four more. Two more were later charged with seditious libel (publishing an article saying the police force had been replaced by thugs). Winnipeg's Mayor Charles F. Gray did not agree with the arrests as he thought the strike was about to collapse, but Robertson and A.J. Andrews, a prominent Winnipeg lawyer and leader of the Citizens' Committee, had decided to make the arrests, apparently believing that the strike leaders were not about to let go of the strike. Two days later, the strike leaders were out on bail.

On Saturday, 21 June, the day that would later be called "Bloody Saturday," despite Mayor Gray's proclamation that no parades would be tolerated, a group of returned soldiers sympathetic to the strike decided to hold a silent parade to protest "the denial of free speech" and "the Russian methods adopted by the present government."[22] The mayor called in the Royal North-West Mounted Police and later the militia. When the parade assembled, the mayor read the Riot Act and the mounted police charged into the crowd. Confusion followed, a partially overturned streetcar was set on fire, and several shots were fired. One person was killed and several were injured, one of whom later died. About one hundred were arrested. On Wednesday, 25 June, the strike collapsed and most strikers went back to work. The next day it was officially called off.

The provincial government agreed to establish a royal commission to investigate the origin and nature of the strike, and the metal workers' hours were reduced from fifty-five to fifty a week. The strikers received no other concessions, no pay raise, no agreement to collective bargaining. Many sympathy strikers had to reapply for their jobs, and some were not rehired. The arrested men were tried and, of the sixteen originally detained, nine were convicted, one acquitted, three deported, and the charges against the others dropped. Seven were subsequently elected to public office, some in 1920 while they were still in prison. One of those elected was J.S. Woodsworth, editor of the *Western Labour News*, who became a member of Parliament and, in 1933, the first leader of the Co-operative Commonwealth Federation (CCF), which later became the New Democratic Party.[23]

Settling the strike removed more than one major worry for the duke. Planning for the visit to Canada of the young, handsome Prince of Wales was already underway, and the duke had thought it unwise for him to travel the country during a period of labour unrest. The duke must have breathed a sigh of relief.

❧

CHAPTER 17

The Duty and Pleasure of Summer 1919

When Evie returned to Ottawa, she brought along her friend and confidante Blanche Egerton, Victor's first cousin, who, at forty-eight, was unmarried. Though Blanche had her own home at Weybridge, outside London, during the war she had spent many days at Carlos Place in London with Victor's mother, her own Aunt Emma. It was Blanche who had written from Carlos Place in February 1918 during an air raid, when both women were frightened and cold as the enemy bombs landed nearby. Undoubtedly, both Victor and Evie were grateful for her attention to Victor's mother. In Canada they enjoyed her company. "She is a splendid person for out here as she enjoys everything and is interested in every one," Evie wrote to Lady Edward.[1] Blanche's letters to Victor's mother, written during her time in Canada, provide a different perspective on some events in the summer and fall of 1919.

Both Evie and Victor were aware of themselves as historical figures, and on her return to Canada, Evie was determined to do her duty, even if it included a western tour. Evie hated the tours, travelling by train, meeting new people every day. She often suffered from lumbago, which was made worse by train travel and by sleeping in a different bed each night. She also worried about having colitis. Many post-menopausal women would sympathize with these difficulties. But Evie's situation was made even more trying by her naturally introverted personality. She was most comfortable with people she knew, so having Blanche with her was helpful. Though Evie had been trained from birth for her role in society, and she was a master at charming the people she met, socializing endlessly exhausted her; she often took to her bed for a day to recover. Victor was just the opposite. He thrived on meeting new people, seeing new parts of the country, finding out about the political and economic situation of each new place. He planned tours that included as many places and functions as he could possibly fit in. He thrilled at seeing and experiencing everything.

Evie still found Victor difficult to pin down when it came to her own need for quiet times. She complained to her mother, "In all the anxiety of the present time, Victor is the calmest and most contented person I know. He has just enough public work to keep him occupied and does not bother about anything else. It makes him rather cross if I try to discuss plans for the future or things to do with the children, so we just go on from day to day without looking forward much. His distaste for bother about things is increasing. We all rather wonder what will happen when he gets home and details have to be faced. He talks of going home for a fortnight in the winter during Charlie's holidays, but that would not give him time to do any estate business."[2]

So, in the summer of 1919, they both focused on doing their duty. Evie wanted to escape to Blue Sea Lake to see her new house. She managed a single day on 24 May, Queen Victoria's birthday, but they had to rush back to Ottawa for Empire Day, celebrated on Sunday, 25 May.[3] The duke spent "the whole morning trying to put together a speech" for the afternoon.[4] The family and staff attended a service at Christ Church Cathedral before meeting a crowd on Parliament Hill in front of Queen Victoria's statue. Schoolchildren and choirs sang, and citizens gathered to hear the duke speak about the legacy of the queen. "She succeeded to a Kingdom. She left an Empire," he concluded his remarks. The secretary of state, the Honourable Martin Burrell, spoke of the young queen solving political problems in her North American colonies by granting self-government to Canada (he meant the granting of responsible government to Nova Scotia and the Province of Canada in 1848, and to Prince Edward Island in 1851 and New Brunswick in 1854). He also spoke of the great unifying force of allegiance to the Throne.[5]

When the weather got unexpectedly warm in early June, Evie's and Victor's social plans were in full swing. Evie wrote to Lady Edward, "We have just had two garden parties, one of 600, the other about 2000, rather trying to shake hands with so many in the middle of a heat wave!"[6] Blanche Egerton told Lady Edward, "We've had the hottest garden party imaginable, never felt anything like it."[7] Victor, on the other hand, reported to his mother, "I must say I like it [the heat] but most people appear to find it rather trying."[8] There was little relief as Rideau Hall did not have air conditioning. Blanche wrote, "It is so hot that we've been motoring after dinner."[9]

A few days later, when they embarked on a tour of the Thousand Islands district of southeastern Ontario, the heat was still intense. The party, including Victor, Evie, Blanche, Dorothy, Rachel, three ADCs – Macmillan, Haddington, and Cator – and Lord Richard Nevill left by special train for Oshawa. Living on the train, they visited shoreline communities along the St Lawrence River, making their way downriver through Belleville, Kingston, and Cornwall in Ontario to Valleyfield, Quebec, and smaller places in between. In each community, there were the usual speeches of welcome before enthusiastic crowds, visits to hospitals and schools, drives around the country, receptions and dinners, all in the scorching heat of an Ontario summer.

As usual, Evie found the touring difficult. Two days into the tour she was upset that they visited two towns in one day, Port Hope and Cobourg,[10] but this time she was determined to do her full part. After a successful day at Belleville, they spent the evening and night at the Rideau Lakes, where the girls could swim and everyone cooled off. Toward the end of the week, she complained to her mother, "We are living on this train, very hot and dusty. A heat wave began before we left Ottawa and it is quite as bad as July – some nights we really can't sleep and the functions in the hot sun are very trying. However, the tour has gone well. The new staff have done admirably and we are all quite pleased. I really think Victor is popular, particularly among the humbler people who like his simple ways. They also think the girls 'so natural' – or 'so plain' as one person expressed it yesterday!"[11]

That same afternoon, while Evie was writing to her mother, Blanche Egerton was writing to Victor's mother from the train beside the Rideau Lakes. "I'm the only one of the party in rude health, at least Victor and I. It does not seem to make any difference to us whether we melt or sleep or what we do. Victor is unfailingly urbane and so civil and cordial to the most unprepossessing of mayors and mayoresses; he is a little more frigid to importunate superiors who run many of the hospitals."

Blanche, who didn't have the same responsibility as Evie, thoroughly enjoyed the tour and regaled Lady Edward with their adventures and follies: "Our first day by boat around the 1000 islands was something too delicious." The boat trip from Kingston to Brockville was on a yacht lent by Mr George Fulford of Brockville.[12] She continued, "I have seen Evie looking dignified and pretty, Victor very solemn, driving around with the perspiring Mayor and Mayoress perched opposite to them on really high music stools, the mayoress so nearly took a header out of the car that Evie had a bilious attack afterward from heat and fright and had to retire from the tour for some hours! Yesterday Victor was made 'Great Father' by the Indians, solemnly walked round in a circle (dressed in a frock coat and top hat) hand-in-hand with dancing chief and four squaws pirouetting round him." Looking out the train window, Blanche wrote, "it is really rather delightful sitting in a siding in a clover field with [the] most delicious wind blowing in – we appreciate it after the grilling functions of the last 7 days. Dorothy and Rachel are picking wild strawberries and I think I must go and help them."[13]

When the tour ended in Valleyfield, Victor left for a fishing trip on the Cascapedia River, which arises out of the Chic-Choc Mountains in the centre of the Gaspé Peninsula and flows south into Chaleur Bay. Like the Restigouche, it is a shallow river with some deeper salmon pools, though it also has some waterfalls that require a portage.

Victor's invitation to fish the Cascapedia arose from work he did for Lord Lansdowne and the Cascapedia Club. Lord Lansdowne had built a cottage on the Cascapedia River in 1884 and named it New Derreen, after his Irish property in County Kerry. He secured a lease from the federal government for exclusive use of a part of the Cascapedia River, paying a small amount for the privilege. He was following in the footsteps of Lord Lorne, who had preceded him as governor general. In 1880, Lorne had been the first to build a cottage on the river to provide some summer comfort for Princess Louise, his royal wife, Queen Victoria's daughter. Lorne had also built two lodges upriver called Middle Camp and Lazy Bogan, places Victor would visit.

Prior to Lord Lorne's tenure, fishing rights to Crown pools had been leased by the government to rich Americans, including R.G. Dun, later of Dun and Bradstreet. The Americans began buying land on the banks in order to have the riparian rights to pools lower than those awarded to the governors general. Lord Lorne, as governor general (1878–83), had been granted land along the river; after his tenure, the privilege was extended to Lord Lansdowne. When Lansdowne left Canada in 1888, he offered his Cascapedia property to Lord Stanley, who succeeded him (1888–93); however, Lady Stanley is reported to have declined living on the river, with its mosquitoes and blackflies. The Stanleys built their own summer house a few miles away at New Richmond on the shores of the Chaleur Bay.[14]

After Lord Stanley's term ended in 1893, the government of Quebec decided not to continue the practice of granting the governors general exclusive use of the river.[15] That left the Americans free to bid for those rights. The departing Lord Stanley turned over New Derreen to the American-owned Cascapedia Club in 1893 and it was used as a clubhouse.[16] In 1918, facing increasing interest in property along the river, the club found they had no records of ownership for part of what had been Lansdowne's property. The club president wrote to Lord Lansdowne asking for his records.

In August 1918, Victor received a letter from Lord Lansdowne saying that he had responded to the president's request by sending the lease and the ground plan for New Derreen, and now he needed Victor's help to clear up the remaining details.[17] Victor wrote to Quebec Premier Sir Lomer Gouin, who reported that while Lord Lansdowne had transferred the property to Lord Stanley, there was no record of what Stanley had done with it. He suggested that the club search for documents in the local registrar's office.[18] When they found nothing, Victor wrote to Lord Stanley's son, Lord Derby, then at the Paris Peace Conference, who managed to find the necessary documents and send them to the club.[19] Victor's reward was a trip to the Cascapedia River in June 1919.

Accompanied by Harry Cator, his ADC, Victor arrived at Matapedia, Quebec, by train on 20 June 1919. They were met by the club president, who drove them by motor over bumpy, dusty roads to New Derreen

Figure 17.1 Cottage at Blue Sea Lake, Quebec, 1919.

Lodge on the Cascapedia River. Victor was thrilled once again to be in the backcountry, still rather wild and untamed despite the road along the river. He told Evie there was little left of the original cottage except the chimney, but the plain and comfortable surroundings suited him. "I have got a bath in my room ... with a lid. Cold water is turned on, but the hot has to be brought in a bucket."[20] On this fishing trip he wrote fewer letters to Evie than he had from the Restigouche. Perhaps Harry Cator was a better companion than the jumpy Tommy Clive had been.

On their first night, the duke and Harry went out fishing at 5:00 p.m. and stayed until 10:00 p.m., when it was too dark to fish. Victor caught five fish and Harry four. The next day they started early and walked upriver for a mile. Victor caught six fish averaging twenty-six pounds. Over three days around New Derreen, they killed twenty-seven fish between them. In his carefully typed records, Victor noted how many fish he caught with each type of fly: Dusty Miller –nineteen; Jock Scott – seven, Black Dose – nine; Silver Doctor – two.[21]

For Victor, the Cascapedia was "the best fishing water I have ever seen,"[22] but the hot, sunny days were perfect for everything except fishing – fishermen believe that fish bite better when the sun is off the water. The limit was twelve each day, and most days they did not reach that, but the fish were even bigger than those he had caught on the Magdalen River. His Cascapedia fish weighed from twenty-six to thirty-three pounds. Each day they fished on into the dark, which was quite late in the June evenings.

During the week, Victor and Harry moved on to Lord Lorne's Middle Camp, walking much of the seven-mile journey and canoeing where they could. After two days of good fishing, they moved on up to another camp, Tracadie, and finally to Lazy Bogan, which was thirty-four miles above New Derreen. Again they had to walk part of the way.[23] There were no horses for towing on this river. At Lazy Bogan, accommodation was in tents. To Victor's surprise, he spent a comfortable night, "not at all cold."[24] Here, Victor began to feel some guilt about fishing in the salmon spawning grounds, though they "certainly had great sport."[25] In three hours, Victor caught eight fish averaging over twenty-three pounds. "It is almost poaching as they come so quick."[26]

At Lazy Bogan, the seasonal limit was twelve fish per angler. Victor and Harry both met their quota by the second day. It was time to retrace their steps downriver. In ten days Victor had killed thirty-seven fish with a total weight of 868 pounds, an average of more than 23 pounds. Harry's total was thirty-five fish.[27] On their last day they became tourists, visiting Lorne Cottage on the Cascapedia and Stanley House in New Richmond before boarding the train.

Though Victor continued to fish in Canada when he could – at Blue Sea Lake, in western Canada, and later in the Dominion of Newfoundland – he never again reached the heights of excitement and pure thrill of fishing in the great Gaspé salmon rivers. This was truly the sport of kings.

In late June, when Victor left for his fishing trip, Evie and her party hurried up to Blue Sea Lake, where the house was almost complete. When they arrived at the newly named New Lismore train stop,[28] across the lake from the new house, the wind was blowing a gale; they could not take canoes across the choppy water. George, the footman, and

Geordie Haddington, an ADC, took Evie and Miss Walton over in a skiff; they shipped a lot of water and got soaked. The family's boat, the *Sally Anne*, was out of order. To ferry the party of thirteen across the lake by skiff would have been a lengthy business. Finally, neighbours, "the DeRosiers, came to the rescue and took the whole day bringing people and luggage across." Evie was concerned. "It is really dangerous to leave us here without a motor boat or a motor [automobile] or horses, as we are utterly cut off from civilization." Despite these worries, she made no plans to go back to Ottawa.[29] Evie blamed Dick Nevill for the complications of their camp life. "We have got a vast retinue of servants ... but it is no use to try and lead the simple life with Dick in control."[30] Blanche Egerton agreed that "the happy-go-lucky life there is rather a thing of the past as an eleven bedroom house with inadequate kitchen won't be as easily run as a picnic in tents."[31]

Though the house was new, again this year there were the usual cottage problems: the plumbing leaked; the boathouse didn't exist yet; the engine of their motor boat, the *Sally Anne*, had given up, Dorothy was sunburned and had blotches on her face from some poisonous plant. Evie was not fazed by these problems, or by the insects. "The mosquitoes range themselves up in squadrons on the netting and march backward and forwards trying to find a mesh large enough to squeeze through," she told Victor, but she did not think that was a reason to quit the cottage.[32] Cousin Blanche, though, declined the first trip to Blue Sea. "It has been so hot that as I don't bathe and am very bad with mosquito bites, and not good at house carpentry I chose the lazy life and left Evie, Dorothy, Macmillan and Ld Haddington to go off to Blue Sea and get the house settled."[33]

By July, the house was finished. It was a delight – two storeys, lots of bedrooms ready for their extended family, a big wraparound verandah where any extras could sleep, but a small kitchen to feed so many. They rarely had fewer than ten people in residence, and sometimes twice that. Victor thought the house looked top-heavy, but when the windows were all open it improved.[34] While Evie was in England, she and Victor had discussed in their letters the installation of a turbine to produce electricity and a pump to bring water from the lake. The exact resolution of those problems did not get mentioned in the letters, but it is apparent that, by late June, the boathouse was built, the plumbing no longer leaked, and the boat engine was running. Even the flower beds against the house were ready. Under Evie's instructions, Harold Macmillan and Geordie Haddington had planted "scarlet runners, cannas, geraniums, asters, petunias, ageratums in groups."[35] By the time Victor was back from Cascapedia in early July, everything was in order.

Evie enjoyed watching the boys and girls at play. However, as she wrote to Victor, "Dorothy and Macmillan gave me a fright yesterday. They started out in the cedar canoe with a bath towel as a sail and disappeared from sight. I got a panic as the wind rose and sent the skiff in one direction and Geordie's kicker, which had just been mounted, in another. They appeared at last, having sailed to the end of the lake and been obliged to paddle back against the wind. The canoe had shipped a lot of water in which they were sitting very happily."[36] Harold Macmillan returned to Ottawa looking "like a small boy at the end of the holidays," but a few days later he returned with the mast and sail for the canoe. "This will save GH [Government House] bath towels," Evie wrote.[37]

With Victor back from his fishing trip and the house prepared, July at Blue Sea was idyllic. Even cousin Blanche seemed to enjoy the properly prepared house. Evie reported to Lady Edward: "Victor loved his fishing but is very happy here doing nothing. It is too hot to exert oneself much though the young ones never seem quiet for more than a few minutes. They swim, generally three times a day, fish for bass in the lake, pick raspberries and strawberries, ... cut down trees, clear paths, sing choruses, play mouth organs, so that one has a feeling of a very busy life."[38]

As they had in previous summers, on Sundays they motored by boat across the lake to the little Anglican church called St. George's-by-the-Lake, where the duke read the lesson.[39] Evie and Blanche took up sketching at Blue Sea. Blanche found it difficult to make pictures of her surroundings. "It is just lake, sky, dense wood, and thin poor little scrub and flatish [sic] hills in the distance," she complained to Lady Edward.[40] Sketching was one of Evie's favourite activities.

Victor's time at the lake that summer proved to be short; he was required in Ottawa.

While Evie was in England, Victor had received a letter from Lord Stamfordham, the king's private secretary, saying that the Prince of Wales – Prince Edward, the eldest son of King George V[41] – was keen to visit Canada as soon as possible.[42] Victor relayed the information to Evie,[43] who replied that she had spoken to his mother, Queen Mary. "H[er] M[ajesty] told me that he must get to know about things in England and marry first and she thought he had better not do the Dominions till he had been married a year because of a probable baby, etc. I could not, for obvious reasons, argue that he should come and stay with us first!"[44] But Evie thought the prince would get his way and not be dictated to by Mama.[45]

The prince, who was then twenty-five, had spent some time with the Canadian Corps in France, and they had "fired his imagination with descriptions of sporting expeditions, trips into the backwoods and other adventures which he could only do 'en garçon.'"[46] In a letter to Evie, Lord Stamfordham stressed that he had impressed upon the young prince that he must also make official visits, receive addresses, and make himself popular with all classes. "The throne is the connecting link which will keep the Empire together," he had told the prince,[47] and "the heir apparent carries *very great* responsibility, especially as regards the overseas Dominions."[48]

Someone warned Evie that the prince must not be bored by too many functions.[49] Dorothy had a solution to that problem. "We will take him to Blue Sea and upset his canoe," she told her mother.[50] She undoubtedly would have done so given the chance. The informer also told Evie quite pointedly that the prince was "an extremely attractive young man," with the obvious implication that she had attractive daughters. "We ought to be all the more careful to let the girls see as many other nice men as possible," Evie wrote to Victor.[51] Whether she would have favoured a marriage between one of her girls and the heir to the British throne is not clear. Perhaps not, as at one point she noted to Victor, "If he is likely to be naughty he had far better stay away as we don't want scandals in Canada. I shall tell Stamfordham so,"[52] which no doubt she did. Evie also told Stamfordham that seven weeks would not be enough for the prince to do his duties in all the big places, see the Prairies, and have some fun.[53] Stamfordham wrote to Victor saying he thought the Prince would be willing to stay long enough to earn "that proud distinction – so odiously described – of a real sport!!"[54]

While Evie was in England, the visit was still just an idea. Stamfordham told Victor that the king did not want the prince to visit any Dominions until the peace was settled, and then probably in the following year. "I understand the parliament buildings will be ready for opening and this would be a good peg upon which to hang the visit!"[55] He meant 1920.

However, when Evie arrived in Ottawa in May 1919, she heard from a Canadian senator that the prince would visit that August. Evie was irate that her well-kept secret was out.[56] Victor also thought, "It is disgraceful that I should not have been told."[57] Apparently, Prime Minister Borden, just before leaving London after the Peace Conference, had had an audience with the king and the Prince of Wales. Borden had then cabled the acting prime minister, Sir Thomas White, to tell him that the king proposed the prince should leave in early August and open the new Parliament Buildings.[58] White replied that "Council heartily approves" and, though the buildings would not be ready, the prince could lay a cornerstone on 1 September, the same date that the original cornerstone had been laid in 1867 by the current prince's grandfather when he was Prince of Wales.[59]

The duke was not happy. Not only had he not been involved in this decision, but he thought it "[v]ery doubtful if it is wise for him to come here with the country in tense condition."[60] The Winnipeg General Strike was still in progress. In addition, it would complicate the duke's own summer travel[61] – and the summer cottage life of Ottawa locals.[62]

Despite the duke's reservations, the prince was coming, and only nine weeks remained to make plans. The duke appointed his military secretary, Colonel Henderson, and Borden appointed Sir Joseph Pope, under-secretary of state for external affairs, to plan the visit. Together, Henderson and Pope began to flesh out the itinerary.

Although Victor loved the heat and the comfort of Rideau Hall, he also wanted to be at Blue Sea with his family. He travelled back and forth, taking whatever time he could afford away from the office to relax at the elegant new house. Planning the prince's visit took most of July.

It was a tedious job. Even though Pope and Henderson were doing most of the work, Victor received memos saying that the prince did not want any "official" breakfast meetings, that he was to land in Halifax on a Sunday, which the duke knew would be inconvenient, and that the plans made for Quebec City had to be changed. Victor was also working on his own tour of western Canada, but he and his party would first go east to greet the prince in August.

By the end of July, the family's summer cottage time was over and they all returned to Ottawa to prepare for their departure. While Victor remained in Ottawa to swear in a new finance minister,[63] Evie took the others to Quebec City. The Citadel was being refurbished for the prince's visit. Blanche Egerton described the scene for Lady Edward: "We had a hectic time at Quebec settling colours of walls and chintz curtains. I think Evie is now content and has nullified Ld Richard's choices!"[64]

Victor finally arrived, and the whole family embarked aboard the yacht HMCS *Hochelaga* to begin their trip down the St Lawrence River. The *Hochelaga*, 193 feet in length, with a full crew, had been a commissioned patrol vessel of the Royal Canadian Navy during the war. At the urging of Sir Charles Fitzpatrick, former chief justice and now the new lieutenant-governor of Quebec, Victor stopped at Murray Bay (now La Malbaie) to visit Sir Lomer Gouin, premier of Quebec. They had a long talk, and though nothing was settled, Victor thought Gouin was "favorably disposed to come or to suggest to some of his colleagues to do so."[65] Probably this refers to the possibility of his joining the federal government – Gouin had resisted entreaties to join the Union government in 1917, but he did eventually win a federal seat and join the Liberals under Mackenzie King in 1921.

The trip down the St Lawrence River had a strict time schedule. The duke was expected in Saint John, New Brunswick, on 15 August to greet the prince. He also wanted to visit the Saguenay area, which he had missed in 1917 when Evie and her crew were there. Their first stop was at Tadoussac, at the mouth of the Saguenay River, where they visited the summer home of the Earl of Dufferin, governor general from 1872 to 1878. For once, young Anne was allowed to come on an extended trip; however, as Blanche told Aunt Emma, "Anne chose to fall in off a very steep rock and swam about till her two sisters presented her each with a leg and she pulled herself out by her sisters' toes."[66] Fortunately Anne had learned to swim at Blue Sea Lake.

Along the Saguenay there were no plans for their reception, since everyone was busy with plans for the Prince of Wales's tour. Blanche wrote to Lady Edward, "we've just seen a few mayors, managers of works, and visited a mill and convent or two then enjoyed ourselves in old clothes, and fished, sketched."[67] Despite Evie's assertions that Victor liked doing nothing, his diary belies that impression. He arranged for himself a very active holiday. The yacht travelled up the Saguenay Fjord between its high, forested hills to the town of Ha! Ha! Bay (now La Baie, part of the city of Saguenay), then the company motored to Jonquière. As well as enjoying meeting mayors and priests, the duke was fascinated with the operations of the pulp and paper mills and met with their owners, Sir William Price and Julien-Édouard-Alfred Dubuc. These men accompanied the duke's party on the train from Jonquière to Lac St-Jean. "First time I have travelled in anything except our own cars and I have no wish to repeat the experience," Victor confided to his diary.[68] Although Victor did like his comforts, he could forgo them in order to visit what seemed to him to be the most remote parts of Canada. In fact, this area had been populated for over four hundred years by French and English immigrants and had been an important part of the fur trade in early Canada. Even before the immigrants arrived, the Montagnais First Nation had claimed it as a major part of their territory.

Now a complication threatened to delay them. Their son Charlie was sailing back to Canada, but they did not know when he would arrive. A message reached them that Charlie was on the ss *Metagama*, a Canadian-owned steamship that had functioned as a troop carrier during the war and was still ferrying returning soldiers back to Canada. The duke and Harold Macmillan worked together to arrange for Charlie to land where they could pick him up. For several days the messages were garbled. Finally they got a message through that he should land at Rimouski on the St Lawrence River. The *Hochelaga* reached Rimouski on 8 August, but the *Metagama* would be delayed another three or four days. They could not afford to wait, so Harold Macmillan stayed to meet Charlie and take him to Campbellton, New Brunswick. For two days the *Hochelaga* journeyed through rough seas. Only Blanche "succumbed"; no one else was seasick, though Evie stayed in bed all of one day.

When they reached Gaspé, they found that the mayor was in Ottawa for the Liberal convention that had just elected William Lyon Mackenzie King as the new leader, replacing the late Sir Wilfrid Laurier. The *Hochelaga* party moved on through Chaleur Bay to Campbellton, where they found Charlie and Harold waiting. Next day, Victor took Charlie fishing on the Restigouche River; father and son stopped for dinner in the luxury of the Restigouche Salmon Club in Matapedia.

The duke departed in time to make his rendezvous with the Prince of Wales in Saint John, New Brunswick. Blanche reported to Lady Edward that while he was away "we've been visiting the haunts of Evie's childhood, walking along sea shores in search of fossils." Evie had spent summers on the Cascapedia River with her father in the 1880s. Blanche continued, "We had a nice meeting with a woman called 'Noni' whom Evie remembered as a little girl of 4 and who remembered Evie as the giver of a wax doll!"[69]

Before reaching Canada, the Prince of Wales stopped at St John's in Newfoundland, then a British Dominion, to a tumultuous welcome.[70] The citizens of Saint John, New Brunswick, the first in Canada to welcome him, thus had a precedent to live up to, and they did it well. When the prince disembarked from HMS *Renown*, "one of the finest war vessels in the Royal Navy,"[71] cheer after cheer rang out as they greeted their future sovereign and "the street crowds seemed to have been infused with new life," the Toronto *Globe* gushed.[72] Saint John declared a two-day holiday to celebrate both the prince and the returned soldiers.[73] The governor general and the prime minister were among the dignitaries on the dock.

The young, handsome prince appeared to enjoy all the events, especially the afternoon of dancing at the lieutenant-governor's reception. The duke, who was also present there, labelled it "a rather tiresome function, especially the dancing." However, that evening he was invited to dine with the prince on board HMS *Dauntless*, and they had a

Figure 17.2 The handsome Prince of Wales with an admirer. He visited Canada from August until November 1919.

nice conversation, which redeemed the day for him.[74] The *Dauntless*, a heavily armed Royal Navy cruiser, had gone out to Newfoundland to meet the prince's ships, HMS *Renown*, which carried the prince, and the light cruiser HMS *Dragon*. All three ships would accompany the prince to Quebec City.

Having greeted the prince on his arrival in Canada, the duke could get back to his family and move on to Quebec City, where he would welcome the prince to the Citadel. Returning to Campbellton, the duke took the *Hochelaga* back up the St Lawrence River, accompanied by Rachel and Charlie. Evie and the others went back by train because Dorothy had complained of headaches on the ship. Though no one mentioned it, her headaches might have had something to do with the fact that Harold Macmillan was going on the train. By this time, Harold and Dorothy were spending a lot of time together. Though Evie worried about the two of them, she could not send him packing before the prince completed his tour.

The family reconvened at the Citadel in Quebec City just in time to get things straight before the prince arrived fresh from triumphant tours of Halifax and Charlottetown. Blanche wrote to Lady Edward: "We are making frantic preparations for the P. of W. Evie has taken to her bed with a bilious headache. We are all quite sure what we've done won't be quite right. I've put palms about, Harry Cator [and] Miss Saunders are doing placement for dinner of 80, Ld R is trying to keep [calm?] the cook, who is in a tantrum. Victor is calmly playing golf. The upholsterer [and] clerk of the works are feverishly rushing round with cushion covers and dabs of paint ... Evie is pleased on the whole with the repainting and reupholstering of the drawing room and ball room. The 'tent room' ... we hope will be so full of people that no one will notice the hideous green carpet and terra cotta border."[75]

Next day, 21 August, the three ships made a show of British sea power as they sailed majestically up the St Lawrence River to drop anchor at the King's Wharf exactly on schedule at 5:00 p.m. Small craft, gaily decorated with colourful pennants, hovered around on the water. On land, the population turned out in the tens of thousands to acclaim Prince Edward Albert, the young Prince of Wales.[76] "Huron Indians left their ox teams on the reserve at Lorette and came into the city to see His Royal Highness." "The quaint Quebec habitant, bulwark against Bolshevism, abandoned the harvest field ... and Veterans who had served in France with the Prince of Wales," were among the cheering crowd. An airplane circled overhead and engaged in "daring stunts." Prominent men, including the duke, stood on the wharf as the mammoth battle cruiser roared out a royal salute, and the prince came down the gangplank and shook hands all around. He then inspected the guard of veterans, many of whom had served with him in France. Red, white, and blue balloons were released from the Citadel on the hill above. His motor car moved through the bunting-clad streets, while he waved his cap to enthusiastic crowds amid a crescendo of cheering.[77]

That night, the duke and duchess hosted a formal dinner at the governor general's residence in the Citadel, followed by fireworks and dancing. The next day, the viceregal couple was offered luncheon on the *Renown* and a tour of the battleship. "She is certainly a wonder and one felt very proud of the navy," the duke noted in his diary.[78] The prince dined that evening at the Garrison Club and then attended a large reception at the Citadel, where again there was dancing. "HRH seemed to enjoy himself, but frequent balls would speedily bring my tenure of office to a close," the duke complained to his diary.[79] During the day, the prince, among other activities, laid wreaths at the monuments of both Montcalm and Wolfe, the two heroes of the Battle of the Plains of Abraham. The prince spoke in French to an old man, a lame habitant, and gave the old man the medal won by his son, who now lay in the soil of France. The prince appeared to be moved by these ceremonies, which delighted the crowds. On his third day, the lieutenant-governor of Quebec, Sir Charles Fitzpatrick, hosted a grand dinner and party at his home, Spencerwood, on the shores of the St Lawrence River. "The house and gardens were illuminated and the *Dragon* came up opposite. Fine effect," the duke noted.[80] Evie thought this one a "rather a dull party with no dancing."[81]

After the prince left Quebec, the duke and his family began to wend their way back to Montreal aboard HMS *Hochelaga*, the duke fitting in visits along the way to smaller Quebec towns – Trois Rivières, Grand Mère, Shawinigan Falls, and Sorel – for the usual receptions and tours. Finally, they were back in Ottawa, where Evie had just one day to press her servants into getting the house ready for the prince. "Tiresome day. Lot of fussing going on," the duke commented.[82]

The prince's triumphal tour through Halifax, Charlottetown, and Quebec City had set the stage for his visit to Toronto, which "fell head over heels in love with ... the blue-eyed boy who will some day rule over the British Empire."[83] Thousands of people crowded the streets in a demonstration of loyalty and affection. The prince responded: "I want to shake hands with the people in rags and tatters and the brave men and women whose self-sacrifice saved the British Empire," he said. "Let them crowd in. Tell the police not to hold them back. I want to shake hands with them all."[84] And he did, so much so that his right hand became swollen and so painful he used his left hand for the rest of the tour.[85]

Banners, bunting, and cheering crowds greeted the prince as his train came into the Ottawa station. Mackenzie King, among the crowd, later wrote in his diary, "As he drove away, standing in his carriage waving his hand to the people, the sight was one of the most thrilling and beautiful I have ever witnessed."[86]

At a formal luncheon, Mackenzie King was "astounded" that he had been seated beside the prince, with Sir Robert Borden on the other side and then the governor general. He described the scene in the large ballroom of the Château Laurier: "table, horse-shoe shaped, beautifully decorated with roses, flowering plants in the centre." The prince told King his hand was painful after so many receptions, and "that some men were merciless in the way they shook hands." King remarked on the grape juice they were served because of Prohibition in Canada. "H.R.H. s[ai]d you can't make a speech on that stuff. He told me he liked a glass of port better than anything else before speaking ... Throughout the luncheon H.R.H. spent a good deal of time going over his speech which he had written out in his own hand on different sheets of paper, Ottawa Govt. House paper. He said he wished we could have the speeches first & the lunch after. I spoke of all speakers having much the same feeling, that a certain amount of nervousness was needed to give effect. He said once one got on one's feet it was so much better, it was the waiting that was trying ... He told me he was not going to Blue Sea Lake but would go out to the Club instead."[87] The prince may have been particularly nervous about this speech before Ottawa and the government elite. However, "when he got up he did really splendidly, spoke with a fine clear, beautiful voice, did not refer much to his notes," Mackenzie King concluded.[88]

Government House held a garden party in his honour. Under sunny skies, and despite his sore hand, the prince shook hands with at least three thousand, as did the duke and duchess. On Monday, 1 September, *The Globe* reported that the governor general and the prince left Rideau Hall in formal British style, in an open carriage drawn by "four magnificent horses driven by uniformed postillions, and grave-looking footmen in scarlet coats rode behind."[89] They made their way to the Parliament Buildings, where the new Centre Block was still under construction, and the prince laid the cornerstone.

Evie summarized the prince's Ottawa visit for Lady Edward: "The Country Club gave a dance for him which he loved. Then we had a dance after the official dinner and another small one the following night which had to end at 12 on account of Sunday, much to HRH's annoyance. He left after dinner on Monday or rather he was to have gone on the train early, but somehow a 'rag' started in the ball room and he was

Figure 17.3 The Prince of Wales greeting General Sir Arthur Currie at a garden party, Rideau Hall, 28 August 1919.

Figure 17.4 Three daughters of the Duke and Duchess of Devonshire (Lady Rachel, Lady Dorothy, and Lady Anne) with their pets on the steps at Rideau Hall.

Figure 17.5 On 1 September 1919, the Prince of Wales laid a cornerstone of the Peace Tower during reconstruction of the Parliament Buildings in Ottawa. It was the fifty-ninth anniversary of his grandfather, the future Edward VII, laying a cornerstone of the original buildings.

dragged away at 11:30 with a melted collar and very disheveled hair, accompanied by his usually most sedate staff in the same condition and quite hoarse from shouting choruses."[90]

The duke was pleased and surprised that the prince's tour was going so well and told his mother: "he certainly has the capacity for doing the right thing in the right way. His speeches are quite admirable and everywhere he has created the most favourable impression."[91] Evie's description was a little more colourful. "The whole of Canada has gone crazy over him and we think his visit will do lots of good. He certainly has great charm, speaks well and has the knack of saying the right thing on every occasion."[92]

The prince departed for the west and the viceregal party planned to do the same, though they would cross paths only once, in Winnipeg. Evie managed a few days' rest at Blue Sea before they departed. The duke could spare only one day for the cottage as he was dealing with another problem. Sir Robert Borden insisted that the prince must leave for England from a Canadian port. The prince had been invited to the United States and planned to go there after his tour of Canada was completed. Apparently, the English planners thought he would leave for home from the United States, but that would not give Canadians the privilege of waving a final goodbye to their future sovereign from their own ports – at least, that's what the prime minister thought. As all communication with the British government went through the governor general (except when the prime minister had an audience with the king), the duke received and sent all the cables. Did the Canadians want the British government to cancel the American tour? That was impossible, as it had been a cabinet decision in Britain, and the United States might take umbrage. No, the Canadians certainly did not want that; they thought he could simply return to a Canadian port. Then what did the Admiralty think? The Foreign Office? Finally, all concerned agreed that he could take a few extra days to return to Halifax for a final farewell.[93]

With that problem resolved, the duke and his entourage headed west. The company included Evie, Blanche Egerton, Miss Saunders, and Dorothy, as well as the three ADCs, Harold Macmillan, Geordie Haddington, and Harry Cator. Anne stayed home in Ottawa with her new governess, Miss Schofield; Charlie and Rachel went to England, Charlie to school and Rachel to stay with Maud for a few weeks.

⚜

CHAPTER 18

The Prince of Wales, and Other Peacetime Pleasures

Now that the war and its aftermath of labour unrest were over, and the visit of the Prince of Wales was going well, the duke and his family could enjoy a more relaxed peacetime existence. Heading across country for Evie's first visit to the West Coast, they were due in Winnipeg for the national Red Cross meeting. The duke, who had been active in the Red Cross since the beginning of his time in Canada, had asked the prince to step briefly into the meeting. He thought the delegates would be impressed with the privilege of a private audience; he was right, and the meeting went well.[1]

About this time, the newspapers were reporting that Dorothy was engaged to the Prince of Wales, a completely unfounded bit of gossip. Dorothy must have been amused, but her father was incensed and asked Lord Richard Nevill in Ottawa to put a stop to it, if he could. Apparently he couldn't as the rumour recurred, and the duke finally realized there was nothing to be done.[2] Meanwhile, Dorothy and Harold were managing to spend most of their time together, though they had no privacy. Only Evie noticed their closeness and worried. Everyone else was focused on the prince.

The governor general's party travelled through the Prairies, but in some places they followed the royal tour a little too closely and, according to Blanche Egerton, found themselves "very flat visitors so soon after the PofW."[3] Blanche described Le Pas, Manitoba, as "a six-year-old place with wonderful air where everyone is expanding, minerals, lumber, fur etc., the country flat as flat but with marvellous sunrises, sunsets."[4] The duke, as usual, was most interested in the prairie harvest, which was less than the bumper crop of 1917 but still better than expected. He wrote to his mother that the optimism and confidence of western Canadians was amazing, "but whenever I ask anyone about it I am always told that to live in this country you must be optimistic."[5]

The itinerary called for three days of real holidays in the Rocky Mountains. On arrival at Jasper Park, they spent only a few minutes with the reception committee before going on horseback up Maligne Canyon to the beautiful azure blue waters of Maligne Lake, with its surrounding glacier-clad mountains. Dorothy described the scene for her grandmother: "We were a very funny party. The first day we started off all riding astride on very uncomfortable Mexican saddles. Cousin Blanche looked splendid but not very happy. She borrowed some beautiful brown corduroy trousers! ... I followed the usual custom there and discarded my skirt. It is quite impossible to climb in a skirt ... We were well escorted by North West Mounted Police and a movie man."[6]

Blanche Egerton, who thought the Rockies indescribably lovely, explained the movie man: "The authorities want to make Jasper into a better Banff, so much was made of Victor's visit; it will be considerably advertized. I don't think a 'movie' of Evie and me walking down a road will be a very good advertizement, but an awful movie man was always dogging our footsteps."[7]

Harold, who had climbed before and "was very pleased at being considered A1 at it,"[8] took Dorothy off climbing one day when the duke was too tired and stiff from the day before. This time they climbed nearby Pyramid Mountain. Dorothy told her grandmother that they "had a wonderful time in the Rockies. I didn't know anything could be so lovely ... The climb was perfectly glorious. We made most of the way up a very narrow twisty path and climbed the rest. They said we could see 70 miles."[9]

Leaving Jasper, the train took them over the Yellowhead Pass, where the railway tracks had been laid less than a decade before. They were lucky to have a clear view of the "magnificent" Mount Robson,[10] the highest peak in the Rocky Mountains at 13,000 feet.

The duke and his party moved on through British Columbia to Prince George and then to Prince Rupert, stopping along the way at such smaller towns as Smithers, Hazelton, and Kitwanga. From Prince Rupert, they took a steamer, the ss *Prince Rupert*, north into Observation Inlet.

The Prince of Wales, and Other Peacetime Pleasures 251

The duke was surprised at the number of "old country" people he met in the smaller towns. "The most curious, was a place called Anyox, 100 miles north of Prince Rupert," he told his mother, where he met the son of a man he knew from Derbyshire. "A very valuable copper mine has been opened ... The mine is practically a mountain of solid copper and is being gradually removed. Unfortunately the fumes from the smelting plant has [sic] destroyed all the vegetation and the whole country looks bleak and derelict. The mountains run right down into the sea and the town, which belongs entirely to the company, is built on the rocks with the roads propped up on wooden causeways."[11]

From Anyox, they sailed down the coast to Vancouver, stopping at Swanson Bay and Ocean Falls to see the lumber, pulp, and paper mills and to greet the local citizens. Evie by this time had a cold and "stopped in bed," which gave her time to write to Lady Edward: "The boat is rather like a glorified penny steamer ... The cabins are good but there is nowhere much to sit as it is wet and foggy and there are 400 passengers, Japs, Chinamen, half breeds, Jews and some Canadians. At this season the salmon canneries along the coast shut down and the weird collection of people employed in them move south to spend the money they have made during the summer – or to find other work."[12]

Dorothy wrote to her grandmother, "All this western part is wonderful country ... farming, lumbering, mining, trapping, shooting and fishing and wonderful scenery. I think it's much better than the east. It's so nice to see large trees again but it seems such a waste to make them into paper. However, that was only because they had to use them up."[13]

They stopped in Vancouver briefly before going on to Victoria. Evie was entranced with the scenery during her first trip to this part of the country: "This coast is wonderfully beautiful. I wish we had had time to see more of Vancouver Island. The roads are good and there are most beautiful motor expeditions."[14] Evie's cold was improving and she carried on with luncheons, dinners, garden parties, and meetings with women's organizations. They drove up the inland coast of Vancouver Island as far as Courtenay, visiting the smaller towns, then returned to Nanaimo for the passage back over the Georgia Strait to Vancouver. Again they visited schools and hospitals and met with women's organizations and returned soldiers. The duke found Capilano Canyon near

Vancouver "far more beautiful than I expected."[15] They probably walked over the suspension bridge that crosses the canyon high above the rushing water below. In 1919 it was a cable-and-wood structure, and though the bridge has been updated it is still a tourist attraction.

They began the journey back east by train, travelling through British Columbia along the Fraser Canyon and then north beside the Thompson River to the small community of Spences Bridge. From there, leaving the river, the train took them back south to Merritt and into Penticton on the southern shore of Okanagan Lake. In each town, the governor general and his party were special visitors and were received with enthusiasm. From Penticton, they boarded a boat called the *Sicamous* and cruised north on Okanagan Lake between the sage-covered clay cliffs, stopping at the fruit-growing towns of Peachland, Summerland, and Kelowna. From the northern end of the lake they motored into Vernon. Blanche Egerton was thrilled with this expedition. She wrote to Lady Edward, "Now we are in the dry belt, most curious and interesting. Today it has looked ugly but yesterday I went with Victor for a perfectly wonderful drive … The fruit is certainly marvellous … I had no idea there could be so many apples in the world."[16] As usual the duke noted the harvest, saying that "the prices are high and the crops excellent."[17]

Returning to Penticton, they travelled east by train across the Monashee Mountains to Tadanac (now part of the city of Trail) on the Columbia River to view the lead-zinc smelting operations. They drove over bad roads through wonderful scenery to fjord-like Kootenay Lake, which lies between the Selkirk and Purcell mountain ranges. The little towns of Balfour, Kaslo, and Bonnington Falls offered receptions and visits to hospitals and schools. Returning to Penticton, they headed north through Princeton, Merritt, and Spences Bridge to Kamloops. From there, they left the dry belt to go into the heart of the Rocky Mountains and visit Revelstoke, located on the twisting Columbia River between the Monashee and Selkirk Mountains. The whole party took a boat trip south on the Arrow Lakes into lumbering communities, and on to more fruit-growing communities where apples, peaches, pears, and cherries were grown in abundance. That day, the duke noted in his diary, "somehow or other a mistake had occurred and there were several places at which we were expected but we had no notice. When we found out, we were able to make it good except at one. I hate disappointing people."[18]

They called at Burton, Edgeworth, and Renata, towns that would not survive the building of the Keenleyside Dam in the 1960s. On the way back, they visited Nakusp, which had telephone but no power in 1919. It is now a thriving small community with a hot springs and outdoor recreation to interest tourists.

Continuing east by train, they stopped at Glacier, a railway whistle stop in Glacier National Park. "First time I have even been on a glacier," the duke wrote, "and was much disillusioned. It is surprising how so beautiful a thing when seen from a distance can be so ugly when actually approached."[19] It was probably dirty and full of cracks. The train was carrying them through the spectacular mountains of the Rogers Pass on a railway line built in the 1880s. The symbolic Last Spike, driven at Craigellachie in 1885, signified the completion of the railway that had been promised to British Columbia in 1871 when the province joined Canada. By 1919, the line from Revelstoke to Golden had been recently improved with the opening of the Connaught Tunnel built for safety reasons, due to the many avalanche disasters that had occurred in that narrow pass over the years. Train was still the only way to traverse this route in 1919. A highway between the two towns, following the big bend of the Columbia River, would be opened only in 1940 and could be described as about two hundred miles of potholed gravel roads. In the 1960s, the paved Trans-Canada Highway, less than one hundred miles, opened through this magnificent but treacherous Rogers Pass.[20]

At Lake Louise in Alberta, the active members of the party – Harold, Dorothy, and Geordie – found some good hiking up Mount St Piran. Dorothy, now a seasoned hiker, thought it was "very easy as there was a trail all the time. It was jolly cold as there was a lot of snow high up," she wrote to her grandmother.[21] The others went by motor to lovely Lake Minnewanka.

Their next stop was the town of Banff in Banff National Park, Alberta. They climbed part of Sulphur Mountain and then went to the hot springs pool among the mountain peaks. Dorothy wrote to Lady Edward, "The baths are all out of doors. It seems odd to be too hot swimming when there's snow on the ground and quite a lot of frost."[22]

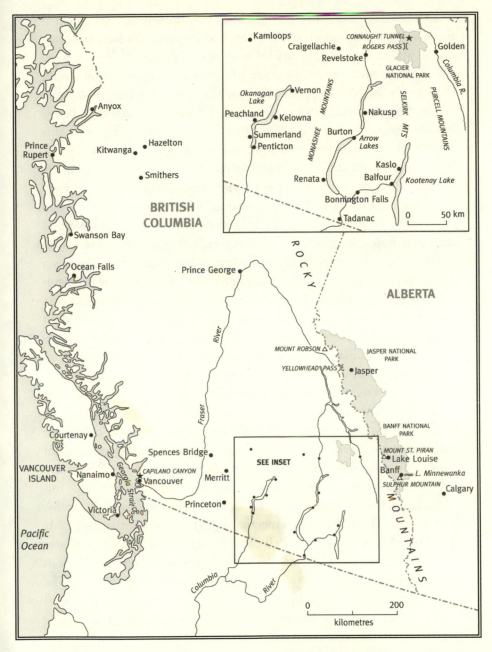

Figure 18.1 Map of the duke and duchess's travels in British Columbia, 1919.

They moved on to spend a day in Calgary for meetings, then called at the farming communities of Kindersley and Rosetown in Saskatchewan on the way to Regina. Dorothy wrote to her grandmother from Regina: "We have at last very nearly come to the end of our tour, though we shall really be very sorry when it's over because it's been great fun. We've suddenly been plunged right into the middle of winter ... It was below zero last night and there's quite a lot of snow. We're in this horrible flat country where there's not a single tree to be seen."[23]

In Ottawa, the duke pronounced himself pleased with the tour. He had travelled 10,300 miles by train and steamer, and there had been additional mileage racked up by motoring, riding, and walking. He had given sixty-six speeches and engaged in many conversations with all sorts of people. He reported to his mother: "I have no hesitation in saying that I found conditions generally better than I expected. There is a certain amount of unrest but I expected to find more ... The opportunities which the country provides are enormous ... The one thing the country wants is population but we must be careful to get the right sort. We have got plenty of the riff raff of Europe and do not want any more. There are plenty of openings but there is no use for anyone to come here who does not mean to put in really hard work."[24]

They had a week to prepare for the return visit of the Prince of Wales to Ottawa. Most of the work fell to servants; Evie stayed in bed for three or four days with lumbago.[25] She told her mother, "If dear old Victor would give me quiet Sundays I believe I could manage the rest all right without lumbago or headaches, but he always promises to have them blank and then fills them as full as other days."[26] Unfazed by the impending arrival of the prince, the duke played golf with Dorothy, Harold, and Geordie between meeting with ministers and visitors. Mr and Mrs Alexander Graham Bell came to luncheon. Sir George Foster came to see the governor general, disturbed about the turn of events in Parliament concerning the railways. The duke wrote in his diary: "The Govt decided to fill up two of the vacancies in the Senate and hope to get their bill. I of course had to sign this O[rder] in C[ouncil] but made a protest."[27] The duke did not approve of the government's method of passing their controversial bill to nationalize the bankrupt Grand Trunk Railway. The government did fill the two Senate vacancies and the bill did become law. The Grand Trunk eventually became part of the Canadian National Railway, which was a Canadian Crown corporation until it was privatized in 1995.

The prince returned to Ottawa on 5 November. Though Dorothy could not think what he would do in Ottawa for five days in bad weather,[28] he was an easy visitor to entertain. He loved dancing, and that's what he did for four nights – at the Country Club, at the May Court Ball in the Château Laurier, at a formal dinner and dance at Government House, and back to the Country Club. Once again, only Sunday kept him from dancing. Attending the service that morning in St Bartholomew's Church, sitting in the governor general's pew, he invested a memorial window honouring those who had fallen in the war.[29] One day he spoke at the Canadian Club, saying how much he had enjoyed being in Canada. And then he was off to the United States, but, as Borden had requested, he would come back to Halifax for a final send-off from Canada.

Having seen the prince onto his train in Ottawa, the duke departed for Toronto for the 11 November ceremonies, the first anniversary of the armistice. A two-minute silence, which had been requested by the king, was well observed. The duke opened Hart House, a cultural centre for students at the University of Toronto, and laid a cornerstone for the memorial tower honouring the university men who had fallen in the war. Vincent Massey, BJ's friend, grandson of Hart Massey for whom the building was named, addressed the assembled dignitaries; Hart House was a gift of the Massey family.[30]

The duke and Sir Robert Borden travelled by train from Ottawa to Halifax to take part in the farewell ceremonies for the prince. It was a run of just under twenty-seven hours, and they played a lot of bridge. The prince had been to Washington and New York and was well fêted in both places. In Halifax, the duke again toured the area devastated by the explosion two years before, noting the impressive progress in building new houses. He "stopped in the *Renown* – very comfortable night," he wrote in his diary.[31] The prince attended a *thé dansant*, an informal afternoon dance, undoubtedly arranged to give the young royal another chance to indulge in his favourite activity. At a formal dinner at the Halifax Club, given by the federal government, Prime Minister Borden proposed the health of the prince, who replied that he was not saying goodbye but only *au revoir*, as he intended to come to Canada again soon. He felt at home and intensely Canadian in this country, and wanted to visit and travel informally.[32] He noted that his travels had revealed how much Canada was the guardian of British institutions on this continent. His final comment was to thank Sir Robert and the government for their hospitality throughout his tour. Harold Macmillan, who travelled to Halifax with the duke, later recalled that "the Prince entertained all the mayors and other functionaries to a great farewell dinner. Whether because of the excellence of the fare or for some other reason, one of them fell into the sea, but was soon fished out amid considerable merriment."[33]

Then it was time for departure. As the Citadel guns boomed a twenty-one-gun salute, HMS *Renown*, bedecked with flags and carrying the future king, sailed out of Halifax Harbour and off to England. The prince had acquitted himself well during his time in Canada. Evie reported to her mother, "He has delighted the girls at each place by dancing till any hours often with one girl a great many times, but he never sits out with them and has not done any of the things we were afraid he would do!"[34] And later, referring to the press saying that Dorothy and the prince were engaged: "Poor Dorothy tried hard to be nice but you can imagine that after so much talk and newspaper paragraphs she was rather stiff and stodgy and he has very little real conversation except about what he has been doing and one uses that up."[35]

Dorothy told her grandmother, "It is perfectly wonderful the impression the Prince of Wales is making out here. Everyone loves him and each place we go to is full of anecdotes about him. One thing that pleases everyone enormously is that he escaped from the rest of the party and went off to a movie! I think the whole of Canada has heard about that and they're so pleased to find that he's exactly like other people."[36]

The prince came at just the right time. Canada needed his freshness and hope for the future. Canadians had put their heart and soul, their money, and a generation of their young men into the war. They were tired and restless. The prince was young, handsome, charming, and full of the energy of youth. His tour cemented Canada to the Empire. He was just unconventional enough that Canadians thought of him as one

Figure 18.2 The Prince of Wales leaving Halifax for home, 25 November 1919. Harold Macmillan is standing behind the Duke of Devonshire.

of their own. (That trait unfortunately would later lead him to abdicate his throne to marry the twice-divorced American Wallis Simpson.)

With the labour problems settled, and the prince's visit having buoyed Canadians' spirits, few problems remained for the governor general. However, late in 1919, coal supplies were running low. Industry had still not recovered from the war and, if forced to close down due to lack of fuel, it would be a huge blow to the economy. Strike activity in the United States had caused that country to ration available coal. Fortunately there was enough coal for household consumption, but the industrial problem loomed large: Canada needed about 2.5 million tons of bituminous coal to keep its industry running in the cold months of November and December. The prime minister sent a letter to the governor general with a copy of his letter to Lord Grey, the British ambassador in Washington, asking for his help in convincing the United States to release more coal for Canada.[37] The duke was worried.[38] There was little he could do other than be aware of the potential problem. Finally, on 11 December, the U.S. strike was over and Canada got its required coal.[39]

As Canada returned to normal postwar life, it was as if a long-closed gate had opened – visitors from Britain began to flood into Rideau Hall. Among the most prominent were Lord and Lady Jellicoe. Viscount Jellicoe was Admiral of the Fleet in Britain and had been Commander of the Grand Fleet during the Battle of Jutland in 1916. His visit was official. He was to advise the Canadian government about how to build their naval power in order to protect the mercantile marine in any future war. His mission was larger than Canada; it included a full tour of the British Empire and a report on postwar strategy for the Royal Navy. He had arrived from Australia and had already visited the city of Esquimalt on Canada's West Coast. In his Canadian Club speech in Ottawa, he said that Britain had lost many merchant vessels during the war, not only to submarines, but also because the German ships were able to evade the ill-equipped British navy.[40] The duke thought it "a most useful and timely speech and it ought to strengthen the hands of the Govt if they are inclined to do anything."[41] The Jellicoes stayed for several days while Lord Jellicoe interviewed ministers. Jellicoe was keen on winter and skated well, something the duke still struggled with.[42] At Rideau Hall, they celebrated Lord Jellicoe's birthday with cake and candles and a present of a fur cap.[43]

Lord Jellicoe presented his report to the governor general on 31 December 1919. He recommended a naval fleet centred around battle cruisers and aircraft carriers. His recommendations were too ambitious for the Canadian government, however. Canada did not have enough trained men to run a large fleet, and the purchase would be too expensive. Canada would concentrate first on local defence of the two coastlines. In 1920, Canada took delivery of two destroyers, *Patriot* and *Patrician*, and a light cruiser, *Aurora*, gifts from Britain, though Canadians were responsible for running costs and any refit required. These ships would serve in conjunction with the two submarines and nine patrol vessels already operated by Canada.[44]

The Jellicoes spent Christmas at Rideau Hall with the Devonshires and the ADCs, the Henderson family, and Mr John Burgon Bickersteth. The duke knew Bickersteth's father, who had been vicar of Leeds Parish

Church. Before the war, the younger Bickersteth had been a lay minister of the Anglican Church in western Canada. His letters from that time had just been published as *The Land of Open Doors: Being Letters from Western Canada 1911–1913*. After serving in the army, he'd returned to Canada in 1919 and was a lecturer at the University of Alberta in Edmonton. The family enjoyed his company, and he wrote in his thank-you note that he had never had a more "ripping" Christmas.[45] Evie described their Christmas for Lady Edward: "Fifteen of us went to early service through a new fall of nice dry snow with lovely sunrise ... There was a great exchange of presents afterwards and a very cheery luncheon. Then some of the party went to skate and some to amuse the old people at a Home for Incurables."[46]

The duke hosted the usual New Year's Day Levee at his office in the East Block for about six hundred and wondered what this new year would bring.[47]

CHAPTER 19

Dorothy and Harold

While Evie was in London in the winter of 1919, she tried her best to introduce Dorothy to eligible young men. Eligible to Evie meant of good English family, including position and breeding, with good manners, and especially adequate money. Canadians, colonials, were not among the eligible, which limited the field considerably while they were living in Canada. In England, she managed to arrange parties, despite the problem of not knowing when young men would be arriving back from the battlefields of Europe. Many of those deemed eligible had died in the war and most survivors had been wounded, among them Harold Macmillan.

Dorothy met Harold at a dance that January, when she was just nineteen. Her mother thought she was not very interested in him, or in any of the other men she met,[1] or really in London life. Evie thought Dorothy preferred the country, where there were fewer available men.[2]

Evie had heard in England from a Lady Evelyn (probably Ivan Cobbold's mother) that Harold's mother said her son was very taken with Dorothy. Evie thought it could not be true because she didn't see any signs of it. Perhaps Dorothy did see the signs. One can imagine that Dorothy enjoyed being the object of attention from a very attractive young man, even if she were not especially interested in him.

Harold kept reappearing. By March, Evie was worried. "He is a dear and very clever but I should not really like it," Evie wrote to Victor.[3] Though Evie did not make her objections clear, she would have known that Harold's family had the successful publishing business, so that money was not an issue. Probably her objection was that he would expect to work as a businessman and was not an aristocrat. After Harold arrived in Canada to serve as an aide-de-camp, she added, "I wonder what you think of Macmillan. We like him so much but I would not care for him to marry Dorothy. I am sure she does not think of him in that way and that it was only because he was coming to us that she made such friends with him. All the same it is just as well that he is not crossing with us."[4] Another time she wrote, "One can only hope that D will prefer Lord Haddington who is coming with us."[5] Lord Haddington was a Scottish peer who had inherited his title from his father in 1917 so he was definitely among the eligible. He was the same age as Harold, twenty-five, but the family thought of him as younger and, in Ottawa, he became seventeen-year-old Rachel's special friend.

When Evie and Dorothy returned to Rideau Hall in May 1919, Harold was well ensconced in his new position, and established in her father's favour. Dorothy was spending much of her time with him.[6] Victor liked talking politics with Harold and, as he told his mother, "He is very intelligent and keen and besides that he plays golf and bridge."[7]

Harold Macmillan was a member of the Macmillan publishing family. His ancestors had built a very successful business which would certainly absorb him if he wished it. Harold's father, the mild-mannered Maurice Macmillan, was a partner in the firm; his mother, an American, had a strong and controlling influence over her youngest and favourite son. Harold had been educated at Summer Fields, the Oxford preparatory school, and moved on to Eton. Both were schools for the social and intellectual elite. In 1912, at the age of eighteen, he had entered Balliol College, Oxford, where he studied the classics, reading Homer, Virgil, Aeschylus, and Sophocles. During his Oxford days, he considered leaving the Anglican Church and becoming a Roman Catholic, but hesitated, perhaps because his mother would certainly have been extremely upset. His Oxford studies were interrupted by the war in 1914.

Though he wanted to enlist immediately, Harold was held back by a case of appendicitis. Recovery from the operation in those years took time, and Harold feared he would miss the excitement, but by mid-October 1914 he was able to join the army. It was not until mid-August 1915 that he was posted to France. In his first battle, at Loos, in late September, he was injured in the head and in his right hand and was sent back to England to recover. Back on active duty by Christmas that year, he and his company returned to France in April 1916, first to Ypres and later south to the Somme. In mid-September, near Ginchy, Harold was trying to take out a German machine-gun nest when he was shot in the left thigh and pelvis. He was in no-man's-land. He rolled into a shell hole, dosed himself with morphine, and played dead while Germans in grey uniforms ran around the lip of his hole and artillery shells fell around him. Drifting in and out of consciousness for over twelve hours, he read Aeschylus's *Prometheus* in Greek, which he had in his pocket. Finally, when it was dark, a party of soldiers came to his rescue and he was sent behind the lines to a French hospital and eventually to London. By the time he reached London, as happened often during that dreadful carnage, the wound was septic. His recovery took the rest of the wartime and longer.[8]

In April, on his arrival in Canada, Harold was still not very healthy, but by late May, Evie thought him "ever so much better and stronger."[9] When they were planting the garden at Blue Sea Lake, "H Macmillan felt obliged to work hard and did it better than G. Haddington but one feels all the time that he is at heart a London young man,"[10] implying that because Dorothy preferred the country, Harold would not make a suitable match for her.

During the summer at Blue Sea Lake, Evie was watchful. "If he has any feelings for D he hides them with great care, though he seems ready for golf in the garden or anything else she wants to do. I think Mrs. M must have greatly exaggerated," she told Lady Edward. Dorothy and Harold had some adventures together that summer. Besides giving Evie a fright by sailing away with a bath towel for a sail and delaying their return, Evie wrote to Lady Edward, "she and Macmillan went to a pond where Dorothy knew there were lovely water lilies. They both fell in up to their waists in black mud but they got the water lillies [*sic*]."[11] And another morning, "Dorothy and Harold got up early to go to Mt. Jacques to see the sunrise."[12] By September, Evie was writing to Lady Edward, "It suits D to have an extremely intelligent companion always at hand but it is hard on him as I am pretty sure she does not really care for him … I don't think he ought to stay on with things in this condition … Victor is very fond of him and will miss him as he is the only man on staff who really talks well."[13] But Evie could not insist that he leave before the prince's visit and their western tour.

By September, when they reached Jasper, Harold and Dorothy had spent several weeks on the train constantly together, surrounded by the others. One day, they went hiking accompanied by the duke and Miss Saunders, "Well on for 9000 ft above sea level so we must have ascended at least 4000 ft," the duke recorded in his diary.[14] Next day, the duke was stiff and chose to fish instead of hiking.[15] Dorothy and Harold climbed Pyramid Mountain with Miss Saunders and a local man as their companions (chaperones).[16] Only a year later did Evie understand what had happened that day. When she returned to Jasper in 1920 someone told her, and she told Victor, that "it was a look he [the local man] caught between D. and H. that prompted him to stay behind with Miss S. No one else here guessed anything as their minds were running on the P. of W."[17] The observant local man gave Harold his opportunity in the romantic setting of the mountain peak looking over valleys of the Rocky Mountains, where Dorothy thought they could see for seventy miles.[18] Harold Macmillan later recalled in his memoir, *Winds of Change*, "it was amidst the wonderful scenery at Jasper Park in Canada that I first knew my affections were returned."[19]

What happened in Jasper in their few moments of privacy? On the top of a mountain, he may have kissed Dorothy and found her passionate, or in some way declared his devotion and discovered it to be reciprocated. Harold knew that an unwelcome proposal of marriage would certainly create a crisis that would send him home immediately. The tour and the visit of the Prince of Wales, for both of which he was an important asset, still had two months to run. On that mountaintop, it is unlikely that they would have talked of marriage. A proposal would have required Dorothy to tell her parents about the relationship between them. Instead they kept it private, a secret between them. How delicious for Dorothy to hold her feelings close, and hide them even from her eagle-eyed mother.

Just two days later, Evie took Harold Macmillan aside in Prince George. She told her mother-in-law, "Harold Macmillan is so obviously devoted that I had to speak to him about his manner to D. We have managed to avoid an actual crisis but it will have to come soon and then he will have to go home. The difficulty is to find a safe substitute. There is always a risk of someone more attractive and less desirable!!"[20] To her mother she wrote, "H. Macmillan got so affectionate that I had to speak to him. He was very nice about it and now behaves with great decorum. We can't make out whether he has any hope or whether he sees that D does not care for him in that way."[21] It seems that Evie was trying to convince herself that Dorothy did not really care for Harold.

When Harold returned from Halifax with the duke, having seen the prince safely off to England, he felt it was time to renew his suit. In early December, Harold wrote to the duchess asking to continue the conversation they had begun in Prince George. They were both in residence at Rideau Hall, but he wrote, "I am taking the liberty of saying what I want to say to you on paper, partly because I cannot overcome a certain shyness and reserve of nature which make it very hard for me to say what I would like to say orally, partly because in this way I think I shall be more certain of making my meaning quite clear to you."

He probably knew that he was a good writer, even a persuasive writer, and that this would give the duchess time to think before she reacted. Harold said he was deeply in love with Dorothy and "the experience is so extraordinary and so absolutely new to me that I cannot understand it. Everything except just this one thing seems unreal and fantastic." There was no question of Dorothy marrying against her parents' wishes, he said, but if she, the duchess, gave him leave, he would take his chances and ask Dorothy to marry him. He did not tell the duchess that he already knew something of Dorothy's feelings. He must have known that the duke loved him dearly and would certainly have approved, so the duchess was the barrier he must surmount. Though, he said, he did not have much to offer Dorothy – "not position or excessive wealth – nothing except the greatest love and devotion"[22] – he was enough in love "to try his fortune." Of course, he knew that Evie knew, thanks to his family's business, he was not completely without monetary resources.

Dorothy had very little experience of male companions except for the ADCs. She had had a romance at fifteen, mostly by letter and telephone, with a distant cousin, Alwyn Cavendish, who was ten years her senior, but when her parents found out, the duke was incensed. "I am afraid the little girl was quite infatuated about him ... The whole thing is very tiresome." He quickly put a stop to it.[23] Then there was a possible flirtation with Mervyn Ridley, who had arrived at Rideau Hall as an ADC in January 1917 and accompanied Dorothy to Washington in

May 1918.[24] A month later, Evie was worried that there was something between him and Dorothy.[25] When Mervyn gave Dorothy a very nice bracelet for her eighteenth birthday, the duke began to worry too.[26] Nothing serious happened between them, though. Mervyn returned to England on the ship with Evie and Dorothy in December 1918,[27] and, in the new year, Evie wrote to Victor: "Mervyn comes 'in and out' a good deal. It is difficult to avoid this when D knows no other men."[28] He accompanied them to Lismore Castle in April. There Evie confronted him, saying that "she did not want the same talk about him and D here as there is in London and Ottawa."[29] He assured her that he saw Dorothy as a child and there was nothing but friendship in his feelings for her. Evie was not sure she believed him but thought that Dorothy did not care for him. Mervyn was not among the eligible; he had a farm in Kenya,[30] and Evie would not have wanted her daughter to live in Africa. And Mervyn told Evie "that he thought it horrible to ask a woman to marry one who had more money than oneself,"[31] meaning that he did not want to marry a woman who had more money than he had. Dorothy was undoubtedly aware of the talk, and perhaps learned then to keep her own counsel about her feelings for male suitors.

Most of the time Dorothy was a sunny, pleasant girl, full of life and mild mischief. She was a nice-looking girl but not strikingly beautiful, and she had no great sense of style. She was educated at home by governesses, which meant probably not very well. There is no evidence in the letters that she read for pleasure. She was less interested in sport than her sister Rachel, but she enjoyed swimming and skating as part of social life. Dorothy did not much like fishing,[32] but taking a canoe out with a towel for a sail must have appealed to her sense of adventure, as did picking water lilies in muddy water. Like Harold, she did not know much about or care for music except for dancing. Like Harold, she had a strong mother who influenced, even controlled, her life. Like Harold, she did not rebel.[33]

Why Dorothy married Harold has been the subject of speculation. Apparently some thought it was to escape from her mother.[34] Writers have described Evie as tough,[35] and as "stingy with money, affection and civility,[36] as "always formidable,"[37] and as "rigid"[38] or "cold, authoritarian and frugal."[39] Most of these writers knew of Evie in her later years after her support system had collapsed – her husband disabled by a stroke, her father dead, her children getting on with their lives. At Rideau Hall, in 1919, Evie still had a loving and understanding husband. She still had Dorothy, Rachel, and Anne at home to worry about, make costumes and plans for, and, as Blanche Egerton said, "Evie liked making plans."⁴⁰ In Canada, Evie was also forty-eight, menopausal, plagued by lumbago and occasional colitis. She never exercised except to walk once in a while. She knew that exercise was important, but thought of it as a way for Victor to lose weight; she was slim and probably didn't think it important for herself. After the fashion of the day, she did nothing to increase her strength and stamina. She did not much like being in Canada. She was trying to do her best for her girls, which to her meant arranging proper marriages.

Dorothy and Evie had very different personalities. Evie was tired out by having to be social for any length of time. Her husband, obviously concerned, often noted in his diary on these occasions that "Evie stopped in bed all day," even if it was in a train. She found the tours especially exhausting and complained of the heat, the discomfort of the trains, the constant socializing. Her lumbago flared. While sometimes she was ill, often she just needed some time to herself. Evie was a classic introvert. She knew very well how to entertain and be social with those she had not met. She had been well trained from birth for this work and was an expert at it. Everyone said she was charming – but it tired her out. Victor was energized by all the meeting and greeting, but not Evie.

Dorothy, when she was at Rideau Hall and at Blue Sea, was probably just finding herself as an individual. A year earlier, in March 1918, one of BJ's letters to his mother is revealing of Dorothy's personality compared to her mother's. Evie had asked BJ to give lessons in literature and Canadian history to Dorothy and Rachel. This was during the difficult winter of 1918. Springy had recently died and his widow and children were still living at Rideau Hall, still in mourning. The war was going badly in France. Evie was depressed and critical of everything. BJ wrote to his mother:

Last Friday we [BJ with Blanche and Dorothy] were sitting together in the Skating Rink when two people came in who had been most kind to them last year at Blue Sea. To Mrs they [sic] a curt nod; Mr they completely disregarded. I leant forward and said "You really must try and be a little polite to people," and walked away. Next morning, I gave Dorothy half an hour's lecture. I told her first that it was common politeness to be nice to people who do things for you ... that social intercourse was a quarter of the work out here, ... that it didn't matter a damn for their own sakes whether the girls were popular or not, but that it mattered a lot for the sake of the regime, ... to all of which Dorothy said "I'm sorry BJ," "I'll try BJ." Next day at the skating party I saw her talking to a knot of people at the tea and helping someone she did not know on with her coat.[41]

BJ's prod was enough to change Dorothy's behaviour. Like her father, she could easily be warm, outgoing, and friendly and it did not exhaust her as it did her mother. In Ottawa, Dorothy's outgoing personality was stifled, not so much by her mother as by her situation. The war had put a damper on the full social life usually offered by governors general at Rideau Hall. Though the young people tried with parties at the Country Club, skiing, and skating, it was not as full a social calendar as they might have had before the war. Dorothy had no serious interests, no chance to study or work toward a career. Marriage was to be her career. There is no doubt from her letters that Dorothy loved Harold. To her, he must have represented a life and a future. Far from looking for an escape, she was moving toward a full life by accepting this marriage.

Biographers have not questioned why Harold was drawn to Dorothy, a woman who did not share his intellectual or spiritual interests. They have simply said that he was infatuated with her, and certainly that was obvious from his and Evie's letters. At that time men did not expect to marry for compatibility with their own interests. Harold's attraction may have rested in part on Dorothy's outgoing personality; perhaps she completed him with her ease in any social situation, something he lacked. His mother's interest in pushing him forward in society may have been a part of it too. He would have known that his mother would approve of a match with the Duke of Devonshire's daughter. However, Harold's love was genuine, a love that lasted all his life.[42]

In response to Harold's letter in December 1919, Evie agreed that he could ask Dorothy to marry him. Perhaps she expected Dorothy to refuse him. As late as 7 October, Evie had told her mother that "We can't make out whether he has any hope or whether he sees that D does not care for him in that way."[43] In early December, when Harold proposed, the duke wrote, "After tea Harold proposed in a sort of way to Dorothy but although she did not refuse him definitely nothing was settled. She seemed to like him but not enough to accept and says she does not want to marry just yet. She seemed in excellent spirits."[44] This seems a rather tentative proposal and response for a couple who had known about their mutual affection for the last two months and more. Perhaps Dorothy was still not sure. Or perhaps she wanted her parents to think this was all new. If she revealed that it was not new, her secret – that she had been keeping important information from them – would have been revealed; to put it in modern parlance, her cover would have been blown. She certainly knew that her mother would need time to adjust to the idea of a son-in-law "in trade."

On 26 December, Evie wrote to Lady Edward that she was pretty sure Dorothy would marry Harold, but Dorothy did not want to be engaged until she had time to think it over in England. "He certainly is a charming man – so clever and understanding – good looking and with nice manners ... I could have wished for rather different in-laws. But everyone loves old Maurice Macmillan and I must say I thought her very pleasant and an interesting talker."[45]

The same day – it must have been later in the day – Victor wrote in his diary that Dorothy and Harold had settled to call themselves engaged. "They both are radiantly happy, but do not wish anything to be said about it."[46] Three days later, Evie wrote to her mother about the engagement: "We are not going to announce it just yet, though everyone must see that there is something up as they will look at each other all the time! ... I had hoped to prevent their getting engaged for a few months, but the child was getting so worried and nervous that is seemed better to give in ... When we could not get anyone close, and had to take Harold, I had a feeling this might happen. She says she thought him much like the nicest of all the men she danced with in London but for a long time she said he was too clever. Now she finds this was a mistake."[47]

Evie's opposition had lasted only three weeks. Victor was more than happy about the engagement. "He is really quite charming and intelligent and absolutely devoted to her and Dorothy is equally confident." Victor looked forward to having a son-in-law interested in politics. "I hope later on he will go in for a political life and I am sure he ought to do well."[48]

Then there was the question of money. Evie wrote to Lady Edward, "Harold seems most vague about money, but thinks his father will allow him enough to marry on. I am afraid that – having always lived very simply himself – he may have rather different views from ours on this subject."[49] To her mother, she wrote, "We have no idea what his father will allow him. If it is very little, they must simply remain engaged till they can think it well over. Eventually he will be quite well off."[50] By 2 January 1920, Harold's father had promised him £3,000 a year and possibly more (about $200,000 Canadian today),[51] so the wedding plans began in earnest. "They will be quite comfortably off, though not rich," Evie noted.[52]

Once the engagement was settled, at least for the family, Evie wrote about her feelings and reservations to her mother:

> I would have liked rather a long engagement but we must come back in May so the marriage will probably be at the end of April as Dorothy hates the idea of coming back here for ever so long and we should all rather [unreadable] another wedding from this house with Maud's fresh on one's mind. They are full of plans about a house in London and a cottage in the country. Dorothy has always disliked London. I have rubbed in the fact that by marrying a business man she makes it her home for life. But she says she does not mind. I have also said a lot about the relations who she may find trying. Otherwise there is no one we should like better than Harold. He does not look strong but is much better than a few months ago. He was wounded 4 times, the last time his thigh and pelvis were terribly smashed and he was on his back for about two years. There are still some pieces of metal in the bones which are all right as long as they don't move.[53]

A few days later, the couple decided to have their engagement officially announced, and it appeared in the Ottawa press on 7 January,[54] though many people knew about it before that.[55] The family and ADCs

Figure 19.1 Lady Dorothy Cavendish and Captain Harold Macmillan were married in St Margaret's Church on the grounds of Westminster Abbey on 21 April 1920.

celebrated with the public 9 January at a ball inaugurating the Cliffside Ski Club, of which the duke was honorary president.[56] The event was attended by the elite of Ottawa. The celebration among the couple's friends was at the Country Club on 14 January where Harold, in Blanche Egerton's words, "made a most finished, polished and amusing speech, and she [Dorothy] looked very pretty in a wonderful bright pink gown which her marvellous maid had made in a day and a night!"[57]

Though Evie did not want Dorothy and Harold to travel across the Atlantic together, she relented and they did so, leaving on 20 January with Blanche Egerton as chaperone. Harold wrote from the ship, the *Empress of France*, to thank Evie for her kindness and noted, "Miss Egerton has been an excellent chaperon, and stayed in her cabin most of the time." Dorothy's cabin was upgraded to "a very much larger and better one, including a sitting room."[58] Was he writing this to needle Evie just a little, since he must have known that she was worried about them travelling together? Perhaps he was just naive about the effect of his words. The soul of decency, Harold would not have taken advantage of the situation.

Evie was still not sure about this wedding and, given that the marriage was ultimately a troubled one, perhaps she was right.[59] She wrote to Lady Edward at the end of January, "Yes, Dorothy seems very happy and devoted to her Harold. He adores her and I think they ought to be very happy together. I wish she had not been in such a hurry to marry, but I always told Victor this would happen if he came to Canada with four daughters and a bunch of ADCs! Victor is looking forward to having Harold as a son-in-law. He is very fond of him and has a great opinion of his character and brains."[60]

About that time the duke recorded in his diary, "Evie very worried over Harold's ancestry especially as women are told that someone in Scotland had had a black baby. I wish people would not put these things into her head."[61]

In England, Dorothy met the family. She wrote to her mother that she was happy to see Maud and baby Arbell and other relatives and BJ, and reported on her meeting with Harold's family: "Poor Harold had a sad homecoming because his mother is most awfully ill ... something to do with the kidneys, but not tuberculosis ... Mr. Mac seemed a dear but was very shy and as I was still more so we didn't get on very well ... I can't in the least make out what is the matter with the brother [Arthur]. He came to the station looking too extraordinary. He's got a black beard, the spottiest face I have ever seen, and he came there in a top hat looking like nothing on earth ... He reads books of Law and plays the clarionette [*sic*]!"[62]

Evie sailed to England in mid-February. Victor stayed in Ottawa for the opening of Parliament in the new building and left in early March.

Dorothy and Harold were married at historic St Margaret's Church, on the grounds of Westminster Abbey, on 21 April 1920, before an august congregation filled with members of royalty and the aristocracy. It was the wedding of the season. Once those in attendance were seated, carriages arrived carrying the king's mother, Queen Alexandra, his sister, Princess Victoria, his son, Prince Albert (later King George VI), and the Duke of Connaught. The small church was packed to bursting, mostly with aristocratic friends of the Devonshires, but also a few notable authors from the Macmillan publishing house, including Henry James and Thomas Hardy.[63] The whole of Victor and Evie's family had convened in London: Eddy, Moucher, Maud, Blanche, Ivan, Rachel, Charlie, Anne, and Lady Edward in her bath chair.[64] The reception at Lansdowne House was a grand affair, though Lord Lansdowne himself did not appear. He said he was too shaky to enjoy a large family gathering.[65]

Dorothy and Harold honeymooned first at Compton Place, the Devonshires' large country house at Eastbourne,[66] and then at Bolton Abbey in the Yorkshire Dales, another family estate, which had thirty thousand acres of farms, woods, and heather moors where they could wander.[67] Evie wrote to her mother as she and Victor were boarding the RMS *Empress of France* for their journey back to Ottawa,[68] "Dorothy writes a glowing account of Bolton and says she did not know that anyone could be so happy. They take their luncheon out every day and walk for miles on the moors."[69]

CHAPTER 20

The End of an Era

Near the end of 1919, Prime Minister Borden felt tired. He had been Conservative Party leader since 1901 and Prime Minister of Canada since he had defeated the Laurier Liberals in 1911. As prime minister, he had lost his first parliamentary battle in 1913 when he proposed the Naval Aid Bill, which was to contribute funds to the British navy. After that, he had sharpened his skills and lost very few battles. He sent Canadians to support the British army in 1914, and, when the flow of volunteers ebbed in late 1916, he crafted a Union government by convincing some Liberals to join him in imposing conscription to ensure Canadian battalions remained at full strength. He ensured his election victory by enfranchising those women who had men at the front and by disenfranchising those people who had emigrated from enemy countries. He removed the potential scourge of an aristocracy from his young nation by eliminating, at least under his watch, the opportunity for Canadians to receive British honours. He saved the bankrupt railways that held the country together.

When Borden went to Europe at the conclusion of the hostilities in 1918, he had one major goal that remained unfulfilled. Canada must become a nation in its own right, not entirely separate from but not merely an appendage of Britain. Canada had, after all, lavished almost sixty thousand young lives, and suffered many more wounded, along with much of its treasure on the European battlefields in support of the Empire. Borden was passionately loyal to the British Empire and British institutions, but he believed that Canada must be represented at the

Peace Conference as a separate nation within the Empire. He noted in his memoirs that "upon the basis of equal nationhood and adequate voice in external relations the salvation of the Commonwealth could be worked out."[1] Though his colleagues wanted him at home to deal with problems they were encountering, Borden decided to stay in Paris to focus on the Peace Conference,[2] afraid that he would lose his place at the table if he left midway. "It would be intolerable," he said, if the Dominions "who numbered their dead by the hundred thousand in the fiercest struggle the world had ever known, should stand outside the council chamber of the Conference, while nations that had taken no direct or active part in the struggle stood within and determined the conditions of Peace."[3]

British Prime Minister David Lloyd George and the Imperial War Cabinet finally agreed that the Dominions and India could each have the same representation as the smaller Allied nations. As well, the British Empire delegation of five members could, from time to time, include members from the Dominions.[4] When that was proposed to a meeting of the Four Great Powers (Britain, France, Italy, and the United States) it met with opposition, especially from President Wilson of the United States. The four powers proposed instead that the Dominions and India should have one delegate while the smaller Allied nations, many of whom had taken no active part in the war, would be entitled to two delegates.[5] This was definitely not acceptable to Borden. Eventually, the Great Powers agreed that Canada, Australia, South Africa, and India were entitled to two delegates each and New Zealand to one. "In numbers at least the representation of the British Empire was sufficiently impressive."[6] One part of Borden's goal had been achieved.[7]

In Ottawa, the governor general followed the press reports of the Peace Conference, though he did not comment in his diary or letters on Canada's representation. In February, a rumour began that Borden had been offered the British ambassadorship in Washington. By the time it reached the duke, it seemed a *fait accompli*. He wrote to Evie: "We have been much excited about Sir Robert Borden and the rumour that he is to go to Washington. I should be very sorry personally and I do not think he would make a particularly good ambassador."[8] It was true that Lloyd George had privately discussed the possibility with Borden, but the latter said he could not make any decision until he saw his colleagues in Canada. Both claimed they did not tell the press.[9] In the end, Borden did not go to Washington.

The duke was confused, as well he might have been, about a 23 January news report. "Curious development at Peace Conference. They have settled to call Russian representatives to a conference on an island in the Sea of Marmara. It is all very perplexing."[10]

The Peace Conference had called a meeting of all the Russian factions at Prinkipo, the largest of the Princes' Islands in the Sea of Marmara near Istanbul, instead of calling the Bolsheviks to Paris, which would have given them legitimacy. In any case, it was not clear who spoke for the Russian people, so they invited both the Bolsheviks and their opponents, the White Russians. Borden, to his pleasure, was asked to be a representative at that meeting. The Bolsheviks agreed to come, though they did not agree to the condition that they must cease hostilities prior to the meeting. The White Russians were appalled at the very suggestion. In the face of increasing criticism of the idea in their home countries, Wilson, Lloyd George, and the French Prime Minister Georges Clemenceau let the suggestion pass without pressing the meeting further.[11]

Borden did get to play a role at the Peace Conference. He was elected vice-chairman of the Greek Committee, whose task was to discuss the borders between Greece, Albania, and Thrace. Three nations – Italy, Greece, and Serbia – each wanted a piece of Albania, and the Albanians wanted Kosovo added to their country. Borden was pleased to be a part of these discussions. In the end, no one was happy with the settlement, which was not completed until 1920.[12]

Borden returned to Ottawa on 26 May. The duke thought he looked tired.[13] He still had to face the crisis of the Winnipeg General Strike, but that was settled by mid-June when the perpetrators were arrested. In September, Borden put the peace treaties, chief among them the Treaty of Versailles, to a vote in the Canadian Parliament to prove that Canada had her own say in these international matters. The duke commented to his mother in a July letter: "Parliament is to meet on Sept. 4 as it has been considered necessary to have a special session to ratify the Peace Treaty, although I can't imagine that anyone will take the slightest notice if Canada does not ratify the treaties."[14] To Borden, though, it was absolutely essential that Canada debate, and eventually ratify, the treaties, and so he made it happen.

By December, the Prince of Wales's popular tour had helped confirm the country's loyalty to Britain and the Empire; the prince had been properly fêted and given a resounding send-off from Canadian shores. Labour unrest had subsided. Now Borden's exhaustion surfaced.

On the morning of 12 December 1919, Borden rang the Duke of Devonshire to ask for a meeting. They met at noon in the duke's East Block office on Parliament Hill. Borden reported the news from his doctors, including two specialists, saying that "he must resign or have a nervous breakdown or worse."[15] The prime minister was fully convinced that it was in the interests of neither the country nor himself that he continue in his post. "He had no suggestion as to a successor," the duke noted in his diary. "It is certainly difficult to see how this govt can last." They discussed who would be able to maintain the coalition of Conservatives and Liberals that Borden had put together. The duke recorded in his diary: "Rowell, Calder and Meighen were the names mentioned but none of them seemed likely. He also mentioned that from a constitutional point I might have to ask Sir George Foster as senior privy councilor. I shall miss Borden, although he has not been as strong lately as I think he might have been."[16] Later that afternoon Borden "communicated with his colleagues" about his doctor's opinion.[17]

By 15 December, the press had found out about Borden's probable resignation, though he would not confirm or deny it.[18] There was still no idea who would succeed him. The following day, Borden noted that he "attended the Governor General to whom I gave a definite intimation of my retirement,"[19] though to the duke it had seemed quite definite earlier. The duke's view of this second meeting was slightly different: "Interesting talk with the PM but he had no further information. The Govt are evidently going to let everything drift and leave it to a caucus. Not a good solution."[20] On 20 December, the duke wrote in his diary: "Very interesting conversation with the PM. He hopes the new arrangements will work, but really there are no new arrangements at all. It is simply going along in the hopes that something will turn up."[21]

He sympathized with Borden's desire for a rest. As he wrote to his mother, "I am sure he would have a bad breakdown if he did not get a real rest. The surprising thing is not that he should be feeling the strain now, but that he did not feel it before. His loss will be a serious blow to the government and it is doubtful if they will last long without him."[22]

That was the point. The government was Borden's coalition; it might not survive without him. The cabinet proposed to Borden on 17 December that he "retain the Premiership and take a vacation of a year."[23] Borden agreed, switched some government posts, put Sir George Foster in charge, attended the governor general's New Year's Day Levee, and left on vacation on 2 January. "Nothing has been definitely settled for the rearrangement of the work," was the duke's worried comment to his diary.[24]

There was probably little the governor general could do. As was his duty, he kept Lord Milner, now secretary of state for the colonies, informed about the situation.[25] Perhaps he expressed his opinion to Borden that the leadership issue should be settled before he left, but the governor general could not ask another member of Parliament to try to form a government while the prime minister was still their leader. There was no general outcry among the public, and, as it had during the Peace Conference, the government muddled on.

Since Sir Robert Borden was still prime minister, the press followed his movements in detail. He travelled to New York and Florida with Lady Borden. Then, leaving his wife behind in West Palm Beach, he sailed with Admiral Lord Jellicoe on HMS *New Zealand* to Havana, Cuba,[26] then to Kingston, Jamaica,[27] and Port of Spain, Trinidad. The press reported that Borden was on his way to South Africa,[28] leaving Canada a "rudderless ship of state" for longer than any other prime minister of an important nation. Instead, Lord Jellicoe's ship sailed directly for England where it arrived on 2 February.[29]

On 31 January, Borden wrote to the duke from the *New Zealand* as they reached latitude 45 degrees, well north of Spain. He was "delighted to leave behind the oppressive heat of the tropics," and, though the sea was rough, he did not mind "being more or less hurled about as if in a railway collision." (They had shared an adventure the previous November when, returning from Halifax where they had seen the Prince of Wales off, their train had crashed into another and Borden had been knocked to the floor. No one was injured, and they laughed about it and resumed their bridge game.[30]) Borden said he had not been in touch with Ottawa since his departure. After a month in England, he returned to the United States, and was inundated with news from home, his "vacation" compromised.[31]

On 26 February 1920, Parliament opened in the new Centre Block, built to replace the building destroyed by fire in 1916. Despite the financial restraints occasioned by the war, the building had been lavishly decorated. The exterior was of locally quarried Nepean sandstone. The use of marble from the Missisquoi quarries in Quebec and Tyndall stone from Manitoba for the interior greatly added to the building's beauty.[32] The Prince of Wales had laid the cornerstone during his visit and now the building was almost ready for occupancy – almost. Some thought it should not be used for the opening of Parliament, but as the duke told his mother, "a good many of them know that if anything in the way of an election took place they would not come back and they did not want to lose the chance of getting in while they can."[33]

For the opening ceremony, "the floor of the House was occupied by an assembly of the political, social and official life of the nation, with the women wearing beautiful gowns," *The Globe* gushed.[34] So much ceremony and display had not been seen since before the war, making it even more poignant.[35] The Duke of Devonshire wore his decorated uniform and, as *The Globe* described it, "the crimson and ermine robes of the Justices of the Supreme Court, the Windsor uniforms of the Privy Councillors, the scarlet gowns of the papal delegates, the khaki of the military officers, the navy blue of the naval officers accompanying His Excellency, all added to the richness and picturesqueness of the spectacle."[36]

By tradition, the Speech from the Throne is given in the Senate Chamber, since neither the governor general nor the senators may enter the House of Commons. In 1920, the new Senate Chamber was not ready for occupancy, so both senators and MPs met in the House of Commons, just for the reading of the speech. The duke, who always worried about reading a Speech from the Throne, was relieved when he "got through it somehow." He held a reception, shaking hands with the many guests. The MPs retired to the Railway Committee Room in the Centre Block for a business session.[37] The following day a *Globe* editorial called the Speech from the Throne "a negligible document," and accused the cabinet of being "hangers-on-to-office." The Union government members "are frightened to move forward, unwilling to make way," the editorial stated.[38] Still nothing happened about the government. Everyone waited for Borden's return and wondered whether he would continue as leader.

Borden returned on 12 May. By that time, the duke had been to England for Dorothy and Harold's wedding and was back in Ottawa with the duchess. Borden did resume government leadership, guiding the last weeks of the parliamentary session. The duke saw him on 13 May and thought he looked better and was in good spirits, but the duke was somewhat irritated that "he was quite incapable of giving any indications of what he is going to do."[39] Just over a month later, on 21 June, Borden told the duke that he could not see how he could continue. A week later, the duke recorded: "Saw the Prime Minister. He says he has definitely made up his mind to retire and discussed various alternatives for his successor."[40]

The duke was again irritated, this time because he had to stay in Ottawa; he had planned a trip to Newfoundland which now had to be put off, but it could not be helped. On 1 July, he prorogued Parliament in the still-unfinished Senate Chamber, but railed to his diary: "the proceedings went off quite as well as could be hoped but it is impossible to make an inspiring ceremony in such bad surroundings. Next year the Senate Chambers ought to be finished and it will be possible to have everything properly done."[41]

The duke had a meeting with Borden that day at which they discussed the party leadership. Sir Thomas White appeared to be the favoured candidate, though Arthur Meighen, minister of the Interior, and Sir Henry Drayton, the finance minister, also seemed probable choices for his successor. Borden met with his caucus later that day and told them of his decision. The members did not want to follow the usual convention of electing a new party leader. This government was not a party, but a coalition of Conservatives and Liberals that Borden had put together. At the suggestion of Sir George Foster, they agreed to each give Borden a letter stating their preferences for leader and ask Borden to name his successor.[42] Borden then met with the press. On 2 July, the governor general noted, "The Press on the whole has got a fairly good appreciation of the position. The references to Sir Robert while not fulsome have a genuine ring and are well expressed."[43]

Borden told the duke that he was trying to get hold of Sir Thomas

White. Although many in the caucus favoured Meighen, Borden thought the cabinet members would not support Meighen unless they were sure that White would not accept.[44] Three days later, the governor general had heard nothing further. "A government must be going on," he fretted.[45] Later that afternoon, Borden appeared and asked the duke to write to White. Borden had been in touch with White, "who asked him not to press his invitation [to come to Ottawa],"[46] however, his colleagues thought that White might agree if he were pressed. The duke discussed the requested letter with Sir Joseph Pope, then wrote asking White to come to Ottawa as soon as possible: "I venture to urge you not to come to any final conclusion as to your course of action until I have had an opportunity of full discussion with you."[47] Colonel Henderson left on the night train to Toronto to deliver the letter personally. Next day, the duke heard from Henderson that White was in Muskoka, a rural district more than a hundred miles north of Toronto, and Henderson was trying to get through to him on the long-distance telephone. Another day lost. "These delays are really very tiresome," the duke complained.[48] Finally, on 7 July, White arrived in Ottawa. He told Borden and then the duke that he was not capable of doing the work because of his health.[49] White was only fifty-four, but he, too, had been burned out by the stresses of war service.

That left Arthur Meighen to be asked to form a government. The duke thought that "Meighen, who is the next choice, will not be nearly so capable of forming a strong administration."[50] However, after a long day of discussions with their colleagues, Borden and Meighen came to Government House at 10:00 p.m. "Meighen was very nice and obviously a little overwhelmed by the responsibility. I am to see him tomorrow and he hopes to get the change of office on Saturday. Borden in the meantime will hold his formal resignation up till then."[51]

This gave Meighen time to try to gather support among the caucus. Only Martin Burrell, minister of Customs and Inland Revenue, and N.W. Rowell, president of the Privy Council and minister of Health, resigned from cabinet. Meighen made an attempt to gather support in Quebec and, specifically, to get Lomer Gouin, who had just resigned as premier of Quebec, to join them in the cabinet, but Gouin refused. By 10 July, Meighen had rallied enough support; the governor general swore him in with Borden present and the formal transition of power was made. By now the duke was feeling somewhat reassured and wrote, "Talk with Meighen. He is making progress. He distinctly improves as one gets to know him better."[52] It was another three days before the full cabinet could be sworn in, though there were few new members. The Borden era was over, but the Union government had survived – for the present.

A few months after Victor and Evie returned to Ottawa from Dorothy and Harold's wedding, Evie wanted to go home again. Dorothy was pregnant and Evie badly wanted to be there when the baby arrived – she had already missed Blanche's first baby, born 1 March 1920. Unfortunately, there were still fifteen months to go in their five-year term. She told her mother, "We have settled that I ought not to go home a third time before the winter season is over so Dorothy will have to have her baby without me."[53]

Victor, in contrast, was depressed that his time in Canada was slipping away. In March 1920, he noted in his diary that two-thirds of his time in Canada was over, forty of his sixty months.[54] Victor was at the height of his career, now very comfortable in Canada, familiar with the landscape and the people, at the centre of politics, which he loved, doing the best job he had ever had, fulfilling his duty for King and Empire. On top of that, Canada was a playground for his favourite sports. From the *Empress of France* as they returned from the wedding, Evie reported to her mother, "Victor is thoroughly happy – all the Canadians on board are so obviously pleased to see him and he feels as much at home with them."[55] She did not need to tell her mother her own reaction.

Evie worried about Rachel, now eighteen and already in full bloom. A year later, her grandfather, Lord Lansdowne, referred to her "radiant ... health and spirits."[56] Rachel excelled at sports – particularly swimming and figure skating; she had almost won competitions at the Minto Skating Club against girls with much longer experience.[57] At the Rideau Hall Saturday afternoon skating parties, it was Rachel's presence that "put a lot more go into the proceedings," according to her father.[58] Evie wanted to avoid yet another daughter marrying an ADC. She had worried in the summer of 1919 when Rachel had been chums with Lord Hugh Molyneux and had told Lady Edward, "They trot about together like two children and he always sits next to her at meals, but they are both such babies that I don't think it matters and he leaves next week."[59] When Molyneux was replaced by Geordie Haddington, Evie worried that a nervous, sleep-deprived Geordie was in love with Rachel and might propose. Though he was an aristocrat – his father had died in 1917 and Geordie was now 12th Earl of Haddington – Evie feared he drank too much and might gamble, and, in any case, Rachel was "*much* too young to marry."[60]

Both Evie and Victor agreed there were problems on their estates that would require their presence in England sometime soon. Though they had sold Devonshire House, their other properties needed attention. Evie had seen, while they were in England, that some of their good caretakers were ill, and there was no one to look after things properly. "Not that Victor himself will as he never bothers much," she told her mother, "but it is better for him to be on the spot."[61]

A story in the press on 2 January 1920 said that the Duke of Devonshire would decline an invitation to extend his stay in Ottawa.[62] At the time he had received no such invitation,[63] but in March, Sir Robert Borden, then on holiday in London, wrote to say he would prefer the duke to serve his full time, or even extend it, and that Borden had spoken to Bonar Law about an extension. Evie, however, lobbied for an early departure. By November, Evie reported to her mother, "Victor has at last written to tell Lord Milner that, if convenient, he would like to get away about June."[64] In January 1921, when they heard that early departure was accepted, Evie knew that Victor was disappointed, but she thought it would be much better to get Rachel home before the expected crisis occurred with an ADC.[65]

While he was dealing with the resignation of Sir Robert Borden and the installation of a new prime minister, Victor chafed at the delay to his Maritime tour and visit to the British colony of Newfoundland. He had needed the king's permission before leaving Canada, and now the king had obliged.

On the afternoon of 13 July, with the new prime minister, Arthur Meighen, duly installed and some additional ministers sworn in, Victor left by train with Colonel Henderson. Evie had left earlier with Maud (she and Arbell had come back from England with Victor and Evie after Dorothy and Harold's wedding), Rachel, Anne, and Walter Dalkeith, the new ADC, as well as a new Blanche, this one Evie's sister's daughter, who had also accompanied them from England.

The family reconvened in Newcastle, New Brunswick, and boarded the familiar yacht, HMCS *Hochelaga*. Their first stop was Prince Edward Island for visits to the small cities of Summerside and Cavendish before motoring on to the island's capital, Charlottetown. They carefully toured both the Protestant and Roman Catholic hospitals and shook hands at garden parties. Meeting the *Hochelaga* again at Souris at the eastern end of the island, they sailed for the Magdalen Islands, Quebec, where they spent another day shaking hands. At last they weighed anchor, heading for Port aux Basques, Newfoundland, and, after landing there just to gather supplies and a guide, sailed on to the tiny community of La Poile on the south coast, a community that boasted seven families, a lobster cannery and a shipbuilding yard.[66]

Once again, Victor thrilled to the exertion of fishing in the rough. Three days of rain and fog was a hindrance, but Victor managed to catch a couple of salmon and everyone seemed to enjoy themselves. They returned to Port aux Basques and sailed north to the west coast village of Humbermouth (now part of the city of Corner Brook) to fish the Humber River. One sunny day, they went south on a rickety train to visit the little village of Harry's Brook, and another day they sailed north to Bonne Bay for more fishing. Although the whole party caught only a few trout and salmon, Victor pronounced the trip a huge success.

Evie's point of view was somewhat different. She reported to her mother, "As you know, yachting does not agree with me, but we have had a very interesting time and have been into a lot of perfectly lovely bays, almost landlocked in some cases and with wooded hills going straight down into the sea."[67] On their way back to Canada, Evie suffered "a perfectly horrible 24 hours from Newfoundland to Sydney. Anne was almost in a state of collapse. The maids were useless. Victor did steward as best he could."[68]

After a day of touring Louisbourg and Glace Bay, Nova Scotia, with the usual receptions, everyone again boarded the *Hochelaga* to cross the inland sea called Bras d'Or Lake to St Peter's, Nova Scotia. After passing through the Strait of Canso to Newcastle, New Brunswick, they boarded the train back to Ottawa.

The family spent much of August at New Lismore, their home at Blue Sea Lake. Maud's daughter, Arbell, now two, delighted her doting grandfather, who thought her the most attractive child he had ever seen.[69] "When Arbell wants to be cheeky she calls Maud 'Maud' instead of mother and then goes off into fit of chuckles and laughters," Evie wrote to her mother.[70] The usual family summer at the cottage included Charlie, who arrived for his holidays and fished with his father. One day Victor took a party in canoes to Cedar Lake north of Blue Sea to fish for bass. Another day, Maud and Rachel, with an ADC, left the fishing party to paddle on to Maniwaki. A thunderstorm came up and they did not come home. When someone went across the lake to the post office at Burbidge Station, there was no news. Victor and Evie spent an anxious night. In the morning there was a telegram at the Burbidge post office: "Survived thunderstorm damp but cheerful."[71] To his relief, when he went back to Ottawa that afternoon, Victor found them on the train.

Part of cottage life was visiting neighbours for tea. Ottawa diarist Ethel Chadwick tells of a swimming party at the architect Allan Keefer's cottage. She encountered the Duchess of Devonshire and "I had to make a bob curtsey in a bathing suit!"[72] In the style of the day, her bathing suit was really a short dress. Another day at Blue Sea, Victor had a message from Colonel Henderson saying that a policeman was on his way to Blue Sea because there had been letters with threats from Sinn Fein. Victor was not anxious for himself, but Sinn Fein and the Irish Republican Army (IRA) were continuing their fight for greater independence from Britain; Victor thought his Irish property, Lismore Castle, may have figured in their sights. The man was supposed to be undercover, but, when he arrived, a footman announced him as a policeman. "As he is here, he had better stay," Victor decided,[73] and they added another to the large gathering at New Lismore.

Soon the pleasant interlude at the lake with fishing, bathing, and visiting had to come to an end. Evie and Victor returned to Ottawa to prepare for another trip west. This tour began with a train trip directly to Edmonton. While Evie, Maud, Rachel, and Blanche, with two ADCs, moved on to Jasper, Victor travelled north through the Peace River country of Alberta. This was new territory for the governor general. Besides the usual formal proceedings, he spent a night in a "very primitive" place called Waterhole and discovered that he had "no wish for a pioneer life." He managed to get in some shooting for prairie chicken and ducks. "Great fun," he enthused.[74] Almost two weeks later, he rejoined the others in Jasper.

Meanwhile, Evie and her party had taken guides, tents, and pack horses into the Maligne Lake area in Jasper National Park. At the time the road went only to Maligne Canyon, just outside the town of Jasper. In mid-September it could be snowy in the high mountains. Partway in they stopped for the night. Evie wrote to Victor, "Our camp was in a thick and rather damp wood, so it was not quite easy to unpack and settle in in the dark. However, we were very comfortable round a big fire till the tepee and supper were ready. We all got up early and washed in an icy cold stream. My ablutions were rather scanty but Maud and Rachel splashed about and said they liked it. I wished I could have done a picture of them very pink and white and slim amongst the trees and moss."[75] They went another fourteen miles to the lake, where accommodation was in a log cabin with two beds and a stove, with tents pitched on the big verandah for the men. As it snowed overnight, the guides said they could not go any farther; there were no trails, and the way would not be clear in the snow. Evie was relieved and stayed in the cabin writing letters while the others went out for walks. She wrote to Victor, "This is an open valley with very park-like shores to the lake but there are huge mountains all round, now entirely covered with snow."[76] And later, "It was too funny to see Maud washing her cold feet in one corner, R doing her hair, Walter shaving, Jack drying his stockings, B performing some mysterious changes of undergarments beneath her upper clothes."[77]

They hoped for a change in the weather, but when there was more wet snow they decided to go back. Evie, riding on a man's saddle, agreed to do the whole twenty-four miles in one day. They left early, stopped for luncheon about halfway back at Medicine Lake, and made it to Maligne Canyon before dark. Evie was proud of herself for not being either stiff or tired. They were all very happy, despite the weather and change of plans.

When Victor joined them, he had one day to ride a little and to hear their stories before they moved on over the Yellowhead Pass by train. Mount Robson afforded a splendid view that day. At Blue River, Victor received a telegram that his mother, Lady Edward Cavendish, had died. Both Victor and Evie were sad, but there was little they could do except carry on. They did cancel some social events.[78] The train took them through to Kamloops and Vancouver, where they boarded the ss *Stadacona* and sailed to Campbell River, about halfway up Vancouver Island on the inland side. They made their way by motor down the island to Victoria, visiting communities in the usual way, then to Vancouver and back east, stopping at a few communities, arriving in Ottawa after five weeks of travelling.

By the fall of 1920, the story of the Devonshires' adventures in Canada was winding down.[79] As he cleared up his papers, Victor noted the tremendous change there had been since the end of the war and how much easier things were.[80] The major events of 1917 through 1919 had given way to a period of calm for the governor general.

By 1920, civil life in Canada had begun to return to a new normal. Many organizations were holding conferences, and the duke opened them, gave welcoming speeches, and entertained the delegates at Rideau Hall. The Canadian Bar Association, the Imperial Press Association, the Boy Scouts, and many others met in Ottawa. The duchess was also busy opening bazaars, meeting with Women's Institutes, the Red Cross, the Victorian Order of Nurses, and the Imperial Order Daughters of the Empire (IODE). Together the duke and duchess frequently held garden parties on the Rideau Hall grounds for a thousand or more, shaking hands with each one. The stream of British visitors continued as family, friends, and acquaintances came to stay at Government House. In the winter of 1921, Rideau Hall skating parties were more popular than ever. The duke reported over eight hundred attending one Saturday.[81] The skating season finished with an evening carnival.[82]

Entertainment was now much more frequent. They went to concerts and plays. On Victor's birthday, they went to see a vaudeville troupe created by Canadian soldiers during the war to entertain the troops. Called The Dumbells, the troupe was touring Canada and later went on to take Broadway by storm.[83] "Movies" were available too, although they were silent except for the efforts of a local piano player. Victor was not very impressed, but Rachel liked them.[84] Victor really enjoyed hockey games, but thought baseball, where he would be asked to throw the first pitch, most tedious.[85] There were also visiting lecturers. Sir Ernest Shackleton, the British hero of Antarctic exploration, came by to tell the story of his trials in attempting to cross Antarctica and how he returned to Britain without any loss of life, in contrast to Robert Scott, his predecessor, who had led a similar but disastrous expedition there earlier.[86]

Victor struggled with speeches in both English and French. He worried about his Armistice Day speeches in 1920. His first was at the Empire Club in Toronto where, more than a year after the Winnipeg General Strike, he urged captains of industry to get together with their employees before any work stoppage could take place. The long *Globe* report quoted his comments in considerable detail.[87] That same evening, the duke spoke to the Royal Canadian Institute about the importance of research, and his remarks were published in their entirety in *The Globe*. In introducing the duke, the president of the institute mentioned the importance of the Cavendish Laboratory, founded by the 7th Duke of Devonshire when he was chancellor of Cambridge University.[88] The duke was relieved to have these speeches behind him.

In Montreal the next day, with no speech to make, he expressed for the only time in his five Canadian years a morose mood: "As usual every prospect of a boring day. If I could go about as ordinary individual there would be plenty to do."[89] After luncheon and later tea with his group of friends, his mood improved.

In Quebec City, the duke met with society leaders and complained about not being able to get below the surface to find out what people really thought – "below the 'dinner' list" as he put it.[90] He preferred events with representative groups where he could feel the pulse of the nation. Victor was good at chatting with people, listening to their views, and coming to his own conclusions about what was really going on in their minds. By now he knew many people rather well.

Victor had one last hunting trip, five days on the Quebec side of the Ottawa River across from Mattawa, Ontario. He wrote to Evie describing three French-Canadian "halfbreed" guides who were "very intelligent" and was impressed that two of them had "been overseas." In a one-room log cabin, seven men slept comfortably on balsam beds. The washing facilities consisted of a single basin. "He [the owner] asked me if I could suggest any improvements and I told him that I thought some more adequate arrangements might be made for washing. He only laughed and said he had noticed that the 'Captain' [Victor's ADC] and I had washed more than anybody who had been here." Hunting for deer with dogs proved unsuccessful since the deer "refused to do its part and did not take to the water." Hunting for moose was equally unsuccessful, but they did get two partridges. Victor loved tramping through the woods all day and slept like a log each night, returning to Ottawa rested and happy.[91]

Parliament opened on 14 February 1921. The *Citizen* noted: "His Excellency the Governor General was escorted by a mounted squadron and received by the Governor General's Foot Guards while a battery on nearby Nepean Point thundered out the customary royal salute."[92]

This was the first year of the return to prewar tradition, with the opening ceremony being held in the new red Senate Chamber, richly decorated with red carpets, red chairs, red on the dais, and red drapings on the throne. The red and ermine cloaks of the justices added to the splendour. Throngs awaited the arrival of His Excellency outside on Parliament Hill. Inside the chamber accommodation was limited, but a number of visitors, including ladies with beautiful gowns, were admitted. Headed by the speaker, members of the House of Commons paraded to the Senate, heard the Speech from the Throne delivered in both English and French, and then withdrew again to the Commons. As usual, the duke worried about making his speech, especially the part in French, but it all went well. This time the chamber was properly prepared; the ceremony could be held with dignity, and was followed by a state dinner and reception.[93]

A few days later, the duke and duchess hosted an event that may have seemed like an anachronism to those who had recently argued, in repudiating British honours, for a more democratic society.[94] At least one person who had previously been thrilled to receive an invitation to any viceregal event, Ethel Chadwick, decided to sit this one out. Her diary does not give her reasons.[95] But the event did attract a substantial group of participants.

Their Excellencies invited the citizens to a formal "drawing-room," where participants could be presented, in order of precedence, to the viceregal couple seated on the red thrones of the newly rebuilt Senate Chamber. Drawing rooms in Canada, begun by Governor General Lord Dufferin and Lady Dufferin in 1872,[96] were modelled on those held at court by Queen Victoria, where, with her royal relatives, she received diplomats and debutantes. For young, unmarried women in Britain, this was a rite of passage to adulthood, a "coming out." This 1921 event in Canada was the first of its kind since the autumn of 1914. The press published instructions for those attending: the event would begin at 9:00 p.m.; doors would not be open before 7:30; ladies intending to be presented for the first time should obtain a presentation card from the aide-de-camp-in-waiting at Government House before the event; carriages could enter Parliament Square by the eastern entrance and leave by the centre or western entrance. Those in cabinet or other high positions were allowed private entrée with their wives, unmarried daughters, and unmarried sisters.

During the event, prior to 9:00 p.m., the governor general received the consuls general of many nations. Then, as strains of music filled the air, Their Excellencies entered the Senate Chamber. The duchess was gracious in a princess-style gown of gold and black brocade, with a long court train of black velvet lined with gold cloth. Her train was carried by two pages dressed in yellow and blue, the Cavendish colours. "Her Excellency wore the orders of Mistress of the Robes, Lady of Justice of the Order of Saint John of Jerusalem, and the coronation medals worn at the coronations of King Edward and King George. Her jewels were a diamond tiara, diamond necklace, and the famous Devonshire pearls. She carried a shower of pale-pink roses."[97] The news reports did not describe the duke's dress but he undoubtedly wore his full uniform with his Order of the Garter sash and medal and his other decorations. The duke and duchess passed through a military guard to the thrones at the head of the Senate Chamber. Lady Rachel and another Rideau Hall guest were the first presented and then stood on the left of the duchess. Their Excellencies received all those presented in order of precedence, beginning with Prime Minister and Mrs Meighen.

This event was intended as a show of affection for Their Excellencies and their household and as a statement of Canada's importance as a nation in the great Empire. The duke thought only 900 people had come and was disappointed,[98] but the *Ottawa Journal* said that about 1,100 had been presented that evening, including guests from many parts of Canada.[99] Although the honours debate in Parliament and in the country had shown some desire for Canadians to divest themselves of British aristocracy and embrace democracy, this event showed that the Empire was not yet dead in the minds of Canadians.

The duke and duchess probably felt it necessary to hold the event since they had not been able to entertain as fully as most governors general because of the war and the construction on Parliament Hill. It did give Evie a chance to wear her medals and jewels and Victor to wear his Order of the Garter. It also re-established the traditional event in which the governor general and his wife received guests as vice-royalty, events that carried on, usually at the opening of Parliament, until the Second World War.

Victor and Evie's return to England in June had been formally agreed to, but there was one more hurdle: it would depend on Victor's successor being appointed. Just a few months remained of Victor's adventure and Evie's quarantine, away from her family and friends. Rumours swirled about the next governor general – perhaps the Duke of Northumberland, or Baron Desborough, or Viscount Byng of Vimy – but there was no confirmation.[100]

While they waited, they embarked on farewell tours of Canada. Their western tour this time took them through the southern Canadian railway route and over the Georgia Strait to Victoria, returning via the more northern Yellowhead Pass through Jasper. On the way out, they visited a ranch belonging to the Prince of Wales about twenty miles south of Calgary. During his tour in 1919, the Prince of Wales had visited an Alberta ranch and was so entranced by the beautiful rolling foothills with the Rocky Mountain peaks on the western horizon that he purchased the adjoining ranch and called it the EP Ranch (Edward Prince).[101] The duke approved. "No pretensions. Saw the stock he brought out from England. Quite good."[102]

Eddy, Moucher, and Maud (Arbell was with her grandparents in Scotland)[103] joined them at Banff, where everyone except the duke and duchess went bathing in the Upper Hot Springs. The duke, as usual, revelled in meeting people, many of whom he now knew well. Evie went to meetings of Women's Institutes, the IODE, the YWCA, and other similar functions, but her mind was on returning home to England. She wrote to Mr Burke, their estate agent, from the train, discussing the servants and their deployment on the family's return.[104]

Victor took Eddy and Moucher on a trip to Georgian Bay. They visited a few towns, attended the usual receptions, saw the Algoma Steel Works in Sault Ste Marie, managed some not very successful fishing, and enjoyed the duke's first visit to this part of Canada. In Montreal, Victor and Evie said goodbye to those they had known best during their tenure in Canada, their friends the Merediths, the Montagu Allans, and the Atholstans.[105] At the Blue Bonnets racetrack (later renamed the Hippodrome de Montréal), the duke enjoyed a ride up the course in a state carriage with an escort of Canadian dragoons.

Finally, on 3 June 1921, the duke received a cable confirming that Lord Byng of Vimy had accepted the post of governor general. Byng was popular in Canada; he had commanded the Canadian troops at their successful battle for Vimy Ridge in 1917. When Evie heard that Byng had appointed a Canadian ADC to his staff, she thought it "would wreck G.H. for all future GGs." She went so far as to dictate a telegram for Victor to send to Byng: "May I mention that Canadian staff has always been strongly deprecated here as dangerous precedent and likely to cause social and racial jealousies – feel sure this objection is very real one."[106] There is no record in the archives of such a telegram and it is unlikely that the duke would have sent it; Byng did have Canadians as aides-de-camp.[107]

That same day, the House of Commons recognized the governor general. The duke was more than pleased: "It is just extraordinary how nice people are and I think they are really sorry that we are going. In the HofC an address was moved to be presented to me and all the speeches were most kind and friendly."[108] The address was moved by Prime Minister Meighen and seconded by Opposition Leader Mackenzie King. It offered words of thanks to His Excellency for his service to the country during "days of storm and stress ... and the difficult period of consequent readjustment." The address noted that he had fully upheld the traditions of the high office and established a place of warm regard in the hearts of the people. Meighen particularly appreciated that he had sought to understand the many parts of the country and that Her Excellency and his family had taken a gracious part with their tact, charm, and simplicity. Mackenzie King spoke of the appropriateness of this address being given on the king's birthday and his appreciation of His Excellency's adherence to the best of British traditions. Sir Robert Borden too spoke, as former prime minister, of the sacrifice with which the duke undertook his duties and "his experience and aptitude for public affairs, rare good judgment, firmness, steadiness, and ... a fine sense of proportion." His own relations with the governor general, he said, were "necessarily of a very intimate nature" and he had appreciated His Excellency's "thoughtful suggestions and wise counsel ... on many occasions of stress and difficulty," and the fact that he was "thoroughly receptive of the constitutional developments which have been somewhat marked in recent years."[109] The feeling was genuine.

The following evening, the duke rode to Parliament in a carriage with four horses for his final prorogation speech. Sitting in the Senate Chamber, he was again delighted with the laudatory speeches presented to him.[110] The members of Parliament and the senators were genuinely appreciative of the duke's handling of his duties, and his steady and wise counsel based on his long experience of political problems.

For a final farewell in Ottawa, the duke gave a speech at a Canadian Club luncheon, where many of his friends came to say goodbye.[111] When the Devonshires finally left Ottawa two weeks later, some ten thousand people gathered to see them off from the Union Station, which was decorated with flags, bunting, and flowering plants. His Excellency inspected the Governor General's Foot Guards. The viceregal family walked over a red carpet to enter the train while the crowd sang "For He's a Jolly Good Fellow" and "Auld Lang Syne."[112] The usually unflappable duke was emotional, moved by the spontaneous tribute. "Big crowd and a great number of personal friends. It was really horrid and

I could hardly help breaking down especially when I came to Sir Robert Borden. It was certainly a good send off. Very unhappy seeing the last of Ottawa."[113]

They headed for Quebec City and the Citadel, visited the lieutenant-governor at Spencerwood, and travelled to Sainte-Anne-de-Beaupré, the beautiful basilica and shrine built to honour Saint Anne, mother of the Virgin Mary. Many believed that Saint Anne could heal illnesses. The duke commented, "It is really rather fine but the humbug and certainty of the whole thing are appalling."[114] His prejudice against Roman Catholics, which the duke had shown privately in his diary several times during his Canadian years, had not abated.[115]

From Quebec City, while Evie stayed at the Citadel, Victor managed another two-week fishing trip at Cape Magdalen, but the water was low and the fish smaller and fewer than in 1917.[116] Saying goodbye in Quebec City was again a wrench. A dinner party at the parliamentary restaurant gave him a chance to thank the men of government and remind them of their great future. He spoke in French first, but then retreated to English.[117]

On 20 July 1921, to the music of "God Save the King" and the booms of a royal salute from the Citadel guns, the *Empress of France* set sail, carrying Victor and Evie away from five years in the colonies.[118]

Afterword

After the Devonshire family returned to England, they took account of what had happened during their almost five years in Canada. Carefully kept travel and financial records from their Canadian years are housed in the Chatsworth archives. During those years, the duke travelled 112,556 miles, including several trips to both coasts and frequent trips to Blue Sea Lake.[1] The records do not include other excursions listed in his diary. He loved travelling, but had to forgo invitations to the Yukon – travel there was difficult – and to the West Indies, which was outside Canada and not part of his mandate, though he did get to Newfoundland, which was not part of Canada at the time.

Detailed financial records show that the duke maintained both stables and a motor department at Rideau Hall. Including salaries and expenses, the stables cost him about 40 per cent more than the motor department. The Government of Canada paid the duke just over $120,000 annually (equivalent to about $2 million Canadian today[2]), which included a salary of $48,666 (valued in 1916 it would be more than $900,000 Canadian today) and allowances for staff salaries, for travel expenses, and for fuel and lighting. The value of a Canadian dollar decreased about 40 per cent from 1916 to 1920 while the duke's salary and expense allotments remained the same. The family spent nearly double their salary and expense allotments during their time in Canada, taking funds from the duke's own resources for travel and other expenses, including the purchase and maintenance of the Blue Sea Lake land and cottage.[3]

After the Devonshires' departure from Canada, the Blue Sea Lake house was put on the market but it did not sell at first. Allan Keefer, the architect who had designed the house,[4] used it with his family for the summer of 1921.[5] The duke had bought the property for $3,000 in 1918 and built the house for around $8,700. The total listed in the financial records for building and equipment from 1918 to 1921 amounted to over $11,000, which appears to include the land purchase, the building, and some expenses for living there.[6] The house and property finally sold in July 1923, for $10,800 (over $150,000 Canadian today).[7] The duke seems to have broken even on it, or better. Apparently the house burned down some years later.[8] The beautiful peninsula on which their house stood is still called Presqu'île Lismore, and there is still a spot where the train stopped on the opposite side of the lake – now just a path since the tracks were removed – which is called New Lismore.

The Duke left a handsome silver cup to be awarded to the winner of the annual international golf competition in which the Canadian Seniors' Golf Association participated.[9] He also left a silver trophy, the Devonshire Cup, to the Ottawa Horticultural Society to be awarded annually for their competition in the Decorative Classes.[10]

The duke's fishing haunts are still serving those who love the Canadian outdoors, though they are not backcountry in the way they were one hundred years ago. Today, much of the Restigouche River is still under the control of the Restigouche Salmon Club, which maintains its lodges and watches over the river and the salmon. The clubhouse in Matapedia is a smaller property now than in 1918. The club also owns about five thousand acres upriver.[11] Currently, the legal fishing season is from 15 April to 30 September. Since the club members want to fish only from about late May to the end of August, during the last decade the club has allowed the public to fish in the river in the early and later parts of the season.[12] In order to preserve dwindling fish stocks, both the provincial and federal governments have instituted catch-and-release policies for sport fishing. Most fish must be gently handled and promptly released; a small number of fish per licence can be kept. In 2011, the Restigouche Salmon Club members released all of the 2,200 fish they caught. The benefits of this program are controversial. Some believe that a fish that has been played to exhaustion and has a hook wound is unlikely to live after being released, or if it lives, to spawn.[13] Others believe that most fish live and the stock will be best preserved by these methods. The details of what tackle to use and how to release a fish is said to be important for fish survival. The quantity and size of the available fish are not as large today as in 1918, but there are still many salmon in the Restigouche River, resulting in an active sports fishing season.[14]

Today, the Cascapedia River is still relatively isolated. Only one major highway reaches the closest town, New Richmond, from Matapedia. A smaller road, now paved and not so dusty as it was in 1919, follows the river north. The Cascapedia still runs clear and quite shallow, though deep enough for the now-motorized flat-bottomed canoes that ply this river. The Cascapedia is only a stone's throw wide for a strong arm, perhaps two hundred yards near New Derreen and narrowing as the canoe travels north. Fishing on much of the river is still in private hands. The Cascapedia River Museum at Cascapedia-St-Jules, Quebec, provides fascinating details of the river's history.

When the Devonshires returned to England, their Canadian experience did influence what happened next. "Despite looking stolid and even sleepy," the duke had shown himself to be "shrewd, tactful, observant, and clear-headed. His authority rested on real though unostentatious ability."[15] The 9th Duke of Devonshire, Lord Victor Christian William Cavendish (Victor), might have harboured ambitions to become viceroy of India. Both his father-in-law, Lord Lansdowne, and his friend Lord Minto had moved from the post of Governor General of Canada to Viceroy of India, and the duke would have known that Lord Dufferin, too, had become Viceroy of India later in his career, after his time as Canada's governor general. Nothing in his diary or letters, however, shows he had any specific ambition for such a post. He did love being involved in government, though. British Prime Minister Andrew Bonar Law appointed him secretary of state for the colonies on 24 October 1922, replacing Winston Churchill. He served under Bonar Law until May 1923, when Law resigned for reasons of ill health. Stanley Baldwin took over as prime minister, and the duke continued as colonial secretary until 22 January 1924.

As secretary of state for the colonies, the duke wrote a report on the problems between white settlers and Asians (Indians) in British East

Africa (Kenya), in which he included a paragraph stating that the interests of the African natives must be paramount. This statement became known as the "Devonshire Declaration" and was influential in the later history of Kenya. Also during his term the Irish Free State was established (December 1922), and the colonial office, under the Duke of Devonshire, was then charged with shaping British policy toward the Free State and collaborating with it on military and intelligence matters.[16] In addition, Southern Rhodesia was added to his responsibilities during his term when it became a self-governing colony with close to dominion status.[17]

When the Baldwin government was defeated in 1924 and Labour took over under Prime Minister Ramsay MacDonald, the duke lost his cabinet position, but the Labour group lasted only a few months and Baldwin was reinstated in late 1924. The duke probably expected to be summoned back to his position in cabinet, but that call never came. He went to Lismore Castle with the family and suffered a debilitating stroke at Easter 1925. He was nearly fifty-seven. He survived, but his personality changed; his career was finished. He became, according to Harold Macmillan, "gruff, unapproachable, even morose, except with little children whom he loved and spoilt."[18] He lived, disabled, until 1938.

Though there are no book-length biographies of the 9th Duke of Devonshire, either as governor general or as an aristocrat in England, there are a few articles and chapters of books about this duke: John Pearson, *Stags and Serpents: The Story of the House of Cavendish* covers all of the family from Bess of Hardwick on, and calls Victor *The Reluctant Duke*; a short section about the 9th Duke of Devonshire appears in Robert H. Hubbard, *Rideau Hall: An Illustrated History of Government House, Ottawa, from Victorian Times to the Present Day*. Online articles appear by Hillmer in *The Canadian Encyclopedia*; on the website of the Governor General,[19] and on other online sites, but the information is slim and sometimes in error.

The Duchess of Devonshire, Lady Evelyn Emily Mary Cavendish (Evie), daughter of the 5th Marquess of Lansdowne, returned to her position as Mistress of the Robes to Queen Mary, which she held until 1953 when the Queen died. She took over the running of the family estates after the duke's stroke. She had homes in London and Chatsworth, and in her later years she lived at Hardwick Hall, where she worked to repair the tapestries on the estate. Hardwick Hall was built in the late sixteenth century by Bess of Hardwick, who began the Cavendish dynasty. (Bess of Hardwick lived from about 1527 until 1608, rose from humble origins, became a friend of Queen Elizabeth I, and left the Chatsworth estate and Hardwick Hall to her son William Cavendish, who continued the family that became the Dukes of Devonshire.[20]) A book about the life of Lady Evelyn, published before the letters at Chatsworth became available, compares the lives of the 9th Duchess of Devonshire and her cook, Dora (Jill Downie, *Storming the Castle: The World of Dora and the Duchess*). The duchess died in 1960 at the age of eighty-nine. Her father, Lord Lansdowne, died in 1927.

The Marquess of Hartington, Lord Edward Cavendish (Eddy), became the 10th Duke of Devonshire on the death of his father in 1938. In 1917 he had married Lady Mary Alice Gascoyne-Cecil (Moucher). She gave birth to two sons, William (Billy) and Andrew, and three daughters, Lady Mary, who lived only a few days, Lady Elizabeth, and Lady Anne. Lady Mary, the duchess, lived until 1988. In 1944, Billy married Kathleen (Kick) Kennedy, sister of John F. Kennedy, later President of the United States. A few months after their marriage, Billy Cavendish was killed in the war. Andrew Cavendish, who, as second son, had not expected to be Duke of Devonshire, became the 11th Duke on the death of his father, Eddy, who had a problem with alcohol and died at age fifty-five in 1950. Andrew married Deborah Vivien Mitford, the youngest of the famous Mitford sisters, in 1941, and died in 2004. His wife Deborah died in 2014. They had three children who lived beyond babyhood, two girls and a boy. Peregrine (his mother called him "Stoker") is now the 12th Duke of Devonshire. The courtesy title of the eldest son of the Duke of Devonshire is usually the Marquess of Hartington (as we have seen, Victor was never the Marquess of Hartington because he was nephew of the 8th Duke), and the courtesy title of the eldest son of the Marquess of Hartington is Lord Burlington. The 12th Duke has a son, William Cavendish, who, his father said, elected, instead of becoming the Marquess of Hartington after his father became the duke, to continue using the name Lord Burlington because he is a professional photographer.[21]

Lady Maud Cavendish Mackintosh travelled extensively during the years of her widowhood. She even travelled to Kenya to visit former aide-de-camp Mervyn Ridley on his farm. She married Brigadier Hon. George Evan Michael Baillie, a Scotsman, on 15 November 1923, with whom she had three children. She wrote the book *Early Memories*, which was published in a limited edition in 1989. A copy resides in the Chatsworth archives. Lady Maud died in 1975, aged seventy-eight.

Her daughter with Angus Mackintosh, Anne Peace Arabella (Arbell) Mackintosh, who was born in 1918, was married twice, and had three children by her first marriage and two by her second. She held the title of 30th Chief of the Clan Chattan confederation (which includes clan Mackintosh) from 1938 to 1942. She died in 2002.

Lady Blanche Cavendish Cobbold had four children, two boys and two girls. Her husband, Ivan Cobbold, was killed by an enemy bomb in England in 1944. When their oldest daughter, Pamela, had her debut, her mother hosted a party for her at which Deborah Mitford, the 11th Duchess of Devonshire, met her future husband, Andrew Cavendish, grandson of Victor, the 9th Duke. Lady Blanche died in 1987, aged eighty-nine.

Lady Dorothy Cavendish married Harold Macmillan of the publishing family in 1920. Harold Macmillan became a Conservative member of Parliament and later Prime Minister of Britain from 1957 to 1963. Dorothy had three children, a boy and two girls. Dorothy died in 1966, aged sixty-five. Harold died in 1986, aged ninety-two. Their son, Maurice Victor Macmillan, became a member of Parliament and a cabinet minister. On retirement, Harold Macmillan wrote a six-volume autobiography beginning with the book *Winds of Change: 1914–1939*. Several books have detailed the lives of Harold and Dorothy. *Troublesome Young Men*, by Lynne Olson, covers the politics and social life of the late 1930s, and *The Macmillans*, by Richard Davenport-Hines, devotes a chapter to Dorothy and Harold. Both books cover the long-term affair of Dorothy and Robert Boothby, which began in the 1930s. Other books include *Harold Macmillan: A Biography*, by Nigel Fisher; *Macmillan: 1894–1956, Volume 1 of the Official Biography*, by Alistair Horne; *Harold Macmillan*, by Charles Williams; and *Supermac: The Life of Harold Macmillan*, by D.R. Thorpe.

Lady Rachel Cavendish married James Grey Stuart, 1st Viscount Stuart of Findhorn, in 1923 when she was twenty-one, and they had three boys. She died in 1977, aged seventy-five.

Lord Charles Cavendish fell in love with the dancer Adele Astaire, who was a sensation with her brother Fred in London. When they married in 1932, Victor gave them Lismore Castle where they lived, travelling extensively. They had a daughter in 1932 and twin sons in 1935, but all the children died soon after birth. Charles became an alcoholic and died at the age of thirty-eight in 1944. Adele did not inherit Lismore and it reverted to the Devonshire estates.

Lady Anne Cavendish had three marriages, and had three children in the first. She died in 1981, aged seventy-two.

Blanche Egerton, who was Victor's first cousin, lived in England at Weybridge. She never married. She died in 1943, aged seventy-one. When she visited Canada in 1919 she was forty-eight.

Captain Vivian Bulkeley-Johnson (BJ), ADC to the Duke of Devonshire from 1916 to 1918, on his return to England worked briefly with the War Cabinet and Air Ministry. He was a London agent for cotton merchants (1922–30) and worked for Rothschilds, a firm of bankers, (1930–52). He married twice. His second marriage, to Cornelia Stuyvesant Vanderbilt, brought him considerable wealth, and they lived on a 240-acre farm. He took an interest in inland waterways and ran a company that operated boats on the Oxford and other canals. He died in 1968, aged seventy-seven.

THE CANADIANS

The Right Honourable Sir Robert Borden (1854–1937) after his retirement in 1920 recovered his health and led an active life. He was often called upon for advice by those in government, especially by Prime Minister Arthur Meighen. Borden wrote books and speeches and began a business career; he became president of Crown Life Insurance Company, president of the new Barclays Bank (Canada), and chairman of the Canadian Investment Fund, the first mutual fund established in Canada.[22] At the invitation of Prime Minister R.B. Bennett, he led the Canadian delegation to the League of Nations in 1930. He left his memoirs, which were published after his death, edited by his nephew Henry Borden (*Robert Laird Borden: His Memoirs*).

The Right Honourable Arthur Meighen (1874–1960) served as Prime Minister of Canada from 1920 until his government was defeated in 1921 by William Lyon Mackenzie King's Liberals. He returned to be the prime minister briefly in 1926. He was appointed to the Senate where he served for a decade, returning to lead the Conservative Party briefly in 1941. He then returned to his law practice.

The Right Honourable Sir George Foster (1837–1931) obtained his title when he was appointed to the British Privy Council at the recommendation of Sir Robert Borden in 1916. He accompanied Prime Minister Borden to Paris during the Peace Conference in 1919. He served as chairman of the Canadian delegation to the first assembly of the League of Nations in Geneva in 1920–21 and was elected vice president of the assembly. He continued as minister of Trade and Commerce until 1921 when he was named to the Senate, where he served his remaining days.

❀

Notes

Documents noted as "DMC," for Devonshire Manuscripts Chatsworth, are quoted by permission of the Duke of Devonshire and the Chatsworth House Trust. Only some documents from the Devonshire Manuscripts had been catalogued when the author accessed them in 2010. Those catalogued have codes including letters and numbers (e.g., G10 3386). Those documents not yet catalogued were stored in boxes labelled as one of the following. References to these letters and documents in the notes are shortened as shown in parentheses:

9th Duke 1, 1916–1921 (9th Duke 1)
9th Duke 2, 1916–1921 (9th Duke 2)
9th Duke 3, 1916–1921 (9th Duke 3)
Theatre store Box 1 (Theatre store 1)
Theatre store Box 2 (Theatre store 2)

Documents noted as "TBC" are quoted or referred to by permission of the Trustees of the Bowood Collection. Bowood is the home of the Lansdowne family. The current marquess has kindly granted permission to quote these documents.

Documents noted as "Chadwick" are from the diaries of Ethel Chadwick, a contemporary and sometime journalist living in Ottawa near Rideau Hall. Her diaries are housed at Library and Archives Canada, MG 30 D258.

· Documents noted as "Sir John Douglas Hazen fonds" are quoted by permission of the University of New Brunswick Archives and Special Collections.

ABBREVIATIONS

DMC: Devonshire Mss Chatsworth
TBC: Trustees of the Bowood Collection
NCC: National Capital Commission library, Ottawa
LAC: Library and Archives Canada

CHAPTER ONE

1 Cannadine, *The Decline and Fall of the British Aristocracy*, 49–54. From the seventeenth century until 1909 the House of Lords had customarily accepted finance bills from the Commons; rejecting the 1909 budget, after a drawn-out political fight and two general elections, led to formally curtailing the discretion of the Lords in 1911.

2 Ibid., 92–4.

3 Cannadine, "The Landowner as Millionaire."

4 Jenkins, *Churchill: A Biography*, 255.

5 Stone, *World War One*, 103; Stokesbury, *A Short History of World War 1*, 154.

6 DMC Baillie, *Early Memories*, 55.

7 Duke's diary, 3 January 1916.

8 Although some peerage documents refer to the 9th Duke of Devonshire as having had the title Lord Hartington before he became duke, the Dowager Duchess of Devonshire told me in 2010 that he had never had that title because he was not the son but the nephew of the 8th Duke of Devonshire. *Burke's Peerage* does not list Lord Hartington as one of his titles.

9 Duke's diary, 29 April 1916.

10 Duke's diary, 7 March 1916.

11 Duke's diary, 2 June 1916.

12 Duke's diary, 6 June 1916.

13 Taylor, *The First World War*, 150.

14 Duke's diary, 13 June 1916.

15 Prince Alexander of Teck had been appointed Governor General of Canada in 1914, after the Duke of Connaught had returned home with his ill wife, but the Duchess of Connaught recovered and the Connaughts returned to Canada. *The Ottawa Evening Journal* (28 June 1916) reported that in 1914 the appointment of Prince Alexander had not been received with wild acclaim because he was royal. "Anything bordering upon placing the Governor Generalship on a hereditary basis would be unacceptable in a country which is and must for a long time remain a democracy." The announcement that the Duke of Devonshire had been appointed was well received in the same article.

The announcement that the king excused Prince Alexander of Teck from the post went to the press on 23 June 1916, the same day that the Duke of Devonshire accepted the post (LAC RG 25-A-2 Vol. 153). There may have been some concern in 1916 about a man titled German Prince of Teck in the Kingdom of Württemberg, and with a German wife, holding a viceregal position in wartime (letter from Sir George Perley to Prime Minister Borden, 4 February 1916 LAC MG 26 H Vol. 49 22847), but he was a soldier with the British Army and fully engaged in the war. Prince Alexander of Teck shed his German title after war and, as First Earl of Athlone, became Governor General of Canada 1940–46, well after the Duke of Connaught. Prince Alexander was the last royal to hold the post.

16 DMC Baillie, *Early Memories*, 56.
17 Pearson, *Stags and Serpents*, 175.
18 Downie, *Storming the Castle*, 70.
19 DMC Clipping from a Montreal newspaper, 18 November 1916, 9th Duke 1.
20 Mitford, *Wait for Me! Memoirs*, 218.
21 DMC Clipping from a Montreal newspaper, 18 November 1916, 9th Duke 1.
22 DMC Lord Lansdowne to the Duchess of Devonshire, 26 March 1913, A2 25.
23 Duke's diary, March 1913.
24 DMC Evie to Aunt Lucy, 8 July 1916, K5676.
25 Ibid.
26 Duke's diary, 25 June 1916.
27 DMC Evie to Lady Edward, 30 October 1916, 9th Duke 1.
28 Duke's diary, 11 July 1916.
29 DMC Scotts Limited receipt, 1 February 1917, 9th Duke 2.
30 Duke's diary, 9 September 1916.
31 DMC Duchess of Connaught to Duchess of Devonshire, 4 July 1916, A11 539.
32 DMC Clipping from Montreal newspaper, 30 September 1916, 9th Duke 1.
33 Duke's diary, 25 September 1916.
34 Diary of Sir George Foster, 6 August 1916, LAC MG 27-IID.
35 Duke's diary, 20–23 September 1916.
36 See www.royal.gov.uk. The document Victor received is dated 28 July 1916 (DMC, Theatre store 1) so the investiture by the king, which took place at Windsor Castle during their visit, was not a surprise.
37 Duke's diary, 15 January 1916.
38 Duke's diary, 22 July 1916.

39 Duke's diary, 21 October 1916. Borden wrote about Hughes, "In my experience his moods might be divided into three categories; during about half of the time he was an able, reasonable, and useful colleague, working with excellent judgment and indefatigable energy; for a certain other portion of the time he was extremely excitable, impatient of control and almost impossible to work with; and during the remainder his conduct and speech were so eccentric as to justify the conclusion that his mind was unbalanced." In Borden, *Robert Laird Borden: His Memoirs*, 463.

40 Cook, *At the Sharp End*, 507–13; LAC: MIKAN 1883256: War Diaries – 44th Canadian Infantry Battalion – October 1916, 8; Nicholson, *Official History of the Canadian Army in the First World War*, 189.

41 Duke's diary, 4 November 1916.

42 DMC Clipping from the *Derbyshire Times*, 18 November 1916, 9th Duke 1.

43 DMC Baillie, *Early Memories*, 57.

44 Downie, *Storming the Castle*, 228.

45 Bulkeley-Johnson, letter to his mother, 11 November 1916, LAC R5076-0-1-E (MG 30-E56).

46 Bulkeley-Johnson diary, 4 November 1916.

47 Bulkeley-Johnson to his mother, 11 November 1916.

48 *The Citizen* (Ottawa), 1 November 1916.

49 *New York Times*, 12 May 1915, http://iht-retrospective.blogs.nytimes.com/2015/05/11/1915-no-remorse-after-lusitania/?_r=0, retrieved 7 July 2015.

50 Duke's diary, 5 November 1916.

51 Bulkeley-Johnson diary, 4–5 November 1916.

52 Ibid.

53 Bulkeley-Johnson to his mother, 11 November 1916.

54 DMC Evie to Lady Edward, 10 November 1916, G10 3386.

55 Duke's diary, 5 November 1916.

56 Duke's diary, 7 November 1916.

57 HMS *Calgarian* ship's log. National Archives UK, ADM 53/36665.

CHAPTER TWO

1 *Halifax Morning Chronicle*, 11 November 1916, 10.

2 DMC Borden to Duke of Devonshire, 8 and 9 November 1916, Theatre store 1.

3 Kitz, *Shattered City*, 7.

4 *The Globe* (Toronto), 13 November 1916; *The Ottawa Citizen*, 13 November 1916.

5 *Halifax Morning Chronicle*, 13 November 1916.

6 Ibid.

7 *New York Times*, 14 October 1911.

8 DMC Official Programme, Reception and Installation of the Right Honourable The Duke of Devonshire as Governor General of Canada at Halifax, Theatre store 1.

9 LAC MG 26 H Vol. 69 #35261.

10 Villeneuve, *Lord Dalhousie*, 20.

11 The Great Seal of Canada. Retrieved from http://www.gg.ca/document .aspx?id=317.

12 *Halifax Herald*, 13 November 1916.

13 Duke of Devonshire to Bonar Law, 11 November 1916, LAC RG 7 G22 Vol. 8 (2).

14 *Halifax Herald*, 13 November 1916.

15 This description is taken from the "Official Programme" that exists both in the Duke's effects at Chatsworth (Theatre store 1) and at the Public Archives of Nova Scotia (V221 #8), from the *Morning Chronicle* (Halifax), 13 November 1916, and the *Halifax Herald*, 13 November 1916.

16 Borden, *Robert Laird Borden: His Memoirs*, 528.

17 Copp, "The Military Effort, 1914–1918," 50.

18 Figures are from Nicholson, *Official History of the Canadian Army in the First World War,* 548. There are recruitment figures by the month but records of casualties – dead and wounded – are for the entire period. Nicholson notes that by 1919, total Canadian casualties included 59,544 deaths and 172,950 non-fatal casualties.

19 Skelton, *Life and Letters of Sir Wilfrid Laurier, Volume II*, 164.

20 Brown and Cook, *Canada 1896–1921*, 379–81.

21 Ibid., 256–62, and Walker, *Catholic Education and Politics in Ontario, Volume 2*, 263–96.

22 Watson, *The Queen's Wish*.

23 DMC Baillie, *Early Memories*, 59.

24 CPR train descriptions from Watson, *The Queen's Wish*, 340–4, and from Pope, *The Tour of their Royal highnesses the Duke and Duchess of Cornwall and York through the Dominion of Canada in the year 1901*.

25 Duke's diary, 12 November 1916.

26 According to J.R. Bartlett, *Dictionary of Americanisms, 1860* (found on https://books.google.ca, 479, retrieved 7 June 2015), after three hurrahs, a tiger sort of growl was commonly used a century ago as a demonstration of approbation, especially in New York.

27 Presumably the band played "God Save the King." While "O Canada" was known at the time and sometimes sung, it did not become the official Canadian anthem until 1980.

28 Description from *The Ottawa Evening Journal*, 13 November 1916; *The Ottawa Citizen*, 13 November 1916; *The Globe* (Toronto), 14 November 1916; DMC *Montreal Daily Mail*, 13 November 1916, 9th Duke 1; Duke's diary, 13 November 1916.

29 Robert Borden, letter to Perley, 15 November 1916. LAC MG 26 H Vol. 69 35892–3.

30 See chapter five in Brown, *Robert Laird Borden: A Biography, Volume II*.

31 Duke's diary, 14 November 1916.

32 *The Ottawa Citizen*, 15 November 1916; *The Globe* (Toronto), 15 November 1916.

33 Duke's diary, 23 November 1916.

34 Duke's diary, 14 November 1916. This description is based on a visit to the governor general's office in the East Block, open to the public, which has been preserved as it was in the late nineteenth century. By 1916 only the pictures of Queen Victoria would have been replaced, with portraits of King George V and Queen Mary.

35 Duke's diary, 25 November 1916, and http://www.scouts.ca/ca/scouts-canada-history.

36 DMC Evie to Lady Edward, 15 November 1916, G10 3387.

37 DMC Evie to Lady Edward, 23 November 1916, G10 3392.

38 Duke's diary, 3 and 7 December 1916; DMC Evie's letters: 1) to her mother-in-law, 23 November 1916; G10 3392; 2) to her mother, 22 December 1916, 9th Duke 3; *The Globe* (Toronto), 11 December 1916.

39 For other pictures of the *Olympic* and other ships painted in dazzle, see: http://www.bbc.co.uk/guides/zty8tfr.

40 DMC Dorothy to her grandmother, 6 December 1916, G10 3397.

41 DMC Evie to Lady Edward, 9 December 1916, G10 3400.

42 DMC Evie to Lady Edward, 4 December 1916, G10 3396.

43 Information about Rideau Hall is found in: Hnatyshyn, *Rideau Hall: Canada's Living Heritage*; MacMillan et al., *Canada's House*; Hubbard, *Rideau Hall*; http://archive.gg.ca/gg/fgg/bios/01/connaught_e.asp.

44 TBC Evie to her mother, 10 December 1916.

45 Duke's diary, 14 February 1916; 13 February 1919; 17 February 1920; 22 February 1921.

46 Information about Rideau Hall grounds from documents housed at the National Capital Commission library (NCC): Federal Heritage Building Review Office, Building Reports, Vol. 20, 86-24, 2011: 85-66 (n.d.) and 86-02 (n.d.); and Robert Hunter, Rideau Hall Outbuildings and Grounds, Staff Report, Architectural History Branch.

47 TBC Evie to her mother, 10 December 1916.

48 The Earl of Minto (1898–1904) succeeded the Marquess of Lans-downe (1883–1888) as Governor General of Canada.

49 DMC Evie to her mother, 7 January 1917, 9th Duke 3.

50 DMC Dorothy to Lady Edward, 13 December 1916, G10 3403; NCC Rideau Hall: Report 85-66, Staff report, architectural History Division, Federal Heritage Buildings Review Office.

51 DMC Dorothy to Lady Edward 13 December 1916, G10 3403.

52 LAC Bulkeley-Johnson to his mother, 26 December 1916.

53 Robert Hunter, NCC Federal Heritage Buildings Review Office, Building-ing Report 86-02, Architectural History Division.

54 TBC Evie to her mother, 11 August 1918.

55 Downie, *Storming the Castle*, 235.

56 These descriptions from: *The Globe* (Toronto), 18 November 1916; DMC Baillie, *Early Memories*, 58; DMC Evie's letter to Lady Edward, 10 November 1916 G3386; TBC Evie's letter to her mother, 10 December 1916.

57 DMC Maud to Lady Edward, 18 January 1917, G10 3418.

58 DMC Baillie, *Early Memories*, 59.

59 DMC Evie to Victor, 5 September 1918, Q5 8664.

60 DMC Evie to Lady Edward, 15 November 1916, G3387.

61 The Ottawa City Directory for 1917 provided information about the Sladen and Crowdy residences. Crowdy also had a cottage at Blue Sea Lake so the Devonshires knew his family.

62 DMC Evie to Lady Edward, 23 November 1916, G10 3392; Duke's diary, 11 March 1916.

63 Duke's diary, 11 March 1916; DMC Evie to Lady Edward, 9 December 1916, G10 3400.

64 Lady Aberdeen (wife of the governor general 1893–98) formed the May Court Club for prominent girls in Ottawa society so that they would elevate the tone of life in the city, promote temperance, and serve as a civilizing influence. Messamore, "The Social and Cultural Role of the Governors General, 1888–1911"; DMC Letters of Evie, Maud, and Blanche, G10 3408; G10 3387; G10 3389; G10 3390; G10 3401; G10 3408; and from websites of the IODE and May Court.

65 LAC Bulkeley-Johnson to his mother, 26 December 1916.

66 DMC Dorothy to Lady Edward, 11 January 1917, G10 3411.

67 DMC Maud to Lady Edward, 18 January 1917, G10 3418. Maud's full description of skijoring makes it sound exciting if dangerous. "Skijoring, hanging on a rope and being dragged on our skis. The rope is tied on a sleigh – there are two cross bars on the rope. Two people hang onto each and we made it still more exciting by having

two ADCs standing behind us on our skis, of course we fell every few minutes and our skis get hopelessly entangled but it was the greatest fun. There were other exciting moments when the bars broke and deposited us flat on or backs in a drift and on another occasion Ld Richard, who was driving us, capsized in his sleigh and was buried in a drift." DMC Dorothy wrote on 16 January 1918 to her grandmother in a letter mistakenly dated 1917 (events she described indicate it was 1918), 9th Duke 1.

68 DMC Maud to Lady Edward, 2 January 1917, G10 3408.

69 An English country dance known in America as the Virginia Reel, often used as a final dance because it was simple and everyone could do it. From: http://www.streetswing.com/histmain/z3covrly.htm, retrieved 29 April 2017.

70 LAC Bulkeley-Johnson to his mother, 26 December 1916.

71 LAC Bulkeley-Johnson to his mother, 3 January 1917.

CHAPTER THREE

1 Bulkeley-Johnson to his mother, 12 December 1916, LAC MG 30-E56, R5076-0-1-E.

2 Drawing-room at Ottawa: *The Globe*, 19 January 1914.

3 DMC Evie to Lady Edward, 15 November 1916, G10 3387.

4 TBC Evie to her mother, 10 December 1916.

5 Bulkeley-Johnson to his mother, 12 December 1916.

6 *The Ottawa Citizen*, 28 January 1916.

7 Ibid.; *The Ottawa Evening Journal*, 27 January 1916.

8 Gwyn, *Tapestry of War*, 192–3.

9 Ibid., 194.

10 Bulkeley-Johnson to his mother, 12 December 1916.

11 Darby and Joan – a devoted old married couple – from the *Canadian Oxford Dictionary*; DMC Evie to Lady Edward, 17 January 1917, G10 3415.

12 DMC Evie to Lady Edward, 23 November 1916, G10 3392.

13 DMC Evie to Lady Edward, 17 January 1917, G10 3414.

14 Ethel Chadwick, a single woman in her early thirties in 1917, kept a diary which is now in Library and Archives Canada (MG 30 D258), and wrote articles from her diary for the Ottawa papers. Much of her social life revolved around Government House and peaked during the Connaughts' tenure (1911–16), when she was a frequent guest and a good friend of the family. The Devonshires invited her along with others to the skating parties and occasionally to Blue Sea Lake, as described later, but she was not on as friendly terms with them or

their ADCs, as she had been with previous incumbents. Ethel remained single, as did so many women after the war.

15 Ethel Chadwick's diary, 20 February 1917, Library and Archives Canada MG 30 D258. From the extensive references in her diary and the length of the descriptions of Government House and its occupants, one can infer that these were among the most important events in her life. As a fashionable, genteel, if impoverished young woman of her time, Ethel read and kept up to date with current literature, as this reference shows. H.G. Wells's novel was published in 1916. Ethel did not have employment but lived in her parents' home. Also, Duke's diary, 20 February 1917.

16 DMC Evie to Lady Edward, 23 November 1916, G10 3392. The title of the book, *The First Hundred Thousand*, refers to the recruitment campaign of Lord Kitchener, British secretary of state for war. Kitchener enlisted huge numbers of volunteers with the famous poster depicting his picture with the text: "Your country needs YOU" for what was referred to as "Kitchener's armies." Advertisements in *The Globe* (Toronto) in early December refer to Beith's book as "the newest, brightest war book" and "the human side of trench warfare." Beith's book follows soldiers and their individual and group tribulations with some humour. Beith wrote under the pen name Ian Hay.

17 Duke's diary, 24 and 25 November 1916.

18 DMC Andrew Bonar Law to the duke, 16 October 1916, 9th Duke 2.

19 Duke's diary, 21 November 1916.

20 *Montreal Star*, 12 December 1916; *Gazette* (Montreal), 12 December 1916, 4.

21 Diaries of William Lyon Mackenzie King, 7 December 1916, http://www.collectionscanada.gc.ca/databases/king/001059-119.02-e.php? &page_id_nbr=6084&interval=20&&PHPSESSID=bk04hjbpq 61tfkdfgss1ge2ps2.

22 Duke's diary, 13, 16, and 23 November 1916.

23 DMC Andrew Bonar Law to the duke, 12 August 1916, Theatre store 1.

24 The first British High Commissioner to Canada was appointed in 1928, after the 1926 Imperial Conference had agreed that the Dominions had the right to their own foreign policy. The Statute of Westminster, 1931, formalized these rights.

25 Messamore, *Canada's Governors General 1847–1878*, 109–14.

26 J.A. Maxwell, "Lord Dufferin and the Difficulties with British Columbia 1874–71." *Canadian Historical Review* 1931, 12(4) 364-389 doi: 10.3138/CHR-012-04-02; Margaret Ormsby, "Prime Minister Mackenzie, the Liberal Party and the Bargain with British Columbia."

Canadian Historical Review 26(2) 1945 148-173. doi: 10.3138/CHR-026-02-04.

27 Section 55 of the British North America Act, 1867, gives this power.

28 Such a crisis did occur a few years later in 1925 when the governor general, Lord Byng, refused to take the advice of then Prime Minister Mackenzie King in what became known as the King-Byng affair.

29 Brown, *Canada's National Policy 1883–1900*, 13–27.

30 These documents confer the powers of the Sovereign onto the Governor General. By the British North America Act of 1867, section 9: "The Executive Government and Authority of and over Canada is hereby declared to continue and be vested in the Queen." The Commission, Letters Patent, and Instructions were found at Chatsworth Archives, Theatre store 1; Letter from Bonar Law, National Archives UK, CO42 Vol. 994 #16 (31321) 12 August 1916.

31 Messamore, *Canada's Governors General*, 19.

32 Bagehot, *The English Constitution*, 44–85.

33 Duke's diary, 27 November 1916. This Government House for Ontario was built in 1915 in what is now Chorley Park. It was abandoned as a home for the lieutenant-governor in 1937 and later torn down, leaving a park. Ontario no longer has an official residence for the lieutenant-governor.

34 DMC Evie to Lady Edward, 4 December 1916, G10 3396.

35 Ferns, "Hendrie, Sir John Strathearn," *Dictionary of Canadian Biography*.

36 DMC Evie to Lady Edward, 4 December 1916, G10 3396; Duke's diary, 27–30 November 1916.

37 DMC Evie to Lady Edward, 4 December 1916, G10 3396.

38 *The Globe* (Toronto), 23 November 1916, 8.

39 DMC Blanche to Lady Edward, 3 December 1916, G10 3395.

40 *The Globe* (Toronto), 30 November 1916.

41 Duke's diary, 29 November 1916.

42 *The Globe* (Toronto), 29 November 1916, 8.

43 The Duchess of Devonshire opened the May Court Club's first Convalescent Home at 199 O'Connor Street on 8 December 1916. From Von Baeyer, *The May Court Club: One Hundred Years of Community Service*, 56.

44 Bulkeley-Johnson to his mother, 12 December 1916.

45 *Gazette* (Montreal), 15 December 1916, 4.

46 Duke's diary 11–18 December 1916; DMC Maud to Lady Edward, 10 December 1916, G10 3401.

47 DMC Evie to Lady Edward, 25 December 1916, G10 3407.

CHAPTER FOUR

1 Duke's diary, 4 January 1918.

2 J. Chamberlain to Governor General of Canada, The Earl of Minto, 23 April 1902, CO42 1007 180.

3 Memorandum about Sir Hugh Graham, LAC MG 26 H Vol. 327 193198–212.

4 Raudsepp, "Graham, Hugh, 1st Baron Atholstan," *Dictionary of Canadian Biography*.

5 Borden wrote to Perley, 17 October 1916 (LAC MG 26 H Vol. 327 193213), enclosing a memorandum about Sir Hugh Graham (LAC MG 26 H Vol. 327 193198–212) and asking Perley to show the information to Bonar Law, then the colonial secretary. Apparently he presented this information only verbally to the duke.

6 In addition to the letter to Perley on 17 October 1916 about the Graham peerage, Borden wrote to Perley on 24 October 1916 about a second honour, this one a knighthood for Charles Riordan (LAC MG 26 H Vol. 327 193218).

7 Duke's diary, 4 December 1916. The interregnum was the period between the Duke of Connaught's last day in office (11 October 1916) and the Duke of Devonshire's installation (11 November 1916). During that period, the chief justice of the Supreme Court served as administrator.

8 Duke's diary, 4 December 1916.

9 Duke's diary, 5 December 1916.

10 Borden to Perley, 5 December 1916, LAC MG 26 H Vol. 327 193239–40.

11 The Ritz-Carlton Hotel opened on 31 December 1912, a luxury hotel designed to cater to the carriage trade, with a bathroom in every room and a kitchen on each floor (so room-service meals could be served course by course), round-the-clock valet service, and a concierge. The hotel is still one of Montreal's finest: http://www.ritzmontreal.com/en/hotel-montreal/history, retrieved 8 November 2016.

12 Borden's diary, 6 December 1916.

13 Borden to Perley, 19 May 1916, LAC MG 26 H Vol. 327 193183.

14 Perley to Borden, 18 May 1916, LAC MG 26 H Vol. 327 193185; Borden told Perley that he had not asked the Duke of Connaught because he did not get Graham's agreement until after Connaught had departed in October (LAC MG 26 H Vol. 327 193198–209, 16 October 1916). (The Duke of Connaught departed from Canada about 14 October 1916.) This does not seem credible since Borden had been trying to get this honour approved since at least May 1916, and B.A. MacNab, editor of the Montreal *Daily Mail*, had written to Borden from Montreal in January 1916 to complain about the possibility of a

barony for Graham with which the writer strongly disagreed (LAC MG 26 H Vol. 327 193182, 13 January 1916, and LAC MG 26 H Vol. 327 193249).

15 Borden noted in his diary that Graham "Then to Ritz and sent for H.G. who broke down and wept when told of difficulties. Utterly crushed. I sent further tgrm to Perley at his suggn. He peppered me with notes during my stay." LAC Borden diary, 6 December 1916; Borden's cable to Perley, 6 December 1916, LAC MG 26 H Vol. 327 193241.

16 Perley to Borden, 9/10 December 1916, LAC MG 26 H Vol. 327 193242.

17 Duke's diary, 14 and 16 December 1916.

18 Duke's diary, 16 December 1916.

19 Borden's diary in LAC, 18 December 1916; also in Borden to Blount, 17 December 1916, LAC MG 26 H Vol. 327 193244.

20 Duke's diary, 18 December 1916.

21 Duke's diary, 26 December 1916.

22 Ibid.

23 Duke's diary, 29 December 1916.

24 DMC Letter from Lord Lansdowne to the duchess, 27 December 1916, F6 2511.

25 DMC Baillie, *Early Memories*, said they became firm friends, 59; Christopher McCreery in *Order of Canada: Its Origins, History and Development*, 25–6, wrote that Devonshire concurred with the Aitken peerage, but the baronetcy was done from London and there is no evidence in his diary that the Duke approved it; quite the opposite. The Aitken baronetcy was completed before the Duke became governor general, and the barony soon after.

McCreery wrote that Sir Hugh Graham was elevated to the peerage through the machinations of Lord Northcliffe and Lord Beaverbrook (26). There is no evidence of either of these men having had anything to do with this peerage. As the story is related here, it was Borden's machinations that brought it to fruition. McCreery also noted that both the governor general and the prime minister did not approve of this peerage, but in the memorandum quoted by McCreery (LAC MG 26 H Vol. 95 50169, 1918 09 17) stating that they both disagreed with an honour, Borden was referring to a knighthood for Campbell Stuart that was forced by Lord Northcliffe in December 1917. See chapter eleven for this story.

26 Borden to Perley, 6 December 1916, LAC MG 26 H Vol. 327 193241.

27 Bonar Law to Sir Robert Borden, 1 May 1916, LAC MG 26 H Vol. 8 1217–18.

28 Borden to Bonar Law, 14 May 1916, LAC MG 26 H Vol. 8 1219.

29 Borden to Duke of Connaught, 17 May 1916, LAC MG 26 H Vol. 8 1222–3.

30 Duke's diary, 17 December 1916.

31 De-la-Noy, *The Honours System*, 97.

32 McCreery, *The Order of Canada*, 27; *The Globe* (Toronto), 11 Feb 1918, 6. Max Aitken had left Canada for England under a cloud of suspicion after a scandal concerning financing of cement companies.

33 "The Great Canadian Cement Caper and the CPR," in Richards, *Lord Beaverbrook*, 71–8.

34 Borden to Bonar Law, 19 May 1916, MG 26 H Vol. 8 1220.

35 Wallace, *The Memoirs of the Right Honourable Sir George Foster*, 179, letter from Duke of Connaught to Sir George Foster dated 9 June 1916.

36 Cook, *Warlords*, 65.

37 Duke's diary, and *The Globe* (Toronto), 15 February 1916.

38 Lord Atholstan took his seat in the House of Lords on 28 April 1920. Duke's diary, 28 April 1920.

39 LAC MG 26 H Vol. 327 193263, 193266, and 193268.

40 LAC R13344-31-0-E, 2 19.

41 *The Globe* (Toronto), 22 August 1917; Baron Atholstan's title was hereditary, the last Canadian peerage to be granted, but it died with him because he did not have a male heir. Sir Joseph Flavelle accepted a baronetcy in June 1917. His was the last hereditary title and he did pass it on, but a baronet is not a peer and does not sit in the House of Lords. Lord Shaughnessy and Lord Strathcona were both barons. Their titles have been passed on and there is now a 5th Lord Shaughnessy and a 4th Lord Strathcona, but both families moved to Britain.

42 LAC MG 26 H Vol. 327 193241.

43 LAC MG 26 H Vol. 327 193243, and Borden to Perley, 13 December 1916, LAC MG 26 H Vol. 9 1998.

CHAPTER FIVE

1 Duke's diary, 6 January 1917.

2 Mitford, *Wait for Me! Memoirs*, x.

3 DMC Evie to her mother, 2 February 1917, 9th Duke 3.

4 DMC Evie to her mother, 7 January 1917, 9th Duke 3; Evie to Lady Edward, 7 January 1917, G1 3409; Evie to Lady Edward, 17 January 1917, G10 3414.

5 DMC Evie to her mother, 2 February 1917, 9th Duke 3.

6 Bulkeley-Johnson to his mother, 29 May 1917.

7 DMC Baillie, *Early Memories*, 59.

8 The journey west included stops at Bolton, Sudbury, White River, Schreiber, Fort William (now Thunder Bay) in Ontario, arriving on the second morning in Winnipeg, Manitoba, and later going on to Portage La Prairie and Brandon.

9 Duke's diary, 28 February 1917. The 20,000-square-foot house still serves as the lieutenant-governor's home.

10 Bulkeley-Johnson to his mother, 17 March 1917.

11 Ibid.

12 Duke's diary, 5 March 1917.

13 DMC Evie to Lady Edward, 5 March 1917, G10 3481.

14 DMC Maud to Lady Edward, 5–7 March 1917, G10 3432.

15 DMC Evie to her mother, 10 March 1917, 9th Duke 3.

16 Duke's diary, 17 March 1917.

17 Duke's diary, 18–25 March 1917, and Bulkeley-Johnson to his mother, 17 March 1917.

18 Bulkeley-Johnson to his mother, 17 March 1917.

19 Duke's diary, 28 March 1917.

20 Bulkeley-Johnson to his mother, 3 April 1917.

21 DMC Maud to Evie, 22 April 1917, N9 6063.

22 Duke's diary, 14 March 1917.

23 Bulkeley-Johnson to his mother, 3 April 1917.

24 TBC Evie to her mother, 19 April 1917.

25 DMC Evie to Lady Edward, 26 June 1917, G10 3453.

26 DMC Evie to Lady Edward, 7 April 1917, G10 3438.

27 Duke's diary, 28 February–2 March 1918.

28 Duke's diary, 21 March 1917; Duke's diary, 25 May 1918, and other references to Evie's attending or entertaining women's organizations.

29 Mitford, *Wait for Me! Memoirs*, 218.

30 Duke's diary, 6 February 1918; and in Chatham, Ontario, 4 June 1918, "Regent persisted in calling on Eve for a speech. She did it very well," Duke's diary, 4 June 1918.

31 Williams, *Byng of Vimy*, 166.

32 Walter Long to governor general, CO42 Vol. 1005 170.

33 DMC Victor to his mother, 12 April 1917, G10 3440.

34 TBC Evie to her mother, 19 April 1917.

35 Ibid.

36 DMC Evie to Lady Edward, 27 April 1917, G10 3444.

37 Victor to his mother, 23 March 1917, G10 3435; Spring Rice to Balfour, 23 March 1917. Letter reproduced in Gwynn, *The Letters and Friendships of Sir Cecil Spring Rice*, Vol. II, 387–8.

38 DMC Victor to his mother, 23 March 1917, G10 3435.

39 DMC Maud to her mother, 2 April 1917, N9 6056.

40 DMC Maud to Victor, 3 April 1917, N9 6057.

41 The President's full speech is available at: http://wwi.lib.byu.edu/index.php/Wilson%27s_War_Message to Congress.

42 DMC Maud to Evie, 6 April 1917, N9 6059.

43 DMC Maud to Evie, 10 April 1917, N9 6060.

44 DMC Evie to Lady Edward, 27 April 1917, G10 3444.

45 DMC Sir Cecil Spring Rice to Victor, 7 April 1917, 9th Duke 2.

46 DMC Evie to Lady Edward, 31 May 1917, G10 3449.

47 DMC Lady Spring Rice to Lady Edward, 3 May 1917, G10 3445.

48 DMC Maud to Evie, 22 April 1917, N9 6063.

49 DMC Lady Spring Rice to Lady Edward, 3 May 1917, G10 3445.

50 DMC Maud to Evie, 29 April 1917, N9 6060.

51 DMC Maud to Victor, 26 April 1917, 9th Duke 1.

52 The North America and West Indies station, a section of the Royal Navy, was responsible for protecting against attacks by German ships and submarines.

53 DMC Maud to Victor, 26 April 1917, 9th Duke 1.

54 DMC Maud to Victor, 19 April 1917, 9th Duke 1.

55 Ibid.

56 Bulkeley-Johnson to his mother, 2 May 1917.

57 Duke's diary, 8 May 1917.

58 Diary of William Lyon Mackenzie King, 2 December 1919, LAC, online; Mackenzie King, who had been Labour minister in Laurier's Liberal government, had lost his seat in the 1911 election and begun working as a consultant to the Rockefeller Foundation. In December 1919, when the conversation with the duchess took place, he was Opposition leader. In 1921, he became prime minister.

59 DMC Evie to Lady Edward, 20 May 1917, G10 3447.

60 That letter is not in the Chatsworth archives, but Victor mentioned in his own letter that Sunday that a letter from Evie had just arrived.

61 DMC Victor to Evie, 20 May 1917, N16 6277.

62 Ibid; Duke's diary, 23 May 1917.

63 DMC Victor to Evie, 20 May 1917, N16 6277.

64 DMC Maud to Evie, 19 May 1917, N10 6140.

65 Duke's diary, 21 May 1916 and 10 September 1916.

66 TBC Evie to her mother, 21 November 1917.

67 Early in 1917, he had been invited to a luncheon and later he had met the duke and duchess at a skating party.

68 Diary of William Lyon Mackenzie King, 28 April 1917, LAC online.

69 Evans, *The Party That Lasted 100 Days*, 70.

70 Correspondence from Sir George Perley, High Commissioner for

Canada, and Walter Long, the colonial secretary, indicates that precedence was an issue of concern. Perley took issue with an apparent breach of protocol when "the proper official order of the self-Governing Dominions – Canada, Australia, New Zealand, South Africa – is not always recognized." He referred to a War Savings meeting of high commissioners held in the Royal Albert Hall which he considered "practically official" (LAC 26 October 1917, R25-2 Vol. 155 Canada House Records). Mr Long's staff member replied that because of the short time available, "other than placing His Majesty's Ministers in the two front rows of the platform, no order of precedence was adopted" (LAC 30 November 1917, RG 25 A-2 Vol 155 Canada House Records).

71 "King, William Lyon Mackenzie," *Dictionary of Canadian Biography Online*, http://www.biographi.ca/009004-119.01-e.php?BioId=42131. As British foreign secretary, Lansdowne had signed an alliance with Japan in 1902.

72 Mason, *The Broken Road*, the story of a prince of India, educated at Eton and Oxford, who on returning to his kingdom, isolated and protected at the end of a broken road, in fury at not being accepted in English society and especially at the impossibility of marrying the English woman he loved, led a rising against the British rulers. He was defeated and the road was built.

73 Diary of William Lyon Mackenzie King, Saturday, 28 April 1917, LAC online.

74 Walker, "Race and Recruitment in World War I."

75 *The Globe* (Toronto), 26 May 1917.

76 DMC Evie to Lady Edward, 31 May 2011, G10 3449.

77 Ibid.

78 *The Globe* (Toronto), 29 May 1917.

79 DMC Evie to Lady Edward, 31 May 1917, G10 3449.

80 Duke's diary, 28 May 1917.

CHAPTER SIX

1 Unfortunately, the building has changed considerably since 1917, so a tour of the building today does not give a clear picture of what they saw, but both the Victor and Evie commented on it in their writings.

2 Duke's diary, 12 and 19 June 1917.

3 DMC Evie to her mother, 13 June 1917, 9th Duke 1.

4 Ibid.

5 Duke's diary, 17 June 1917.

6 Ibid.

7 Spencerwood, which in 1917 was the lieutenant-governor's residence, burned down in 1966. The estate is no longer the viceregal residence but a public park, still glorious, called Bois de Coulogne. http://www.capitale.gouv.qc.ca/parcs-et-places-publiques/parcs/parc-du-bois-de-coulonge/historique, accessed 29 April 2016.

8 Nicholson, *Official History of the Canadian Army in the First World War*, 215.

9 *The Globe* (Toronto), 15 May 1917, 5.

10 Quoted in Granatstein and Hitsman, *Broken Promises*, 26.

11 Armstrong, *The Crisis of Quebec*, 129–30; Brown and Cook, *Canada 1896–1921*, 263; http://www.cbc.ca/archives/entry/van-doos-a-battalion-is-born.

12 Armstrong, *The Crisis of Quebec*, 129.

13 The Ontario government passed Regulation 17 in 1912, which allowed bilingual instruction in only some of the province's schools. French Canadians were enraged because they believed this did not meet the agreement of Confederation and they tried to have the Dominion government disallow the legislation. The Dominion said the law should stand, but the Quebecers took the issue to the Judicial Committee of the British Privy Council, which ruled that the regulation was constitutional but the committee established to enforce its policy in Ottawa was ultra vires. From Barber, "Ontario Schools Question," *The Canadian Encyclopedia*, 1329.

The Manitoba Schools Question erupted in 1890 when Manitoba abolished public funding of Catholic schools. Most of the French-Canadian population of Manitoba was Catholic and saw this as an abrogation of their rights. After two Privy Council decisions, the issue was settled in 1896 with an agreement between Prime Minister Laurier and Premier Thomas Greenway of Manitoba that allowed some religious instruction in the public schools. From Crunican, "The Manitoba Schools Question," *The Canadian Encyclopedia*, 1084.

14 *The Ottawa Evening Journal*, 31 May 1917.

15 DMC Memo from the Duke of Devonshire to Walter Long, Colonial Secretary, 31 July 1917, Theatre Store 1.

16 DMC Letter from Laurier to Borden, 6 June 1917, in PM's letters and other notes, 1917, 1918, 1919, 1920, Theatre store 1.

17 DMC The duke's notes of his conversation with Sir Robert Borden, 6 June 1917, Theatre Store 1.

18 DMC Evie to her mother, 13 June 1917, 9th Duke 3.

19 DMC Evie to Lady Edward, 31 May 1917, G10 3449.

20 Duke's diary, 9 June 1917.

21 Duke's diary, 15 June 1917.

22 By January 1918, the Bonne Entente movement had failed in a flurry of recrimination. From Hawkes, *The Birthright*, 376.

23 Quoted in Armstrong, *The Crisis of Quebec*, 78.

24 Ibid., 141.

25 Bourassa, "Conscription" pamphlet published by *Le Devoir*, 1917.

26 Duke's diary, 14 and 15 June 1917.

27 Duke's diary, 22 June 1917.

28 Duke's diary, 23 June 1917.

29 Charlie wrote that this yacht "in winter is used to cut ice from Quebec to Montreal which is very hard work, and in summer it is used to take the Governor General about the place," DMC Charlie Cavendish to his grandmother, Lady Edward, 27 June 1917, G10 3454.

30 This time Evie took Maud, Dorothy, Rachel, Charlie, and Anne, as well as Miss Walton, the governess, and Angus. Blanche was still recovering from foot surgery.

31 DMC Evie to her mother, 8 July 1917, 9th Duke 3.

32 Clarkson, "Visit to Tadoussac, Sept 14, 2000."

33 DMC Charlie to Lady Edward, 27 June 1917, G10 3454.

34 DMC Evie to Lady Edward, 26 June 1917, G10 3453.

35 Benoit, "Price, Sir William," *Dictionary of Canadian Biography*.

36 LAC RG 25 G1 Vol. 1207.

37 Duke's diary, 2 July 1917; DMC Victor to his mother, 2 July 1917, G10 3457; *The Globe* (Toronto), 2 July 1917, 3; DMC Draft of letter from the duke to the king, 3 July 1917, Theatre store 1.

38 Victor had returned to Ottawa with Mervyn Ridley, ADC, for the fiftieth anniversary of Confederation ceremonies. Blanche was still in Ottawa. Anne stayed in Quebec City with her governess, Miss Walton. The maids were not on board. The ship had a captain and a steward.

39 Bulkeley-Johnson to his mother, 12 July 1917.

40 DMC Evie to Lady Edward, 30 June 1917, G10 3455.

41 Ibid.

42 "Bog-ayaliath" is the best transcription of the word in Bulkeley-Johnson's letter, but no trace of such a name can be found on the web. The flower that he calls "calmia" is listed as kalmia or mountain laurel, a flowering evergreen shrub.

43 M. Victor Fafard was keeper of the lighthouse at Pointe des Monts from 1889–1926, http://www.pointe-des-monts.com/histoire/, retrieved 9 November 2016.

44 Bulkeley-Johnson to his mother, 12 July 1917.

45 This event was commemorated in 1937 when the newly incorporated town of Baie Comeau was named after him.

46 Frenette, "Comeau, Napoléon-Alexandre (baptized Alexandre-Napoléon)," *Dictionary of Canadian Biography.* Comeau's book, *Life and Sport on the North Shore of the Lower St. Lawrence and Gulf* (Quebec: Daily Telegraph Printing House, 1909) is available at: http://ia600402.us.archive.org/18/items/lifesportonnorthoocomerich/lifesportonnorthoocomerich,pdf retrieved 9 November 2016.

47 Bulkeley-Johnson to his mother, 12 July 1917; DMC Evie to Lady Edward, 30 June–2 July 1917, G10 3455.

48 Mostly the family called it by the English name, Magdalen, and the English is used here. In French it is Rivière Madeleine or Cap Madeleine. The family in their letters variously called it Madeleine River or Cap Magdalen. It is now a small settlement called Sainte-Madeleine-de-la-Rivière-Madeleine.

49 Bulkeley-Johnson to his mother, 12 July 1917.

50 Bulkeley-Johnson called him "Chipman" and the duke called him "Shipman." It's not clear which is correct, but probably Shipman because it is used more often and later in time by the duke. For consistency, he is called Shipman here.

51 Bulkeley-Johnson to his mother, 12 July 1917.

52 DMC Evie to her mother, 8 July 1917, 9th Duke 3.

53 DMC Maud to Lady Edward, 17 July 1917, 9th Duke 1.

54 Bulkeley-Johnson to his mother, 12 July 1917.

55 DMC Evie to her mother, 8 July 1917, 9th Duke 3; Maud to Lady Edward, 17 July 1917, 9th Duke 1.

56 Bulkeley-Johnson to his mother, 12 July 1917.

57 DMC Maud to Lady Edward, 17 July 1917, 9th Duke 1.

58 DMC Dorothy to Lady Edward, 15 July 1917, 9th Duke 1.

59 DMC Evie to her mother, 8 July 1917, 9th Duke 3.

60 Bulkeley-Johnson to his mother, 12 July 1917.

61 Duke's diary, 5 July 1917.

62 Duke's diary, 13 July and 18 July 1917.

63 Bulkeley-Johnson to his mother, 12 July 1917.

64 DMC Lord Lansdowne to Victor, 20 August 1917, P33 8220B.

65 Bulkeley-Johnson to his mother, 16 July 1917.

66 Mackay, *Anticosti: The Untamed Island,* 25.

67 Jackson, *The Last of the Whigs,* 23.

68 Bulkeley-Johnson to his mother, 16 July 1917.

69 Ibid.

70 Details of Anticosti history are taken from Mackay, *Anticosti: The Untamed Island,* 67.

71 Bulkeley-Johnson to his mother, 12 July 1917.

72 MacKay, *Anticosti: The Untamed Island,* 71.

73 Henri Menier changed the name of this bay to Baie-Sainte-Claire after his mother. MacKay, *Anticosti: The Untamed Island*, 62.

74 Bulkeley-Johnson to his mother, 16 July 1917.

75 Ibid.

76 DMC Victor to his mother, 22 July 1917, 9th Duke 1.

77 Duke's diary, 11 July 1917.

78 Mackay, *Anticosti: The Untamed Island*, 13.

79 Ralph was apparently someone in England who Angus thought was Maud's fiancé but Ralph did not surface in any of the saved letters in the Chatsworth archives. There are a few mentions of Ralph, sometimes appearing for dinner, in the duke's diary during 1916 when the family was in England, but no last names except a Ralph Cavendish, who may or may not have been this Ralph.

80 DMC Evie to Victor, 22 July 1917, 9th Duke 1.

81 DMC Evie to her mother, 8 July 1917, 9th Duke 3.

82 Bulkeley-Johnson to his mother, 12 July 1917.

83 Ibid.

84 DMC Evie to Lady Edward, 18 July 1917, 9th duke 1.

85 DMC Evie to her mother, 22 July 1917, 9th Duke 3.

86 DMC Evie to Aunt Lucy, 8 July 1916, K5 4676.

87 Bulkeley-Johnson to his mother, 16 July 1917.

88 DMC Evie to Victor, 22 July 1917, 9th Duke 1.

89 DMC Evie to her mother, 1 August 1917, 9th Duke 3.

90 DMC Evie to her mother, 22 July 1917, 9th Duke 3.

91 DMC Evie to Victor, 22 July 1917, 9th Duke 1.

92 Duke's diary, 29 July 1917.

93 DMC Evie to Victor, 30 July 1917, 9th Duke 1.

CHAPTER SEVEN

1 DMC Laurier to Borden, 6 June 1917; Borden to the governor general, 7 June 1917; Borden to Laurier, 7 June 1917, PM's letters and other notes, 1917–20, Theatre store 1.

2 Duke's diary, 25 July 1917.

3 Duke's diary, 23 July 1917.

4 DMC Shane Leslie to the governor general, 23 July 1917, Q22 8731 (A, B, C). Shane Leslie was Sir John Randolph Leslie, 3rd Baronet, an Irish-born diplomat and writer. In 1917 he was in Washington working with British Ambassador Sir Cecil Spring Rice. Attached to the letter are the duke's notes saying they were sent to Spring Rice on 1 August 1917. The notes include answers to some of Leslie's criticisms and a line saying that the duke did not know who (overwritten as "where") Shane Leslie was, but he would be willing to talk to him.

Since the letter is dated the same day that the duke returned from Quebec City, it is possible that Sladen's discussion was actually with Shane Leslie, who may have been in Ottawa and delivered the letter. Shane Leslie was a first cousin of Winston Churchill (their mothers were sisters), but there is no evidence Leslie was a cousin to the duke.

5 Duke's diary, 24 July 1917.

6 Sir Joseph Pope, who had been John A. Macdonald's secretary for many years (1882–91), was under-secretary of state, 1896–1909, and then the first permanent head of the Department of External Affairs, 1909–25. From Farr, *The Canadian Encyclopedia*.

7 Lord Shaughnessy was president of Canadian Pacific Railway. Regehr, "Shaughnessy, Thomas George, 1st Baron Shaughnessy," *Dictionary of Canadian Biography*.

8 Sifton was influential in the anti-reciprocity campaign in 1911 that brought the Conservatives under Borden to power. Hall, "Sifton, Sir Clifford," *Dictionary of Canadian Biography*.

9 Ford, "Some Notes on the Formation of the Union Government in 1917."

10 *The Globe* (Toronto), 24 July 1917.

11 DMC Shaughnessy to the duke, 29 July 1917, Theatre store 1; Diary of Sir Lomer Gouin, LAC R7648 Vol. 73.

12 Duke's diary, 24 July 1917.

13 Duke's diary, 5 August 1917.

14 Ford, "Some Notes on the Formation of the Union Government in 1917."

15 This description of the meeting from: DMC The Duke of Devonshire's "Notes on Conference at Government House, Thursday August 9th, 1917," a report that accompanied his letter to Walter Long of 10 August 1917, Theatre store 1; and from the Diary of Sir Lomer Gouin, Library and Archives Canada, R7648 Vol. 73.

16 Ibid.

17 DMC The governor general to Walter Long, 10 August 1917, Theatre store 1. From Gouin's notes we know that each participant spoke in turn and there was little spontaneous conversation.

18 DMC The Duke of Devonshire's "Notes on Conference at Government House," 9 August 1917, Theatre store 1.

19 The meeting is also described in Borden, *Robert Laird Borden, His Memoirs*, 740.

20 Duke's diary, 9 August 1917.

21 DMC Lord Lansdowne to the Duke of Devonshire, 20 August 1917, P33 8220 (A).

22 DMC Governor General to Walter Long, 31 July 1917, Theatre store 1.

23 Duke's diary, 17 August 1917.

24 Duke's diary, 23 August 1917.

25 Borden, *Robert Laird Borden, His Memoirs*, 742–3.

26 Duke's diary, 28 August 1917.

27 *The Globe* (Toronto), 28 August 1917.

28 *The Globe* (Toronto), 29 August 1917. CNR incorporated the Grand Trunk and its subsidiary, the Grand Trunk Pacific, as well as the Intercolonial, the Canadian Northern, and the National Transcontinental. Tucker and Marshall, "Canadian National Railways."

29 Armstrong, *The Crisis of Quebec*, 197.

30 "Seven Arrested for Explosions" *Observer* (Utica, NY), 1 September 1917; "Say Blackwell made the Bombs, Will be Charged with the Murder of Lord Ahtelstan [*sic*]," *Standard* (Bedford, Mass.), 5 September 1917. LAC Lord Atholstan R13344 Vol 2.

31 Duke's diary, 24 July 1917.

32 The Income War Tax Act, the first of its kind in Canada, was considered a conscription of wealth. The Railway Bill brought together the Canadian Northern Railway and others into what became the Canadian National Railway. There were two franchise bills. The first, the Military Voters Act, allowed all military personnel to vote, even if they were in the theatre of war. The second, the Wartime Elections Bill, was the first act in Canada to give votes to women in a federal election; however, only women who were relatives of soldiers (wives, mothers, sisters) could vote. The bill also disenfranchised persons from enemy-alien countries naturalized after 31 March 1902. The franchise bills were very controversial. Foot, "Election of 1917," *Canadian Encyclopedia*.

33 English and Panneton, "The Wartime Elections Act," *Canadian Encyclopedia*.

34 For provincial elections, Manitoba had enfranchised women in January 1916, but the other provinces had not yet followed suit. In several provinces, women already had the vote in municipal elections, though in some provinces this was restricted to widows and spinsters or to rate-payers.

35 Borden's Union cabinet consisted of five westerners: A.L. Sifton, J.A. Calder, and T.A. Crerar, Liberals; M. Burrell and A. Meighen, Conservatives; nine from Ontario: General S.C. Mewburn, N.W. Rowell, H. Guthrie, and Senator G.D. Robertson, Liberals; and E. Kemp, T. White, J.D. Reid, T.W. Crothers, and F. Cochrane, Conservatives; four from Quebec: C.C. Ballantyne, Liberal, and C.J. Doherty, P.E. Blondin, and A. Sevigny, Conservatives; three from the Maritimes:

F.B. Carvell and A.K. Maclean, Liberals, and G.E. Foster, Conservative. Each region of the country was thus represented in each of the Liberal and Conservative sections of the Union government, but the representation from Ontario was largest. See Borden, *Robert Laird Borden: His Memoirs*, 757–8.

36 DMC Victor to Evie, 26 August 1917, N16 6284.

37 Borden, *Robert Laird Borden: His Memoirs*, 667.

38 Brown and Cook, *Canada 1896–1921*, 275.

39 Borden, *Robert Laird Borden: His Memoirs*, 607 and 668. The proposed imperial conference was never held, but by 1926 relations had changed, and in 1931 the Statute of Westminster placed the legal seal on these changes. Ibid., 676.

40 Borden to Perley, 13 October 1917, LAC Documents on Canadian External Relations (DCER) #25.

41 Perley to Borden, 16 October 1917, LAC, DCER #26.

42 Colonial secretary to governor general, 19 October 1917, DCER #27.

43 Governor general to colonial secretary, 22 October 1917, CO42 V 1001, 353–4.

44 Duke's diary, 20 October 1917.

45 Governor general to colonial secretary, 22 October 1917, CO 42 V 1001, 353–4.

46 Hazen to J.J. Robidoux, 16 October 1917, Sir John Douglas Hazen fonds, UNB Archives MG H13 Box 25 file 2.

47 Hazen to Colonel Murray MacLaren, 7 November 1917, Sir John Douglas Hazen fonds, UNB Archives MG H13 Box 25 file 2.

48 Hazen to J.B.M. Baxter, 16 October 1917, Sir John Douglas Hazen fonds, UNB archives MG H13 Box 25 file 2.

49 Colonial secretary to governor general, 26 October 1917, DCER #30.

50 Governor general to colonial secretary, 31 October 1917, DCER #31.

51 Governor general to colonial secretary, 5 November 1917, DCER #32; and Hazen to Colonel Murray MacLaren, 7 November 1917, Sir John Douglas Hazen fonds, UNB archives MG H13 Box 25 file 2.

52 Duke's diary, 28 October 1917.

53 Borden, *Robert Laird Borden: His Memoirs*, 767.

54 Wilson, *The Imperial Policy of Sir Robert Borden*, 73–5. Wilson covers the progress of Borden's work on this issue in detail and calls it "Borden's last great achievement as a statesman of the Empire." In April 1920 the decision became public and was announced in British and Canadian Parliaments 10 May 1920. It was not until 1927 that a representative was actually appointed.

CHAPTER EIGHT

1 DMC Evie to her mother, 10 August 1917, 9th Duke 3.

2 DMC Evie to Victor (undated except for Thursday – probably 16 August 1917), 9th Duke 1.

3 DMC Evie to her mother, 16 August 1917, 9th Duke 3.

4 Canadian Pacific discontinued passenger service in 1963. The train right-of-way is now a bicycle or walking track. Ballantyne, "Maniwaki Requiem."

5 Duke's diary, 18 August 1917.

6 Ethel Chadwick's diary, 18 August 1917, LAC MG 30 D258.

7 Ethel Chadwick's diary, 30 August 1917, LAC MG 30 D258.

8 DMC Maud to Lady Edward, from Woods Hole, 27 August 1917, 9th Duke 1.

9 Duke's diary, 20 August 1917.

10 The Dominion Police was the security force in eastern Canada. In 1920 the force merged with the police force of western Canada, the Royal North-West Mounted Police, to become the Royal Canadian Mounted Police.

11 Edmond, *Rockcliffe Park: A History of the Village.*

12 DMC Evie to Lady Edward, 19 August 1917, 9th Duke 1.

13 Bulkeley-Johnson to his mother, 29 August 1917, LAC MG 30 E56.

14 DMC Evie to Lady Edward, 1 September 1917, 9th Duke 1.

15 DMC Dorothy to Lady Edward, 6 September 1917, 9th Duke 1.

16 DMC Charlie to Lady Edward, 9 September 1917, 9th Duke 1.

17 DMC Victor to his mother, 23 August 1917, 9th Duke 1.

18 Duke's diary, 19 August 1917.

19 DMC Evie to Victor, 31 July 1917, 9th Duke 1.

20 DMC Evie to her mother, 1 August 1917, 9th Duke 3.

21 DMC Evie to her mother, 10 August 1917, 9th Duke 3.

22 DMC Evie to her mother, 16 August 1917, 9th Duke 3.

23 DMC Maud to Evie, from Woods Hole, 18 August 1917, N9 6073.

24 DMC Maud to Evie, from Woods Hole, 21 August 1917, N9 6074.

25 DMC Blanche Egerton to Evie, 12 September 1917, G9 3322.

26 DMC Angus to Evie, 21 August 1917, N9 6075.

27 DMC Angus to Evie, from Boston, 28 August 1917, N9 6078.

28 DMC Telegram from Maud and Angus to Evie, from Boston, 29 August 1917, N9 6079.

29 Bulkeley-Johnson to his mother, 3 September 1917, LAC MG 30 E56.

30 Ethel Chadwick's diary, 30 August 1917, LAC MG 30 D258.

31 Ethel Chadwick's diary, 1 September 1917, LAC MG 30 D258.

32 DMC Evie to Victor, 2 September 1917, 9th Duke 1.

33 DMC Telegram from Mackintosh to the duke and duchess, 1 September 1917, N9 6081.
34 Figures calculated using the Bank of England Inflation Rate calculator (http://www.bankofengland.co.uk/education/Pages/resources/inflation tools/calculator/default.aspx) and the Bank of Canada currency converter (http://www.bankofcanada.ca/rates/exchange/daily-converter/).
35 TBC Evie to her mother, 15 October 1917.
36 DMC Telegram to Lady Edward, 31 August 1917, 9th Duke 1.
37 DMC Evie to Lady Edward, 1 September 1917, 9th Duke 1.
38 DMC Blanche Egerton to Evie, 12 September 1917, G9 3322.
39 DMC Evie to Lady Edward 30 September 1917, 9th Duke 1.
40 Duke's diary, 24 October 1917. The Memorial is in Bell Memorial Park in Brantford, Ontario.
41 LAC Image of Dr Alexander Graham Bell presenting a silver telephone to the Duke of Devonshire, Governor General of Canada, at the Bell Homestead, Brantford, Ontario, 24 October 1917. Copy negative C-066614.
42 Duke's diary, 10 October 1917.
43 Duke's diary, 12, 19, and 21 October 1917.
44 DMC Blanche Egerton to Evie, 18 November 1917, G9 3333.
45 DMC Evie to Lady Edward, 24 October 1917 and 5 November 1917, 9th Duke 1.
46 Ibid.
47 The full guest list was published in *The Ottawa Evening Journal*, 5 November 1917, along with the list of presents and who they came from.
48 Evie to Lady Edward, 24 October 1917, 9th Duke 1; Duke's diary, 2 November 1917.
49 *The Ottawa Evening Journal*, 5 November 1917.
50 DMC Evie to Lady Edward, 5 November 1917, 9th Duke 1.
51 Ibid.
52 DMC Victor to his mother, 1 November 1917, 9th Duke 1.
53 *The Ottawa Citizen*, 3 November 1917.
54 *The Globe* (Toronto), 5 November 1917.
55 DMC Victor to his mother, 1 November 1917, 9th Duke 1.
56 DMC Miss Walton (governess) to Lady Edward, 6 December 1917, 9th Duke 1.
57 LAC Mackenzie King diaries, 3 November 1917, www.collections canada.gc.ca/databases/king/001059-100.01-e.php.
58 *The Globe* (Toronto), 5 November 1917.
59 Ibid.

60 DMC Miss Walton (governess) to Lady Edward, 6 December 1917, 9th Duke 1.

61 *The Globe* (Toronto), 5 November 1917.

62 DMC Evie to Lady Edward, 5 November 1917, 9th Duke 1.

63 What we now know as Meech Lake was "Meach's Lake" in all letters and newspapers in 1917.

64 DMC Evie to Lady Edward, 5 November 1917, 9th Duke 1.

65 Duke's diary, 3 November 1917.

66 DMC Florence Spring Rice to Lady Edward, 5 November 1917, 9th Duke 1.

67 DMC Evie to Lady Edward, 24 October 1917, 9th Duke 1.

68 TBC Duchess to her mother, 21 November 1917.

69 DMC Evie to Victor, 20 November 1917, and Florence Spring Rice to Lady Edward, 30 November 1917, 9th Duke 1.

70 DMC Florence Spring Rice to Lady Edward, 5 November 1917, 9th Duke 1.

CHAPTER NINE

1 *The Globe* (Toronto), 5 November 1917.

2 Duke's diary, 7 November 1917.

3 DMC Victor to his mother, 9 November 1917, 9th Duke 1.

4 Duke's diary, 11 November 1917.

5 The small towns they stopped at included: Chapleau in Ontario; Gladstone, Minnedosa, and Birtle in Manitoba; Bredenbury, Yorkton, and Wynyard in Saskatchewan; and McLeod in Alberta. From DMC Duke's journal of the trip, Theatre store 1.

6 DMC Victor to Evie, 14 November 1917, N16 6290.

7 DMC Evie to Victor, 18 November 1917, 9th Duke 1.

8 Bulkeley-Johnson to his father, 14 November 1917, LAC MG 30 E56.

9 DMC Duke's journal of the trip, Theatre store 1.

10 Alberta retains a Government House in Edmonton but it is no longer the official residence of the lieutenant-governor (http://history.alberta. ca/governmenthouse/default.aspx); British Columbia maintains a Government House in Victoria, home of the lieutenant-governor, though the one the duke visited burned down in 1957 (http://www.lt gov.bc.ca/gov-house/history/history.html); Saskatchewan's Government House in Regina is no longer the residence, but is the office of the lieutenant-governor and used for ceremonial occasions (http://www.govern menthouse.gov.sk.ca/our-history); Manitoba's Government House in Winnipeg, built in 1883, still serves as the lieutenant-governor's home (http://www.lg.gov.mb.ca/history/house/history.html).

11 Duke's diary, 16 November 1917.

12 DMC Duke's journal of the trip, Theatre store 1.

13 Ibid.

14 DMC Victor to his mother, 18 November 1917, 9th Duke 1.

15 DMC Victor to Evie, 18 November 1917, N16 6293.

16 DMC Evie to Victor, 27 November 1917, 9th Duke 1.

17 Bulkeley-Johnson to his mother, 20 November 1917, LAC MG 30 E56. British Columbia drove on the left until 1920, http://www.world standards.eu/cars/driving-on-the-left/.

18 Bulkeley-Johnson to his mother, 21 November 1917, LAC MG 30 E56.

19 BJ thought it was one of his best speeches. Bulkeley-Johnson to his mother, 21 November 1917, LAC MG 30 E56. *The Globe* (Toronto), 23 November 1917, 11 reported its contents.

20 Victory Loans were Canadian government appeals for money to finance the war effort in World War I and World War II. The successful campaign led to Canada Savings Bonds in 1946. Hillmer, "Victory Loans," *The Canadian Encyclopedia*.

21 DMC Victor to Evie, 23 November 1917, N16 6297; Duke's journal of the tour, Theatre store 1.

22 Bulkeley-Johnson to his mother, November 1917, LAC MG 30 E56.

23 DMC Duke's journal of the tour, Theatre store 1.

24 DMC Victor to Evie, 14 November 1917, N16 6290.

25 DMC Duke's journal of the tour, Theatre store 1.

26 DMC Evie to Lady Edward, 22 November 1917, 9th Duke 1.

27 *The Globe* (Toronto), 3 December 1917. In all of Canada, 820,035 people out of a total population of 7,891,000 bought Victory Bonds. *The Globe* (Toronto), 26 January 1918.

28 Bulkeley-Johnson to his mother, 9 December 1917.

29 Duke's diary, 9 December 1917.

30 TBC Evie to her mother, 15 December 1917.

31 Quoted from Lord Lansdowne's letter as printed in *The Globe* (Toronto), 30 November 1917.

32 Ibid.

33 Keegan, *The First World War*, 341.

34 DMC Victor to his mother, from the viceregal train, 30 November 1917, 9th Duke 1.

35 DMC Victor to Evie, from the viceregal train, 30 November 1917, N16 6303.

36 Newton, "The Lansdowne 'Peace Letter' of 1917."

37 Ibid.

38 *The Times* (London), 1 December 1917.

39 DMC Evie to Victor, 1 December 1917, 9th Duke 1.

40 *New York Times*, 1 December 1917.

41 Ibid.
42 DMC Blanche Egerton to Evie, 2 December 1917, G9 3335.
43 DMC Blanche Egerton to Evie, 9 December 1917, G9 3336.
44 DMC Lord Sandhurst to Victor, 5 December 1917, H4 3962.
45 *The Globe* (Toronto), 1 December 1917, 6.
46 Skelton, *Life and Letters of Sir Wilfrid Laurier.*
47 DMC Evie to Victor, 2 December 1917, 9th Duke 1.
48 TBC Evie to her mother, 2 January 1918.
49 Duke's diary, 1 December 1917.
50 Duke's diary, 2 December 1917.
51 *New York Times*, 1 December 1917.
52 Wilson, "Fifth Annual Message," 4 December 1917.
53 Duke's diary, 17 January 1918.
54 Duke's diary, 30 January 1918.
55 Duke's diary, 1 February 1918.
56 Duke's diary, 5 March 1918.
57 Keegan, *The First World War*, 342.
58 *New York Times*, 6 March 1918.
59 Macmillan, *Paris, 1919*, 158.
60 Duke's diary, 6 December 1917.
61 DMC Evie to Victor, 7 December 1917, 9th Duke 1.
62 Duke's diary, 8 December 1917.
63 Kitz, *Shattered City.*
64 DMC Miss Walton to Lady Edward, 6 December 1917, 9th Duke 1.
65 DMC Charlie Cavendish to Lady Edward, 21 December 1917, 9th Duke 1.
66 *The Globe* (Toronto), 24 December 1917, 8.
67 *Halifax Morning Chronicle*, 22 December 1917.
68 *The Globe* (Toronto), 24 December 1917, 8.
69 Quotes about the Halifax Explosion are taken from: *The Globe* (Toronto), 24 December 1917; *Halifax Morning Chronicle*, 22 December 1917; letter from the duke to his mother, 24 December 1917, DMC 9th Duke 1; the Duke's diary, 21 December 1917.

CHAPTER TEN

1 Bulkeley-Johnson to his mother, 25 December 1917.
2 The U.S. Army in World War I. Retrieved from http://www.history.army.mil/books/AMH-V2/AMH%20V2/chapter1.htm. Six months later there would be 900,000 U.S. soldiers in the European theatre of war.
3 Keegan, *The First World War*, 329–30.
4 Ibid., 367–8.

5 Ibid., 340–1.

6 Duke's diary, 14 December 1917.

7 DMC Victor to his mother, 24 December 1917, and 6 January 1918, 9th Duke 1.

8 Bulkeley-Johnson to his mother, 12 December 1916, LAC MG 30 E56.

9 DMC Victor to his mother, 6 January 1918, 9th Duke 1.

10 Duke's diary 17 January 1918.

11 TBC Evie to her mother, 4 March 1918.

12 DMC Victor to his mother, 6 January 1918, 9th Duke 1.

13 TBC Evie to her mother, 3 January 1918.

14 Bulkeley-Johnson to his mother, 9 January 1918, LAC MG 30 E56.

15 DMC Ambassador Spring Rice to British Foreign Secretary A.J. Balfour, 12 January 1918, Theatre store 1.

16 Ibid.

17 Ibid.

18 DMC Victor to his mother, 16 January 1918, 9th Duke 1.

19 DMC Evie to Lady Edward, 16 January 1918, 9th Duke 1.

20 DMC Victor to his mother, 16 January 1918, 9th Duke 1.

21 Duke's diary, 9 January 1918.

22 Duke's diary, 10 January 1918.

23 DMC A copy of his speech is in Theatre store 1.

24 *New York Times*, 13 January 1918.

25 Duke's diary, 12 January 1918.

26 *New York Times*, 13 January 1918.

27 *New York Times*, 3 January 1918.

28 DMC Evie to Lady Edward, 16 January 1918, 9th Duke 1.

29 DMC Victor to his mother, 16 January 1918, 9th Duke 1.

30 Lord Northcliffe owned both the London *Daily Mail* and the *Times* of London.

31 DMC Evie to her mother, 22 December 1916, 9th Duke 3.

32 Bulkeley-Johnson to his mother, 14 February 1918, LAC MG 30 E56.

33 DMC Evie to Lady Edward, 7 April 1917, G10 3438.

34 Bulkeley-Johnson to his mother, 14 February 1918, LAC MG 30 E56.

35 *Ottawa Citizen*, 14 February 1918, 1.

36 "Notes on the Manner in which Canadian business is Transacted in Washington." Memo prepared by Sir Cecil Spring Rice, forwarded to Sir Joseph Pope, 13 February 1918, LAC RG 5 G-1 Vol. 1222 File 200. Also the same document, addressed to the governor general, i s contained in Documents on External Relations, 31 January 1918, number 24.

37 Bulkeley-Johnson to his mother, 14 February 1918.

38 Ibid.

39 Gwynn, *The Letters and Friendships of Sir Cecil Spring Rice*, 435.

40 *New York Times,* 17 February 1918.

41 Sir Cecil Spring Rice to a friend, from Gulhek, Persia, 22 July 1899. Quoted in Gwynn, *The Letters and Friendships of Sir Cecil Spring Rice*, 284.

42 Information about Sir Cecil Spring Rice not specifically referenced is from Gwynn, *The Letters and Friendships of Sir Cecil Spring Rice*, and from Burton, *Cecil Spring Rice: A Diplomat's Life.*

43 DMC Evie to Lady Edward, 7 January 1918, 9th Duke 1.

44 DMC Blanche Egerton to Evie, 16 February 1918, G9 3444.

45 TBC Evie to her mother, 17 May 1918.

46 DMC Evie to Lady Edward, 27 January 1918; the duke to Lady Edward, 27 January 1918, 9th Duke 1.

47 TBC Evie to her mother, 4 March 1918.

48 TBC Evie to her mother, 17 May 1918.

49 *The Globe* (Toronto), 3 March 1918, 2; Duke's diary, 28 February 1918.

50 TBC Evie to her mother, 4 March 1918.

51 Information for this paragraph is from *The Globe* (Toronto) and *The Ottawa Citizen* and from the duke's diary, 1–5 March 1918.

52 Duke's diary, 14 April 1918.

53 Duke's diary, 28 March 1919; Duke to his mother, 31 March 1919, 9th Duke 1.

54 TBC Evie to her mother, 4 March 1918.

55 TBC Evie to her mother, 1 April 1918.

56 Bulkeley-Johnson to his mother, 14 February 1918. Mrs Massey was the wife of Vincent Massey, with whom BJ had become friends at Oxford and with whom he remained in contact. In 1952 Vincent Massey became the first Canadian-born governor general.

57 Duke's diary, 6 April 1918.

58 *The Globe* (Toronto), 6 April 1918, 1.

59 Ibid.

60 Ibid.

61 Duke's diary, 6 April 1918.

62 The Russell Theatre, which held over 1,500, was torn down in 1928 to make room for Confederation Square. Alberti, "Russell Theatre," *The Canadian Encyclopedia Online.*

63 Duke's diary, 7 April 1918.

64 Duke's diary, 29 March, 1918; Reading the Riot Act means that an official such as the mayor could charge the assembly to disperse within a specified time or face arrest.

65 One of these, *The Quebec Chronicle,* was owned by Major General

David Watson, who was in France as head of the Fourth Canadian Division, the man whom the duke had met in October 1916.

66 TBC Evie to her mother, 1 April 1918.

67 Information for this section on the riots comes from *The Globe* (Toronto), 29 March to 6 April 1918; the duke's diary, 29 March to 4 April 1918; Armstrong, *The Crisis of Quebec 1914–1918*, 226–46; Borden, *Robert Laird Borden: His Memoirs*, 789; Granatstein and Hitsman, *Broken Promises*, 89; Marx, "The Emergency Power and Civil Liberties in Canada," 52–3; and Auger, "On the Brink of Civil War: The Canadian Government and the Suppression of the 1918 Quebec Easter Riots," *Canadian Historical Review*. There is a difference of opinion between authors Marx and Auger about whether what the government imposed on Quebec City in 1918 was martial law; Marx says there was no martial law in Canada from Confederation until his article was published in 1970 (before the October Crisis), while Auger says martial law was imposed in 1918. This discrepancy appears to be in their interpretations of what constitutes martial law.

68 Duke's diary, 13 April 1918.

69 Duke's diary, 14 April 1918.

70 Duke's diary, 13 April 1918.

71 *The Globe* (Toronto), 13 April 1918; Duke's diary, 7 May 1918.

72 Duke's diary, 18 May 1918.

73 *The Globe* (Toronto), 18 May 1918.

74 Governor general to Walter Long, 14 July 1917, LAC RG 7 G22 Vol. 8.

75 Walter Long, internal memo, 11 September 1917, LAC CO 42 Vol. 1001 164.

76 Governor general, no clear addressee, n.d., LAC CO 42 Vol. 1001 171–3.

77 Governor general, presumably to Walter Long, 31 July 1917, LAC CO 42 Vol. 1001 165–6. Education is a provincial matter in Canada.

78 Governor general, review of request from British Columbia, not clear to whom it was sent, n.d., LAC CO 42 Vol. 1001 167–70.

79 Ibid.

80 Ibid.

81 Duke's diary, 9 October 1917.

82 LAC Long to Perley, 30 April 1918, RG 25 G-1 Vol. 1166 File 2308.

83 Sir Robert Borden to Walter Long, 2 August 1918, LAC CO 42 Vol. 1010 346; Walter Long to governor general, 22 August 1918, LAC RG 25 G-1 Vol. 1166 File 2308.

84 Long to governor general, 22 August 1918, LAC RG 25 G-1 Vol. 1166 File 2308.

85 Governor general to colonial secretary, 17 January 1918, LAC RG 25 G-1 Vol. 1221.

86 Colonial secretary to governor general, 9 February 1918, LAC RG 25 G-1 Vol. 1221.

87 Colonial secretary to governor general, 26 March 1918, LAC RG 25 G-1 Vol. 1221.

88 Colonial secretary to governor general, 4 May 1918, LAC RG 25 G-1 Vol. 1221.

89 Colonial secretary to governor general, 14 May 1918, LAC RG 25 G-1 Vol. 1221.

90 Colonial secretary to governor general, 16 May 1918, LAC RG 25 G-1 Vol. 1221.

91 Maurice Hankey to Colonial Office, 13 April 1918, LAC CO 42 Vol. 1010 127.

92 Governor general to Colonial Office, 13 April 1918, LAC CO 42 Vol. 1010 130–1.

93 Walter Long to Battersbee, internal memo for transmission to Sir Robert Borden, 17 April 1918, LAC CO 42 Vol. 1010 101–3.

94 Information for this paragraph is taken from Stone, *World War One*, chapter six, and from Keegan, *The First World War*, 355. The British raid on Zeebrugge was 23 April 1918. Apparently the raid, though it blocked the harbour, did not interrupt German submarine operations. It did, however, renew hope in the west.

95 Duke's diary and Ethel Chadwick's diary, 15 May 1918.

96 DMC Evie to Lady Edward, 28 May 1918, 9th Duke 1.

97 Duke's diary, 24 May 1918.

98 DMC Evie to Lady Edward, 28 May 1918, 9th Duke 1.

99 Ibid.

100 Duke's diary, 28 May 1918.

101 DMC Blanche Egerton to Evie, 9 June 1918, G9 3350.

102 Duke's diary, 10 June 1918.

103 DMC Duke to Lady Edward, from the viceregal train at Stratford, 12 June 1918, 9th Duke 1.

104 Ibid.

105 Duke's diary, 13 June 1918.

106 Duke's diary, 18 June 1918.

107 DMC Duke to Lady Edward, 22 June 1918, 9th Duke 1.

108 Duke's diary, 13 May 1918.

CHAPTER ELEVEN

1 Walter Long to governor general, 25 April 1917, LAC RG 7 G22 Vol. 14.

2 Walter Long to governor general, 1 November 1917, LAC MG 26 H Vol. 8 1341–2. Canada was allotted thirteen places in the first two classes that carried knighthoods for male or female civilians.

3 Duke's diary, 10 November 1917.

4 Haley, "Stuart, Sir Campbell Arthur (1885–1972)," *Oxford Dictionary of National Biography.*

5 Duke's diary, 17 December 1917.

6 Borden to Perley, 17 December 1917, MG 26 H 1299.

7 Borden to Lord Northcliffe, 31 January 1918, LAC MG 26 H Vol. 8 1293–4.

8 Long to Duke of Devonshire, 15 April 1918, LAC CO 42 Vol. 1007 161.

9 Sir Charles Gordon to Borden, 25 February 1918, LAC MG 26 H Vol. 8 1289–91.

10 Borden to Sir Charles Gordon, 4 March 1918, LAC MG 26 H Vol. 8 1292.

11 Brown, "Gordon, Sir Charles Blair," in *Dictionary of Canadian Biography.*

12 Borden to Duke of Devonshire, 30 December 1917, LAC MG 26 H Vol. 9 1450.

13 Governor general to Borden, 17 January 1918, LAC MG 26 H Vol. 165 89610–11; Borden to governor general, 22 January 1918, MG 26 H Vol. 165 89612–13.

14 *Saturday Night,* 6 April 1918, LAC CO 42 Vol. 1007 181. Clipping sent with a letter from the Duke of Devonshire to the colonial secretary, 11 April 1918, LAC CO 42 Vol. 1077 176.

15 Borden's diary and duke's diary, 18 February 1918.

16 Borden to governor general, 11 March 1918, LAC CO 42 Vol. 1007, 151–5.

17 Duke's diary, 11 March 1918.

18 Duke's despatch, CO 42 Vol. 1000, 309–11, 20 March 1918. Note that this file in LAC microfilm of CO 42 is unreadable. This file was obtained from the original files in the National Archives, London.

19 Governor general to colonial secretary, 23 March, 1918, LAC CO 42 Vol. 1007 141–6.

20 Ibid.

21 Walter Long to Duke of Devonshire 15 April 1918, LAC CO 42 Vol. 1007 163.

22 Long to Duke of Devonshire, 15 April 1918, LAC CO 42 Vol. 1007, 161–3; The baronetcy for Flavelle must have been signed by the duke but did not occasion any comment in his diary. He knew Flavelle

quite well and on one occasion thought he would make a good prime minister. Duke's diary, 19 December 1916.

23 Duke's diary, 4 April 1918.

24 House of Commons Debates, Parliament of Canada (Hansard), 8 April 1918, 518.

25 Governor general to colonial secretary, 25 May 1918, LAC CO 42 Vol. 1007, 265–6.

26 Duke's diary, 23 May 1918.

27 Borden's diary, 21 May 1918, LAC MG 26 H.

28 Cook, *Warlords: Borden, Mackenzie King, and Canada's World Wars*, 65.

29 For example, the Lanark County Council Chamber, Perth, Ontario, voted on 23 November 1918 to "heartily endorse" the resolution re: the abolition of titles in Canada, LAC MG 26 H1(a) Vol. 75 50174; Fort William letter (LAC MG 26 H Vol. 81 42029) and several others arrived.

30 *The Globe* (Toronto), 23 May 1918, 4.

31 John Simpson to Sir Robert Borden, 11 April 1918, LAC MG 26 H Vol. 81 42023.

32 Colonel Cantley to A.E. Blount, Clerk of the Senate, 2 December 1918, LAC MG 26 H Vol. 9 1500–1; Sir John Carson to Sir Robert Borden, 11 October 1917, LAC MG 26 H Vol. 9 1436–7.

33 George Fiddes to Walter Long, LAC CO 42 Vol. 1007, 136.

34 Finlay to Long, 17 May 1918, LAC CO 42 Vol. 1010 176.

35 Grant of Honours to persons in Canada, LAC CO 42 Vol. 1007 136, 28 March to 24 April 1918.

36 George Curzon to Walter Long, 1 June 1918, LAC CO 42 Vol. 1010 168.

37 Borden to Long, 9 August 1918, LAC CO 42 Vol. 1010 352; Long to Devonshire, 9 August 1918, LAC CO 42 Vol. 1011 337.

CHAPTER TWELVE

1 Duke's diary, 1 July 1918.

2 There were no legal limits in 1918; the rule of eight fish per person was a Restigouche Salmon Club limit.

3 Victor to Evie, 3 July 1918.

4 "Salmon Angling on the Restigouche," *Scribner's Magazine*.

5 Vanderweide, "Crushing the Barrier with Restigouche Salmon."

6 DMC Victor to his mother, 7 July 1918, 9th Duke 1.

7 *Charter, Bylaws, Officers and Members of the Ristigouche Salmon Club. 1966.*

8 DMC Ristigouche Salmon Club Fishing Rules and Division of Up-River Waters 1918, Theatre store 1.

9 *Charter, Bylaws, Officers and Members of the Ristigouche Salmon Club. 1966.*

10 Duke's diary, 1 July 1918.

11 DMC Victor to Evie, 3 July 1918, N16 6311.

12 DMC Victor to Evie, 7 July 1918, N16 6313.

13 Dubé, *Stolen Treasure*, 4.

14 DMC Victor to Evie, 7 July 1918, N16 6313.

15 DMC Victor to Evie, 4 July 1918, N16 6312.

16 DMC Victor to Evie, 10 July 1918, N16 6316.

17 Fish rise when the air is cooler than the water. Sun on the water makes the air hotter. Conversation with Peter Dubé, owner of Hotel Restigouche and fishing guide, 20 September 2011.

18 DMC Victor to Evie, 7 July 1918, N16 6313.

19 Duke's diary, 7 July 1918.

20 "Salmon Angling on the Restigouche," *Scribner's Magazine.* I am indebted to Irene Doyle's article "My Restigouche River Run" for leading me to this article, http://www.restigouche.net/en/chroniques/nature/2001-17.shtml, retrieved 10 November 2016.

21 DMC Victor to Evie, 7 July 1918, N16 6313.

22 Indian House was designed by New York architect Stanford White, who was a member of the Club, http://new-brunswick.net/new-brunswick/restigouche/restigouche2.html, retrieved 10 November 2016.

23 DMC Victor to his mother, 7 July 1918, 9th Duke 1.

24 DMC Victor to Evie, 8 July 1918, N16 6314.

25 DMC Victor to Evie, 9 July 1918, N16 6315.

26 Ibid.

27 Duke's diary, 6 July 1918.

28 DMC Victor to Evie, 9 July 1918, N16 6315.

29 Duke's diary, 7 July 1918.

30 DMC Victor to Evie, 11 July 1918, N16 6317.

31 DMC Victor to Evie, 7 July 1918, N16 6313, and 8 July 1918, N16 6314.

32 DMC Victor to Evie, 7 July 1918, N16 6313.

33 DMC Victor to Evie, 8 July 1918, N16 6314.

34 DMC Victor to Evie, 10 July 1918, N16 6316.

35 Ibid.

36 DMC Victor to Evie, 3 July 1918, N16 6311.

37 DMC Victor to Evie, 10 July 1918, N16 6316.

38 Although "caught" fish would be more common in current parlance, in 1917 the duke always used "killed."

39 DMC Restigouche Fishing records, Theatre store 1.

40 DMC Victor to Evie, 11 July 1918, N16 6317.

41 Duke's diary, 11 July 1918.

42 *Charter, Bylaws, Officers and Members of the Ristigouche Salmon Club. 1966.* The largest catches in this 1966 record were in the war years, 1941–44, but in the 1950s the catch began to decline. Note that "Restigouche" is used in English, "Ristigouche" in French. There is no record of what they did with all the fish but Peter Dubé of the Motel Restigouche said the Restigouche Salmon Club had ice houses to store the fish, and members sent them to their homes in the United States.

43 DMC Evie to Victor, 29 June 1918, Q5 8646, and 5 July 1918, Q5 8650.

44 Deed of sale, Registre foncier du Québec No. 30554, 28 November 1918.

45 DMC Evie to Lady Edward, 5 July 1918, 9th Duke 1.

46 TBC Evie to her mother, 14 July 1918.

47 DMC Evie to Victor, 5 July 1918, Q5 8650.

48 DMC Victor to Lady Edward, 25 July 1918, 9th Duke 1.

49 DMC Evie to Lady Edward, 5 July 1918, 9th Duke 1.

50 Ethel Chadwick's diary, 18 July 1918, LAC MG 30 D258. Ethel and her friends were invited for a swimming party. They were staying across the lake at the Lemoines' cottage. Evie's watercolour sketches, mentioned by Ethel Chadwick, seem to have disappeared.

51 DMC Dorothy to Lady Edward, 8 July 1918, 9th Duke 1.

52 DMC Evie to Lady Edward, 14 July 1918, 9th Duke 1.

53 DMC Victor to Lady Edward, 25 July 1918, 9th Duke 1.

54 Duke's diary, 29 July 1918.

55 TBC Evie to her mother, 27 July 1918.

56 Bulkeley-Johnson to his mother, 1 August 1918. BJ was not up to working and went home with Prince Arthur, the Duke of Connaught, who visited Ottawa for a few days in August after completing a mission to the Emperor of Japan. They left Halifax on HMS *Shannon* in late August.

57 DMC Victor to Lady Edward, 16 August 1918, 9th Duke 1.

58 TBC Evie to her mother, 27 July 1918.

59 Duke's diary, 29 July 1918.

60 DMC Evie to Victor, 27 August 1918, Q5 8661, and Evie to Lady Edward, 14 July 1918, 9th Duke 1.

61 DMC Evie to Victor, 27 August 1918, Q5 8661.

62 DMC Evie to Victor, 1 September 1918, Q5 8663.

63 DMC Evie to Victor, 5 October 1918, Q5 8667.

64 DMC His Excellency the Duke of Devonshire's Household Accounts, 1918 to 1921.

65 All dates quoted here are in the Gregorian calendar, which is used now; at the time, Russia used the Julian calendar. When Russia adopted the Gregorian calendar in 1918 it had to drop about thirteen days.

66 Duke's diary, 17 March 1917.

67 Duke's diary, 15 May 1918.

68 Walter Long to governor general, 20 July 1918, LAC RG 25 G-1 Vol. 1224 File 630.

69 Quoted in Moffat, "Forgotten Battlefields: Canadians in Siberia, 1918–1919."

70 Borden, *Robert Laird Borden: His Memoirs*, 869.

71 Swettenham, "Allied Intervention in Siberia 1911–1919."

72 Isitt, *From Victoria to Vladivostok*.

73 Ibid., 2.

74 Moffat, "Forgotten Battlefields: Canadians in Siberia, 1918–1919," 82.

CHAPTER THIRTEEN

1 DMC Evie to Victor, 1 September 1918, Q5 8663.

2 DMC Evie to Victor, 5 September 1918, Q5 8664.

3 DMC Dorothy to her mother, 4 September 1918, A28 1029.

4 DMC Victor to Evie, 25 August 1918, N16 6324.

5 DMC Victor to Evie, 27 August 1918, N16 6325.

6 Duke's diary, 30 Aug 1918; DMC Victor to Evie, 31 Aug 1918, N16 6327.

7 Duke's diary, 2 September 1918.

8 DMC Victor to Evie, 1 September 1918, N16 6328; Duke's diary, 31 August 1918.

9 Calculated from Bank of Canada website: http://www.bankofcanada.ca/rates/related/inflation-calculator/.

10 DMC Victor to Lady Edward, 7 September 1918, 9th Duke 1. Victor's mathematics is slightly wrong: 480 acres x 30 bushels/acre x $2.20 per bushel comes to $31,680 in 1918, which converts to about $433,000 in 2016. But the overall impression of a large financial profit remains.

11 DMC Victor to Evie, from Regina, 3 September 1918, N16 6329. (For comparison, the expected 90 million bushels of wheat in Saskatchewan in 1918 converts to 2.44 million metric tonnes, while the 2011 yield was 11.5 million tonnes for a total of more than 423 million bushels. From *Saskatchewan Ministry of Agriculture Fact Sheet 10.01 2012.02.13*, http://www.agriculture.gov.sk.ca/Default.aspx?DN=b6db783f-c302-419a-bc84-a772363ed736.

12 DMC Lord Lansdowne to Evie, 8 September 1918, F6 2526.

13 DMC Prince Arthur to Victor, 23 September 1918, 9th Duke 2.

14 DMC Borden to the duke, 13 September 1918, Theatre store 1.

15 TBC Evie to her mother, 20 September 1918.

16 TBC Evie to her mother, 25 September 1918.

17 Ibid.

18 DMC Evie to Lady Edward, 3 October 1918, 9th Duke 1.

19 DMC Duke's diary, 25 September 1918.

20 DMC Victor to Evie, 5 October 1918, N16 6335.

21 DMC Evie to Victor, 11 October 1918, Q5 8670.

22 TBC Evie to her mother, 27 October 1918.

23 DMC Evie to Lady Edward, 3 October 1918, 9th Duke 1.

24 TBC Evie to her mother, 25 September 1918.

25 Duke's diary, 28 September 1918.

26 DMC Victor to Evie, 3 October 1918, N16 6334. Government House in Quebec City was called Spencerwood. Lieutenant-governors of Quebec lived there until it burned down in 1966. After that, the property became a public park called Bois-de-Coulogne.

27 *New York Times*, 5 October 1918.

28 Barry, *The Great Influenza*, 260.

29 Cunningham, *Diseases in History: Flu*. On page 23 Cunningham notes that a person infected with influenza usually becomes infectious in about twenty-four hours and remains so for three to four days.

30 DMC Victor to Evie, 9 October 1918, N16 6339.

31 DMC Victor to his mother, 11 October 1918, 9th Duke 1.

32 DMC Victor to Evie, 5 October 1918, N16 6335.

33 DMC Evie to Victor, 12 October 1918, Q5 8671.

34 Ibid.

35 DMC Victor to Evie, 11 October 1918, N16 6340.

36 DMC Victor to his mother, 8 October 1918, 9th Duke 1.

37 DMC Evie to Victor, 11 October 1918, Q5 8670.

38 Duke's diary, 12 October 1918.

39 DMC Evie to Victor, 13 October 1918, Q5 8672.

40 Ibid.

41 DMC Victor to Evie, 13 October 1918, N16 6341.

42 Information from the duke's diary, 11, 12, 13 October 1918; DMC Correspondence between Victor and Evie, Q5 8669; Q5 8670; Q5 8671; Q5 8672; N16 6340; N16 6341.

43 DMC Evie to Lady Edward, 19 October 1918, 9th Duke 1.

44 Influenza (Seasonal) World Health Organization, April 2009, http://www.who.int/mediacentre/factsheets/fs211/en/, retrieved 10 November 2016.

45 Pettigrew, *The Silent Enemy: Canada and the Deadly Flu of 1918*, 140.

46 Cunningham, *Diseases in History: Flu*, 56.

47 TBC Evie to her mother, 27 October 1918.

48 DMC Evie to Lady Edward, 19 October 1918, 9th Duke 1.

49 Angus Mackintosh's grave at Arlington National Cemetery is noted at: http://www.cwgc.org/find-war-dead/casualty/4010498/MACKIN TOSH,%20ANGUS%20ALEXANDER.

50 TBC Evie to her mother, 27 October 1918.

51 Ibid.

52 Ibid.

53 DMC Evie to Victor, 16 October 1918, Q5 8673.

54 DMC Victor to Evie, 17 October 1918, N16 6343.

55 *The Globe* (Toronto), 1 October 1918, 6; quoted advice from the Massachusetts Health Department.

56 *The Globe* (Toronto), 2 October 1918, 8.

57 DMC Victor to his mother, 18 October 1918, 9th Duke 1.

58 Pettigrew, *The Silent Enemy: Canada and the Deadly Flu of 1918*, 43 and 48.

59 Bacic, "The Plague of the Spanish Flu: The Influenza Epidemic of 1918 in Ottawa."

60 TBC Evie to her mother, 2 November 1918.

61 Duke's diary, 30 September and 30 October 1918.

62 DMC Victor to Evie, 30 October 1918, N16 6354.

63 CPR Train Time Table, 29 October 1916, Canadian Pacific archives.

64 Duke's diary, 10 November 1918.

65 Ibid.

66 Ethel Chadwick diary, 11 November 1918.

67 *The Ottawa Citizen*, 11 November 1918, 2; *The Ottawa Journal*, 11 November 1918, 15.

68 Although www.thepeerage.com gives another version of this child's names, the record of her christening held in the Diocesan Archives of the Anglican Church in Ottawa confirms that she was christened Anne Peace Arabella.

69 DMC Evie to Lady Edward, 16 November 1918, 9th Duke 1.

70 Duke's diary, 11 December 1918.

71 Duke's diary, 6 December 1917.

72 DMC Victor to his mother, 8 October 1918, 9th Duke 1.

73 *Daily Gleaner* (Fredericton), 1 October 1918, published an article in anticipation of his visit.

74 Duke's diary, 3 December 1918.

75 Duke's diary, 12 December 1918.

76 Cameron, *Trotsky in Amherst*.

77 Duke's diary, 13 December 1918.

78 Cameron, *Trotsky in Amherst*.

79 DMC Evie to Victor, 12 December 1918, Q5 8683.

80 Duke's diary, 9 December 1918.

81 Duke's diary, 12 December 1918.

82 Francis, *Seeing Red*, 53–60.

83 Ibid., 61.

84 DMC Miss Walton to Evie, 20 January 1919, N8 6044.

85 Duke's diary, 28 December 1918.

86 DMC Henderson to Evie, 6 January 1919, N8 6038.

87 DMC Henderson to Evie, 15 January 1919, N8 6042. Prohibition in Ontario was not rescinded until 1927 but the duke was only voluntarily following the Prohibition rules from January 1918.

88 DMC Richard Nevill, the comptroller, to Evie, 14 January 1919, N8 6041.

89 Duke's diary, 8 February 1918.

90 Duke's diary, 11 January 1919.

91 Duke's diary, 9–10 January 1919. Because of his failing eyesight, in 1913 Pearson sold the *Daily Express* which eventually passed in 1916 to Sir Max Aitken, later Lord Beaverbrook.

92 DMC Miss Walton to Evie, 7 January 1919, N8 6039. "The Mole" was the stone breakwater at Zeebrugge.

93 DMC Victor to Evie, 6 February 1919, N16 6358.

94 Duke's diary, 20 January 1919.

95 DMC Miss Saunders to the duchess, 18 January 1919, N8 6043.

96 DMC Blanche to Evie, 21 January 1919, G5 3242.

97 DMC Victor to his mother, 10 February 1919, 9th Duke 1.

98 *The Globe* (Toronto), 14 February 1919. In 2012, the Government of Canada could not find any information about the gargoyle of the Duke of Devonshire on the Parliament Buildings. Email from Thomas Bigelow, Curatorial Services, House Proceedings, Government of Canada, 12 November 2012.

99 *The Globe* (Toronto), 19 May 1919.

100 Duke's diary, 20 May 1919.

101 Duke's diary, 19–26 May 1919; *The Globe* (Toronto), 19–27 May 1919.

102 *The Globe* (Toronto), 18 February 1919.

103 DMC Victor to his mother 19 February 1919.

104 Parliament was still being held in the Victoria Museum – now the Museum of Nature on Metcalfe Street – pending completion of the Centre Block of the Parliament Buildings, which had burned in February 1916.

105 What is now Sussex Drive was then called Sussex Street according to *The Globe* (Toronto), 19 February 1919.

106 DMC Victor to Evie, 22 February 1919, N16 6362.

107 DMC Victor to his mother, 2 March 1919, 9th Duke 1.

108 Duke's diary, 9 August 1919.

CHAPTER FOURTEEN

1 LAC MG 26 H Vol. 8 1265; Vol. 8 1227; Vol. 9 1645–6.

2 Perley to White, 10 February 1919, LAC MG 26 H Vol. 9 1794.

3 Borden to White, 26 March 1919, LAC MG 26 H Vol. 9 1798.

4 Governor general to colonial secretary, 15 April 1919, LAC RG 7 G22 9 (3).

5 Borden to White, 4 January 1919, LAC MG 25 H Vol. 9 1777.

6 Borden to White, 31 January 1919, LAC MG 26 H Vol. 9 1787.

7 Ibid.

8 House of Commons Debates, Parliament of Canada (Hansard), 14 April 1919, 1441.

9 House of Commons Debates, Parliament of Canada (Hansard), 14 May 1919, 2395.

10 It would take another forty-eight years before the present system of honours, the Order of Canada, came into being. The Order of Canada was announced 17 April 1967, and the first awards were presented 1 July 1967. A distinguishing feature of the award is that nominations are made by members of the community and evaluated by an advisory committee, which forwards recommendations to the governor general. The government is not involved.

11 Duke's diary, 23 May 1919.

12 British government internal memo: Titles: Hansard report and press cuttings: 16–24 June 1919, author unreadable. LAC CO 42 Vol. 1011 263–4.

13 British government internal memo: 23 June 1919, LAC CO 42 Vol. 1011 (page number unclear, probably 260).

14 DMC Evelyn Cecil to Duke of Devonshire, 15 July 1919 and 24 September 1919 re: decorations for The Order of Hospital of St John of Jerusalem in England, 9th Duke 2. Milner to governor general, 28 July 1919, re: Italian honours for Canadians, LAC MG 26 H Vol. 9 1535.

15 Borden to governor general, 22 September 1919, LAC MG 26 H Vol. 8 1283A–1283B.

16 House of Commons Debates, Parliament of Canada (Hansard), 22 May 1919, 2749.

17 House of Commons Debates, Parliament of Canada (Hansard), 23 May 1919; LAC CO 42 Vol. 1011 349. The document was engrossed, meaning it was prepared in a large formal script.

18 Viscount Milner to the king, 2 August 1919, LAC CO 42 Vol. 1011 339–40; LAC CO 42 1015 152, 16 August 1919.

19 Milner to the governor general, 7 August 1919. LAC MG 26 H Vol. 95 50203.

20 LAC CO 42 Vol. 1011 263. 24 June 1919.

21 Author unclear, probably Walter Long, internal memo 9 July 1919, LAC CO 42 Vol. 1011 333.

22 Minutes of the War Cabinet meeting, 13 August 1919, National Archives UK, NA CAB 23/11.

23 LAC CO 42 Vol. 1014, 14 October 1919 (page number obscured).

24 Birkenhead to Milner, 26 November 1919, LAC CO 42 Vol. 1014 308–9.

25 McCreery, *Order of Canada: Its Origins, History, and Developments*, 55.

26 *Globe and Mail* (Toronto), 21 June 1999, A3.

27 *Globe and Mail* (Toronto), 17 March 2000, A16.

28 Conrad Black is listed on the United Kingdom Parliament website as ineligible to participate in the work of the Lords because of leave of absence taken June 2015, http://www.parliament.uk/mps-lords-and-offices/lords/-ineligible-lords/, accessed 24 September 2015.

29 Of Canada's remaining titles: Sir Joseph Flavelle passed his peerage through his son, Sir Ellsworth Flavelle, to his grandson, Sir Joseph David Flavelle,who died without male issue in 1985, extinguishing the title. (Bliss, "Flavelle, Sir Joseph Wesley," *Dictionary of Canadian Biography*.) Sir Campbell Stuart was awarded a KBE (Knight Commander of the Order of the British Empire), a non-hereditary title. The remaining peerages awarded to Canadians include the Beaverbrook barony – on his death in 1964 Sir Max Aitken passed both his titles (baronet and baron) to his son, Sir John William Maxwell Aitken, who disclaimed his peerage for life but retained the baronetcy; his son, Sir Maxwell William Humphrey Aitken, is currently 3rd Baron Aitken and has male issue – and the Shaughnessy peerage (see note 41 in Chapter 4).

CHAPTER FIFTEEN

1 DMC Evie to Victor, 15 December 1918, Q5 8684.

2 Ibid.

3 DMC Evie to Victor, 18 December 1918, 9th Duke 1.

4 DMC Lord Lansdowne to Victor, 16 December 1918, 9th Duke 2.

5 The baby's name was written variously Anne Peace or Ann Peace or Arbell. Her baptism record at St Bartholomew's Anglican Church in

Ottawa shows her name as Anne Peace Arabella. Finally, they settled on using Arbell, short for Arabella.

6 DMC Evie to Victor, 29 December 1918, 9th Duke 1.

7 Ibid.

8 DMC Evie to Victor, 21 February 1919, 9th Duke 1.

9 DMC Evie to Victor, 26 December 1918, 9th Duke 1.

10 DMC Evie to Victor, 22 February 1919, 9th Duke 1.

11 DMC Evie to Victor, 6 March and 1 April 1919, 9th Duke 1; and Victor to Evie, 9 April 1919, N16 6372.

12 DMC Evie to Victor, 12 February, 27 March, and 1 April 1919, 9th Duke 1.

13 DMC Evie to Victor, 26 December 1918, 9th Duke 1.

14 During the war, Devonshire House contained the offices of the Women's Voluntary Aid Detachment (VAD) which provided medical assistance, and the Women's Auxiliary Army Force (WAAF) which provided women for non-combat army work including cooks, waitresses, clerks, and motor drivers. Letter from Katherine Furse, Commander-in-Chief, Women's VADs, to the Duke of Devonshire, 12 February 1917, 9th Duke 2.

15 DMC Evie to Victor, 22 March 1919, 9th Duke 1.

16 DMC Evie to Victor, 18 December 1918, 9th Duke 1; Victor to Evie, 14 January 1919, N5 6844; Victor to Evie, 20 February 1919, N16 6361; Duke's diary, 7 August 1919; Devonshire House, Piccadilly, was built by the 3rd Duke about 1740 and was a centre of social life for subsequent Devonshire families. After the sale in 1919, the house was demolished and the site rebuilt by industrialists.

17 DMC Evie to Victor, 18 December 1918, and 12 March 1919, 9th Duke 1. Chiswick House is now a public park maintained by the Chiswick House and Gardens Trust.

18 DMC Evie to Victor, 6 March 1919, 9th Duke 1.

19 DMC Evie to Victor, 1 April 1919, 9th Duke 1.

20 Ibid.

21 DMC Victor to Evie, 20 January 1919, N5 5846.

22 DMC Victor to Evie, 10 March 1919, N16 6366.

23 DMC Evie to Victor, 12 February 1919, 9th Duke 1.

24 DMC Evie to Victor, 26 December 1918, N5 5839.

25 DMC Evie to Victor, 12 December 1918, Q5 8683.

26 DMC Evie to Victor, 1 April 1919, 9th Duke 1.

27 Thorpe, *Supermac*, 52.

28 DMC Evie to Victor, 12 January 1919, 9th Duke 1.

29 DMC Evie to Victor, 28 January 1919, 9th Duke 1.

30 DMC Evie to Victor 12 January 1919, 9th Duke 1.

31 DMC Evie to Victor 20 January 1919, 9th Duke 1.

32 DMC John D. Cobbold, Ivan's father, to Evie, 15 March 1919, 9th Duke 2.

33 DMC Evie to Victor, 7 April 1919, 9th Duke 1.

34 DMC Evie to Victor ,16 March 1919, 9th Duke 1.

35 DMC Evie to Victor, 27 March 1919, 9th Duke 1.

36 DMC Evie to Victor, 24 April 1919, 9th Duke 1.

37 DMC Evie to Victor, 7 April 1919, 9th Duke 1.

38 DMC Evie to Victor, 22 March 1919, 9th Duke 1.

39 DMC Evie to Lady Edward, 6 April 1919, 9th Duke 1.

40 DMC Evie to Victor, 24 April 1919, 9th Duke 1.

41 DMC Blanche Egerton to Victor, 14 April 1919, 9th Duke 2.

42 DMC Evie to Victor, 22 March 1919, 9th Duke 1.

43 DMC Lord Richard Nevill to Victor, 1 May 1919, 9th Duke 1.

44 DMC Lord Lansdowne to Victor, 1 May 1919, 9th Duke 2.

45 DMC Blanche Egerton to Victor, 30 April 1919, 9th Duke 2.

46 Duke's diary, 30 April 1919.

47 DMC Evie to Victor, 7 April 1919, 9th Duke 1.

48 Evie to Victor, 27 November 1917, 9th Duke 1.

49 DMC Evie to Victor, 12 February 1919, 9th Duke 1.

50 DMC Evie to Victor, 7 December 1918, Q5 8682.

51 DMC Victor to Evie, 26 December 1918, N5 5839.

52 Duke's diary, 18 May 1919.

CHAPTER SIXTEEN

1 DMC Evie to Victor, 28 January 1919, 9th Duke 1.

2 DMC Evie to Victor 3 February 1919, 9th Duke 1.

3 DMC Evie to Victor 13 February 1919, 9th Duke 1.

4 DMC Evie to Victor, 28 January 1919, 9th Duke 1; Victor to Evie, 31 January 1919, N16 6357.

5 DMC Victor to his mother, 19 February 1919, 9th Duke 1.

6 *The Globe* (Toronto), 15 March 1919, 17.

7 Hagedorn, *Savage Peace*, 86–8; Frances, *Seeing Reds*, 138; Bumsted, *The Winnipeg General Strike of 1919*.

8 *Saturday Night*, 22 February 1919, as quoted in Francis, *Seeing Reds*, 139.

9 DMC Victor to Evie, 6 February 1919, N16 6358.

10 Duke's diary, 15 May 1919.

11 *The Globe* (Toronto), 25 May 1918, 4.

12 Bumsted, *The Winnipeg General Strike of 1919*, 13.

13 Meighen was temporarily replacing Charles Doherty, who was attending the Peace Conference with the prime minister.

14 Francis, *Seeing Reds*, 187; Bumsted, *The Winnipeg General Strike*, 34–5.

15 Francis, *Seeing Reds*, 33.

16 Ibid., 186.

17 DMC Victor to his mother, 11 May 1919, 9th Duke 1.

18 Armstrong, *The Crisis of Quebec*, 233.

19 Duke's diary, 30 May 1919.

20 *The Globe* (Toronto), 30 May 1919, 1.

21 Duke's diary, 11 June 1919.

22 From *Western Labour News*, 20 June 1919, quoted in Francis, *Seeing Reds*, 111.

23 Much of the information about the Winnipeg General Strike of 1919 was taken from three books: Francis, *Seeing Red*, Bumsted, *The Winnipeg General Strike*; and Kramer and Mitchell, *When the State Trembled*. These three provide detailed accounts of the Winnipeg Strike, its background, and consequences. Articles in *The Globe* (Toronto), 13 March 1919 to 27 March 1920, about labour unrest and the strike were an invaluable source of daily details.

CHAPTER SEVENTEEN

1 DMC Evie to Lady Edward, 5 June 1919, 9th Duke 1.

2 TBC Evie to her mother, 19 June 1919.

3 Both Evie and Victor called it Empire Day, but the press referred to the ceremony as simply a memorial for the centenary of Queen Victoria's birth.

4 Duke's diary, 26 May 1919.

5 *Ottawa Journal*, 26 May 1919, 3.

6 DMC Evie to Lady Edward, 5 June 1919, 9th Duke 1.

7 DMC Blanche Egerton to Lady Edward, 3 June 1919, 9th Duke 1.

8 DMC Victor to his mother, 10 June 1919, 9th Duke 1.

9 DMC Blanche Egerton to Lady Edward, 3 June 1919, 9th Duke 1.

10 Duke's diary, 13 June 1919.

11 TBC Evie to her mother, 19 June 1919.

12 Senator George Taylor Fulford (1858–1905) made millions selling patent medicine, "Pink Pills for Pale People." He built a large home on the banks of the St Lawrence River at Brockville which, in 1919, was the family home of his son, George T. Fulford II, Jr. The large house, with its gardens, is now a National Historic Site and the Fulford Museum (Bator, "Fulford, George Taylor," *Dictionary of Canadian Biography*).

13 DMC Blanche Egerton to Lady Edward, 19 June 1919, 9th Duke 1.
14 All three of these summer homes – the Lorne, Lansdowne, and Stanley cottages – still exist and are now in private hands. The story of the governors general and their cottages is told in Carmichael, *The Grand Cascapedia River*, 30–57.
15 DMC Sir Lomer Gouin to the Duke of Devonshire, 26 October 1918, Theatre store 1.
16 DMC Lord Lansdowne to Duke of Devonshire, 27 September 1918, and letter from Edward Sheldon, president of the Cascapedia Club, to Lord Lansdowne, 29 August 1918, Theatre store 1.
17 DMC Lord Lansdowne to Duke of Devonshire, 27 September 1918, Theatre store 1.
18 DMC Duke of Devonshire to Edward W. Sheldon, 26 October 1918, Theatre store 1.
19 Duke's diary, 20 June 1919; DMC Letter from Lord Derby to Duke of Devonshire, 20 January 1919, and letter from Edward Sheldon to the Duke of Devonshire, 11 February 1919, Theatre store 1.
20 DMC Victor to Evie, 22 June 1919, N16 6377.
21 DMC Cascapedia fishing records, Theatre store 1.
22 Duke's diary, 21 June 1919.
23 DMC Victor to Evie, 29 June 1919, N16 6378; Duke's diary, 26 June 1919.
24 Duke's diary, 28 June 1919.
25 Duke's diary, 27 June 1919.
26 Ibid.
27 DMC In his carefully typed records Victor records his own fishing figures, Theatre store 1. The number that Harry caught each day is recorded in the duke's diary but not the weights.
28 There was no station at New Lismore, just a train stop, which the CPR named after their property. Ethel Chadwick called it the Devonshires' flag station and the duke called it a wharf. The name is still there, though there is no train now.
29 DMC Evie to Victor, 22 June 1919, 9th Duke 1.
30 Ibid.
31 DMC Blanche Egerton to Lady Edward, 9 June 1919, 9th Duke 1.
32 DMC Evie to Victor, 9 June 1919, 9th Duke 1.
33 DMC Blanche Egerton to Lady Edward, 9 June 1919, 9th Duke 1.
34 DMC Victor to Evie, 24 March 1919, N16 6368.
35 DMC Evie to Victor, 9 June 1919, 9th Duke 1.
36 DMC Evie to Victor, 26 June 1919, 9th Duke 1.
37 DMC Evie to Victor, 28 June 1919, 9th Duke 1.
38 DMC Evie to Lady Edward, 21 July 1919, 9th Duke 1.

39 Duke's diary, 26 August 1917; Duke's diary, 28 July, 11 August, 18 August 1918.

40 DMC Blanche Egerton to Lady Edward, 12 July 1919, 9th Duke 1.

41 His full name was Prince Edward Albert Christian George Andrew Patrick David. The family called him David but he signed his letters to Evie "Edward" or "Edward P." He was born 23 June 1894. He became King Edward VIII in 1936 on the death of his father King George V, and abdicated his throne later in 1936 in order to marry twice-divorced Wallis Simpson. The British government and the colonies, including Canada, did not agree to the king's plan to marry Mrs Simpson, which caused him to abdicate.

42 DMC Lord Stamfordham to the Duke of Devonshire, 9 December 1918, 9th Duke 2.

43 DMC Victor to Evie, 26 December 1918, N5 5839.

44 DMC Evie to Victor, 6 January 1919, 9th Duke 1.

45 DMC Evie to Victor, 12 January 1919, 9th Duke 1.

46 DMC Lord Stamfordham to the Duchess of Devonshire, 13 January 1919, N8 6040.

47 Ibid.

48 Ibid.

49 DMC Evie to Victor, 12 January 1919, 9th Duke 1.

50 Ibid.

51 Ibid.

52 DMC Evie to Victor, 1 March 1919, 9th Duke 1.

53 Ibid.

54 DMC Lord Stamfordham to Duke of Devonshire, 28 March 1919, 9th Duke 2.

55 DMC Lord Stamfordham to Duke of Devonshire, 10 February 1919, 9th Duke 2.

56 DMC Blanche Egerton to Lady Edward, 19 May 1919, 9th Duke 1.

57 Duke's diary, 18 May 1919.

58 Borden to White, 16 May 1919, LAC RG 25 G-1 Vol. 1243, No. 530.

59 White to Borden, 17 May 1919, LAC RG 25 G-1 Vol. 1243, No. 530.

60 Duke's diary, 19 May 1919.

61 Duke's diary, 18 and 20 May 1919.

62 DMC Blanche Egerton to Lady Edward, 3 June 1919, 9th Duke 1.

63 Duke's diary, 2 August 1919. Sir Thomas White had been finance minister as well as acting prime minister while Borden was at the Peace Conference. He resigned from cabinet, though he retained his seat in Parliament.

64 DMC Blanche Egerton to Lady Edward, 3 August 1919, 9th Duke 3.

65 Duke's diary, 3 August 1919.

66 DMC Blanche Egerton to Lady Edward, 12 August 1919, 9th Duke 3.
67 Ibid.
68 Duke's diary, 6 August 1919.
69 DMC Blanche Egerton to Lady Edward, 16 August 1919, 9th Duke 3.
70 *The Globe* (Toronto), 13 August 1919.
71 *The Globe* (Toronto), 21 August 1919.
72 *The Globe* (Toronto), 16 August 1919.
73 *The Ottawa Citizen*, 16 August 1919.
74 Duke's diary, 15 August 1919.
75 DMC Blanche Egerton to Lady Edward, 20 August 1919, 9th Duke 3.
76 *The Globe* (Toronto), 22 August 1919.
77 Ibid.
78 Duke's diary, 22 August 1919.
79 Ibid.
80 Duke's diary, 23 August 1919.
81 DMC Evie to Lady Edward, 4 September 1919, 9th Duke 3.
82 Duke's diary, 27 August 1919.
83 *The Globe* (Toronto), 26 August 1919.
84 *The Globe* (Toronto), 28 August 1919.
85 Mackenzie King's diary, 29 August 1919, describes a conversation about the Prince's sore hand from shaking hands so much. King's diary is available online at http://www.collectionscanada.gc.ca/data bases/king/index-e.html. Among several publications, *The Globe* (Toronto), 5 November 1919, 9, notes his using his left hand to shake hands.
86 Mackenzie King's diary, 28 August 1919.
87 Mackenzie King's diary, 29 August 1919.
88 Ibid.
89 *The Globe* (Toronto), 2 September 1919, 1; Duke's diary, 1 September 1919.
90 DMC Evie to Lady Edward, 4 September 1919, 9th Duke 3.
91 DMC Victor to his mother, 1 September 1919, 9th Duke 3.
92 DMC Evie to Lady Edward, 4 September 1919, 9th Duke 3.
93 Governor general to Colonial Office, September 1919, CO42 1011 579, 580 and CO42 1015 188–9, 194, 198, 200–4.

CHAPTER EIGHTEEN
1 Duke's diary, 9 September 1919.
2 Duke's diary, 10 and 19 September 1919.
3 DMC Blanche Egerton to Lady Edward, from Saskatoon, Saskatchewan, 17 September 1919, 9th Duke 3.

4 Ibid.

5 DMC Victor to his mother, 19 September 1919, from Edmonton, Alberta, 9th Duke 3.

6 DMC Dorothy to Lady Edward, from the SS *Prince Rupert*, 29 September 1919, 9th Duke 3.

7 DMC Blanche Egerton to Lady Edward, 24 September 1919, from Jasper, Alberta, 9th Duke 3.

8 Ibid.

9 DMC Dorothy to Lady Edward, 29 September 1919, 9th Duke 3.

10 Duke's diary, 24 September 1919.

11 DMC Duke to his mother, 30 October 1919, 9th Duke 1. Today Anyox is a ghost town – the mine fell victim to the depression of the 1930s.

12 DMC Evie to Lady Edward, from the SS *Prince Rupert*, 29 September 1919, 9th Duke 3.

13 DMC Dorothy to her grandmother, 29 September, 1919, 9th Duke 3.

14 Ibid.

15 Duke's diary, 7 October 1919.

16 DMC Blanche Egerton to Lady Edward, 9 October 1919, 9th Duke 1.

17 Duke's diary, 9 October 1919.

18 Duke's diary, 17 October 1919.

19 Duke's diary, 19 October 1919.

20 The author drove the bumpy, dusty "Big Bend" highway, which followed the Columbia River, many times in the 1950s. The narrow gravel road had tall trees on each side that cast shadows over the road, making it impossible to see the potholes. The tedious 200-mile journey took four hours, relieved only by a coffee break at the halfway point where the highway, and the river, curved south.

21 DMC Dorothy to Lady Edward, from Regina, 24 October 1919, 9th Duke 1.

22 Ibid.

23 Ibid.

24 DMC Victor to his mother, from Ottawa, 30 October 1919, 9th Duke 1.

25 DMC Blanche Egerton to Lady Edward, 31 October 1919, 9th Duke 1; and Duke's diary 31 October and 1, 2, 3, 4 November 1919.

26 TBC Evie to her mother, 30 October 1919.

27 Duke's diary, 6 November 1919.

28 DMC Dorothy to Lady Edward, 26 October 1919, 9th Duke 1.

29 *The Ottawa Citizen*, 31 August 1919.

30 *The Globe* (Toronto), 12 November 1919. Massey was the first Canadian-born governor general (1952–59). Hart House remains an important feature of the University of Toronto.

31 Duke's diary, 24 and 25 November 1919.

32 "Prince Leaves for Home Isle," *The Globe* (Toronto), 22 November 1919.

33 Macmillan, *Winds of Change*, 116.

34 TBC Evie to her mother, 30 October 1919.

35 TBC Evie to her mother, 11 November 1919.

36 DMC Dorothy to her grandmother, 26 October 1919, 9th Duke 1.

37 DMC Borden to the governor general, 29 November 1919, Theatre store 1.

38 DMC Duke to his mother, 5 December 1919, 9th Duke 1.

39 Duke's diary, 11 December 1919.

40 *The Globe* (Toronto), 1 December 1919.

41 Duke's diary, 29 November 1919.

42 Duke's diary, 3 December 1919.

43 Duke's diary, 5 December 1919.

44 Canada's Naval History, http://www.warmuseum.ca/cwm/exhibitions/navy/galery-e.aspx?section=2-D-1&id=1&page=0; Schleihauf, "'Necessary Stepping Stones': The Transfer of *Aurora*, *Patriot*, and *Patrician*."

45 DMC John B. Bickersteth to the duchess, 30 December 1919, G4 3218; Bickersteth, *The Land of Open Doors*.

46 DMC Evie to Lady Edward, 26 December 1919, 9th Duke 1.

47 Duke's diary, 1 January 1920.

CHAPTER NINETEEN

1 DMC Evie to Victor, 24 January and 28 January 1919, 9th Duke 1.

2 DMC Evie to Victor, 22 February 1919, 9th Duke 1; TBC Evie to her mother, 31 July 1919.

3 DMC Evie to Victor, 22 March, 1 April, and 7 April 1919, 9th Duke 1. All mention her unease with the relationship between Dorothy and Harold.

4 DMC Evie to Victor, 7 April 1919, 9th Duke 1.

5 DMC Evie to Victor, 22 March 1919, 9th Duke 1.

6 DMC Evie to Lady Edward, 4 September 1919, 9th Duke 3.

7 DMC Victor to Lady Edward, 16 April 1919, 9th Duke 1.

8 Harold's injury on the Somme from Macmillan, *Winds of Change*, 88, and Williams, *Harold Macmillan*, 44–5. Information about Harold's early life from Williams, *Harold Macmillan*, 5–58, and Thorpe, *Supermac*, 9–65.

9 DMC Evie to Lady Edward 25 May 1919, 9th Duke 1.

10 DMC Evie to Victor, 9 June 1919, 9th Duke 1.

11 DMC Evie to Lady Edward, 17 July 1919, 9th Duke 1.

12 Duke's diary, 26 July 1919.

13 DMC Evie to Lady Edward, 4 September 1919, 9th Duke 3.

14 Duke's diary, 22 September 1919.

15 Ibid.

16 Duke's diary, 23 September 1919.

17 DMC Evie to Victor, undated letter, Q2 8488.

18 DMC Dorothy to her grandmother, 29 September 1919, 9th Duke 3.

19 Macmillan, *Winds of Change*, 116.

20 DMC Evie to Lady Edward, on board the SS *Prince Rupert*, 29 September 1919, 9th Duke 3.

21 TBC Evie to her mother, 7 October 1919.

22 DMC Harold Macmillan to the Duchess of Devonshire, undated, G4 3207. All the quotations in this paragraph are from his letter. The duke noted in his diary, 7 December 1919, that Harold proposed "in a sort of way," so the discussion between Harold and the duchess must have occurred shortly before that.

23 Duke's diary, 11 March 1916.

24 Duke's diary, 15 May 1918.

25 Duke's diary, 23 June 1918.

26 Duke's diary, 28 July 1918.

27 Duke's diary, 8 December 1918.

28 DMC Evie to Victor, 4 January 1919, 9th Duke 1.

29 DMC Evie to Victor, 1 April 1919, 9th Duke 1.

30 Bulkeley-Johnson to his mother, 31 January 1917, LAC MG 30-E56.

31 DMC Evie to Victor, 1 April 1919, 9th Duke 1.

32 DMC Evie to Lady Edward, 21 July 1919, 9th Duke 1.

33 Horne, *Macmillan*, 12.

34 Ibid., 57.

35 Olson, *Troublesome Young Men*, 40.

36 Williams, *Harold Macmillan*, 71.

37 DMC Blanche Egerton to Lady Edward, 9 October 1919, 9th Duke 1.

38 Davenport-Hines, *The Macmillans*, 171.

39 Davenport-Hines, "Cavendish, Victor Christian William," *Oxford Dictionary of National Biography*, 16.

40 DMC Blanche Egerton to Lady Edward, 9 October 1919, 9th Duke 1.

41 Bulkeley-Johnson to his mother, 18 March 1918, LAC MG 30-E56.

42 Both Williams, *Harold Macmillan*, and Thorpe, *Supermac*, make this point.

43 TBC Evie to her mother, 7 October 1919.

44 Duke's diary, 7 December 1919.

45 DMC Evie to Lady Edward, 26 December 1919, 9th Duke 1.

46 Duke's diary, 26 December 1919.

47 TBC Evie to her mother, 29 December 1919.
48 DMC Victor to his mother, 29 December 1919, 9th Duke 1.
49 DMC Evie to Lady Edward, 26 December 1919, 9th Duke 1.
50 TBC Evie to her mother, 29 December 1919.
51 Duke's diary, 2 January 1920; £3,000 in 1920 is equivalent to about £120,000 in 2015 (nearly $200,000 Canadian).
52 DMC Evie to Lady Edward, 2 January 1920, 9th Duke 1.
53 TBC Evie to her mother, 3 January 1920.
54 *The Ottawa Citizen*, 7 January 1920; *Ottawa Journal*, 7 January 1920.
55 Duke's diary, 4 January 1920.
56 *The Ottawa Citizen,* 10 January 1920.
57 DMC Blanche Egerton to Lady Edward, 16 January 1920, 9th Duke 1.
58 DMC Harold Macmillan to the duchess, 28 January 1920, A28 1032.
59 See Olson, *Troublesome Young Men*, and Davenport-Hines, *The Macmillans* for information about the later lives of Harold and Dorothy, including Dorothy's affair with Harold's colleague, Robert Boothby.
60 DMC Evie to Lady Edward, 29 January 1920, 9th Duke 1.
61 Duke's diary, 30 January 1920.
62 DMC Dorothy to her mother, 30 January 1920, A28 1033.
63 The wedding is described in detail in Williams, *Harold Macmillan*.
64 Duke's diary, 21 April 1920.
65 DMC Lord Lansdowne to Evie, 11 April 1920, F6 2527.
66 Duke's diary, 23 April 1920.
67 For a description of Bolton Abbey see Mitford, *Wait for Me!* 190.
68 DMC Victor to his mother, 1 May 1920, 9th Duke 1.
69 TBC Evie to her mother, 1 May 1920.

CHAPTER TWENTY

1 Borden, *Robert Laird Borden: His Memoirs*, 879.
2 Ibid., 885.
3 Ibid., 895.
4 Ibid.
5 Many nations had delegates at the Paris Peace Conference (1919), including Belgium, Greece, Japan, and China. Canada had two seats, variously occupied by Sir Robert Borden, Sir George Foster, the Honourable A.L. Sifton, and the Honourable C.J. Doherty. Canada's signature, indented under the British Empire along with Australia, New Zealand, South Africa, gave it a seat at the new international organization, the League of Nations.
6 Borden, *Robert Laird Borden: His Memoirs*, 895.

7 Ibid., 895; and *The Globe* (Toronto), 16 January 1919.

8 DMC Victor to Evie, 14 February 1919, N16 6360.

9 Borden, *Robert Laird Borden: His Memoirs*, 911–12.

10 Duke's diary, 23 January 1919.

11 Macmillan, *Paris 191*, 74–7.

12 Macmillan provides a concise description of the arguments and result in *Paris 1919*, 347–65.

13 Duke's diary, 26 May 1919.

14 DMC Victor to his mother, 31 July 1919, 9th Duke 3.

15 Duke's diary, 12 December 1919.

16 Ibid.

17 Borden, *Robert Laird Borden: His Memoirs*, 1016.

18 *The Globe* (Toronto), 15 December 1919.

19 Borden, *Robert Laird Borden: His Memoirs*, 1017.

20 Duke's diary, 16 December 1919.

21 Duke's diary, 20 December 1919.

22 DMC Victor to his mother, 18 December 1919, 9th Duke 1.

23 Quoted from Borden's diary in Brown, *Robert Laird Borden*, 178–9.

24 DMC Victor to his mother, 26 December 1919, 9th Duke 1.

25 Governor general to Lord Milner, 15 December 1919, LAC CO 42 Vol. 1012 476.

26 *The Globe* (Toronto), 9 January 1920, 1; 10 January 1920, 5.

27 Borden, *Robert Laird Borden: His Memoirs*, 1020.

28 *The Globe* (Toronto), 13 January 1920.

29 Borden, *Robert Laird Borden: His Memoirs*, 1022–3.

30 DMC Borden to the governor general, 31 January 1920, Theatre store 1.

31 Brown, *Robert Laird Borden*, 180.

32 *The Globe* (Toronto), 16 February 1920, 3.

33 DMC Victor to his mother, 17 February 1920, 9th Duke 1.

34 *The Globe* (Toronto), 27 February 1920, 1.

35 Ibid.

36 Ibid., 4.

37 Duke's diary, 26 February 1920.

38 *The Globe* (Toronto), 27 February 1920, 6.

39 Duke's diary, 13 May 1920.

40 Duke's diary, 21 June 1920.

41 Duke's diary, 1 July 1920.

42 Brown, *Robert Laird Borden*, 181–2.

43 Duke's diary, 2 July 1920.

44 Brown, *Robert Laird Borden*, 182.

45 Duke's diary, 5 July 1920.

46 Ibid.; DMC Draft letter from the governor general, probably to the colonial secretary, about 10 July 1920, Theatre store 1.

47 DMC Governor general to Sir Thomas White (copy), 5 July 1920, Theatre store 1.

48 Duke's diary, 6 July 1920.

49 Duke's diary, 7 July 1920. White had been finance minister since 1911 and had served as acting prime minister during Borden's absence at the Peace Conference. He had resigned as finance minister in August 1919 for health reasons, though he remained a member of Parliament until 1921.

50 Duke's diary, 7 July 1920.

51 Ibid.

52 Duke's diary, 19 July 1920.

53 TBC Evie to her mother, 20 August 1920.

54 Duke's diary, 11 March 1920.

55 TBC Evie to her mother, 8 May 1920.

56 DMC Lord Lansdowne to Evie, 16 April 1921, F6 2530.

57 DMC Victor to his mother, 18 March 1919, 9th Duke 1.

58 DMC Victor to Evie, 6 February 1919, N16 6358.

59 DMC Evie to Lady Edward, 25 May 1919, 9th Duke 1.

60 DMC Evie to Victor, 16 February 1920, Q2 8487.

61 TBC Evie to her mother, 30 January 1921.

62 *The Globe* (Toronto), 2 January 1920.

63 Duke's diary, 2 January 1920.

64 TBC Evie to her mother, 2 November 1920.

65 TBC Evie to her mother, 30 January 1921.

66 Duke's diary, 20 July 1920.

67 TBC Evie to her mother, 28 July 1920.

68 Ibid.

69 Duke's diary, 26 and 28 March 1920.

70 TBC Evie to her mother, 20 August 1920.

71 Duke's diary, 31 August 1920.

72 Ethel Chadwick's diary, 25 August 1920, LAC MG 30 D258.

73 Duke's diary, 22 August 1920.

74 Duke's diary, 20 September 1920.

75 DMC Evie to Victor, 15 September 1920, Q2 8493.

76 Ibid.

77 DMC Evie to Victor, 17 September 1920, Q2 8494.

78 TBC Evie to her mother, 25 September 1920.

79 Because Victor's mother had died, the details of their life in these last months come from the duke's diary, some letters from Evie to her mother, and the press. Both Victor and Evie had written to Lady Edward

almost weekly and she obviously saved every letter, and some from her grandchildren too. The letters have made their way to the Chatsworth archives and have given us an intimate view into their life at Rideau Hall and elsewhere in Canada. When they were apart, they tended to write to each other every few days, and these letters are also at Chatsworth. However, Evie and Victor spent much of these last few months in Canada with each other, so there are few letters between them.

80 Duke's diary, 30 May 1921.
81 Duke's diary, 8 January 1921.
82 Duke's diary, 26 February 1921.
83 Duke's diary, 31 May 1920.
84 Duke's diary, 28 November 1919 and 22 March 1921; DMC Evie to Victor, 17 December 1920, Q2 8495.
85 Duke's diary, 14 May 1921 and 18 November 1919.
86 Duke's diary 23 February 1921.
87 *The Globe* (Toronto), 12 November 1920, 9.
88 Ibid., 18.
89 Duke's diary, 12 November 1920.
90 Duke's diary, 17 January 1921.
91 Duke's diary, 18–23 November 1920; and DMC Victor to Evie, 19 November 1920, N16 6385.
92 *The Ottawa Citizen*, 14 February 1921.
93 Duke's diary, 14 February 1921; *Ottawa Journal*, 15 February 1921; *The Ottawa Citizen*, 14 February 1921; *Toronto Daily Star*, 14 February 1921.
94 Duke's diary, 19 February 1921. The "drawing room" was held on Saturday, 19 February 1921.
95 Ethel Chadwick's diary, 19 February 1921, LAC MG 30 D258.
96 Hamilton-Temple-Blackwood, *My Canadian Journal 1872–1878*.
97 *Ottawa Journal*, 19 February 1921.
98 Duke's diary, 19 February 1921.
99 *Ottawa Journal*, 19 February and 21 February 1921; *The Ottawa Citizen*, 19 and 21 February 1921.
100 Duke's diary, 29 January 1921 and 28 May 1921.
101 The Prince of Wales, later King Edward VIII, had by then purchased a ranch in the foothills of the Rocky Mountains south of Calgary. He owned the EP Ranch until 1962, when it was sold. He visited several times both before and after his marriage.
102 Duke's diary, 13 April 1921.
103 DMC Baillie, *Early Memories*, 76.
104 DMC The duchess to Mr Burke, 22 April 1921, 9th Duke 1.
105 Duke's diary, 11–13 June 1921.

106 DMC Evie to Victor, 7 June 1921, Theatre store 2.

107 Diary of Mackenzie King, 12 August 1921, describes the arrival of Lord and Lady Byng: "The note of youth and vigour and absence of aide was noticeable in Lord Byng and of naturalness and pleasantness in Lady Byng. A refreshing contrast to the heaviness of the Duke of Devonshire and the formal exclusiveness of the Duchess."

108 Duke's diary, 3 June 1921.

109 House of Commons Debates, Parliament of Canada (Hansard), 3 June 1921, 4433–5.

110 Duke's diary, 4 June 1921.

111 Duke's diary, 18 June 1921.

112 *The Globe* (Toronto), 20 June 1921, 3.

113 Duke's diary, 18 June 1921.

114 Duke's diary, 20 June 1921.

115 Duke's diary, 20 April 1917; 15 June 1917; 17 September 1919.

116 DMC Victor to Evie, 21 June 1921, 9th Duke 3.

117 Duke's diary, 19 July 1921; *La Presse* (Montreal), 20 July 1921; *The Ottawa Citizen*, 20 July 1921, 21.

118 *La Presse* (Montreal), 20 July 1921.

AFTERWORD

1 DMC Travelling Records of His Excellency the Duke of Devonshire, K.G., etc. Governor General of Canada 1916 to 1921.

2 All current equivalent values were calculated by using the Bank of Canada's and the Bank of England's inflation calculators and conversions.

3 DMC His Excellency the Governor General's Household Accounts, 1917–21.

4 Edmond, *Rockcliffe Park: A History of the Village.*

5 Ethel Chadwick's diary, 6 September 1921, LAC MG 30 D258.

6 DMC His Excellency the Governor General's Household Accounts, 1917–21.

7 Land title documents: Canton de Bouchette, 23 Rang 7; DMC Evie to Victor, 1 September 1918, Q5 8663.

8 Personal communication from Bob Cameron, whose grandfather built a cottage on the lake.

9 Barclay, *Golf in Canada*, 456.

10 The Devonshire Trophy is still awarded annually as a Show Year prize for the highest aggregate in Design–Open by the Ottawa Horticultural Society. Email from Jayne Huntley of the Ottawa Horticultural Society; http://www.ottawahort.org/book/pain/166_Trophies_and_awards.doc.

11 One building of the Restigouche Salmon Club's Matapedia property burned down in the 1970s, and several of the original buildings have been rebuilt. Conversation with manager of the Restigouche Salmon Club, 21 September 2011.

12 Vanderweide, "Crushing the Barrier with Restigouche Salmon," and interview with Peter Dubé, 20 September 2011.

13 Conversation with Peter Dubé, 20 September 2011. See also Dubé, *Stolen Treasure*.

14 Reiss, Reiss, and Reiss, "Catch and Release Fishing Effectiveness and Mortality," *Acute Angling*.

15 Davenport-Hines, "Cavendish, Victor Christian William," Oxford Dictionary of National Biography.

16 McMahon, *British Spies and Irish Rebels*, 92.

17 Wood, *So Far and No Further!* 9; Palley, *The Constitutional History and Law of Southern Rhodesia 1888–1965*, covers the details of the constitutional change in 1923.

18 Macmillan, *Winds of Change,* 193.

19 The Governor General of Canada website, https://www.gg.ca/docu ment.aspx?id=15415&lan=eng.

20 The life of Bess of Hardwick is well told in Lovell, *Bess of Hardwick: the First Lady of Chatsworth*.

21 Personal conversation with the 12th Duke of Devonshire.

22 Brown, *Robert Laird Borden*, 189–90.

Bibliography

PRIMARY SOURCES

Archival Sources
Anglican Church of Canada: Diocese of Ottawa Archives
Search for the baptismal record for Anne Peace Arabella Mackintosh in
St Bartholomew's Church.

Brant County Museum, Brantford, Ontario
Photographs of the Duke of Devonshire with Sir Alexander Graham Bell,
1917.

Canadian Pacific Archives
Passenger Service timetables for Maniwaki subdivision: 1916, 1918, 1920,
showing Blue Sea (1916); Blue Sea and New Elsmere (1918);
Blue Sea and New Lismore (1920).

Devonshire Manuscripts, Chatsworth, UK (DMC)
Letters and documents 1916–21, including:
Diary of the Duke of Devonshire, 31 December 1912 to 31 December
1915.
Documents given to the Duke of Devonshire by the Duke of Connaught,
October, 1916.
Letters concerning the visit of the Prince of Wales 1919.
Letters of the children of the Duke and Duchess of Devonshire.
Letters of the Duchess of Devonshire to the duke's mother, to her own
mother, to the duke, and to her friends and other relatives.
Letters of the Duke of Devonshire to the duchess.
Letters from friends of the Duke of Devonshire.
Letters from the Prime Minister of Canada.

Letters Patent of the Duke of Devonshire concerning his role as Canadian governor general.

Official letters from the Colonial Office to the Duke of Devonshire.

Library and Archives Canada

The Canada Gazette, Extra 11 November 1916. https://www.collections canada.gc.ca/databases/canada-gazette/093/001060-119.01-e.php?document_id_nbr=6249&f=g&PHPSESSID=mpdsfg9v4mhgkhsjcinmfm5mn7.

Colonial Office fonds for Canada, MG 11-CO42 Vols 999, 1000, 1001, 1002, 1005, 1007, 1009, 1010, 1011, 1012, 1014, 1015, 1017, 1020.

Documents on External Relations (DCER) Vol. 1 1909–18; Ministry of External Affairs, 1967.

MG 26 H Sir Robert Borden fonds, diary.

MG 26 H Volumes 8, 9, 49, 79, 81, 89, 95, 165, 327.

MG 26 H13 *The Diaries of William Lyon Mackenzie King* online. Library and Archives Canada. http://www.collectionscanada.gc.ca/databases/king/index-e.html.

MG 27 II House of Commons Debates: Parliament of Canada: (Hansard) debates concerning British honours for persons customarily resident in Canada.

MG 27 IID7 Sir George E. Foster Collection: Diary of Sir George Foster.

MG 27 IIE6 Vol 1. Austin Ernest Blount fonds

MG 28 I 315 Echo Beach Fishing Club fonds.

MG 30 D 528 Ethel Chadwick fonds.

MG 30 E56 (R5076-0-1-E) Vivian Bulkeley-Johnson fonds.

R13344-31-0-E Sir Hugh Graham – "Did He Deserve a Peerage" – article by Henry Dalby.

R13344-67-X-E News clippings (re. plot to kill Lord Atholstan)

R13344-70-X-E Vol. 2 Lord Atholstan – biographical material and memorial tribute.

R4694-0-8-E (MG27 IIB4) Fonds: Duke of Devonshire: including Diary of the Duke of Devonshire, 1 January 1916 to 15 August 1921.

R7648-0-6-F (MG27-IIIB4) Volume 73 Fonds: Lomer Gouin.

RG 7 G22 Correspondence with the Colonial Office, 1784–1923, Vols 8, 9, 10, 14–16.

RG 9-III-D-3 Volume: 4939 War Diaries of the 44th Canadian Infantry Battalion, October 1916.

RG 18-A-1 (Duke of Devonshire) Style and titles of Duke of Devonshire.

RG 25-A-2 Vol. 153, 154, 155, 156, 281 Canada House Records.

RG 25-A-3-a Appointment of His Grace the Duke of Devonshire as Governor General of Canada.

RG 25 G-1 Vols 155, 156, 1166, 1191, 1203, 1207, 1216, 1217, 1221, 1222, 1224, 1242, 1243, 1244, 1246.

The National Archives (United Kingdom)
ADM 53/36665 HMS *Calgarian* ship's log.
CO 42 (a few of the copies of these files held in Library and Archives Canada were unreadable and consulted in the UK National Archives).

Newspapers 1916–21
The *Daily Mail* (London)
The Globe (Toronto)
The *Halifax Morning Chronicle*
The Montreal *Gazette*
The New York Times
The Ottawa Citizen
The Ottawa Evening Journal
La Presse (Montreal)
The Times (London)
Toronto Daily Star

And newspaper clippings from Chatsworth files:
The *Derbyshire Times*
The Montreal *Daily Mail*
The *Montreal Standard*

Public Archives of Nova Scotia at Halifax
Official Programme of the Reception and Installation of the Right Honourable Duke of Devonshire.

Registre foncier Gouvernement du Québec Canton de Bouchette
Duke of Devonshire's Purchase of the Blue Sea Lake property, 18 November 1918.
Sale of the property, 6 July 1923.

The Trustees of the Bowood Collection, home of the Marquess of Lansdowne (TBC)
Letters from the Duchess of Devonshire to her mother, 1916–21.
Photograph: Wedding of Lady Evelyn Fitzmaurice and Victor Cavendish (later 9th Duke of Devonshire), 9 July 1892.

University of New Brunswick Archives
John Douglas Hazen fonds, MG H13 Box 25.

Angus Alexander Mackintosh's grave in Arlington Cemetery, Washington, DC.

Anyox, British Columbia: "Anyox." Wikipedia. https://en.wikipedia.org/wiki/Anyox.

"Daily Currency Converter." Bank of Canada. http://www.bankofcanada.ca/rates/exchange/daily-converter/.

Deployment numbers of U.S. Army soldiers in Europe: "The U.S. Army in World War 1, 1917–1918." U.S. Army Center of Military History. http://www.history.army.mil/books/AMH-V2/AMH%20V2/chapter1.htm.

"Field Marshal His Royal Highness the Prince Arthur, Duke of Connaught and Strathearn, about the changes made to Rideau Hall during his time as Governor General of Canada." Governor General of Canada. Accessed 17 April 2017, http://archive.gg.ca/gg/fgg/bios/01/connaught_e.asp.

Flowers found in Pont-des-Monts, Quebec: "Kalmia." Wikipedia. https://en.wikipedia.org/wiki/Kalmia.

"The Great Seal of Canada." The Governor General of Canada. http://www.gg.ca/document.aspx?id=317.

"Inflation calculator." Bank of England. http://www.bankofengland.co.uk/education/Pages/resources/inflationtools/calculator/index1.aspx.

"Influenza (Seasonal)." World Health Organization. http://www.who.int/mediacentre/factsheets/fs211/en/.

The lieutenant-governors' residences in:

Victoria: "The History of Government House." Lieutenant Governor of British Columbia. http://www.ltgov.bc.ca/gov-house/history/history.html.

Edmonton: "Government House." Alberta Government. https://www.alberta.ca/government-house.aspx/default.aspx.

Regina: "About Government House." Government of Saskatchewan. http://www.governmenthouse.gov.sk.ca/about/.

Winnipeg: "Government House." Lieutenant Governor of Manitoba. http://manitobalg.ca/history/government-house/.

Quebec City: "Spencerwood, Quebec City, QC." McCord Museum. http://collections.musee-mccord.qc.ca/en/collection/artifacts/VIEW-4333?Lang=1&accessnumber=VIEW-4333, and https://en.wikipedia.org/wiki/Government_House_(Quebec).

North-West Mounted Police: "North-West Mounted Police." In *The Canadian Encyclopedia*. Historica Canada. http://www.thecanadianencyclopedia.ca/en/article/north-west-mounted-police/.

Official websites of the Imperial Order Daughters of the Empire, http://www.iode.ca/, and May Court club of Ottawa, http://www.maycourt.org/

Stanford White, architect of Indian House on the Restigouche River: "About Camp Harmony." Camp Harmony. http://www.campharmony. ca/about.html.

Wheat yields 2011 to compare with 1918. Saskatchewan Ministry of Resources Fact Sheet. Government of Saskatchewan. Accessed 16 May 2012, http://www.agriculture.gov.sk.ca/Default.aspx?DN=b6db783f-c302-419a-bc84-a772363ed736,; and for 2015, http://publications.gov. sk.ca/documents/20/83874-50681_GSK_AG%20StatBro_Eng-2016% 20Acres_a5_HR%20-%20web.pdf.

Personal Interviews

Bob Cameron, Ottawa

The Dowager Duchess of Devonshire, Edensor, England

Peter Dubé, Matapedia, Quebec

The 12th Duke of Devonshire, Chatsworth, England

Mary Robertson, Coordinator of the Cascapedia River Museum, Cascapedia-St-Jules, Quebec

SECONDARY SOURCES

Alberti, Louis-Gerard. "Russell Theatre." In *The Canadian Encyclopedia.* Historica Canada. http://www.thecanadianencyclopedia.ca/en/article/ russell-theatre-emc/.

Armstrong, Elizabeth. *The Crisis of Quebec, 1914–1918.* Toronto: McClelland and Stewart, 1974.

Auger, Martin F. "On the Brink of Civil War: The Canadian Government and the Suppression of the 1918 Quebec Easter Riots," *Canadian Historical Review* 89, no. 4 (2008). doi:10.3138/chr.89.4.503.

Bacic, Jadranka. *The Plague of the Spanish Flu: The Influenza Epidemic of 1918 in Ottawa.* Ottawa: The Historical Society of Ottawa, 1999.

Bagehot, Walter. *The English Constitution,* 2nd edition, 1873. http://www. efm.bris.ac.uk/het/bagehot/constitution.pdf.

Baillie, Maud. *Early Memories.* Copyright Judith Cameron, 1989. (This book was written by Lady Maud Cavendish after her second marriage and privately published; a copy is kept at Chatsworth.)

Ballantyne, Bruce. "Maniwaki Requiem." *Canadian Rail,* no. 394. Saint-Constant, Quebec: Canadian Railroad Historical Association, September–October 1986.

Barber, Marilyn. "Ontario Schools Question." In *The Canadian Encyclopedia.* Edmonton: Hurtig Publishers, 1985.

Barclay, James. *Golf in Canada: A History.* Toronto: McClelland and Stewart, 1992.

Barry, John M. *The Great Influenza: The Epic Story of the Deadliest Plague in History*. New York: Viking, 2004.

Bartlett, J.R. "Tiger," *Dictionary of Americanisms, 1860*. Accessed 17 April 2017, https://books.google.ca/books?id=bntXAAAAYAAJ& printsec=frontcover&dq=j.r+bartlett+dictionary+of+americanisms&hl =en&sa=X&ved=0ahUKEwjjw-rh-I3TAhUa8YMKHbiyAR0Q6AEIIDAB #v=onepage&q=j.r%20bartlett%20dictionary%20of%20americanisms &f=false.

Bator, Paul Adolphus. "Fulford, George Taylor." In *Dictionary of Canadian Biography*, Vol. 13, University of Toronto/Université Laval, 2003–. Accessed 17 April 2017, http://www.biographi.ca/en/bio/fulford_george_ taylor_13E.html.

Beloff, Max. *Imperial Sunset, Volume 1: Britain's Liberal Empire 1897– 1921*. New York: Alfred A. Knopf, 1970.

Benoit, Jean. "Price, Sir William." In *Dictionary of Canadian Biography*, Vol. 15, University of Toronto/Université Laval, 2003. Accessed 17 April 2017, http://www.biographi.ca/en/bio/price_william_15E.html.

Bickersteth, John Burgon. *The Land of Open Doors: Being Letters from Western Canada 1911–1913*. Toronto: The Musson Book Company, 1914. Republished by University of Toronto Press, Scholarly Publishing Division, 1976, and as an ebook, 2016.

Bliss, Michael. "Flavelle, Sir Joseph Wesley." In *Dictionary of Canadian Biography*, Vol. 16, University of Toronto/Université Laval, 2003–. Accessed 17 April 2017, http://www.biographi.ca/en/bio/flavelle_ joseph_wesley_16E.html.

Borden, Henry (Ed.). *Robert Laird Borden: His Memoirs, Volumes 1 & 2*. Toronto: Macmillan, 1938.

Bourassa, Henri. "Conscription." Pamphlet published by *Le Devoir* 1917, Library and Archives Canada, Amicus no. 2699909.

Brown, Robert Craig. *Canada's National Policy 1883–1900: A Study in Canadian-American Relations*. Princeton, New Jersey: Princeton University Press, 1964.

– "Gordon, Sir Charles Blair." In *Dictionary of Canadian Biography*, Vol. 16, University of Toronto/Université Laval, 2003–. Accessed 17 April 2017, http://www.biographi.ca/en/bio/gordon_charles_blair_16E.html.

– *Robert Laird Borden: A Biography, Vol. II, 1914–1937*. Toronto: Macmillan, 1980.

Brown, Robert Craig, and Ramsay Cook. *Canada 1896–1921: A Nation Transformed*. Toronto: McClelland and Stewart, 1976.

Bumsted, J.M. *The Winnipeg General Strike of 1919: An Illustrated History*. Winnipeg: Watson & Dwyer, 1994.

Burton, David H. *Cecil Spring Rice: A Diplomat's Life*. London: Associated University Presses, 1990.

Cameron, Silver Donald. *Trotsky in Amherst*. Accessed 16 January 2017, http://www.silverdonaldcameron.ca/trotsky-amherst.

Cannadine, David. *The Decline and Fall of the British Aristocracy*. New Haven: Yale University Press, 1990.

– "The Landowner as Millionaire: The Finances of the Dukes of Devonshire c. 1800 – c. 1926." In *Aspects of Aristocracy: Grandeur and Decline in Modern Britain*. New Haven: Yale University Press, 1994.

Carmichael, Hoagy B. *The Grand Cascapedia River: A History, Vol. 1*. Far Hills, New Jersey: Anesha Publishing, 2006.

Charter, Bylaws, Officers and Members of the Ristigouche Salmon Club. 1966. Club House, Matapedia, Quebec.

Clarkson, Adrienne. "Visit to Tadoussac, September 14, 2000." Accessed 17 April 2017, http://archive.gg.ca/media/doc.asp?lang=e&DocID=1179.

Comeau, Napoleon Alexandre. *Life and Sport on the North Shore of the Lower St. Lawrence and Gulf*. Quebec: Daily Telegraph Printing House, 1909. Complete copy now available at http://ia600402.us.archive.org/18/items/lifesportonnorthoocomerich/lifesportonnorthoocomerich.pdf.

Cook, Tim. *At the Sharp End: Canadians Fighting the Great War, 1914–1916*. Vol. 1. Toronto: Penguin, 2007.

– *Shock Troops: Canadians Fighting the Great War, 1917–1918*. Vol. 2. Toronto: Penguin, 2008.

– *Warlords: Borden, Mackenzie King, and Canada's World Wars*. Toronto: Allen Lane, 2012.

Copp, T. "The Military Effort, 1914–1918." In *Canada in the First World War: Essays in Honour of Robert Craig Brown*, edited by David Mackenzie. Toronto: University of Toronto Press, 2005.

Crosby, Alfred W. *America's Forgotten Pandemic: The Influenza of 1918*. Cambridge: Cambridge University Press, 1989.

Crunican, Paul E. "The Manitoba Schools Question." In *The Canadian Encyclopedia*. Edmonton: Hurtig Publishers, 1985, 1084.

Cunningham, Kevin. *Diseases in History: Flu*. Greensboro, North Carolina: Morgan Reynolds, 2009.

Davenport-Hines, Richard. "Cavendish, Victor Christian William, 9th Duke of Devonshire, (1868–1938) politician and governor-general of Canada." In *Oxford Dictionary of National Biography*. Oxford: Oxford University Press, 2004–16.

– *The Macmillans*. London: Heinemann, 1992.

De-la-Noy, Michael. *The Honours System: Who Gets What and Why*. London: Virgin Books, 1992.

Downie, Jill. *Storming the Castle: The World of Dora and the Duchess.* Toronto: Key Porter Books, 1998.

Dubé, Peter. *Stolen Treasure.* Bloomington, Indiana: Authorhouse, 2009. Also available at www.tresorvole.info/StolenTreasure.pdf.

Edmond, Martha. *Rockcliffe Park: A History of the Village.* Ottawa: The Friends of the Village of Rockcliffe Park Foundation, 2005.

English, John. *The Decline of Politics: The Conservatives and the Party System, 1901–1920.* Toronto: University of Toronto Press, 1977.

English, John, and Daniel Panneton. "The Wartime Elections Act." In *The Canadian Encyclopedia.* Edmonton: Hurtig Publishers, 1985. Also http://www.thecanadianencyclopedia.ca/en/article/wartime-elections-act/.

Evans, Hilary, and Mary Evans. *The Party That Lasted 100 Days: The Late Victorian Season.* Colchester, UK: TBS The Book Service, 1976.

Farr, D.M.L. "Sir Joseph Pope." In *The Canadian Encyclopedia.* Historica Canada. Accessed 17 April 2017, http://www.thecanadianencyclopedia.ca/en/article/sir-joseph-pope/.

Ferns, Thomas H. "Hendrie, Sir John Strathearn." In *Dictionary of Canadian Biography*, Vol. 15, University of Toronto/Université Laval, 2003–. Accessed 17 April 2017, http://www.biographi.ca/en/bio/hendrie_john_strathearn_15E.html.

Fisher, Nigel. *Harold Macmillan: A Biography.* London: Weidenfeld and Nicolson, 1982.

Foot, Richard. "Election of 1917." In *The Canadian Encyclopedia.* Historica Canada. Accessed 17 April 2017, http://www.thecanadianencyclopedia.ca/en/article/election-of-1917/.

Ford, Arthur R. "Some Notes on the Formation of the Union Government in 1917." *Canadian Historical Review* 19 (4) December 1938.

Francis, Daniel. *Seeing Reds: The Red Scare of 1918–1919, Canada's First War on Terror.* Vancouver: Arsenal Pulp Press, 2010.

Frankland, Noble. *Witness of a Century: The Life and Times of Prince Arthur Duke of Connaught 1850–1942.* London: Shepheard-Walwyn, 1993.

Frenette, Pierre. "Comeau, Napoléon-Alexandre (baptized Alexandre-Napoléon)." In *Dictionary of Canadian Biography*, Vol. 15, University of Toronto/Université Laval, 2003–. Accessed 17 April 2017, http://www.biographi.ca/en/bio/comeau_napoleon_alexandre_15E.html.

Geggie, Norma, and Stuart Geggie. *The Gatineau Fish and Game Club, 1894–1994,* 2nd edition. Ottawa: n.p., 2009.

Granatstein, J.L., and J.M. Hitsman. *Broken Promises: A History of Conscription in Canada.* Toronto: Oxford University Press, 1977.

Gray, Charlotte. *Nellie McClung.* Toronto: Penguin Canada, 2008.

Gwyn, Sandra. *Tapestry of War.* Toronto: HarperCollins, 1992.

Gwynn, Stephen, ed. *The Letters and Friendships of Sir Cecil Spring Rice; A Record,* Vols 1 and 2. New York: Houghton Mifflin, 1929.

Hagedorn, Ann. *Savage Peace: Hope and Fear in America 1919.* New York: Simon & Shuster, 2007.

Haley, William. "Stuart, Sir Campbell Arthur (1885–1972)," rev. Robert Brown. In *The Oxford Dictionary of National Biography.* Oxford: Oxford University Press, 2004. Accessed 7 Aug 2016, http://www.oxford dnb.com/view/article/31732.

Hall, David J. "Sifton, Sir Clifford." In *Dictionary of Canadian Biography,* Vol. 15. University of Toronto/Université Laval, 2003–. Accessed 17 April 2017, http://www.biographi.ca/en/bio/sifton_clifford_15E.html.

Hamilton-Temple-Blackwood, Hariot Georgina, Duchess of Dufferin and Ava. *My Canadian Journal 1872–1878.* Don Mills, Ontario: Longmans Canada, 1969.

Hawkes, Arthur. *The Birthright: A Search for the Canadian and the Larger Loyalty.* Toronto: Dent, 1919. Accessed 17 April 2017, https://archive. org/details/birthrightsearchoohawkrich.

Hay, Ian (pseudonym of Ian Hay Beith). *The First Hundred Thousand.* Project Gutenberg. http://www.gutenberg.org/ebooks/12877.

Heard, Andrew. *Canadian Constitutional Conventions: The Marriage of Law and Politics.* Toronto: Oxford University Press, 1991.

Hicks, Bruce M. "The Crown's 'Democratic' Reserve Powers." *Journal of Canadian Studies,* Vol. 44 (2) Spring 2010, 5–31.

Hillmer, Norman. "Victor Cavendish, 9th Duke of Devonshire." In *The Canadian Encyclopedia.* Historica Canada. http://www.thecanadian encyclopedia.ca/en/article/victor-cavendish-9th-duke-of-devonshire/.

– "Victory Loans." In *The Canadian Encyclopedia.* Historica Canada. Accessed 17 April 2017, http://www.thecanadianencyclopedia.ca/en/article/victory-loans/.

Hnatyshyn, Gerda. *Rideau Hall: Canada's Living Heritage.* Ottawa: Friends of Rideau Hall, 1994.

Horne, Alistair. *Macmillan: 1894–1956: Volume 1 of the Official Biography.* London: Macmillan, 1988.

Horrall, S.W. "Dominion Police." In *The Canadian Encyclopedia.* Historica Canada. http://www.thecanadianencyclopedia.ca/en/article/dominion-police/.

Houghton, Walter E. *The Victorian Frame of Mind: 1830–1870.* New Haven: Yale University Press, 1957.

Hubbard, R.H. *Rideau Hall: An Illustrated History of Government House, Ottawa, from Victorian Times to the Present Day.* Toronto: University of Toronto Press, 1977.

Isitt, Benjamin. *From Victoria to Vladivostok: Canada's Siberian Expedition, 1917–19.* Vancouver: UBC Press, 2010.

Jackson, Patrick. *The Last of the Whigs: A Political Biography of Lord Hartington, Later Eighth Duke of Devonshire (1833–1908).* London and Toronto: Associated University Presses, 1994.

Jenkins, Roy. *Churchill: A Biography.* New York: Farrar, Straus and Giroux, 2001.

Keegan, John. *The First World War.* Toronto: Vintage Canada, 2000.

Kitz, Janet F. *Shattered City: The Halifax Explosion and the Road to Recovery.* Halifax: Nimbus, 1989.

Knox, Gilbert. *The Land of Afternoon.* Ottawa: The Graphic Publishers, 1924.

Kramer, Reinhold, and Tom Mitchell. *When the State Trembled: How A.M. Andrews and the Citizens' Committee Broke the Winnipeg General Strike.* Toronto: University of Toronto Press, 2010.

Lascelles, Allan. *Government House, Ottawa.* Ottawa: n.p., 1934.

Lovell, Mary S. *Bess of Hardwick: The First Lady of Chatsworth.* London: Little Brown, 2005.

Mackay, Donald. *Anticosti: The Untamed Island.* Toronto: McGraw-Hill Ryerson, 1979.

Mackenzie, D., ed. *Canada and the First World War: Essays in Honour of Robert Craig Brown.* Toronto: University of Toronto Press, 2005.

Macleod, R.C., and Peter Diekmeyer. "Royal Canadian Mounted Police." In *The Canadian Encyclopedia.* Historica Canada. http://www.thecana dianencyclopedia.ca/en/article/royal-canadian-mounted-police/.

Macmillan, Harold. *Winds of Change: 1914–1939.* London, Macmillan, 1966.

MacMillan, Margaret. *Paris, 1919.* New York: Random House, 2004.

– *Stephen Leacock.* Toronto: Penguin Canada, 2009.

MacMillan, Margaret, Marjorie Harris, and Anne L. Desjardins. *Canada's House: Rideau Hall and the Invention of a Canadian Home.* Toronto: Alfred A. Knopf Canada, 2004.

MacNutt, Stewart W. *Days of Lorne.* Westport, Connecticut: Greenwood Press, 1978.

Maine, Basil. *The King's First Ambassador: A Biographical Study of H.R.H. The Prince of Wales.* London: Hutchison, 1935.

Marx, Herbert. "The Emergency Power and Civil Liberties in Canada." *McGill Law Journal* 16, no. 1 (1970): 39–91. http://lawjournal.mcgill.ca/ userfiles/other/4841543-marx.pdf.

Mason, A.E.W. *The Broken Road.* London: Nelson and Sons, 1914.

McCreery, Christopher. *Order of Canada: Its Origins, History, and Developments.* Toronto: University of Toronto Press, 2005.

McMahon, Paul. *British Spies and Irish Rebels: British Intelligence and Ireland, 1916–1945*. Woodbridge, Suffolk, UK: The Boydell Press, 2008.

Messamore, Barbara. *Canada's Governors General 1847–1878*. Toronto: University of Toronto Press, 2006.

– "The Social and Cultural Role of the Governors General, 1888–1911." In *Imperial Canada: 1867–1911*, edited by Colin M. Coates. University of Edinburgh, Centre of Canadian Studies, 1997, 78–108.

Mitford, Deborah, Duchess of Devonshire. *Wait for Me! Memoirs*. New York: Farrah, Strauss and Giroux, 2010.

Moffat, Ian C.D. "Forgotten Battlefields: Canadians in Siberia, 1918–1919." *Canadian Military Journal* 8, no. 3, Autumn 2007, 73–83. Also available at http://www.siberianexpedition.ca/about/links.php.

Murrow, Casey. *Henri Bourassa and French Canadian Nationalism: Opposition to Empire*. Montreal: Harvest House, 1968.

Neatby, H. Blair. "King, William Lyon Mackenzie." In *Dictionary of Canadian Biography*, Vol. 17, University of Toronto/Université Laval, 2003–. Accessed 17 April 2017, http://www.biographi.ca/en/bio/king_william_lyon_mackenzie_17E.html.

Newton, Douglas. "The Lansdowne 'Peace Letter' of 1917 and the Prospect of Peace by Negotiation with Germany." *The Australian Journal of Politics and History*, March 2002, Vol. 48 (1) 16–39.

Nicholson, G.W.L. *Official History of the Canadian Army in the First World War: Canadian Expeditionary Force 1914–1919*. Ottawa: Queen's Printer and Controller of Stationery, 1962.

Nicolson, Nigel. *Great Houses of Britain*. London: Weidenfeld and Nicolson, 1965.

Olson, Lynne. *Troublesome Young Men: The Rebels Who Brought Churchill to Power and Helped Save England*. Toronto: Doubleday Canada, 2007.

Ouellet, Yves. *Tadoussac: The Magnificent Bay*. Laval, Quebec: Guy Saint-Jean Editeur, 2000.

Palley, Claire. *The Constitutional History and Law of Southern Rhodesia 1888–1965 with Special Reference to Imperial Control*. Oxford: Clarendon Press, 1966.

Pearson, John. *Stags and Serpents: The Story of the House of Cavendish and the Dukes of Devonshire*. London: Macmillan, 1983.

Pettigrew, Eileen. *The Silent Enemy: Canada and the Deadly Flu of 1918*. Saskatoon, Saskatchewan: Western Producer Prairie Books, 1983.

Pope, Joseph. *The Tour of Their Royal Highnesses the Duke and Duchess of Cornwall and York through the Dominion of Canada in the Year 1901*. Ottawa, S. E. Dawson, 1903. LAC Amicus No. 14238002.

Raudsepp, Enn. "Graham, Hugh, 1st Baron Atholstan." In *Dictionary of*

Canadian Biography, Vol. 16, University of Toronto/Université Laval, 2003–. Accessed 17 April 2017, http://www.biographi.ca/en/bio/graham_hugh_1848_1938_16E.html.

Regehr, Theodore D. "Shaughnessy, Thomas George, 1st Baron Shaughnessy." In *Dictionary of Canadian Biography*, Vol. 15, University of Toronto/Université Laval, 2003–. Accessed 17 April 2017, http://www.biographi.ca/en/bio/shaughnessy_thomas_george_15E.html.

Reiss, Paul, M. Reiss, and J. Reiss. "Catch and Release Fishing Effectiveness and Mortality." *Acute Angling*. Accessed 17 April 2017, www.acuteangling.com/Reference/C&RMortality.html.

Richards, David Adams. *Lord Beaverbrook*. Toronto: Penguin Canada, 2008.

The Round Table in Canada. Toronto: Rous and Mann, 1917. Library and Archives Canada, Amicus no. 16608022.

"Salmon Angling on the Restigouche." *Scribner's Magazine* Vol. 0003 Issue 5, May 1888. http://digital.library.cornell.edu/cgi/t/text/pageviewer-idx?c=scri&cc=scri&idno=scri0003-5&node=scri0003-5%3A8&view=pdf&seq=585.

Schleihauf, William. "'Necessary Stepping Stones': The Transfer of *Aurora, Patriot* and *Patrician* to the Royal Canadian Navy after the First World War." *Canadian Military History*, Vol. 9, Number 3, Summer 2000, 21–8. http://scholars.wlu.ca/cmh/vol9/iss3/4/.

Skelton, O.D. *Life and Letters of Sir Wilfrid Laurier, Volume I 1841–1896* and *Volume II 1986–1919*. Edited with an introduction by David M.L. Farr. Toronto: McClelland and Stewart, 1965.

Swettenham, J.A. "Allied Intervention in Siberia 1911–1919." Report No. 83, *Historical Section (G.S.) Army Headquarters*, 20 October 1959. http://www.siberianexpedition.ca/about/links.php.

Taylor, A.J.P. *The First World War: An Illustrated History*. London: Hamish Hamilton, 1963.

Thompson, Francis. *Chatsworth: A Short History*. London: Country Life, 1951.

Thorpe, D.R. *Supermac: The Life of Harold Macmillan*. London: Pimlico Random House, 2010.

Tucker, Albert, and Tabitha Marshall. "Canadian National Railways." In *The Canadian Encyclopedia*. Historica Canada. Accessed 16 January 2017, http://www.thecanadianencyclopedia.ca/en/article/canadian-national-railways/.

Vanderweide, Harry. "Crushing the Barrier with Restigouche Salmon." TFN *Destinations*, July 1996. Accessed 20 January 2010, www.the-fishing-network.com/magazine/vo3/no6/destination.html.

Villeneuve, René. *Lord Dalhousie: Mécène et Collectionneur.* Ottawa: Musée des beaux-arts du Canada, 2008.

Von Baeyer, Edwinna. *The May Court Club: One Hundred Years of Community Service.* Ottawa: The May Court Club, 1999.

Wade, Mason. *The French Canadians: 1760–1967,* Vols 1 and 2 (revised edition in two volumes). Toronto: Macmillan Canada, 1968.

Walker, Franklin A. *Catholic Education and Politics in Ontario, Volume 2, A Documentary Study.* Toronto: Federation of Catholic Education Associations of Ontario, 1976.

Walker, James W. St G. "Race and Recruitment in World War I: Enlistment of Visible Minorities in the Canadian Expeditionary Force." *Canadian Historical Review,* LXX, 1, 1989, 1–26.

Wallace, Stewart W. *The Memoirs of the Right Honourable Sir George Foster P.C., G.C.M.G.* Toronto: Macmillan, 1933.

Watson, Joseph. *The Queen's Wish: How it was Fulfilled by the Imperial Tour of T.R.H. The Duke and Duchess of Cornwall and York through the Dominion of Canada in the Year 1901.* Toronto: W. Briggs, 1902. LAC Amicus #19497501.

Williams, Charles. *Harold Macmillan.* London: Phoenix, 2009.

Williams, Jeffrey. *Bing of Vimy: General and Governor General.* London: Les Cooper in Association with Secker & Warburg, 1983.

Wilmott, H.P. *World War 1.* New York: Dorling Kindersley, 2003.

Wilson, Harold A. *The Imperial Policy of Sir Robert Borden.* Gainesville, Florida: University of Florida Press, 1966.

Wilson, Woodrow. "Fifth Annual Message," 4 December 1917. The American Presidency Project. http://www.presidency.ucsb.edu/ws/index.php?pid=29558#axzz1boHucxBh.

– "Wilson's War message to Congress, 2 April 1917." World War I Document Archive. http://wwi.lib.byu.edu/index.php/Wilson%27s_War_Message to Congress.

Wood, J.R.T. *So Far and No Further! Rhodesia's Bid for Independence During the Retreat from Empire 1959–1965.* Victoria, BC: Trafford Publishing, 2004.

Index

Page numbers in italics refer to illustrations

Aberdeen, Lady, 46, 61, 311n64
Aberdeen, Lord, 46
Agricultural College (Guelph), 60–1
aides-de-camp, 43, 44, 49, 99, 108, 127, 184, 206, 219–20, 266
Aikins, James, 73, 130
Aitken, William Maxwell (1st Baron Beaverbrook), 64, 69–70, 71, 167, 214, 316n25, 317n32, 344n91, 346n29
Albert, Prince. *See* King George VI
Alberta, 136, 159, 254–6, *255*, 287, 292–3, 330n10; Banff, 135, 136, 184, 251, 254, 293; Calgary, 68, 135, 136, 138, 223, 226, 256, 292; Edmonton, 135, 136, 226, 261, 287; Jasper, 251, 265, 287, 292; Lake Louise, 136, 254; viceregal visit to, 135, 136, 251, 254–6, 287–8, 292–3
Alexander of Teck, Prince, 8, 306n15
Alexandra, Queen, 274
Algonquin, sinking of, 78
Allan, Hugh Montagu, 62, 293
Allan, Mrs (wife of H.M. Allan), 62
Allan Shipping Line, 18, 62
Andrews, A.J., 227
Anglin, Francis, 51, 52, 122, 123, 127, 185, 188

Anticosti Island, 100–6; Ellis Bay, 100, 102, 104; English Bay (Baie Ste Clair), 102, 103; Fox Bay, 102
Arthur, Chester, 180
Arthur, Prince. *See* Connaught, Duke of
Asquith, Herbert, 67, 140, 141
Astaire, Adele, 302
Astaire, Fred, 302
Australia, 117, 260, 276

Bagehot, Walter, 56, 59, 60; and elements of the British constitution, 59, 60
Baillie, George Evan Michael, 301
Baker, Newton, 207
Baldwin, Stanley, 298, 299; Baldwin government, 299
Balfour, Arthur, 3, 9, 37, 78, 80, 84, *85*, 85–6, 140, 151, 152, 153, 154
Banting, Frederick, 214
Beaverbrook, Lord. *See* Aitken, William Maxwell
Beck, Adam, 171
Beith, Ian Hay, 53–4; *The First Hundred Thousand*, 54, 313n16
Belcourt, Napoléon-Antoine, 122
Belgian Relief Committee, 145
Bell, Alexander Graham, 129, 256
Bennett, R.B., 214–15, 302
Bickersteth, John Burgon, 260–1; *The Land of Open Doors*, 261

Birkenhead, Lord, 214

Black, Conrad (Baron Black of Crossharbour), 215, 346n28

Blue Sea Lake: Burbidge Station, 121, 122, 124, 126, 127, 185, 186, 187, 286; Devonshire family property at, 109, 120–5, 126–7, 128, 171, 185–90, 191, 194, 203, 208, 230, 234, 235–7, 238, 239, 241, 246, 248, 264, 268, 286, 296–7; New Lismore, name of property, 186, 286; New Lismore train stop, 235, 297, 350n28; "Presqu'ile Lismore," 187, 297; St George's-by-the-Lake Church, 188, 237

Boer War, 33, 45, 65

Bolton Abbey (Yorkshire), 18, 274

Bonar Law, Andrew, 26, 54, 55, 57, 58, 67, 69, 70, 71, 143, 166, 284, 298

Bonne Entente, 92, 322n22

Boothby, Robert, 301

Borden, Henry, 303; *Robert Laird Borden: His Memoirs*, 303

Borden, Lady (wife of Robert), 31, 49, 130, 204, 279

Borden, Robert, 15–16, 23–4, 29, 31, 32, 33–5, 34, 36, 37, 49, 54, 61, 64, 65–71, 72, 83, 89, 90–1, 94, 110–14, 115, 116–19, 130, 141–2, 145, 161, 162, 163, 164, 166, 167, 172–8, 191–2, 193, 197, 203, 206, 211–13, 215, 224, 239, 246, 249, 257, 258, 259, 275–9, 281–3, 284, 294, 295, 302–3; and attempt to create coalition government, 90–1, 110–11, 113–14; and British honours for Canadians, 61, 64–71, 172–8, 211–12, 213, 215, 275, 316n25; and communication with Imperial government, 166–7, 191; and conscription, 89, 90–1, 110–14, 115, 142, 161, 162, 275; and election campaign (1917), 141–2; and foreign policy independence for Canada, 116–19, 164, 173, 191, 275–6, 277; memoirs of, 116, 276,

303; resignation of, 278–9, 281–2, 284; role of at Peace Conference, 275–6, 277; and support for Sam Hughes, 33–4, 308n39; and troop commitments, 29, 89–90, 275; and Union government, 91, 114–15, 116, 118, 145, 148, 275, 283, 326n35

Bourassa, Henri, 92, 110, 162; and conscription, 92, 110, 162

Bowes-Lyon, Elizabeth, 81

Bowes-Lyon, Frenella, 81

Bowes-Lyon, John Herbert, 80–1

Bowood House (Wiltshire), 217

Boy Scouts of Canada, 37, 94, 135, 288

Britain: and Canada's request for a representative in Washington, 117–19; and communication with Canadian government, 58, 116, 164–7, 191; as constitutional monarchy, 56; and dispute over honours for Canadians, 64–71, 172–8, 211–15, 275, 290–1, 292; Duke of Devonshire's reputation in, 12, 64, 68–9, 118, 165, 213, 215; and the Lansdowne Letter, 139–44, 150, 152; and loyalty to British Empire in Canada, 26, 29, 59, 89, 117, 258, 275, 292; role played by in World War I, 5–7, 16–17, 134, 148, 168, 191, 192, 260, 276; and War Mission to United States, 80, 85, 117, 128, 152, 172. *See also* England

British Columbia, 56, 136, 137, 165, 251–4, 255; Anyox, 252; Capilano Canyon, 252–3; Glacier National Park, 254; Golden, 254; Nanaimo, 135, 137–8, 252; Revelstoke, 135, 140, 253, 254; Rogers Pass, 254; Tadanac (now part of Trail), 253; Vancouver, 135, 137, 252–3, 288; viceregal visit to, 135, 136, 137–8, 251–4, 255; Victoria, 135, 136, 137, 252, 288, 292, 330n10

British North America Act, 29, 55, 57, 58, 314n27, 314n30

Broken Road, The, 83, 320n72
Brown, George, 56
Browning, Montague, 81
Bulgaria, 140, 202
Bulkeley-Johnson, Vivian (BJ), 19–
20, 21, 41, 43, 44, 46–8, 49, 50,
51–2, 60, 61, 73–4, 75, 76, 77, 79,
81, 92, 93, 94–6, 97, 98–9, 100–
102, 103–105, 107, 108, 121, 122,
123–4, 126, 127, 134, 135, 136,
137, 138, 148, 149, 150–1, 154–5,
156, 160, 183, 188, 194, 201, 216,
219, 257, 268–9, 273, 302; career
and marriages of, 302; death of,
302
Burrell, Martin, 230, 282
Butchart, Jennie, 138
Butchart, Robert, 138
Butchart Gardens, 138
Byng, Viscount of Vimy, 292, 293,
314n28, 360n107

Cabot Lodge, Henry, 153, 155
Cahan, Charles, 206
Calgarian, 18–19, 19, 21, 23
Canada: cost of living in, 29; French-
English tensions in, 29–30, 89–92;
and granting of British honours, 61,
64–71, 129, 172–8, 211–15, 292;
labour unrest in, 206, 223–8, 250,
259, 278, 289; and movement towards independence, 29, 58, 65,
117, 129, 172–8, 191, 215, 275–6,
277; "racial" prejudice in, 84, 90,
293. *See also* Canada, in World
War I
Canada, in World War I: casualties,
17, 29, 116, 134, 136, 148, 159,
194, 245, 258, 275; and conscription, 56, 89–92, 110–16, 120, 125,
131, 134, 142, 148–9, 161–3, 164,
191–2, 193–4, 275; and labour
shortages, 29; and recruitment, 29,
30, 89–90, 113; troop commitments of, 29, 89–90, 113, 190–2,
275; and War Mission to United
States, 119

Canadian Club, 54, 62, 137, 154,
160, 198, 209, 257, 260, 294;
Women's, 77, 198
Canadian National Railway, 115,
256–7
Canadian Northern Railway, 114,
115
Canadian Pacific Railway, 30, 61, 64,
108, 111, 121, 134, 137, 202, 203;
and the viceregal train, 30–1, 60,
73, 87, 134, 139, 140, 147, 202,
203, 231, 279
Canadian Patriotic Fund, 37, 55, 61
Canadian Vickers Limited, 129, 198
Carlos Place (London, home of Lady
Edward Cavendish), 216, 229
Carpenter, Alfred, 207
Cartier, George-Étienne, 56
Cascapedia Club, 8, 232, 233–5; and
New Derreen Lodge, 232, 233–4,
235, 298
Cascapedia River, 8, 120, 184, 232–
5, 237, 242, 298
Cator, Harry, 220, 231, 233, 234,
235, 244, 249
Cavendish, Alwyn, 266
Cavendish, Andrew (11th Duke of
Devonshire), 300, 301
Cavendish, Anne, 13, 18, 37–8, 39,
41, 45, 46, 53, 108, 131, 155, 168,
185, 187, 194, 202, 207, 208, 240–
1, 247, 249, 268, 274, 285, 302;
death of, 302
Cavendish, Blanche, 13, 18, 32, 41,
43, 45–6, 50, 53, 60, 73, 108, 109,
126, 127, 131, 133, 156, 159, 169,
185, 194, 203, 204, 207, 208, 218,
220–2, 268, 274, 283, 301; children of, 301; death of, 301; marriage of to Ivan Cobbold, 220–2
Cavendish, Charles (Charlie), 13, 18,
37–9, 39, 41, 45, 93, 95, 96, 108,
120, 122, 123, 125, 128, 146, 171,
185, 202, 203, 207, 218, 219, 230,
241, 242, 243, 249, 274, 286;
death of, 302; marriage of to Adele
Astaire, 302

Cavendish, Deborah (Dowager
Duchess of Devonshire), 77, 300,
301; *Wait for Me!*, 77
Cavendish, Dorothy, 13, 18, 37–9,
39, 41, 45, 46, 53, 95, 98, 99, 109,
120, 123, 124–5, 128, 131, 132,
169, 185, 187, 188, 194, 203, 206,
216, 217, 218, 220, 221, 222, 231,
232, 236, 237, 238, 243, 247, 249,
250, 251, 252, 254, 256, 257, 258,
266–74; and affair with Robert
Boothby, 301; children of, 301;
courtship and marriage of to
Harold Macmillan, 262–3, 264–6,
267–74, 272, 281, 283, 285, 301;
death of, 301; and rumours of engagement to the Prince of Wales,
250, 258
Cavendish, Edward (father of the 9th
Duke of Devonshire), 8, 9
Cavendish, Edward (10th Duke of
Devonshire), 3, 5, 13, 17, 72, 77,
130, 222, 274, 293, 300; children
of, 300; death of, 300; marriage of
to Lady Mary Alice Gascoyne-
Cecil, 72, 77, 300
Cavendish, Edward, Lady (mother of
the 9th Duke of Devonshire), 12,
37, 128, 157, 216, 222, 229, 274,
358–9n79; death of, 288
Cavendish, Frederick, 8, 12
Cavendish, John, 5, 12
Cavendish, Lucy, 12, 13, 108
Cavendish, Maud, 4, 8, 13, 18, 30,
32, 41, 42, 43, 45–6, 47, 50, 53,
60, 62, 63, 72, 73, 73, 74–5, 78–
83, 95, 96, 98, 107–9, 122, 123,
125–6, 127–8, 129, 130, 133, 139,
148, 152, 160, 193, 194, 197–8,
199, 200, 201, 202, 203, 206, 216,
217, 221, 222, 249, 271, 273, 274,
285, 286, 287, 293, 301; and birth
of Arabella Peace, 197; death of,
301; and death of Angus Mackintosh, 200; *Early Memories*, 301;
and marriage to George Evan

Michael Baillie, 301; proposal, engagement, and wedding to Angus
Mackintosh, 107–9, 125, 127–8,
129–30, 131, 131–2, 132, 134,
222, 271; and trip to England
(1919), 206, 216–17; in Washington, 78–82, 108, 133
Cavendish, Moyra, 130
Cavendish, Peregrine (12th Duke of
Devonshire), 300
Cavendish, Rachel, 13, 18, 37–9, 39,
41, 45, 53, 93, 95, 99, 109, 120,
123, 124, 127, 128, 129, 131, 132,
156, 171, 185, 187, 194, 202, 203,
207, 208, 231, 232, 243, 247, 249,
263, 267, 268, 274, 283–4, 285,
286, 287, 289, 291–2; death of,
302; and marriage to James Grey
Stuart, 302
Cavendish, Richard, 12, 216–17, 220
Cavendish, Spencer Compton (8th
Duke of Devonshire), 4, 8, 9, 10,
11, 11, 300
Cavendish, William (1st Earl of
Devonshire), 9, 300
Cavendish, William, Lord Burlington
(son of 12th Duke of Devonshire),
300
Chadwick, Ethel, 51, 53, 121–2, 127,
168, 203–4, 286, 291, 312n14,
313n15
Chaplin, Charlie, 207
Charlotte, Queen, 25
Chatsworth, 7, 9–10, 12, 13, 14, 17,
18, 45, 138, 218–19, 299, 300;
Chatsworth archives, 99, 296, 301
Chiswick House (London), 18, 218
Chrétien, Jean, 215
Churchill, Winston, 5, 9, 298
Clemenceau, Georges, 277
Clive, Tommy, 179, 181, 184, 185,
187, 206, 234
Cobbold, Ivan, 220–2, 262, 274,
301; death of, 301; marriage of to
Lady Blanche Cavendish, 220–2
Cobbold, Pamela, 222, 301

Comeau, Alexandre, 96; *Life and Sport on the North Shore of the Lower St. Lawrence*, 96

Compton Place (Eastbourne), 18, 218, 274

Connaught, Duchess of, 12, 13–14, 41, 49, 50, 51, 76, 121, 160

Connaught, Duke of, 8, 12, 15, 19, *19*, 23, 33, 35, 36, 40, 41, 43, 49, 51, 53, 54, 55, 61, 66, 69, 70, 76, 94, 121, 166, 188, *189*, 194, 197, 203, 208, 274, 340n56

conscription, 56, 89–92, 99, 106, 109, 110–16, 120, 125, 131, 134, 142, 148–9, 161–3, 164, 193–4, 275; and anti-conscription demonstrations and riots, 115, 161–3, 164, 193–4; exemption from, 161, 162, 164; and the Military Service Act, 111, 113, 115, 161, 162, 163, 226; opposition to in Quebec, 90–1, 92, 110, 113, 134, 148–9, 161–3, 193–4. *For "conscription of wealth," see* Income War Tax Act

Conservative Party of Canada, 33, 34, *34*, 66, 90, 91, 111, 116, 275, 278, 281, 303

Co-operative Commonwealth Federation (CCF), 228

Corbett (Royal Navy captain), 20, 21, 22

Cottrell (South Wales, Mackintosh home), 216, 217

Crowdy, James, 45, 122, *123*, 188

Currie, Arthur, 247

Curzon, George, 178

Daily Mail (London), 153, 208

Daily Telegraph (London), 139, 144

Dalhousie, Lord, 25

Dalkeith, Walter, 285, 287

Dauntless, 242–3, 244

Davies, Louis, 24, 25

Derby, Lord, 233

Desborough, Baron, 292

Devonshire, Duchess of (Evelyn Cavendish), *xvii*, 11, *15*, 85, *170*; and concern for marriage prospects of daughters, 3, 13, 108, 127–8, 188, 219–20, 238, 243, 250, 262–3, 264, 265–6, 267, 268, 269–70, 273, 283–4; and concern for propriety, 49–52; criticism of, 160, 267–8; death of, 300; and dislike of touring, 169, 186, 229, 231, 268; and family trip down St Lawrence River, 93, 94–9, 120, 240–1; and final departure from Canada, 294–5; health concerns of, 74, 83, 229, 256, 268; household and family responsibilities of, 37, 45, 46, 77, 98, 218; interest of in moving to Canada, 3, 11–13; introverted personality of, 229–30, 268, 269; life in Canada with her parents, 10, 87–8, 120, 242; marriage of to Victor Cavendish, 10, *11*, 109; as Mistress of the Robes, 11, 14, 291, 299; and nervousness in public speaking, 77; prejudices of concerning Canadians, 77–8, 138, 159; prejudices of concerning mixed-race marriage, 83–4, 273; public duties of, 10, 14, 60, 61, 62, 77, 198, 252, 268, 293; response of to the Lansdowne letter, 142–3, 144, 150; and search for a cottage property, 93, 106, 120–1; and servants, 18, 42–3, 93, 97–8, 121, 186, 187, 194, 206, 245, 256, 285, 293, 300; and trip to England (1919), 203, 204, 206, 216–22, 223, 238, 262; in Washington, 133, 136–7, 139, 145; and work with women's groups, 61, 77, 158–9, 198, 252, 288, 293. *See also, for other family members, entries under* Cavendish

Devonshire, 4th Earl and 1st Duke of, 9

Devonshire, 6th Duke of, 4

Devonshire, 7th Duke of, 4, 8, 218, 289

Devonshire, 8th Duke of. *See* Cavendish, Spencer Compton

Devonshire, 9th Duke of (Victor Cavendish), *xvi*, *11*, *32*, *39*, *84*, *85*, *170*, *195*, *259*; accession to the title, 8; arrival and reception of in Canada, 23–32; and British honours for Canadians, 61, 64–71, 129, 174–5, 213, 215; and collaboration with Robert Borden, 33–5, 166, 278, 294; and communication between Canadian and Imperial governments, 116, 164–6, 191, 249; and concern with labour unrest, 223, 224, 225–6; and conscription crisis, 56, 91–2, 99, 106, 109, 110, 120, 134, 149; death of, 300; decision to accept appointment as governor general, 3–8, 9, 13; discomfort of with Roman Catholicism, 205, 209–10, 295; early career of, 9, 21, 22, 59, 188; and enthusiasm for agriculture, 4, 9–10, 12, 40, 59, 60–1, 163, 168, 195–7, 250–1, 253; extroverted personality of, 230, 289–90, 293; and final departure from Canada, 294–5; and foreign policy independence for Canada, 116, 129, 174–5; and gout, 169, 182, 183–4, 188; investiture of, 14; and love of fishing and hunting, 10, 92–3, 99–100, 125, 171, 179–85, 188, 191, 232–5, 242, 285, 286, 290, 293, 295; marriage of to Evelyn Petty-Fitz-Maurice, 10, *11*; and the New Year's Levee, 47, 261, 279; popularity of, 59, 205, 231, 252, 283, 292, 293–4; post-Canada career of, 298–9; and preparations for journey to Canada, 13–14, 17–20; and the Prince of Wales's tour, 228, 238–40, 242, 243, 244–5, 248–50; properties of, 3–4, 8–9, 12, 13, 17–18, 77, 100, 218, 230, 274, 284, 299–300; public duties of, 61, 62–3, 73–4, 88, 135–6, 169, 194, 198, 205, 231, 288; and public speaking, 55, 63, 88, 150, 152, 171, 205, 280, 289, 290; reputation of in Britain, 64, 68–9, 118, 165, 213, 215; response of to the Lansdowne letter, 143–4; sadness at leaving Canada, 283, 294–5; salary paid to, 296; and special meeting on conscription and coalition, 111–14; successor to, 292, 293; suffers a stroke, 267–8, 299; tours and visits undertaken by, 59–63, 73–5, 82, 87–92, 115–18, 128, 129, 133, 134–9, 145, 146–7, 150–2, 169–71, 194–6, 205–7, 231–2, 240, 249, 250–6, 264, 281, 284–6, 287–8, 292–3, 296; visit of to Canadian troops in France, 16–17. *See also, for other family members, entries under* Cavendish

Devonshire House (London), 3, 17–18, 187, 217; sale of, 218, 284; wartime uses of, 17–18, 218, 347n14

Diana, Princess of Wales, 156

Dickens, Charles, 72; *David Copperfield*, 72

Diefenbaker, John, 215

Doherty, Charles, 225

Dominion Police, 66, 122, 134, 161, 328n10

Dominions, role and status of, 23, 57–8, 86, 117–19, 165, 275, 313n24; and Imperial Conference (1926), 58; at Peace Conference, 276; and Resolution IX, 117

Dragon, 243, 244, 245

Drayton, Henry, 281

Dubuc, Julien-Édouard-Alfred, 241

Dufferin, Lady, 49, 58–9, 291

Dufferin, Lord, 49, 56–7, 58–9, 93, 240, 291, 298

Dumbells, The, 289

Dun, R.G., 233

Edward, Prince of Wales, 126, 228, 238–9, 242–9, 243, 247, 248, 250, 258–9, *259*, 265, 278, 280, 292–3,

351n41, 359n101; and EP Ranch, 293, 359n101; visit of to Canada, 228, 238–49, 243, 250, 256, 257–9, 264, 265, 266, 278, 279, 280; visit of to United States, 249, 257
Edward VII, King, 239, 248, 291
Egerton, Blanche, 126, 128, 129, 141, 157–8, 169, 222, 229, 231–2, 236, 237, 240, 241, 242, 244, 249, 250, 251, 253, 268, 272, 273, 302; death of, 302
election of 1917, 90–1, 110–16, 134, 141–2, 145
Elizabeth I, Queen, 9, 300
Elizabeth II, Queen, 81
Empire Club, 289
England: Canadians living in, 211; constitution of, 56, 59; fear for relatives in, 157–8; labour unrest in, 223; traditional social roles in, 54, 59, 83, 154; visitors from, 53–4, 85, 85, 188, 207, 260, 288. *See also* Britain

Fafard, M. (lighthouse keeper), 96, 322n43
Fiddes, George, 177–8
Finlay, Viscount, 178
Fitzpatrick, Charles, 36, 49, 148–9, 161, 162, 163, 209, 240, 245
Flavelle, Joseph, 175, 317n41, 337–8n22, 346n29
Ford, Henry, 171
Fortescue, George, 219
Foster, George, 14, 58, 70, 111, 112, 113, 158, 159, 173, 256, 278, 279, 281, 303; and Daylight Saving, 159
France, 3, 5, 33, 45, 72, 87, 89, 90, 93, 94, 101, 102, 105, 116, 134, 144, 145, 148, 164, 167, 168, 172, 191, 192, 238, 241, 244, 245, 263–4, 268, 276, 277; Duke of Devonshire's visit to Canadian troops in, 16–17; role played by in World War I, 6, 92, 134, 148, 168, 191, 192; and War Mission to United States, 81

French, John, 164
Fulford, George, 232, 349n12

Garneau, George, 91–2
Gascoyne-Cecil, Mary Alice, Lady (Moucher), 72, 77, 130, 222, 274, 293, 300; children of, 300
George III, King, 25
George V, King, *xvi*, 3, 14, 24, 25, 26, 26, 30, 36, 55, 93, 94, 136, 143, 175, 178, 208, 211, 214, 238, 239, 291, 294
George VI, King, 81, 274
Germany, role of in World War I, 6, 37, 112, 134, 139, 140, 142, 143, 148, 151, 157, 160, 164, 167–8, 185, 190–1, 197, 203, 260, 264; and submarine warfare, 20–1, *38*, 72, 78, 79, 185, 260
Globe (Toronto), 24, 49, 60, 70, 85, 114, 130, 141, 144, 146, 147, 158, 160, 177, 178, 208, 209, 242, 246, 280, 289
Gordon, Charles, 128–9, 172, 173
Gouin, Lomer, 87, 90, 91, 111, 112, 113, 168, 171, 179, 233, 240, 282
Governor General of Canada, role of, 55–9, 166; and authority over foreign and defence policies, 57; and personal influence, 58–9; and "reserve powers," 56, 57–8
Graham, George, 111, 112, 113
Graham, Hugh (Baron Atholstan), 61, 65–9, 70, 115, 193, 293, 315n14, 315n15, 316n25, 317n41; and "Elmwood," 193–4, 197, 199, 200
Grand Trunk Railway, 256–7
Gray, Charles F., 227, 228
Grey, 4th Earl, 24
Grey, Lord (British ambassador to U.S.), 259
Grieve, Mackenzie, 208–209
Gwatkin, Willoughby, 50–1, 163, 226
Gwynn, Sandra, 51; *The Tapestry of War*, 51

Haddington, George, Lord (Geordie), 220, 231, 236, 237, 249, 254, 256, 263, 264, 284

Haig, Douglas, 16

Halifax, Nova Scotia, *19*, 22, 23–4, 37, 38, 55, 73, 116, 118, 129, 134, 145–7, 161, 205, 206, 244, 245, 249, 257–8, 259, 266, 279; arrival and reception of viceregal party at, 23–6; the Citadel, 23, 258; Halifax Harbour, 22, 23, 145, 258; Province House, 24–5. *See also* Halifax Explosion

Halifax Explosion, 139, 145–7, 148, 152, 206, 257; casualties in, 145–6, 147; and visit from duke and duchess, 146–7

Hamilton, Mary Cecilia Rhodesia, Lady, 72, 82, 85, 206

Hankey, Maurice, 167

Hardinge, Lord, 140

Hardwick, Bess of, 9, 18, 299, 300

Hardwick Hall, 18, 300

Hardy, Thomas, 274

Hawker, Harry, 208–9

Hazen, John Douglas, 117–18, 119

Henderson, Harold, 16, 18, 24, 25, 32, *32*, 42, 43, 44, 73, 120, 132, 134, 135, 146, 149, 150, 151, 194, 207, 239, 240, 260, 282, 285, 286

Henderson, Peggy, 42, 124, *131*, 138, 188, 260

Henderson, Roderick, 42, 46, *131*, 138, 188, 260

Henderson, Violet, Lady, 42, 44, 124, 260

Hendrie, John, 60, 130

Hochelaga, 240, 241–2, 243, 245, 285, 286

Holst, Gustav, 155; "I Vow to Thee My Country," 155–6

honours, British: Knight Grand Cross, 14, 173; Order of the British Empire, 172–3, 177, 211, 346n29; Order of the Garter, 14, 137, 291, 292; Order of St Michael and St George, 14, 214

honours, British, granting of to Canadians, 61, 64–71, 172–8, 211–15, 275, 290–1, 292, 315n14, 316n25, 317n41; civilian vs military, 211–12; hereditary vs knighthoods, 64, 65, 69, 70, 173–4, 175–6, 177–8, 211, 212–13, 317n41, 346n29; procedure for, 64–5, 66, 70, 175, 211, 214; proposal to abolish, 65, 70–1, 174, 175–6, 212–14; proposal to include women in, 215; reaction to in Canada, 70, 173, 177, 215; and response from London, 177–8

Hood, Horace, 6

Hudson's Bay Company, 106

Hughes, Charles Evans, 21

Hughes, Sam, 14, *15*, 15–16, 33–5, 36, 52, 54, 308n39; resignation of, 34–5

Imo, and Halifax Explosion, 145

Imperial Order Daughters of the Empire (IODE), 14, 45, 77, 159, 199, 288, 293; Soldiers' Club, 45, 168

Imperial War Cabinet, 178, 191, 214, 276, 302

Imperial War Conference, 68, 72, 90, 117, 178

Income War Tax Act, 115–16, 326n32

India, 7, 8, 10, 117, 276, 298

Industrial Workers of the World (IWW), 206, 224

influenza epidemic (1918), 193, 198–201, 202; casualties from, 198, 200, 202; and efforts to prevent spreading, 198, 199, 202; number of cases, 199, 202; origins of, 193, 199

Ireland, 8, 10, 18, 77, 100, 164, 219; and conscription, 164; and Easter Rising (1916), 164; and Irish Free State, 299; and Irish Republican Army (IRA), 286; and labour unrest, 223; and Sinn Fein, 164, 286

Italy, 276, 277; role played by in World War I, 134, 192

James, Henry, 274

Japan, 153, 188, 191, 192; and immigration to Canada, 83

Jellicoe, Lord, 6, 260, 279; recommendations of for Canadian navy, 260

Joffre, Joseph, 81

John, Prince, 208

Jusserand, Jean-Jules, 81

Keefer, Allan, 122, 189–90, 286, 297

Keefer, Thomas, 122

Kemp, Edward, 35, 211, 226

Kennedy, John F., 300

Kennedy, Kathleen (Kick), 300

Kenyon-Slaney, Rodolph, 20, 43, 44, 48, 50, 51–2, 72, 82, 146, 206; marriage of to Lady Mary Hamilton, 72, 82, 85

Kerensky, Alexander, 140, 190

King, William Lyon Mackenzie, 55, 81–2, 83–4, 130–1, 163, 210, 215, 240, 242, 245–6, 294, 303, 314n28, 319n58

Kingsmill, Charles, 120

Kitchener, Lord, 7, 54, 313n16

labour unrest, 223–8; in Britain, 223; in Canada, 206, 223–8, 250, 259, 278, 289; in the United States, 224, 259–60

Lady Grey, 93, 94, 95, 99, 100, 108

Lang, Cosmo Gordon, 160

Lansdowne, Charles, Lord, 12

Lansdowne, Lord (5th Marquess, father of the Duchess of Devonshire), 3, 4, 6, 7–8, 10, 12–13, 57–8, 68–9, 83, 99–100, 113, 128, 139–44, 197, 216, 217, 222, 232, 233, 274, 283, 298, 299; and controversial letter calling for negotiated peace, 139–44, 150, 152; death of, 300; as Governor General of Canada, 7, 57–8; as Viceroy of India, 8

Lansdowne, Maud, Lady (mother of the Duchess of Devonshire), 3, 4, 8, 10, 12–13, 40, 88, 142, 216, 217, 220

Lansdowne House (London), 3, 4, 222, 274

Lansing, Robert, 152

Laurier, Lady (wife of Wilfrid Laurier), 48, 49, 130, 168, *170*

Laurier, Wilfrid, 30, 31, 33, 36, 49, 66, 90–1, 94, 110, 112–13, 114, 130, 134, 142, 162, 168, *170*, 210, 242; and conscription, 90–1, 110, 134, 162; death of, 209; state funeral for, 209–10

Laurier government, 83, 111, 275

Leacock, Stephen, 47

League of Nations, 139–40, 144, 150, 302, 303, 356n5

Leblanc, Pierre-Évariste, 31, 87, 89, 130

Le Devoir, 92, 162

Lemoine, Pauline, 121–2, 127

Lenin, Vladimir, 140, 190, 206

Leslie, Shane, 110, 324n4

Lessard, Major–General François-Louis, 161

Liberal Party of Canada, 30, 33, 91, 110, 111, 112, 113, 114, 115, 116, 118, 129, 131, 142, 210, *210*, 240, 242, 275, 278, 281, 303; and conscription, 91, 112, 131; and reciprocity, 111; and Western Liberal convention (1917), 111, 112, 114

Lismer, Arthur, 38; Olympic *with Returned Soldiers*, 38

Lismore Castle (Ireland), 18, 77, 97, 99, 164, 186, 219, 221, 222, 267, 286, 299, 302

Llandovery Castle, sinking of, 185

Lloyd George, David, 67, 68, 69, 141, 142, 143, 144, 151, 178, 197, 203, 276, 277

London, England, 3, 7, 10, 52, 55, 69, 72, 157, 168, 216–18, 221, 223, 262, 264, 270, 271, 274, 302; and celebration of fiftieth anniversary of Confederation, 94

Long, Walter, 67–8, 69, 70, 77, 112, 113, 114, 116, 117–19, 165, 166–7, 173, 175, 191

Lorne, Lord (Marquess of), 24, 96, 232–3, 235
Louise, Princess, 232
Lusitania, sinking of, 7, 21, 62, 205

MacCallum, Grant, 146
Macdonald, John A., 56, 58, 64
MacDonald, Ramsay, 299
MacKay, Thomas, 39, 40
Mackenzie, Alexander, 64
Mackintosh, Angus, 43, 44, 50, 51, 76, 79, 81, 82, 93, 95, 100, 107–9, 125, 126, 127–8, 129, *131*, 133, 148, 152, 155, 194, 197, 198, 201, 217, 301; death of, 199–200, 201, 204; engagement and wedding of to Lady Maud, 127–8, *131*, 131–2, *132*; health concerns of, 107, 108, 109, 125, 194
Mackintosh, Anne Peace Arabella, 205, 206, 216, 217, 273, 285, 286, 293, 301; birth of, 197, 201; christening of, 198, 202, 205, 346–7n5; death of, 301
Mackintosh, Mrs (wife of the Mackintosh of Moy), 216–17, 293
Mackintosh of Moy (Mackintosh of Mackintosh), 108, 127, 127–8, 201, 205, 216–17, 293
Macmillan, Arthur, 273
Macmillan, Harold, 219–20, 231, 236, 237, 241, 242, 243, 249, 250, 251, 254, 256, 258, 259, 262–6, 267–74, 299; death of, 301; education of, 263; political career of, 301; war service and injuries of, 263–4, 271; wedding of to Lady Dorothy, 272, 274, 283, 285, 301; *Winds of Change*, 265, 301
Macmillan, Maurice Victor (son of Dorothy and Harold), 301
Macmillan, Maurice, 263, 270, 271, 273
Macmillan, Mrs (Harold's mother), 262, 263, 264, 269, 270, 273
Magdalen River, 95, 97–100, 106, 323n48; Cape Magdalen, 98, 99,

100, 106, 107, 108, 295; fishing at, 97, 99–100, 125, 182, 235, 295
Malouin, M., 101, 104
Malouin, Mme, 104
Manchester Guardian, 141
Manitoba, 17, 24, 29, 73–5, 90, 102, 130, 195, 280; Brandon, 195; Dauphin, 195; Deer Lodge Military Convalescent Hospital, 73, 73–4; Le Pas, 250; and the Manitoba Schools Question, 90, 321n13; viceregal visit to, 138–9, 194–6, *195*; Winnipeg, 73, 73–5, 77, 82, 135, 136, 138–9, 248, 250. *See also* Winnipeg General Strike
Marina, sinking of, 20–1
Martin-Zédé, Georges, 102–3, 104–5
Mary, Queen, 8, 11, 14, 30, 36, 94, 208, 238, 299
Mary, Queen of Scots, 9
Massey, Hart, 257
Massey, Mrs (wife of Vincent Massey), 160
Massey, Vincent, 19, 160, 257
May Court Club, 46, 61, 311n64; May Court Ball, 257; May Court Convalescent Home, 61
McClung, Nellie, 149, 159
McLachlan, James D., 199
Meach's Lake, 120, 132, 330n63
Meighen, Arthur, 225, 227, 278, 281, 282–3, 285, 292, 294, 302, 303
Menier, Gaston, 101, 103, 106
Menier, Henri, 100, 101–5
Meredith, H. Vincent, 61, 293
Metagama, 241
Military Service Act, 111, 113, 115, 161, 162, 163, 226
Military Voters Act, 115, 275, 326n32
Milner, Lord, 211, 213, 214, 279, 284
Minto, Larry, 202
Minto, Lord, 8, 298
Mitford, Deborah Vivien. *See* Cavendish, Deborah
Molyneux, Hugh, Lord, 220, 284

Monck, Charles (4th Viscount), 40, 56

Mont Blanc, and Halifax Explosion, 145

Montreal, 18, 45, 54, 55, 61–3, 66, 67, 76, 108, 129, 130, 172, 188, 193, 194, 198, 202, 208, 245, 289, 293; anti-conscription riots in, 115; influenza in, 202; Ravenscrag, 62; Ritz-Carlton Hotel, 67, 76, 315n11

Morris (doctor), 182–3

Moy Hall (Scotland), 201

National Council of Women, 14, 82, 159

"Naughty Nine," 50–2

Naval Aid Bill, 275

Nevill, Richard, Lord, 43, 44, 46, 47, 62, 107, 130, 134, 149, 156, 194, 201, 208, 222, 231, 236, 240, 244, 250

New Brunswick, 69, 108, 118, 125–6, 179, 180, 205, 230, 240, 241, 242, 285; Campbellton, 241, 242, 243; Fredericton, 205; St Andrews by-the-Sea, 108, 109, 125–6; Saint John, 240, 242; viceregal visit to, 205, 240, 242, 285

New Democratic Party, 228

New Lismore. *See* Blue Sea Lake: Devonshire family property at

New York Bar Association, 150, 152

New Yorker Staats–Zeitung, 141

New York Times, 141, 143, 144, 152

Newfoundland, 117, 235, 243, 281, 284, 296; family fishing trip to, 281, 284–5; St John's, 208, 242

New Zealand, 117, 276

Nicholson, G.B., 212–13

Nickle, W.F., 174, 175, 176, 177, 212, 213, 215; and the Nickle Resolution, 214–15

Norris, Tobias, 195, 227

Northcliffe, Lord, 117, 128–9, 139, 153, 154–5, 172–3, 316n25

Northumberland, Duke of, 292

Nova Scotia, 230; Amherst Internment Camp, 205–206; Sydney, 205, 206, 285; viceregal visit to, 205–7, 286. *See also* Halifax; Halifax Explosion

Olympic, 37–8, *38*; and dazzle camouflage, 38

Ontario, 90, 130, 145; and French-language school instruction, 29–30, 90, 321n13; and Prohibition, 125, 149; viceregal visits to, 60, 61, 77, 82, 128, 129, 135, 169–71, 231–2, 293

Order of Canada, 215, 345n10

Order of the Hospital of St John of Jerusalem, 213, 291

Ottawa, 10, 18, 26, 31, 32, 37, 40, 46, 122, 129, 130, 145, 146, 194, 202, 203–4, 208, 222, 230, 245–8, 256, 257–8, 271–2, 291–2, 294–5; armistice celebrations in, 203–4; arrival of viceregal party at, 31–2, 32; Ashbury College, 45, 194; celebration of fiftieth anniversary of Confederation in, 94, 99; Château Laurier, 31, 50, 54, 246, 257; Christ Church Cathedral, 85, 127, 130, 131, *131*, 160, 230; the "drawing room" event, 291–2, 311n64; influenza epidemic in, 202; and the "Naughty Nine," 50–2; Parliament Hill, 40, 94, 204, 230, 278, 290, 291, 292, 294; St Bartholomew's Church, 155, 156, 205, 257; St Patrick's Basilica, 209; social life in, 49–52, 53, 59, 80, 86, 272, 280; visit of the Prince of Wales to, 245–8, 247, 256, 257–8. *See also* Parliament Buildings

Ottawa Citizen, 50, 116, 203, 290

Ottawa Journal, 130, 203–4, 292

Paris Peace Conference (1919), 144, 191, 211, 224, 233, 239, 276–7, 279, 303, 356n5; representation of Dominions at, 276

Parliament Buildings, 35–6, 94, 208,

239, 246, 248, 273, 281, 294; Centre Block fire and rebuilding, 35, 36, 94, 204, 246, 280, 292; gargoyles on, 208; and new Senate Chamber, 290, 291, 294; and temporary relocation of Parliament, 209

Patenaude, Esioff-Léon, 91
Patricia, Princess, 121
Pearson, Arthur, 207
Pearson, Lester B., 215
Percy, Eustace (1st Baron Percy of Newcastle), 80–1
Perley, George, 32, 66, 67–8, 70, 94, 117, 166, 167, 172, 211, 222
Pfeiffer, Richard, 199
Plains of Abraham, Battle of, 87, 91, 245
Pope, Joseph, 66, 111, 154, 163, 164, 166, 239, 240, 282
Price, William, 93, 241; Price Brothers, 93
Prince Edward Island, 230, 285; Charlottetown, 244, 245, 285; viceregal visit to, 285
Prohibition, 125, 135, 149–50, 159, 246

Quebec, 8, 29, 31, 97, 104, 106, 125, 145, 148–9, 164–5, 179, 180, 233, 240, 280, 282, 290; and boat travel on St Lawrence River, 93, 94–9, 120, 240–1, 245; conscription in, 89–91, 110, 111, 113, 134, 148–9, 161–3, 164, 226; Huron Village of Lorette, 199; and language rights, 29–30; Matapedia, 179, 180, 180, 182, 184, 233, 242, 297, 298; Prohibition in, 149; Sainte-Anne-de-Beaupré, 295; viceregal visits to, 61–3, 87–92, 93, 94–99, 120, 231, 245, 285, 289. See also Blue Sea Lake; Cascapedia River; Restigouche River; Restigouche Salmon Club
Quebec City, 23, 26, 40, 86, 87–92, 93, 108–109, 120, 130, 194, 198,

200, 240, 243, 244–5, 295; anti-conscription riots in, 161–3, 164, 226; the Citadel, 87–8, 88, 194, 199, 202, 240, 243, 244–5, 295; influenza epidemic in, 198, 199, 202; Plains of Abraham, 87, 91, 245; Spencerwood, 89, 198, 245, 295, 321n7

Railway Bill, 115, 326n32
Reading, Lord, 128–9, 152, 154–5, 167
Red Cross Society: British, 10, 18, 77; Canadian, 14, 46, 55, 62, 77, 137, 138, 158, 159, 169, 199, 211, 250, 288
Renown, 242, 243, 244, 257, 258
Restigouche River, 168, 171, 179, 193, 232, 234, 242, 297–8
Restigouche Salmon Club, 171, 179, 180, 180–5, 186, 242, 297–8
Rhodes, Edgar, 224
Richardson (MP), 175, 176
Rideau Hall (Ottawa), 10, 20, 32, 35, 38, 39, 39–41, 42, 42–3, 85, 85, 121, 125, 131, 186, 204, 231, 239, 246, 247, 266, 296; entertaining at, 49–54, 61, 83, 117, 121, 129, 130, 131, 149, 153, 154, 158, 168, 171, 172, 189, 207, 222, 230–1, 246, 247, 257, 260, 269, 288; Prohibition at, 149–50, 158, 207, 344n87; Rideau Cottage, 42; servants at, 18, 37, 42–3; skating, skiing, and other sports at, 40, 45, 46, 53, 121, 155, 156, 207, 268–9, 283, 288; staff at, 37, 43–5, 129–30, 188, 205, 266, 296
Ridley, Mervyn, 43, 44, 92, 93, 98, 100, 120, 122, 131, 148, 150, 151, 169, 187, 188, 201, 206, 220, 266–7, 301
Robertson, Gideon, 225, 227
Rockcliffe Park, Village of, 45, 122
Rockefeller, John D., Jr, 164
Rogers, Robert, 114
Roosevelt, Theodore, 153

Root, Elihu, 152
Ross, Frank, 97, 98, 100
Rowell, Newton, 114, 204, 278, 282
Royal Canadian Institute, 289
Royal Canadian Navy, 24, 240, 260;
   Aurora, *Patrician*, and *Patriot*, 260
Royal North-West Mounted Police,
   136, 228, 251
Russia, 76, 83, 134, 140, 143, 144,
   153, 185, 190–2, 223, 277; and
   revolution, 76, 83, 190, 191, 206;
   and Treaty of Brest-Litovsk, 144,
   148, 190

Saguenay River, 93, 106, 120, 240–1
Sandhurst, Lord, 141
Sargent, John Singer, 10
Saskatchewan, 158, 194, 196, 256;
   Battleford, 135; Regina, 135, 136,
   138, 139, 145, 256; Saskatoon,
   135; viceregal visit to, 135, 136,
   138, 139, 196, 256
Saturday Night magazine, 173–4,
   224
Saunders (private secretary to the
   duchess), 41, 44–5, 53, 146, 200,
   203, 208, 244, 249, 265
Schofield (governess), 249
Scotland, 108, 128, 131, 201, 221,
   293; and labour unrest, 223
Scott, D'Arcy, 122, 126, 127
Scott, Robert, 289
Shackleton, Ernest, 289
Shaughnessy, Thomas, 61, 64, 108,
   111, 112, 113, 317n41
Sherwood, Percy, 66, 121, 122, 127,
   134
Shipman (or Chipman) (doctor), 97,
   100, 323n50
Shrewsbury, 6th Earl of, 9
Siberia, Allied Expedition to, 190;
   and Canadian Expeditionary Force,
   191, 192
Sifton, Clifford, 90, 111, 112, 113,
   114, 116
Simpson, Wallis, 259, 351n41
Sladen, Arthur, 45, 110

Smith, F.E., 154–5
Smuts, Jan, 117
Socialist Party of Canada, 223
South Africa, 45, 117, 167, 276, 279
Southern Rhodesia, 299
Spring Rice, Anthony, 153, 155, 156,
   188, 207, 268
Spring Rice, Betty, 153, 156, 188,
   207, 268
Spring Rice, Cecil, 31, 53, 76, 78, 80,
   84, 85, 118, 119, 126, 130, 133,
   134, 139, 142, 151, 152–6, 157,
   157; death of, 155, 157, 268; "I
   Vow to Thee My Country," 155–6
Spring Rice, Florence, 31, 53, 76, 80,
   109, 126, 130, 133, 134, 139, 151,
   152, 153, 154, 155, 156, 157, 188,
   207, 218, 268
Stamfordham, Lord, 178, 238–9
Stanley, Lord, 233
Stiles (personal maid to the Duchess
   of Devonshire), 98
Strathcona, Lord, 70, 317n41
Stuart, Campbell, 128–9, 172–3, 175,
   177, 316n25, 346n29
Stuart, James Grey (Viscount Find-
   horn), 302
Sun, The, 141

Taché, M., 104
Taylor (valet to the 9th Duke of Devonshire), 98, 182, 183, 184
Thomson, Roy (1st Baron Thomson
   of Fleet), 215
Titanic, 37
Toronto, 37, 60, 61, 62, 63, 73, 77,
   115, 130, 160, 161, 169, 208, 227,
   245, 257, 282, 289; armistice ceremonies in, 257; Chorley Park, 60,
   314n33; Hart House, 257; influenza epidemic in, 202; visit of
   the Prince of Wales to, 245
tours and visits of the Duke and
   Duchess of Devonshire: to Brantford, Ontario, 129; to Georgian
   Bay, Ontario, 171, 293; to Guelph,
   Ontario, 60–1, 169; to Halifax,

116, 117–18, 129, 147, 206, 257, 258; to Hamilton, Niagara, southern Ontario, 82, 169–71; to Maritime provinces, 205–7, 284–6; to Montreal, 55, 61–3, 129, 198, 293; to Newfoundland, 281, 284–6; to northern Ontario, 73, 128; to prairies and western Canada, 73–5, 133, 134–9, 145, 194–6, 248, 249, 250–6, 255, 264, 265–6, 287–8, 292–3, 318n8; to Quebec City, 87–92, 244–5, 289–90; to Thousand Islands district (Ontario), 231–2; to Toronto, 60, 61, 73, 77, 115, 169, 257, 289; to United States, 150–2
Townshend, General, 6
Trotsky, Leon, 206
Turgeon, M., 104
Turkey, 202

Union government, 91, 111, 114–5, 116, 118, 134, 145, 148, 149, 225, 240, 275, 279, 280, 281–3, 326n35; choosing new leader of, 281–3
United States, 65, 111, 119, 144, 159, 181, 193, 202, 276, 279, 300; anti-British feeling in, 153, 154; and dispute over fisheries, 57–8; influenza epidemic in, 193, 201, 202; labour unrest in, 224, 259–60; and presidential election (1916), 21–2, 31; role played by in World War I, 21, 76, 78–9, 84, 112, 139, 140, 143, 148, 152, 154, 168, 190, 191, 276; sending aid after Halifax Explosion, 147, 152; and visit of the Prince of Wales, 249, 257; Washington, DC, 75, 76, 78–80, 82, 85, 117, 133, 150–2, 155, 172, 193, 198, 200, 201, 204, 257

Vanderbilt, Cornelia Stuyvesant, 302
Vanderbilt, William K., 180
Victoria, Princess, 274
Victoria, Queen, 10, 19, 49, 58, 230, 232, 291

Victorian Order of Nurses, 14, 158, 159, 288
Victory Loan campaign, 137, 138, 331n20
Viviani, René, 81

Walton (governess), 38, 41, 45, 53, 120, 123, 131, 146, 207, 236
War Measures Act, 162, 223
Wartime Elections Act, 115, 326n32
Watson, David, 17, 334–5n65
Wells, H.G., 53, 313n15; *Mr. Britling Sees It Through*, 53
Western Labour News, 225, 228
White, Thomas, 191, 212, 224, 239, 281–2, 358n49
Wilson, Woodrow, 21–2, 76, 78–9, 80, 137, 139, 140, 142–3, 144, 150–1, 153, 155, 276, 277; and the "Fourteen Points," 150; and "peace letter," 140
Winnipeg, 223, 224, 225, 226, 227, 248, 250; strike of 1918, 225
Winnipeg General Strike, 224–8, 239, 277, 289; aftermath of, 228; and "Bloody Saturday," 227–8; causes of, 225; and Citizens' Committee of One Thousand, 225, 227; and Metal Trades Council, 225, 226; and One Big Union (OBU), 224; and sympathetic strikes, 226–7
Winnipeg Trades and Labor Council, 223
Women's Auxiliary Army Forces (WAAF), 18, 347n14
Women's Christian Temperance Union (WCTU), 149
Women's Conference (Ottawa 1918), 158–9
Women's Institutes, 288, 293
Women's Volunteer Aid Detachment (VAD), 18, 347n14
Woodsworth, J.S., 228
World War I, 4–7, 15–17, 20–1, 23, 26, 29, 59, 86, 90, 94, 134, 137, 138, 139–44, 148–9, 159, 160, 163, 164, 166–8, 171, 184–5, 190–

2, 197, 202–3, 229, 241, 250, 258, 268, 289, 301; and Allied expedition to Siberia, 190–2; and armistice declaration, 203–4; casualties of, 140, 168, 219, 262; and conscription, 56, 89–92, 110–16, 134, 142, 148–9, 161–3, 164; and labour shortages, 29, 195; restraints occasioned by, 24, 25, 41, 49, 94, 130, 131, 137, 158, 171, 269, 280, 292; and Treaty of Versailles, 277; United States' entry into, 21, 76, 78–9, 84, 112, 139, 140, 143, 152, 154; and women's contributions to war effort, 152, 160. *See also* World War I, battles of

World War I, battles of: Caporetto, 134; Flers-Courcelette, 29; Gallipoli, 5, 6, 7; Jutland, 6, 7, 260; Kut-Al-Amara, 6, 7; Lens, 116; Loos, 263; Marne, 81; Messines Ridge, 168; Mount Kemmel, 168; Neuve Chapelle, 43; Nivelle Offensive, 148; Passchendaele, 140, 148; Somme, 16–17, 264; Verdun, 6, 7; Vimy Ridge, 77–8, 160, 293; Ypres, 12, 43, 107, 264; Zeebrugge (Belgium), 168, 207